☀ INSIGHT GUIDES

PeRU

DISCOVERY
CHANNEL

APA PUBLICATIONS **L**

Part of the Langenscheidt Publishing Group

ABOUT THIS BOOK

INSIGHT GUIDE
PERU

Editorial
Project Editor
Pam Barrett
Managing Editor
Alyse Dar
Editorial Director
Brian Bell

Distribution

UK & Ireland
GeoCenter International Ltd
The Viables Centre, Harrow Way
Basingstoke, Hants RG22 4BJ
Fax: (44) 1256 817988
United States
Langenscheidt Publishers, Inc.
36–36 33rd Street 4th Floor
Long Island City, NY 11106
Fax: 1 (718) 784 0640
Canada
Thomas Allen & Son Ltd
390 Steelcase Road East
Markham, Ontario L3R 1G2
Fax: (1) 905 475 6747
Australia
Universal Publishers
1 Waterloo Road
Macquarie Park, NSW 2113
Fax: (61) 2 9888 9074
New Zealand
Hema Maps New Zealand Ltd (HNZ)
Unit D, 24 Ra ORA Drive
East Tamaki, Auckland
Fax: (64) 9 273 6479
Worldwide
Apa Publications GmbH & Co.
Verlag KG (Singapore branch)
38 Joo Koon Road, Singapore 628990
Tel: (65) 6865 1600. Fax: (65) 6861 6438

Printing

Insight Print Services (Pte) Ltd
38 Joo Koon Road, Singapore 628990
Tel: (65) 6865 1600. Fax: (65) 6861 6438

CONTACTING THE EDITORS
We would appreciate it if readers
would alert us to errors or out-
dated information by writing to:
Insight Guides, P.O. Box 7910,
London SE1 1WE, England.
Fax: (44) 20 7403 0290.
insight@apaguide.co.uk

www.insightguides.com

This guidebook combines the
interests and enthusiasms of
two of the world's best-known
information providers: Insight
Guides, whose titles have set
the standard for visual travel
guides since 1970, and Discovery Channel, the world's premier
source of non-fiction television
programming.

The editors of Insight Guides
provide both practical advice and
general understanding about a
destination's history, culture,
institutions and people. Discovery Channel and its website,
www.discovery.com, help millions of viewers explore their
world from the comfort of their
own home and also encourage
them to explore it first-hand.

How to use this book

This book has been structured
both to convey an understanding
of the country, its people and its
culture, and to guide readers
through its sights and activities.
◆ To understand modern Peru,

The contributors

This new edition was thoroughly updated by **Nick Caistor** and edited by **Alyse Dar**. It builds on earlier editions by **Tony Perrottet**, **Andrew Eames** and **Pam Barrett**. The editors looked for writers with a combination of affection for and detachment from their specialist subject.

The chapters on pre-Inca civilizations and the colonial period were written by **Adriana von Hagen**. **Peter Frost**, who has lived for many years in the Inca capital of Cuzco, contributed the chapters on Inca society and Machu Picchu. Many of the revamped chapters build on those written by **Mary Dempsey**, who settled in Lima in the 1980s. Others were originally shaped by **Kim MacQuarrie**, **Lynn Meisch**, **Julia Meyerson**, **Robert Randall**, **Katherine Renton**, **Mike Reid**, **Michael Smith**, **Simon Strong**, **Lesley Thelander**, **Betsy Wagenhauser**, and **Barry Walker**.

Jane Holligan, a Lima-based freelance writer, contributed the chapter on Peru's recent political situation. **Diana Zileri** wrote about Afro-Peruvian music; the essay on Gene Savoy was written by **John Forrest**.

As in the previous edition, much of the photography was by **Eduardo Gil**, but many other talented photographers contributed their work, principally **Sue Cunningham**, **Andreas Gross**, **Eric Lawrie**, and **Heinz Plenge**.

The book was copy-edited by **Paula Soper**, proofread by **Sylvia Suddes** and indexed by **Elizabeth Cook**.

you need to know something about its past. The **Features** section covers the history and culture of the country in a series of lively and informative essays.
◆ The main **Places** section provides a complete guide to all the sights worth seeing. Places of special interest are coordinated by number with full-color maps.
◆ The **Travel Tips** section provides information on travel, accommodation, restaurants, outdoor activities and more. Information may be located quickly by using the index printed on the back cover flap. The flap also acts as a useful bookmark.

Map Legend

— ·· —	International Boundary
– – – –	Department Boundary
—•—	National Park/Reserve
– – – –	Ferry Route
✈ ✈	Airport: International/ Regional
🚌	Bus Station
P	Parking
❶	Tourist Information
✉	Post Office
✝ † ⳨	Church / Ruins
†	Monastery
☾	Mosque
✡	Synagogue
🏰 🏯	Castle / Ruins
∴	Archaeological Site
∩	Cave
🛉	Statue/Monument
★	Place of Interest

The main places of interest in the Places section are coordinated by number with a full-color map (e.g. ❶), and a symbol at the top of every right-hand page tells you where to find the map.

INSIGHT GUIDE
PERU

CONTENTS

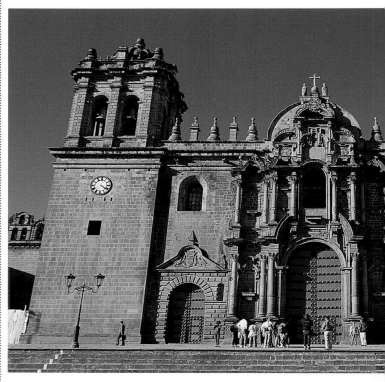

Introduction

History

Features

Cusco Cathedral

Travel Tips

◆**Full Travel Tips index
is on page 321**

ANCIENT AND MODERN

With a legacy of rich cultures and some of the world's most spectacular scenery, Peru is facing today's realities

Despite its rugged and often inhospitable landscape, Peru ranks among the world's great centers of ancient civilization. The sun-worshiping Incas are the most famous in a long line of highly developed cultures that thrived thousands of years before the arrival of Europeans. Their remains fascinate travelers and archeologists alike. Along with the stunning Inca ruins near Cusco and the great city of Machu Picchu, Peru is home to the Nazca lines etched on its coastal deserts, the Colla burial *chullpas* near Lake Titicaca, the enormous adobe city of Chan Chan and the Moche burial site of the Lord of Sipán. These cultures left no written records, just mysterious and beautiful works in gold, silver, and stone.

But ancient ruins are only a fraction of the story. Although the traditional American world was shattered by the bloody Spanish Conquest in the 1500s, the legacy of ancient cultures is very much alive. Roughly half of Peru's 27 million people are of pure Amerindian origin; often living in remote mountain villages, they still speak the Quechua or Aymara tongue of their ancestors, and many of their beliefs and customs are a mixture of traditional Andean ways and the culture imposed by the Spanish conquistadors. There are also more than 50 ethnic groups who live in Peru's Amazon region, some of whom still shun contact with the outside world.

Peru is also one of the most spectacular countries on earth. Its variety is astonishing: scientists have ascertained that of 103 possible ecological zones, Peru has 83 within its borders. As a result, the country can offer virtually every conceivable scenic attraction: the Peruvian Andes draw trekkers and mountain climbers from all over the world; over half of Peru lies within the Amazon jungle; and the world's driest desert runs the entire length of its coast.

In the 21st century, Peru is still being formed as a modern nation. Separated by geographical differences and an often violent past, Peruvians today are justly proud of their heritage and their country's riches. Peru is one of the world's great travel destinations. ❏

PRECEDING PAGES: vivid tapestries from Cusco; the solemn bride and groom; festival of Virgen del Carmen; reed boat on the Islas de los Uros.
LEFT: the generation gap is easily bridged in rural Peru.

LAND OF EXTREMES

Mountains, deserts, and jungle combine to make the Peruvian landscape a varied and breathtaking one, where nature is firmly in control

Bordered to the north by Ecuador and Colombia, to the east by Brazil and Bolivia, to the south by Chile, and to the west by the waters of the Pacific, Peru is the third-largest country in South America. Ask Peruvians about their homeland and they will cut it into geographical slices – coastal desert, highlands, and jungle – pointing out that theirs is the only South American nation which contains all three. It is this challenging geography that has given Peru its varied legacy of ethnic cultures, foods, music, and folklore.

Peruvians often use superlatives to describe the country's features. They include Lake Titicaca, the world's highest navigable lake at 3,856 meters (12,725 ft) above sea level, and Mount Huascarán, Peru's biggest Andean peak and South America's fourth-highest mountain at 6,768 meters (22,200 ft). The River Amazon, the world's greatest river system, and its namesake rainforest make up much of the country, and the globe's deepest canyons (Colca and Cotahuasi) lie just outside Arequipa.

Settled among those wonders are 27 million Peruvians, 8 million of them crowded into Lima and the surrounding area. About 45 percent of the nation are Amerindian – mostly Quechua-speakers, with a small proportion of Aymara-speaking peoples. Some 37 percent are *mestizos* (of mixed white and native blood), 15 percent are of European extract, and 3 percent are either descendants of black slaves, brought to work the mines, or Japanese and Chinese immigrants. Spanish and Quechua are the official languages. Some 90 percent of the country's residents are Roman Catholic, although the religious rites they practice bear traces of pre-Christian religions.

Barren beaches

The Spanish conquistadors' first glimpse of Peru was along its 2,500-km (1,500-mile)

coastal desert – one of the driest in the world. Visitors familiar with South America's Caribbean coast find Peru's sandy beaches unsettling, with their harsh backdrop of dunes or cactus-covered cliffs. But when conquistador Francisco Pizarro arrived in 1532 the coast was less desolate. The Amerindians had developed

sophisticated irrigation systems, and fields of vegetables and grains were grown in the desert. Today, agricultural settlements still flourish around the oases formed by rivers running down from the Andean slopes, forming fertile valleys in the otherwise bare terrain.

At the southern end of the coast, Chile's appropriation of some of this desert land more than a century ago in the War of the Pacific (1879–83) meant the loss of a hidden treasure – tracts rich in the nitrates sought for fertilizers. Still, the coast has brought wealth to Peru despite its inhospitable landscape and dearth of water (only a cup of measurable precipitation every two years is recorded in some areas). Fish

---

PRECEDING PAGES: the dense Amazon rainforest.
LEFT: trucking through the desert.
RIGHT: remains of Yungay, destroyed by a mudslide.

stocks are plentiful in the coastal waters, making Peru one of the world's foremost exporters of anchovies.

It is the cold, fish-bearing current running along the hot coast from the south that keeps rain away from the desert. So little moisture accumulates above the Humboldt Current (named for the 19th-century German explorer Alexander von Humboldt) that ocean winds heading toward the mountains rarely carry condensation. What they do bring to the land, however, is a thick, dense fog that causes havoc with air traffic and covers Lima for much of the year with a gloomy mist known as *garúa*.

The exceptions to the rainless norm are the freak showers, and sometimes floods, when El Niño, a warm current traveling from the equator, comes too close to the coast. El Niño means "the Christ-child," and it gained its name because it arises around Christmas. Its disruptive effects have always been a fact of life in Peru, but an unusually fierce current in 1997–98 spread the effects much farther afield and brought the phenomenon to international attention. The northern coast in particular suffered very badly from the floods and mudslides brought on by heavy rainstorms.

Mountain and jungle

Above all, it is the highlands that are associated with Peru. Here Quechua-speaking women weave rugs and garments, condors soar above the Andes, and wild vegetation camouflages Inca ruins. Although breathtaking to look at, the Sierra seems brutally inhospitable: the thin, cold air here combines with a rugged landscape to make the Andes an obstacle to transportation, communication, and development.

Nevertheless, nearly half of Peru's population is scattered across the Sierra, on poor rocky land where alpacas and llamas graze while subsistence crops are grown on terraced farmland exploited since Inca times more than 600 years ago.

Although the Incas found a way to survive in the Andes, cutting terraces into steep hillsides, building aqueducts which astound modern hydraulic engineers, and erecting massive forts and cities in isolated valleys, they met a formidable foe in the shape of the jungle – the one region even they could not penetrate.

LEFT: Mount Alpamayo in the Cordillera Blanca.

Three-fifths of Peru is jungle, divided into the hot, steamy Lower Amazon and the so-called High Jungle, or *ceja de la selva* (eyebrow of the jungle). The latter is the area where the mountains meet the Amazon, a subtropical expanse where Peru's coffee and much of the world's coca crop is grown.

Peru has a policy of protecting the rainforest through legislation and by designating virgin areas as national parks. Extending from the Andean foothills to the east of Cusco into the low jungle is the Parque Nacional Manu, which has one of the world's most impressive concentrations of wildlife; more than 850 bird species alone have been spotted from the park's research station. A few hours away by river from Puerto Maldonado is the Reserva Nacional Tambopata-Candamo, which contains more than 1,110 butterfly species and a quantity of insects that are found nowhere else on earth.

Land of earthquakes

Nature has dealt this country many cruel blows. Peru straddles the Cadena del Fuego (the Chain of Fire), a geologic fault line running the length of the continent. The line passes along the coast, cutting directly through Arequipa which, over the centuries, has borne the brunt of the seismic damage.

In the Sierra, earthquake damage is aggravated by the breaching of highland lakes, sending tons of water and mud down onto towns, burying residents alive. The worst recorded disaster of this type occurred in 1970 in Yungay, near Huaraz, when tremors opened the banks of a lake above the city and 18,000 people were swept into a chasm by the resulting alluvion. The ghastly site is marked by the tops of three palm trees – which once stood on the Plaza de Armas – protruding from the earth.

The broad range of weather conditions across the country makes labels such as "winter" and "summer" of little practical use. Lima residents refer to their hot sunny months (December to April) as summer, and the rest of the year, when the fog sets in, as winter. In the Sierra, winter is the rainy months (October to May). Snow is uncommon in inhabited highland areas, although the highest Andean peaks are snow-covered throughout the year. The jungle, meanwhile, is hot and humid all year. ❏

LEFT: terraces in the Valle del Colca, near Arequipa.

Decisive Dates

INITIAL PERIOD 1800–800 BC
Irrigation and agriculture initiated, with maize as the staple food; pottery and simple weaving techniques emerge.

EARLY HORIZON PERIOD 800–300 BC
The Chavín culture brings innovations in textiles, metallurgy, and carving.

EARLY INTERMEDIATE PERIOD 300 BC–AD 600
The Nazca and Moche cultures flourish. The first

Nazca lines are drawn in the southern desert; the Moche people of the north coast create Las Huacas del Sol y de la Luna. Finds from the Moche grave of the Lord of Sipán show that they were skilled metalworkers.

MIDDLE HORIZON PERIOD AD 600–1000
The Wari (or Huari) Empire, with its capital near Ayacucho, exerts its influence throughout Peru.
c.AD 1000: The Sicán culture, in the Lambayeque valley area, produces fine gold, silver, and copper work.

LATE INTERMEDIATE PERIOD (C.1000–1470)
Various cultures emerge; most important are the Chimu, the Chachapoyas, the Chancas, and the Incas.
c.1000–1400: The people of the Chachapoyas cul-

ture construct the great walled city of Kuélap, in the Amazonas region.
c.1300: The Chimu people build Chan Chan, the largest adobe city in the world.

THE INCA EMPIRE 1438–1532
1438: The Incas, led by Pachacutec, win a decisive battle against the northern-based Chancas and extend their empire from Cusco across a vast swathe of South America. They assimilate the crafts and techniques of the conquered people and introduce their own: terracing, irrigation, and architecture.
1527: Huascar, great grandson of Pachacutec, ascends the throne in Cusco, while his half-brother Atahuallpa rules the northern empire from Quito. Civil war ensues, with Atahuallpa emerging victorious.

THE SPANISH CONQUEST 1532–69
1532: Spanish conquistadors, led by Francisco Pizarro, arrive in Tumbes and march to Cajamarca. Atahuallpa is imprisoned, and a huge ransom demanded.
1533: Atahuallpa is executed by the Spaniards, who then take Cusco and ransack Coricancha, the treasure-filled Temple of the Sun. Manco, Huascar's half-brother, is installed as a puppet leader.
1535: Pizarro founds Lima, the capital of the Viceroyalty of Peru.
1536: Manco rebels against the Spanish and besieges Cusco but is defeated at Sacsayhuamán. He retreats to Vilcabamba.
1538: Diego de Almagro, Pizarro's original partner, leads an opposing faction. Civil war breaks out. Almagro is defeated and garrotted.
1541: Pizarro is assassinated by Almagro supporters.
1544: Manco is murdered by Spanish prisoners at Vilcabamba, but the city eludes the Spanish until 1572.
1548: Viceroy Pedro de Gasco is murdered.
1569: Tupac Amaru, the last Inca, is killed.

THE COLONIAL PERIOD 1569–1821
1570s: Francisco de Toledo, the fifth viceroy, establishes *reducciones*, the forced resettlement of indigenous peoples; he formalizes the *encomienda* system, whereby Amerindians provide land and tribute to their landlords; he also legalizes the *mita*, an Inca system of forced labor which, under Spanish control, becomes a form of virtual slavery.
Early 1600s: A Catholic campaign to stamp out native religions results in many Amerindian beliefs and rites being given a Christian veneer.
1700: The colonial system is firmly established throughout the Andes.
1700–13: The War of the Spanish Succession in Europe

sees the Habsburg dynasty replaced by the Bourbons, who try to improve the economy and reduce corruption.
1759: Charles III ascends the throne of Spain and opens up trade and commerce in Peru.
1780: Rebellion against the Spanish led by José Gabriel Condorcanqui, known as Tupac Amaru II, who is defeated and executed in 1781.
1784–90: Viceroy Teodor de Croix institutes reforms, setting up a court to deal with Amerindian claims.
1814: An Amerindian uprising led by Mateo Garcia Pumacahua captures Arequipa and wins creole support before being put down by royalist troops.
1820: After liberating Chile, the Argentinian general José de San Martín invades Peru, helped by the recently formed Chilean navy under British command.

MODERN HISTORY

1821: San Martín enters Lima in July and proclaims Peru's independence, although most of the rest of the country remains under the rule of the viceroy.
1822: San Martín leaves Peru for self-imposed exile after his meeting with Simón Bolívar in Guayaquil.
1824: Rebels headed by General José de Sucre crush royalist forces at the Battle of Ayacucho.
1824–26: Bolívar's presidency.
1826–65: Following Bolívar's departure a period of turmoil ensues, with 35 presidents in 40 years.
1840: First guano and nitrate fertilizer contracts with Britain, which comes to control Peru's economy.
1866: A Spanish attack on the port of Callao fails.
1869: Spain signs peace treaty with Peru.
1870s: US-backed railroad boom begins.
1877: Peru bankrupted by foreign debts.
1879–83: War of the Pacific with Chile over sodium nitrate deposits in Tarapaca province.
1883: Peace Treaty. Tarapaca is ceded to Chile.
1904: Construction of Panama Canal started and new era of US economic influence in Latin America begins.
1924: Exiled Victor Raúl Haya de la Torre founds Alianza Popular Revolucionaria Americana (APRA).
1931: Haya de la Torre is allowed back to Peru to contest elections, but is defeated. Numerous Apristas are killed in the subsequent uprising.
1941: Border war with Ecuador.
1948: Military coup brings General Odría to power.
1963–68: President Fernando Belaunde initiates land reforms, but a coup sends him into exile.
1968: General Juan Velasco takes over. Sweeping land reforms and nationalization are introduced. Quechua is recognized as the second language.

LEFT: Francisco Pizarro, *El Conquistador*.
RIGHT: Alberto Fujimori.

1968–75: Nationalist military regime.
1975: General Morales Bermúdez stages a bloodless coup. Economic problems increase.
1980: Belaunde returns to power in democratic elections. Terrorist organization Sendero Luminoso (Shining Path) becomes a serious threat.
1983: Powerful El Niño floods devastate industry.
1985: APRA leader Alán García wins elections. His policies lead to hyperinflation.
1990: Alberto Fujimori becomes president.
1992: Fujimori's "auto-coup." Congress suspended. Tough economic programs win IMF approval. Anti-terrorism measures lead to the capture and prosecution of Sendero leaders over the next few years.

1995: Fujimori is re-elected to a second term and his Cambio 90-Nueva Mayoria alliance gains majority in Congress.
1996–97: Guerrillas of Tupac Amaru group killed at end of siege of Japanese ambassador's residence.
1996–2000: President Fujimori's second term in office characterized by failure to reduce poverty.
2000: Fujimori wins third term when main opponent Alejandro Toledo withdraws. Mass protests start, and Fujimori flees to Japan following charges of corruption.
2001: Alejandro Toledo sworn in as first elected indigenous president of modern Peru.
2003: Toledo imposes state of emergency after a strike by teachers, farmers, and government officials.
2004: Fatal mudslides hit Machu Picchu. ❏

LOST EMPIRES:
PERU BEFORE THE INCAS

Centuries before the Incas ruled Peru there were societies creating adobe cities,
woven garments, and exquisite objects of gold and silver

Civilization in the Andes has long been equated with the Incas. Almost every account of Peru by 16th-century Spanish chroniclers told of fabled Inca wealth, and lauded their achievements in architecture and engineering, inevitably comparing them to the feats of the Romans. However, archeologists working on the Peruvian coast and highlands have now shown that the origins of Peruvian civilization reach back four millennia, some 3,000 years before the Incas emerged from their highland realm to forge Tahuantinsuyu, their enormous empire of the four quarters of the world *(see page 40)*.

It wasn't until the beginning of the 20th century, when scientific archeology was first carried out in Peru, that the true antiquity of the civilization began to emerge. No-one imagined at the time that civilization in the New World could be almost as ancient as that of the Old. Data emerging from Peru, however, shows that the earliest monumental architecture is roughly contemporary with the pyramids of Egypt and pre-dates the large-scale constructions of the Olmec in Mesoamerica by more than 1,000 years.

The beginnings of civilization

The first traces of human settlement in Peru have been found along the coast, where some 50 river valleys slice through the desert, creating fertile oases interspersed by arid expanses of sand. In the years 2500–1800 BC, a time known to archeologists as the Cotton Preceramic, small communities thrived along the coast, harvesting the rich Pacific Ocean for its bounty of shellfish, fish, and marine mammals. On river floodplains they cultivated cotton and gourds and hunted for deer. In the *lomas*, lush belts of fog vegetation located a few miles inland, they gathered wild plants. Before the introduction of true weaving, they created

twined and looped textiles of cotton and sedge, some decorated with intricate designs that attest to technological and esthetic skills.

Toward the end of the Cotton Preceramic, larger settlements emerged, such as that of

Paraíso just north of Lima, which covered 58 hectares (143 acres). Over 100,000 tons (90,000 tonnes) of quarried stone were used here to build monumental platforms. At Aspero in the Supe Valley, 145 km (90 miles) north of Lima, the largest mound, built of rubble and stone blocks, is 10 meters (33 ft) high and measures 30 by 40 meters (98 by 130 ft) at its base. Both of these centers were surrounded by sprawling residential areas containing burial grounds and thick midden, or waste, deposits.

The Initial Period

Some time around 1800 BC, at the beginning of what is known as the Initial Period, these

LEFT: gold figurine in the Museo Brüning.
RIGHT: Moche lord unearthed at Sipán.

fishing communities began to move inland. Although the majority of sites documented from this time average only 20 km (12 miles) from the coast, they were far enough up-valley to tap the rivers and construct irrigation canals, substantially increasing the ancient Peruvians' subsistence base. Evidence from the middens indicates that in addition to cotton and gourds they grew squash, peppers, lima and kidney beans, peanuts, and avocados, and supplemented their diet with marine products. Maize, which would become an Andean staple, was introduced somewhat later, possibly from Mesoamerica where it was first domesticated.

Facing Moxeke lies Huaca, or Mound A – once almost 6 meters (20 ft) high and 135 meters by 135 meters (450 ft by 450 ft) wide. Here, access to storage areas was controlled by wooden doorways, and the images of two fanged felines guard one of two entrances.

These architectural monuments, with U-shaped platforms and sunken circular courtyards, have been documented from sites just south of Lima to the Moche or Trujillo valley, 595 km (370 miles) north of Lima. Near Trujillo stands the Huaca de los Reyes, which also contained elaborate adobe friezes of felines, once painted red, yellow, and cream, long faded by

Two further revolutionary inventions belong to this period: the introduction of pottery and of simple weaving techniques.

In the Casma Valley, 275 km (170 miles) north of Lima, large Initial Period settlements flourished at sites such as Moxeke-Pampa de las Llamas. Located 18 km (11 miles) inland, the complex once covered an area of 2.5 sq. km (1 sq. mile) dominated by two mounds. The 27-meter (90-ft) high pyramid of Moxeke, excavated in the early 20th century, is decorated with awesome adobe friezes of snarling felines and human attendants, which are painted red, blue, and white. The temple facade has been reconstructed at Lima's Museo de la Nación.

TREASURES IN STORE

Many of the ancient sites really should be seen, as their sheer size is impressive and a visit allows you to appreciate their atmosphere. But to see most of their treasures you must go to one of the museums where the finds are kept.

The Tello Obelisk and many other Chavín carvings, as well as weavings from Paracas, are now in the Museo de la Nación in Lima, as is a wonderful collection from the Sicán tombs. And to see treasures from Sipán, and a variety of Moche and Chimu finds, pay a visit to the excellent Brüning Museum in Lambayeque and the Museum of Sicán (see page 178).

the desert sun. The arms of the U-shaped temple point upriver, toward the Andes and the source of water, a constant preoccupation on the rainless coast.

The Initial Period also saw the construction of sites such as Sechín, which is also in the Casma Valley, and was first excavated some 80 years ago by J.C. Tello, a renowned Peruvian archeologist. Here, carved on stone monoliths surrounding an adobe temple, a macabre procession of victorious warriors and their dismembered victims commemorates a battle – although who the victors or the vanquished were is still uncertain.

Nonetheless, excavations have unearthed ceremonial structures with fire-pits, where offerings were burned. Llamas had already been domesticated by this time, serving both as beasts of burden and as an important food source. Llama caravans carried highland produce – potatoes and other Andean tubers and grains – to the coast, where they were exchanged for goods from the warm coastal valleys: dried fish and shellfish, seaweed, salt, cotton, peppers, and coca leaves, to supplement the heavy inland diet. The guinea pig *(cuy)*, an Andean delicacy, was probably also domesticated about this time.

Sierra cultures

The emergence of complex societies on the coast was paralleled by developments in the highlands, where archeologists have documented the rise of ceremonial architecture at sites such as Huaricoto in the Callejón de Huaylas, 250 km (155 miles) northeast of Lima. Unfortunately, preservation of organic matter is not as good in the highlands as it is on the arid coast, and so the archeological record for this area is not as complete.

LEFT: an erotic Moche drinking vessel.
ABOVE: a carved gourd found in a Moche tomb.
ABOVE RIGHT: an emphatically priapic Moche vessel.

The Early Horizon

In the highlands, construction began around 800 BC at the ceremonial center of Chavín de Huantar, near Huaraz *(see page 200)*. Perhaps one of the most famous sites of ancient Peru, Chavín was believed until recently to have been the inspiration for the similar art style that spread throughout much of coastal and highland Peru. The period (approximately 800–300 BC) is often referred to as the Chavín Horizon.

However, research over the past 35 years has shown that Initial Period developments on the coast (including U-shaped temples, circular sunken courtyards, stirrup-spout ceramics, and an elaborate iconography featuring fanged felines and snarling gods) culminated at Chavín, and did not originate there as some had thought.

Perhaps because the culture was based midway between the coast and the jungle, Chavín iconography even incorporated jungle fauna into its elaborate system. The Tello Obelisk, on view at Lima's Museo de la Nación, features a fierce caiman.

The spread of the Chavín cult brought with it innovations in textiles and metallurgy, and coastal sites contemporary with the Chavín temple were perhaps branch shrines of a powerful Chavín oracle. Painted cotton textiles found at Karwa, near the Bay of Paracas, about

cal birds used to adorn fans, which probably came from the jungle. Traces of the use of cameloid fiber in north-coast weavings, again probably alpaca, also appear at this time.

Metalworking techniques, such as soldering and repoussé, and gold-silver alloys were first used by ancient Peruvians on the north coast during the Early Horizon period. The Moche were to add to the repertoire of metalworking skills a few centuries later.

The Nazca and Moche cultures

The decline of Chavín influence led to the emergence of regional cultures in river valleys

170 km (105 miles) south of Lima, for example, depict deities reminiscent of those carved on stone slabs at Chavín de Huantar.

The weavings found buried with mummy bundles at Paracas and dated to about 300 BC are perhaps the finest ever produced in ancient Peru. Because of the hundreds of mummy bundles buried in stone-lined pits this is sometimes known as the Necropolis Phase. By this time almost every weaving technique known today had been invented by the Peruvians. Evidence for a far-flung trade network is also visible at Paracas: obsidian from the highland region of Huancavelica; cameloid fiber, probably alpaca, also from the highlands; and feathers of tropi-

on the coast and in highland valleys during a time known as the Early Intermediate Period, which lasted until about AD 600. In the Nazca Valley, weavers and potters followed the Paracas tradition, but instead of producing painted and incised pottery they began to make ceramics decorated with a variety of vividly colored mineral pigments, some showing scenes of domestic life.

On an arid plain north of modern-day Nazca, the Nazca people etched giant images by brushing away surface soil and stones to reveal the lighter colored soil beneath. Images of birds, some measuring 60 meters (200 ft) across, predominate, but they also drew killer whales, a monkey (90 meters/300 ft across), and a spider (45 meters/150 ft long). All these creatures feature on Nazca ceramics. The straight lines and trapezoids appeared a few hundred years later.

There are numerous theories about why the lines were drawn. Maria Reiche, who spent much of her life studying the phenomenon *(see page 241)*, believed they formed part of an astronomical calendar; Erich von Daniken attributes them to visitors from outer space – a theory given little credence by archeologists. More recent theories suggest that the geoglyphs were paths linking sacred sites, or that they were linked to mountain worship and fertility.

(temples of the Sun and the of Moon) south of Trujillo, the Moche held sway over 400 km (250 miles) of desert coast. The Temple of the Sun, one of the most imposing adobe structures ever built in the New World, was composed of over 100 million mudbricks.

The Moche built irrigation canals, aqueducts, and field systems that stretched for miles, connecting neighboring valleys, and cultivated maize, beans, squash, peanuts, and peppers. In their *totora* reed boats they fished and hunted for sea lions, and captured deer along the rivers. They kept domesticated dogs and traded for luxury goods such as turquoise from Argentina,

Indeed, many of the animal images can be tied to Andean fertility concepts, and some of the lines point to the mountains in the distance, the source of valuable water.

The ancient Nazca lived in settlements dispersed around the Nazca drainage area. They worshiped at the ceremonial center of Cahuachi, downriver from the modern city of Nazca.

On Peru's north coast, the Moche people flourished in the Moche or Trujillo Valley, known in ancient times as Chimor. From their early capital at the huacas del Sol y de la Luna

LEFT: shining image of the Sun diety.
ABOVE: a mask from the Sicán site, Lambayeque.

QUEEN OF THE DESERT

Maria Reiche, the German mathematician who dedicated her life to studying the Nazca lines, first went to Peru in the 1930s. Her interest began when she became the translator for Paul Kosok, an irrigation expert who first spotted the lines from the air.

She spent years taking measurements and making charts and, having concluded that the lines were part of an astronomical calendar, wrote a book about her findings: *Mystery on the Desert.* Reiche was awarded the Order of the Sun – the country's highest honor – and became the first living person to be depicted on a Peruvian stamp. She died in 1998.

and lapis lazuli from Chile, which they crafted into jewelry, and exotic seashells from the Gulf of Guayaquil.

Famed for their ceramics, Moche potters created realistic portrait heads and fine line drawings of gruesome sacrificial ceremonies. The most imaginative and skilled metalsmiths in ancient Peru, they perfected an electrochemical-plating technique that gilded copper objects.

The Lord of Sipán

The discovery in 1987 of the tomb of a Moche lord at Sipán, near the modern city of Chiclayo some 800 km (500 miles) north of Lima, has

torrential rains and destroyed irrigation canals, causing widespread famine.

The Middle Horizon Period

With the fall of Moche in the north and the decline of Nazca to the south, a powerful southern highland kingdom exerted its architectural and artistic influence over large areas of Peru between AD 600 and 1000, wiping out the styles of the conquered peoples in the process. The capital of this empire was Wari (or Huari), a large urban center near the modern city of Ayacucho *(see page 315)*. Archeologists have excavated Wari military sites at Piquillacta near

provided much new data on the ancient Moche, including evidence that most valleys under Moche influence had their own powerful regional governors. The lord had been buried with hundreds of pieces of funerary pottery, as befitted his status, but also with an astonishing amount of gold and silver *(see page 178)*. Discoveries at Sipán also link its metalwork to similar pieces looted from the site of Loma Negra near Piura, on the far north coast.

Sometime between AD 650–700 the Moche Kingdom came to an end. It is thought that the El Niño phenomenon – when the warm waters flowing from the equator replace the cold waters of the Humboldt Current – could have produced

FORTUITOUS FINDS

For years archeologists had hoped to discover more about the lives of the Moche people, but in 1987 it was a band of *huaqueros*, or grave robbers, who stumbled on the tomb of the Lord of Sipán which provided so much information about the ancient culture, as well as some glorious artifacts.

Alerted by local police, Dr Walter Alva, the curator of the Brüning Museum, was astonished to see that among the rich booty stashed in the thieves' rice sack was a hammered sheet of gold fashioned into a face with lapis lazuli eyes. This item alone would have been worth tens of thousands of dollars on the black market.

Cusco, at Cajamarquilla near Lima, and at Marca Huamachuco, which is in the highlands to the east of Trujillo.

The Wari style is strongly reminiscent of the ceramics and sculpture from the Bolivian *altiplano* site of Tiahuanaco, which flourished between 200 BC and AD 1200. Situated at the southern end of Lake Titicaca at 3,856 meters (12,725 ft) above sea level, Tiahuanaco was the highest urban settlement in the New World. Its people employed an ingenious cultivation system that archeologists estimate could have sustained a city of some 40,000 people.

Tiahuanaco farmers cultivated potatoes, *oca*,

The Sicán discoveries

With the decline of Wari influence, regional cultures again flourished in the coastal valleys. In the north the Lambayeque or Sicán culture appears to have been centered some 50 km (30 miles) north of Chiclayo. Here a team of archeologists have used radar techniques to assist in excavating a number of tombs. These elaborate burial sites have yielded fascinating evidence of the Sicán culture.

The burial chamber of one obviously important male was surrounded by numerous female skeletons, thought to be weavers, which may well have been sacrificial victims. The remains

and *olluco* (Andean tubers) as well as quinoa and *cañiwa* (grains) on raised fields known as *camellones* in Spanish, formed by digging lake-fed canals and heaping up the resulting soil to construct raised fields about 10 meters (33 ft) wide. During the day the sun heated the water in the canals, which radiated its warmth at night to protect the crops from frost.

Recent experiments have shown that crops which were grown in this way could have produced harvests that were seven times greater than the average yield.

LEFT: wall carvings at Sechín.
ABOVE: the Lord of Sipán, as he was found.

of a richly decorated expanse of cloth were also unearthed. Scores of gold, silver, and copper masks and vessels were discovered, including an exquisite gold alloy mask with emerald eyes, which suggest that the site was an important metalworking center. The size of the complex also suggests that it was the capital of what must have been an extremely wealthy and powerful culture.

But the complex appears to have been abandoned in about AD 1100. The remnants of the population moved a few miles south to Túcume, where they constructed 26 large, flat-topped adobe pyramids and numerous smaller structures.

Heyerdahl's project

These pyramids were excavated by a team under the direction of Norwegian explorer Thor Heyerdahl, best known for his *Kon-Tiki* voyage. Unlike most pre-Columbian sites, Túcume has eluded looters because the Spanish conquerors spread the rumor that it was haunted. So ingrained was the belief that Heyerdahl had to have a purification ceremony performed before the dig could begin in 1987.

Although he recorded numerous graves containing silver figurines and textiles worked in tropical feathers, Heyerdahl showed most enthusiasm over artifacts that support his theory

that ancient Americans were capable of long-distance navigation and were the first settlers in Polynesia. Chief among such finds were a wooden oar and a balsa raft frieze on a long section of wall at the site. Túcume was conquered by the Chimu people a few centuries later, and subsequently used by the Incas.

The Chimu culture

It was probably around 1300, during the period known to archeologists as the Late Intermediate (*circa* 1000–1400), that construction began at Chan Chan (near Trujillo), the Chimu capital near the ancient Moche site of the temples of the Sun and the Moon. It seems that Chan Chan (*see page 174*) was then continuously occupied by the Chimu dynasty until it fell to the powerful Inca armies of Tupac Yupanqui in about 1464.

Rising to prominence in the north while the Incas gained power in the south, the Chimu realm stretched 965 km (600 miles) along the coast, from the Chillon Valley in the south to Tumbes in the north. Spanish chroniclers of the 17th century recorded a Chimu myth of the arrival on a balsa raft of the dynasty's legendary founder, Taycanomo. Details of his life are largely mythical, but he probably did exist. The legend spoke of ten Chimu kings, who ruled for about 140 years, which gives the early 14th-century date for the founding of Chan Chan.

There are nine rectangular compounds at Chan Chan, the largest adobe city in the world, each corresponding to a Chimu monarch. Each compound served as an administrative center as well as a palace, a royal storehouse, and, on the king's death, his mausoleum. The succeeding monarch then built a new one, and the deceased ruler's compound was maintained by his family and loyal retainers.

Around the royal compounds, in small, crowded dwellings, lived a population of about 50,000, chiefly weavers, potters, and metalsmiths who supplied the royal storehouses. Today the sprawling mudbrick capital of Chan Chan is a bewildering labyrinth of ruined adobe walls, some 7.5 meters (25 ft) high and stretching for 60 meters (200 ft). At its height in 1450 the city covered 23 sq. km (9 sq. miles). The eighth compound, or Tschudi Complex, has been partially restored and gives some idea of what the capital must have been like. Remains of adobe friezes showing patterns of waves, fish, seabirds, and fishing nets, all vital to the survival of these coastal people, can still be seen adorning some of the walls.

The Chachapoyas culture

Contemporary with the Chimu was the Chachapoyas culture (AD 700–1470), which flourished in the northern highlands. The remains of Kuélap, a huge stone city, stand above the River Utcubamba, but apart from the fact that the people who built such massive, fortified structures must have felt under threat, we have little information about them. ❑

LEFT: mummy found at Paracas.
RIGHT: the Tello Obelisk from the Chavín culture.

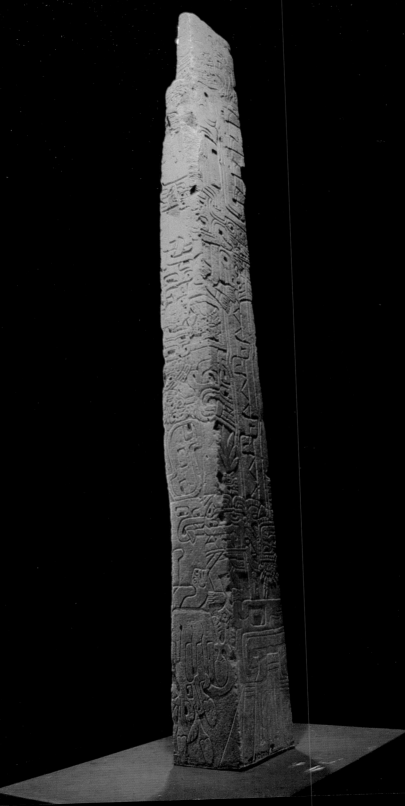

THE INCAS

The Peruvian empire of the Children of the Sun was short-lived,
but its legacy remains a source of inspiration

Peru's pre-Hispanic history is a long one, filled with the marvels of ancient civilizations that fed multitudes by irrigating deserts, wove textiles so fine they cannot be reproduced even today, and built adobe cities that have survived millennia of earthquakes. Some, like the Chimu, Moche, Nazca, Wari, and Chavín, left behind traces that have allowed archeologists and scholars to reconstruct pieces of their societies. Others may always remain nameless and obscure. However, no group is as well-known, or perhaps as astounding, as the Incas – the magnificent culture dominating much of the continent when the Spanish conquistadors arrived.

The Inca nation – the Children of the Sun – was a small regional culture based in the central highlands. Like the Chimu, Chancay, Ica, and other groups, they exerted local autonomy over large population centers and had distinct styles of textiles and pottery. But in the early 1400s, under the reign of Pachacutec, the Incas began an expansion – one of the greatest and most rapid that has ever been recorded.

In little more than 50 years, Inca domination was extended as far north as modern Colombia and south to present-day Chile. Amerindian groups that resisted were summarily vanquished and relocated as punishment. Others, through peaceful negotiations, joined the kingdom with little loss of regional control provided that they were prepared to worship Inti, the sun, as their supreme god and paid homage to the Inca leaders.

As each regional culture fell, Inca teachers, weavers, builders, and metallurgists studied the conquered people's textile techniques, architecture, gold-working, irrigation, pottery, and healing methods. As a result, they quickly accumulated massive amounts of information more advanced than their own.

By the time the Spanish arrived, Cusco, the Inca capital, was a magnificent urban gem; irrigated deserts and terraced mountainsides were producing bountiful crops, storehouses of food had eliminated hunger, and Inca military might had become legendary.

Although the accuracy of Spanish chronicles are suspect, and the Incas themselves left no written records, scholars, anthropologists,

and archeologists have managed to piece together fragments of a magnificent world.

A strict world order

Inca society was clearly hierarchical and highly structured, but not necessarily tyrannical or repressive. Everyone had a place and a part to play. Food and resources were stored and distributed so that all were fed and clothed. There was no private property, and everything was communally organized. It may have been a society in which the majority accepted their role without feeling exploited.

The Inca polity was a pyramidal system of government, with the ruling Inca (as the emperor

---

LEFT: Pre-Inca Colla burial *chullpa* at Sillustani.
RIGHT: the fortress at Sacsayhuamán.

was called) and his *coya*, or queen, at the apex. Under him stood the nobility, the "Capac Incas," supposedly the true descendants of Manco Capac, the founding Inca, and belonging to some 10 or 12 *panacas*, or royal houses. Each emperor founded a *panaca* when he came to power, so the current ruler's was the only one headed by a living man. The other *panacas* centered their lives and cults around the mummified remains of a former Inca. The city of Cusco was filled with the huge palaces built by Inca rulers to house their personal retinue, their descendants, born to their many wives and concubines, and, finally, their own mummy.

The *panacas* of Cusco co-existed with a similar number of *ayllus* – large kinship groups – of lesser nobility, the so-called "Incas-by-privilege," who were early inhabitants of the Cusco region, pre-dating the Incas. They held lands, had ritual and economic functions, and many other aspects of life in common. The *panacas* and noble *ayllus* belonged to two separate divisions, Upper and Lower Cusco, whose relationship was both competitive and complementary.

Below these two groups stood the regional nobility, who were not Incas at all but held aristocratic privileges along with intricate blood relationships and with reciprocal obligations to the ruling caste. Everyone in the empire was bonded to the whole by such connections, except for one large, amorphous group, the *yanacona*, who were a domestic class serving the *panacas*. They received no formal benefits and, although they could reach a high status, their loyalty was usually negotiable. Many of them defected to the Spaniards after the Inca Atahuallpa's capture in 1532.

The privileges of power

The nobility reserved many privileges for themselves, granting them selectively to outsiders. Polygamy was common, but exclusively aristocratic. Likewise, chewing coca leaves and wearing vicuña wool were privileges of the ruling caste. Noble males wore huge, ornate gold plugs in their pierced ears. Their beautifully woven tunics carried heraldic symbols called *tokapu*. All citizens wore the clothes and hairstyles befitting their station and ethnic group. The streets of Cusco were colorful, for hundreds of groups were represented in the city, each with its own distinctive costume.

Scores of local languages existed, but the lingua franca of the empire was Quechua, a language spoken today from northern Ecuador to southern Bolivia. The origins are obscure, but the Incas are believed to have acquired it from some other group. The nobles also used a private language, possibly a "high" chivalric dialect with elements of both Quechua and the Aymara language of the Lake Titicaca region.

The ruling lords were fond of hunting, and a royal hunt was a spectacular affair. Animals were not slaughtered indiscriminately, but culled. Young females of most species were

---

TAKING CARE OF MUMMY

The royal mummy, housed in the *panaca*, was attended to as royally after the death of the ruler as during his lifetime. It was consulted through seers and mediums on all important matters. It received daily offerings of food and drink, and at certain festivals it was taken out on its royal litter and paraded around Cusco.

Other members of the Inca nobility were also mummified after their deaths, and housed in lesser shrines. At one annual festival it was the custom for the royal mummies to be carried about the countryside, revisiting the places they had most enjoyed during their time on earth.

released for future reproduction. The myth of power within the Inca state held that the emperor was a divine being unlike ordinary mortals, descended from the sun via his founding ancestor, Manco Capac. He gave voice to the desires and intentions of this deity.

The sun may have become the supreme Inca deity after the rise of the ninth emperor, Pachacutec; before that, the supreme deity was Viracocha, an almighty creator also worshiped by other cultures. Inca religion was not confined to the sun and Viracocha. Cusco's great temple, the Coricancha, or Court of Gold, contained shrines to the moon, lightning, the Pleiades,

many of them housing the mummies of lesser nobles, and all of them connected by imagined lines that radiated from Coricancha like the spokes of a wheel. This system of sacred geography, known as the *ceque* system, was closely linked to the ritualistic and economic life of Cusco. The *panacas* and *ayllus* had care of individual *huacas* and groups of *ceque* lines.

Holy concubines

Also important in Inca worship were the *acllas*, or chosen women. The Spanish drew a simplistic parallel between them and the Roman vestal virgins, labeling them Virgins of the Sun.

venus, and the rainbow. There were also shrines to scores of local deities – idols or sacred relics brought to Cusco by innumerable regional peoples. The Incas did not attempt to erase local religions but included their gods in an ever-expanding pantheon.

Beside local and celestial deities there were the *apus* – the spirits of great mountains – and the *huacas*: stones, caves, grottoes, springs, and waterfalls, believed to contain spirit powers. More than 300 *huacas* existed around Cusco,

LEFT: working the land during a *mita* (the chronicle of Huaman Poma de Ayala).
ABOVE: the 12-angled stone in Cusco.

Some may have been virgin devotees of certain deities, but chastity was not a major preoccupation of the Incas, and young people were not expected to be sexually abstinent. The *acllas* were a diverse group, selected from throughout the empire for their talents and beauty. Many were concubines of the Inca, some were destined to become wives of selected nobles, others served the main temple, producing weavings and foods whose destination was the sacrificial fires of the Coricancha. It is also likely that some belonged to a caste of astronomer-priestesses associated with the cult of the moon, whose divine incarnation was the *coya*, sister and principal wife of the emperor.

The young Inca nobles were educated by *amautas*, scholars who transmitted cultural knowledge, often in the form of mnemonic songs and verses. Music and poetry were respected arts among the nobility, as was painting. An immense "national gallery", called Puquín Cancha, was destroyed during either Pizarro's conquest or the preceding civil war.

The Inca calendar featured an array of important festivals, which marked stages of life and the agricultural calendar. The summer and winter solstices were the greatest celebrations, held with numerous sub-festivals. The *Capac Raymi* summer solstice, for example, also featured the

coming-of-age celebrations for the new crop of young nobles. The males underwent trials, including ritual battles, and a death-defying race. Another great ceremony was *Sitwa*, in September, when foreigners had to leave Cusco, and the Incas engaged in a ritual of purification, casting out sickness and bad spirits.

Cusco itself was a holy city as well as the administrative capital of the empire. It was the centre of Tahuantinsuyu – the formal name of the Inca empire, meaning the four quarters of the world. The great royal roads to the four *suyus* began at the main square. Here all things came together, and soil from every province was ritually mingled with that of Cusco.

The four *suyus* corresponded roughly to the cardinal points. The northern quarter was the Chinchaysuyu – northern Peru and modern Ecuador. The south was the Collasuyu – Lake Titicaca, modern Bolivia and Chile. The Antisuyu was the wild Amazon forest to the east. The Kuntisuyu was the region west of Cusco, much of it also wild and rugged country, but including the south and central Peruvian coast.

A rural empire

Tahuantinsuyu was not significantly urbanized. There was the great complex of Chimu, on the north coast and, of course, Cusco. And there were a few large administrative centers along the spine of the Andes, housing a mainly transient population, which mustered and distributed the resources of entire regions. But most of the population lived in small rural communities scattered across the land.

The complex organization of the Inca state rested on a foundation of efficient agriculture. Everyone from the highest to the lowest was involved to some degree in working the land. Even the emperor ritually tilled the soil with a golden foot-plow, to inaugurate the new planting season, and it is notable that virtually any Inca ruin, no matter what its original function, is surrounded and penetrated by agricultural terraces and irrigation channels. Fields of corn stood in the very heart of Cusco.

Corn was the prestige crop. The great irrigated terracing systems whose ruins we see today were mainly devoted to its cultivation. Other Inca staples were potatoes and some other indigenous Andean root crops, plus beans, quinoa – a species of the beet family – and the related amaranth. The huge altitude range of the tropical Andes allowed the Incas to enjoy a great variety of foods, but it also required them to develop many localized crop strains for particular micro-climates. This they did, with typical thoroughness, at several experimental agriculture centers, whose ruins survive today.

The Incas' great food surpluses enabled them to divert labor to a variety of enterprises. They created a vast road network, so expertly laid that much of it still exists. They built astonishing structures of stone, so finely worked and of blocks so large that they required staggering amounts of time and effort. They employed thousands of artisans to produce works of gold and silver, pottery, and fine textiles. And they raised great armies, able to march thousands of miles without carrying provisions, so extensive was their network of storehouses.

The system that made these works possible was called *mita*. It was a kind of community tax, paid in labor. Every community sent some of its able-bodied young men and women for a limited period into the service of the state.

The period varied according to the hardship of the work – mines, for example, were a tough assignment, and accordingly brief. Working in a state pottery was easier, and correspondingly longer. Some communities – such as the famous one which rebuilt the Apurímac suspension bridge, Q'eshwachaca, each year – rendered their *mita* in a specific task. One *ayllu* provided the emperor with inspectors of roads, another with inspectors of bridges, and one even supplied the state with spies.

The life of a transient *mita* worker was rewarded by institutional generosity and punctuated by public festivals of spectacular drunkenness. Peasants who were otherwise tied to their villages for life mingled with groups from exotic locations worlds away, and caught a glimpse of the dazzling world of the Inca nobility. It was probably the most exciting time of their lives. Later the Spanish took over this institution and turned it into near slavery in their *encomienda* system.

Binding the Andes to Cusco

About every 10 km (6 miles) along the great skein of roads that knitted the empire together stood a *tambo*, a kind of lodge, with storage facilities for goods in transit and communal quarters for large groups of people. Closer together were little huts that served as relay stations for the *chasquis*, the relay message-runners, who could allegedly cover the 2,400 km (1,500 miles) between Quito in Ecuador and Cusco in ten days.

Every major bridge and *tambo* had its *quipucamayoc*, an individual who recorded everything that moved along the road. Their instrument was the *quipu*, a strand of cord attached to color-coded strings, each carrying a series of knots tied so as to indicate a digital value. The *quipucamayocs* were the accountants of the empire. *Quipus* may also have served as a cumbersome means of sending messages, with

certain types of knot being assigned a syllable value, so that a row of knots formed a word.

Crimes of property were rare; stealing was regarded as an aberration and dealt with ruthlessly when it occurred. Offenders suffered loss of privileges, with public humiliation and perhaps physical punishment. Serious or repeated crimes were punished by death, the victim being thrown off a cliff or imprisoned with poisonous snakes and dangerous animals.

A combination of techniques sustained the growth of the Inca empire. Military conquest played a part, but so did skillful diplomacy; some of the most important territories may have

DIVIDE AND RULE

Another institution, less benign than the *mita*, was the *mitmaq*. Loyal Quechuas were sent to distant, newly incorporated provinces whose inhabitants were proving troublesome, in order to pacify and "Inca-ize" the region. The recalcitrant ones displaced by the incoming group were then moved into the Inca heartland, where they were surrounded by loyal Quechuas, and either indoctrinated into believing that the ways of the empire were not so bad after all, or else too isolated from fellow malcontents to cause trouble. It was a system that cannot have been popular, but it was a lot less harsh than those employed by many empire builders.

LEFT: Inca funeral garb.
RIGHT: a *quipu*, used for keeping records.

been allied confederates rather than subordinate domains. The glue holding the empire together was the practice of reciprocity: ritual generosity and favors to local rulers on a huge scale, in exchange for loyalty, labors, and military levies, women for the Inca nobility, products specific to the region, and so on. The emperor maintained fabulous stores of goods to meet his ritual obligations and create new alliances.

The path to power

The Incas were perhaps not imperialist, in our sense of the word, at the outset. There was an ancient Andean tradition of cultural influences,

spreading out by means of trade and pilgrimage from important religious centers such as Chavín, and later Tiahuanaco. It is likely that Cusco started in this way, too; later the Incas extended their sway in southern Peru by means of reciprocal agreements and blood alliances.

Then, in 1438 came the pivotal war of survival against the Chancas, a powerful group from the north. The historical existence of the Chancas has never been confirmed by archeology, but the Inca version was that the man who took the title Pachacutec – "transformer of the world" – defeated the invading Chancas at the gates of Cusco. Subsequently he transformed Inca culture, and launched the expansion which

would be continued by his son, Tupac Yupanqui, and grandson, Huayna Capac. As the Incas extended farther from their center, they confronted groups with ideas and identities increasingly different from their own. Thus, continued expansion increasingly required the use of force.

When the Incas used military force they used it sparingly. Many opponents surrendered without a fight when they saw the size of the army sent against them. The Incas still preferred to cut off an enemy's water supply, or starve him into submission, rather than confront him directly in battle.

War and warriorhood were an important part of Andean life from early times, yet they surely cannot have been of paramount value to the Incas. If they had, then military tactics and technology would have been at their peak, whereas in fact their weapons and methods of warfare were still extremely primitive – far inferior to their attainments in administration, architecture, agriculture, and engineering – and had not evolved since the earliest times of Andean culture. They fought with clubs, stones, and all-wooden spears. Even the bow and arrow, though known to them, was not widely used in battle. The gulf between their fighting capacity and that of the steely Spanish conquistadors was tragically wide.

Many groups the Incas had conquered, such as the Huanca from Peru's central highlands, resented Inca domination. They had to be held in place by threat of force, and later they happily deserted to fight with the Spanish.

In the years just before the Spanish invasion, Pachacutec's grandson, Huayna Capac, was far from his homeland, fighting in the

BROTHERS AT WAR

Ironically, it was Huayna Capac's desire to unite his domain through marriage which achieved the opposite result and led to civil war. He had married the daughter of Duchicela, King of Quito, and the son of this marriage, Atahuallpa, became the Inca's favorite. But his other son, Huascar, was descended from Inca lineage on both sides and was therefore the legitimate heir.

When Huascar ascended the throne in 1527, civil war broke out and lasted for five years. Eventually Atahuallpa emerged victorious and established his capital at Cajamarca, shortly before the arrival of the Spanish conquerors.

mountains along the present northern frontier of Ecuador with Colombia. Quito, the base from which the campaigns were launched, had become a *de facto* second capital, and a northern aristocracy had formed. On the death of Huayna Capac the two groups fell into violent conflict, resulting in civil war between Huascar and Atahuallpa.

Artists in stone

Like other peoples of the New World, the Incas had not discovered how to smelt iron ore, but their use of other metals was quite sophisticated. They had mastered many techniques for working gold and silver, and created bronze alloys of varying types for different uses.

None of these metals was much use for working stone, which was one of the glories of the Inca civilization. Modern research shows that the finely fitted stones were primarily cut and shaped using hammer-stones of harder rock. This process was laborious, but not as slow as we might imagine. The Incas' vast manpower and their reverence for stone enabled them to persevere through the many years it took to complete such astounding structures as Machu Picchu and Sacsayhuamán.

How they moved and fitted the stones remains a mystery. Rollers and pulleys have been proposed, yet no theory explains how the combined efforts of 2,500 men – the number believed necessary to haul the largest stones up the ramp at Ollantaytambo – were simultaneously applied to a single stone. As for fitting, a common suggestion is simple trial and error: stones were set and then removed; high spots were marked; adjoining faces were then smoothed, and the process repeated, until the stones fitted together perfectly. It sounds plausible – until one sees the stones: boulders so colossal that the mere thought of lifting them makes one nervous.

Despite their wondrous skills, the Incas never invented the wheel, nor a form of writing. Andean terrain is extremely steep, and the Incas' only draft animal was the small, lightly built llama, unable to pull a load exceeding 45 kg (100lb). So the absence of a wheel is understandable. Thus, lacking the first reason to

devise a wheel, the Incas never discovered its other uses, such as making pots. They did, however, inherit the distaff spindle for spinning thread, which has been used in the Andes for thousands of years.

Another invention the Incas lacked was the arch. To span great gaps they built sturdy suspension bridges. In buildings they used the trapezoidal aperture. This shape – tapering upwards, with a stone or wooden lintel across the top – will take a fair amount of weight from above. All four walls of almost every Inca building also leaned slightly inward, making them very stable. This technique, combined

with the brilliantly interlocking joins of their stonework, made their buildings almost earthquake-proof – a useful feature in Peru.

The absence of any form of writing is harder to explain. The *tokapu* textile symbols and the *quipus* were the closest they came. Quechua is full of ambiguities, puns, and multiple meanings, relying heavily on context for its true sense. It is the language style of an oral culture, but whether this is the cause or the effect of having no written language is impossible to say. While the Incas lacked certain things we take for granted, this did not prevent their creating a sophisticated civilization, whose echoes still reverberate throughout the Andes. ❏

LEFT: Inca administrators cross a straw suspension bridge (the chronicle of Huaman Poma de Ayala).
RIGHT: a *chasqui* (Inca message runner).

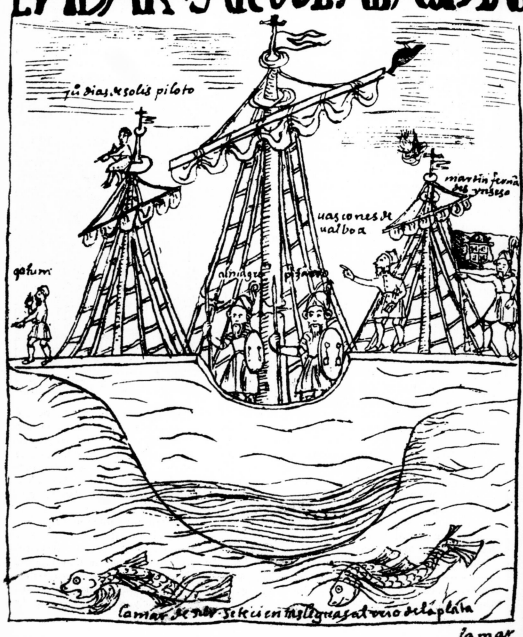

iu dias.de solis piloto

uascones de ualboa

martin fernā deb ynseso

almagro pisaro

gofum

la mar de nev se ki cien msliguas al rio dela plata

la mar

THE CONQUEST

Lust for gold made the Spanish conquest of Peru one of
the bloodiest episodes in the history of empire

It was in 1532 that a motley collection of Spanish conquistadors first appeared on the fringes of the Inca empire, the largest and most powerful empire that South America had ever known. In the months to come, these 62 horsemen and 106 foot soldiers commanded by a professional soldier named Francisco Pizarro would march to the heart of Peru and brutally seize control of the Inca throne. Within a decade, a glittering Andean world would be firmly in the grip of the Spaniards, its glories stripped and its people virtually enslaved.

Few historical events have been as dramatic or cruel as the conquest of Peru. Although only a handful in number, the invading Spaniards had on their side an astonishing streak of good luck, complete technological superiority, and a lack of principle that would have made Machiavelli shudder. Apparently experiencing no emotions other than greed and fear, they were repeatedly able to trick their way into the confidence of the Inca rulers and nobility, only to betray them. By the time the Incas realized the ruthlessness of their foes, it was too late.

The invasion of America

Cautiously marching into Peru's coastal desert, Pizarro and his men were in the front ranks of Spain's explosion into the New World. It had been only four decades earlier, in 1492, that Christopher Columbus had landed in the West Indies – the same year that Castile drove the last Moors from European soil. With no foe inside its boundaries and a need to bolster national pride and replenish the royal coffers, Spain soon directed the violent energies of its soldiers across the Atlantic. In 1519, Hernán Cortés, with 500 men and 16 horses, conquered the fabulously wealthy Aztec empire in Mexico. Panama was settled, and conquistadors were soon looking toward the newly found Pacific Ocean as a route to even further riches.

Although the existence of Peru was still no

more than a rumor at that time, it was only seven years later that two already relatively wealthy soldiers from Spain's barren Extremadura region, Francisco Pizarro and Diego de Almagro, led two expeditions down the west coast of South America before stumbling on the city of Tumbes and gathering information about the Inca empire. Intoxicated by the prospect of conquering a new Mexico, Pizarro went back to Spain, where he gained permission from the Spanish Crown to undertake the conquest. He then recruited a band of adventurers from his home town, Trujillo, before setting sail again, together with an ambitious priest named Hernando de Luque.

By the time Pizarro returned to Tumbes in 1532 with his 168 men, it was in ruins. In a stroke of fortune that would determine the fate of Peru, the Spaniards had found the Inca empire in an unparalleled crisis, weakened for the first time by a bitter civil war. Several years earlier, a virulent disease – probably smallpox, spreading like

LEFT: the conquistadors set sail for the New World.
RIGHT: Francisco Pizarro, their Spanish leader.

wildfire among the Amerindians from European settlements in the Caribbean – had struck down the supreme Inca, Huayna Capac. His two elder sons, half-brothers, had been untouched by the plague: Huascar, based in the capital city of Cusco, and Atahuallpa, heading the imperial army in Quito, in present day Ecuador. In the subsequent civil war, Atahuallpa's troops were victorious, but the empire was rocked and badly weakened by the struggle *(see box on page 42)*.

When Pizarro landed, Atahuallpa had only just become the undisputed Inca. He was heading in triumph south from Quito to the capital when news arrived that a group of tall, bearded

men had entered his lands. Atahuallpa was camped not far from the Spaniards' route of march. The Inca decided that he would meet the strangers himself.

Into the Andes

Pizarro and his force turned away from the barren coast to climb the rough road into the Andes. Although exhausted by the thin, high-altitude air, the conquistadors marveled at the first signs of the Inca civilization: steep valleys were lined with rich terraces of maize; shepherds stood by with flocks of ungainly llamas; and powerful stone fortresses overlooked the Spaniards' path. But the Inca warriors and their

subjects watched the advancing strangers impassively: Atahuallpa had given orders that they should not be hindered.

Finally Pizarro arrived at Cajamarca. Stretching into the valley beyond were the tents of the Inca's army and entourage. Pizarro entered the near-deserted town and sent his brother Hernando with a group of horsemen to meet Atahuallpa. The Inca received the envoys with all the pomp and splendor of his magnificent court. When permitted to speak, the Spaniards used a translator to convey that Pizarro "loved [the Inca] dearly" and wished to meet him. Atahuallpa agreed to a meeting in Cajamarca the following day.

Only that night did the Spaniards fully appreciate what they had got themselves into. Pizarro had no definite plan, and the conquistadors heatedly debated what should be done. They were several days' march into an obviously huge empire. Outside, the camp fires of the Incan army lit up the surrounding hillsides "like a brilliantly star-studded sky." They were terrified, but the lust for gold was even stronger than fear.

The capture of the Inca

Next morning, the Spaniards prepared an ambush. Hidden in Cajamarca's main square, the soldiers waited tensely all morning without any sign of movement in Atahuallpa's camp. Many began to suspect that their treacherous plan had been detected and they would all be slaughtered outright. It was not until nearly sundown, after Pizarro had once again sent envoys to promise that "no harm or insult would come to him," that the Inca decided to pay his visit.

MUTUAL DISTRUST

One contemporary chronicler recorded the Spaniards' surprise and awe at the sight of Atahuallpa's army and entourage in the valley outside Cajamarca: "Nothing like this had been seen in the Indies up to then. It filled all us Spaniards with fear and confusion. But it was not appropriate to show any fear, far less to turn back. For had they sensed any weakness in us, the very Indians we were bringing with us would have killed us."

One can only speculate about how the Inca leaders and their soldiers felt on seeing the Spaniards, clad in armor and mounted on strange, unknown beasts with "golden shoes" upon their four feet.

Atahuallpa and his nobles arrived in full ceremonial regalia. "All the Indians wore large gold and silver discs like crowns on their heads," one observer wrote. Atahuallpa himself wore a collar of heavy emeralds and was borne on a silver litter by 80 blue-clad nobles. Surrounding him were "five or six thousand" men, either unarmed or carrying clubs and slings. But Atahuallpa found no Spaniards in the square, and called out impatiently: "Where are they?"

Friar Vicente de Valverde emerged from the darkness with a translator and a copy of the Bible. What happens next is confused by the chroniclers, but has been pieced together by

Pizarro gave his signal. Cannons blasted and the Spaniards piled into the plaza with their battle cry of "Santiago!" Cavalry crashed into the horrified Amerindian ranks and began a wholesale slaughter: the natives "were so filled with fear that they climbed on top of one another – to such an extent that they formed mounds and suffocated one another."

Retreat had been blocked, and none of the entourage escaped alive. Pizarro himself hacked a path straight for the Inca and grabbed his arm. He suffered the only wound to befall the Spanish troops, inflicted by one of his own men who went to stab the Inca. Pizarro deflect-

John Hemming in his classic *Conquest of the Incas*. It appears that Valverde began to explain his role as a priest. Atahuallpa asked to look at the Bible, never having seen a book. "He leafed through [the Bible] admiring its form and layout. But after examining it he threw it angrily down amongst his men, his face a deep crimson." This "sacrilege" was all that the Spaniards needed to justify their actions. Valverde began screaming: "Come out! Come out, Christians! Come at these enemy dogs who reject the things of God!"

LEFT: Atahuallpa offers gold in exchange for freedom.
ABOVE: the meeting between Pizarro and Atahuallpa.

ed the blow, cutting his hand. Atahuallpa was rushed away from the carnage and locked, ironically enough, in the Temple of the Sun.

The royal prisoner

The Spanish could hardly believe their luck in capturing Atahuallpa. The Inca Empire, already divided by the civil war, was now without its absolute leader. On the instructions of the Spaniards, Atahuallpa issued orders from captivity, and his stunned people could only obey.

The conquistadors took whatever they wanted from the surrounding camp. Inca soldiers looked on as Hernando de Soto demanded men as porters, women as slaves, llamas for food – and, naturally, as much gold, silver, and jewelry as his squadron could carry. Atahuallpa, seeing that the Spaniards were interested above all in precious metal, assumed that they must either eat it or use it as a medical remedy (as depicted in drawings by the 16th-century indigenous chronicler Waman Puma). Atahuallpa offered a ransom for his freedom: a room of 88 cubic meters in size would be filled once over with gold and twice with silver.

The Spaniards were amazed at the offer, and Pizarro hastened to agree – summoning a secretary to record the details as a formal pledge and give a stamp of legality to the deal. In return, Pizarro promised to restore Atahuallpa to Quito. It was a blatant lie, but one that served the conquistadors' purpose brilliantly: the whole Inca empire was mobilized to supply them with booty. Llama trains from Quito to Lake Titicaca were soon starting out, loaded down with precious statues, jugs, and dishes.

Abuse and murder

Meanwhile, a small group of Spaniards went to Jauja, where Atahuallpa's greatest general, Chalcuchima, was stationed. Trustingly, the general obeyed Atahuallpa's instructions that he should accompany the Spaniards back to

A TRUE LEADER

While awaiting the arrival of the promised treasure, the Spaniards became impressed by their royal prisoner. One of Pizarro's men later wrote that "Atahuallpa was a man of 30 years of age, of good appearance and manner, although somewhat thick-set … He spoke with much gravity, as a great ruler." The Inca possessed an incisive intellect, grasped Spanish customs quickly, and learned the secrets of writing and the rules of chess. During the time he remained a prisoner, Atahuallpa's servants and wives maintained the royal rituals, bringing the Inca his cloaks of vampire-bat skin and burning everything he touched or wore.

Cajamarca, thus giving Pizarro the only other man who might have led a coordinated resistance to his invasion. Having treated the general well until his arrival at Cajamarca, they then tortured him to obtain more information about gold, and set about burning him at the stake. He was released "with his legs and arms burned and his tendons shrivelled."

Atahuallpa now realized that he had made a grave mistake in cooperating with the invaders, and that they had no intention of releasing him or leaving his empire. In mid-April 1533, Pizarro's partner Diego de Almagro arrived from Panama, with 150 Spanish reinforcements, before leaving again for Spain with news of the conquest and booty for Holy Roman Emperor Charles V. The influx of treasure into Cajamarca turned it into an undisciplined boom town and made the Spaniards bolder. But rumors began that Inca forces were massing to rescue their leader.

Many Spaniards became convinced that they were in danger so long as Atahuallpa remained alive. Others saw the value of the Inca as a prisoner, and argued that it would be difficult to justify an execution. Chroniclers record that a captured native claimed to have seen an Inca army marching on Cajamarca. Pizarro panicked and called an emergency council. It was obvi-

tism… His exhortations did him much good. For although he had been sentenced to be burned alive, he was in fact garrotted by a piece of rope that was tied around his neck."

News of the execution horrified Atahuallpa's supporters, especially when it was learned that there was no Inca column advancing on the city. When news arrived in Europe, educated opinion was equally appalled. Even Holy Roman Emperor Charles V was upset about the execution, protesting that it offended the divine right of kings upon which his own rule – and that of all contemporary monarchs – was based. But by then the Spanish Crown's share of booty

ous that the Inca could no longer be counted on to support Spanish rule. The council quickly decided that he should die.

Pizarro's secretary coldly recorded the sordid proceedings. The Inca was "brought out of his prison… and was tied to a stake. The friar [Valverde] was, in the meantime, consoling and instructing him through an interpreter in the articles of our Christian faith… The Inca was moved by these arguments and requested bap-

FAR LEFT: the Spaniards ambush Atahuallpa. LEFT: the Inca taken hostage. ABOVE: Atahuallpa asks Pizarro if the Spaniards eat gold (left and above, Huaman Poma de Ayala). ABOVE RIGHT: the Inca taken to execution.

was arriving from Peru and such scruples could be overlooked. The priceless art and sculpture of the great Inca empire went straight to the smelters of Seville.

Onward into the heartland

In August 1533, the Spaniards marched on Cusco. It seems an audacious project, but it is important to realize that a large part of the Inca Empire's population, especially around the southern Sierra, welcomed the news of Atahuallpa's death. To those who had backed his brother Huascar in the civil war, Atahuallpa was a usurper and his troops from Quito an enemy occupying force. It should also be remembered that the invaders were not dealing with a united people, but with a collection of disparate groups, some of whom were happy to be part of the Inca Empire, while others still resented the Inca yoke and were willing to fight on the side of the Spaniards. Realizing this, Pizarro was now ready to pose as the liberator of the Andes.

At Jauja, a contingent of Atahuallpa's army tried to make a stand. The Spanish cavalry charged and routed them immediately. This first armed clash of the conquest revealed a pattern that would be repeated: the native foot soldiers were no match for the mounted and well-armored Spaniards. Horses gave the conquis-

tadors mobility and allowed them to strike downward on their opponents' heads and shoulders, while the strange animals also created fear and confusion amongst the Incas.

The Spaniards' steel armor was almost impenetrable to the natives' bronze hand-axes, clubs, and maces. And Pizarro's men were some of the most experienced fighters Europe had to offer. Again and again the invaders would use their technological advantage to press home victories against apparently overwhelming odds.

Pizarro founded Jauja as the new Peruvian capital and pressed on. What followed was a desperate race to cross the several rope bridges spanning the Andean gorges before the Quitans

could destroy them. On one occasion the Amerindians attempted an ambush, and managed to kill several Spaniards in hand-to-hand battle. Pizarro decided that the captured general Chalcuchima had planned the attack and ordered him to be burned alive. But the attack had been to no avail: there was a final pitched battle in the pass before Cusco, and the Quitans' morale broke. They slipped away from the Urubamba Valley under cover of night and left the Inca capital to the invaders.

Dividing up the spoils

Pizarro and his men marched unopposed into the nerve-center of the Inca world, the "navel of the universe," Cusco. "The city is the greatest and finest ever seen in this country or anywhere in the Indies," Pizarro wrote back to Charles V. "We can assure Your Majesty that it is so beautiful and has such fine buildings that it would be remarkable even in Spain." But the invaders barely had time to marvel at the precise Inca masonry and the channels of water running through every street before installing themselves in various Inca palaces and starting on the serious business of pillaging the city.

Pizarro realized that his small force would not survive a true popular uprising, and so attempted to keep the looting of Cusco relatively orderly – at least until reinforcements arrived. He offered his men tracts of land and the right to the unpaid labor of the local population. This attempt to induce the Spaniards to become settlers, and to produce rather than destroy, would later become institutionalized in Latin America as the *encomienda* system. After "founding" the city in the name of the Spanish king, Pizarro

GOLD FRENZY

The contemporary historian León-Portilla described, with obvious distaste, the conquistadors' frenzy of insatiable greed in the gold-laden Coricancha, the Temple of the Sun: "Struggling and fighting among each other, each trying to get his hands on the lion's share, the soldiers in their coats of mail trampled on jewels and images and pounded the gold utensils with hammers to reduce them to a more portable size... They tossed all the temple's gold into a melting pot to turn it into bars: the laminae that covered the walls, the marvelous representations of trees, birds, and other objects in the garden."

rode back to the barren coast of Peru and created his colonial capital, facing the sea: modern-day Lima, where his statue still stands.

Pizarro had also accepted the offer of the 20-year-old Manco, another of Huayna Capac's sons, to become the new Inca. Manco wanted the Spaniards to restore him to his father's crown, and the conquistadors were happy to have him as a puppet leader in the southern Sierra. He was installed as leader in Cusco while two groups of Spaniards headed toward Quito to take on the retreating imperial army that remained loyal to Atahuallpa's memory.

The reality of conquest

Under Manco Inca's nominal rule, Cusco seemed tranquil enough. But it wasn't long before the puppet ruler began to see the Spanish "liberators" in their true colors. Their greed and brutality grew in proportion with their confidence; they were obviously in Peru to stay.

Manco was distressed to see the Inca world crumbling before his eyes. The natives of Cusco refused to obey him, while many of his subject tribes began to assert their independence. The swelling ranks of Spaniards began forcing the locals into press-gangs, extorting gold from nobles and raping Inca women. They harassed Manco Inca for treasure, captured his wife, and pillaged his property.

Manco could tolerate no more and announced his intention to rebel. Vast numbers of native soldiers were mobilized, and Manco slipped away from Cusco into the mountains. It was 1536, and the great rebellion had begun.

Incas on the offensive

Manco's troops quickly took Sacsayhuamán, the great fortress overlooking Cusco whose massive stone blocks still awe visitors today. Chroniclers record that the Inca force was about 100,000 strong against the Spaniards' 80 cavalry and 110 foot soldiers, commanded by Francisco Pizarro's brother, Hernando. Their defenses were bolstered by large contingents of native forces, but the outlook for the Spaniards was grim: Cusco was surrounded and, for all they knew, they might have been the last Spanish outpost in Peru.

The Inca attack finally began with slingshot

LEFT: the Inca rebellion.
RIGHT: the siege of Cusco.

stones, made red-hot in camp fires, hailing down onto Cusco's thatched roofs, setting them alight. But the roof of the building where the main body of Spaniards was hiding remained untouched. Even so, Manco Inca's forces captured most of the city. The Spaniards decided on a desperate plan: to counter-attack the strategic fortress of Sacsayhuamán.

Another of the Pizarro brothers, Juan, led 50 horsemen in a charge straight at the native lines. Despite their overwhelmingly superior numbers, the Incas still did not have a weapon that could seriously injure the Spanish cavalry. Although Juan Pizarro was killed, the conquis-

tadors forced their way to a safe position on the hill opposite Sacsayhuamán. They prepared a night attack using medieval European siege tactics, and took the outer terrace of the fortress.

The Spanish hold on

The capture of Sacsayhuamán was the key to Cusco's defense. Although the city remained surrounded for another three months, the Incas found it impossible to take. Fighting continued with extraordinary cruelty. Captured Spaniards had their heads and feet cut off. Amerindian prisoners were impaled or had their hands chopped off in Cusco's main square.

The rebellion was more successful in other

parts of the empire. Francisco Pizarro organized several relief expeditions from Lima, but the Incas had learned to use geography against the Spanish. One group of soldiers was caught in a narrow gorge by a hail of rocks; most were killed, the remainder captured. Another force was trapped, and their heads sent to Manco Inca. Now the victorious natives marched on Lima.

The attack on the town came from three sides, but in the flat coastal plains the Spanish cavalry proved invincible. A determined charge routed the main Amerindian force, and the commanding general was cut down in his tracks.

Meanwhile the Spaniards went onto the Nicaragua, while Diego de Almagro returned with troops from a failed expedition to Chile. When Almagro relieved Cusco in April 1537, Manco Inca decided that his cause was lost and retreated with his forces into the remote Vilcabamba Valley. The Spaniards chased him as far as Vitcos, but became distracted by looting. The Inca escaped under cover of darkness, carried in the arms of 20 fast runners. The Spaniards would have time to regret their greed: deep inside the subtropical valley, behind an almost impenetrable series of narrow gorges and suspension bridges, Manco created an Inca court-in-exile that would sur-

offensive in Cusco, with an attack on Manco in the nearby terraced fortress of Ollantaytambo. Amazon Amerindians, who were experts in the use of bows and arrows, kept the conquistadors at bay, while others used weapons captured from the Spaniards. Manco was seen at the crest of the fortress riding a captured horse and directing his troops with a lance. The conquistadors beat a hasty retreat and the siege dragged on – but the tide had turned.

Reconquering Peru

Spanish governors from other parts of the Americas were quick to come to Pizarro's aid. Reinforcements soon arrived from Mexico and

WHEN THIEVES FALL OUT ...

The Spaniards' behavior toward each other was a source of amazement to the Incas and the other inhabitants of the empire. Not only were the all-powerful conquerors now falling out among themselves, but they had already shown themselves capable of stealing from one another.

Theft had been a rare and sternly punished event in the Inca Empire, and it severely dimmed the aura of the Spaniards as golden-haired superior beings when it was learned that they stole not only from the vanquished people, which although deplorable was perhaps understandable, but also from each other.

vive in various forms for another 35 years.

By now there was a new twist to the complicated politics of the conquest: Almagro and Francisco Pizarro, the original partners in the invasion, had never reached agreement on how the empire should be divided between them, so the plotting between the two former allies plunged Peru into civil war.

No sooner had Manco Inca fled than the three surviving Pizarro brothers united against Diego de Almagro, pitting Spaniard against Spaniard on Andean battlefields. Eventually, in 1538, the Pizarrist faction defeated Almagro outside Cusco, and the general was garrotted.

prised in his Lima palace by a group of supporters of his murdered partner, Diego de Almagro. He was able to kill one of his attackers before being hacked to death. His corpse was thrown into a secret grave.

Pizarro's ally Bishop Vicente de Valverde – the priest who had first attempted to convert Atahuallpa – tried to escape to Panama, but the ship was wrecked off the island of Puna, and it is believed that cannibalistic natives devoured the hypocritical cleric.

The deaths of Pizarro and Valverde seem a fitting end to the first stage of the conquest. But the era that was beginning would be no less bru-

Victory and revenge

At 63 years of age, Francisco Pizarro was at the peak of his bloodstained career. Although no longer active on the battlefield, he was undisputed governor of a Peru which, although Manco Inca still occasionally harassed Spanish travelers from his jungle hideaway, was firmly under control. He possessed fabulous wealth and had been made a Marquis by the grateful Spanish Crown. But on June 26, 1541, Pizarro's past caught up with him: he was sur-

LEFT: the fortress of Sacsayhuamán, where the greatest battle of the conquest took place.
ABOVE: the Spaniards turn on one another.

tal. Now that most of the easily appropriated Inca treasures had been seized and distributed, the Spanish began to exploit the population mercilessly. The conquistadors who had received land and the right to native labor under the *encomienda* system became the elite of the new colony. They extorted tithes in the form of grain, livestock, and labor, and forced the Amerindians into a brutal form of feudalism.

In 1542 a new viceroy arrived from Spain to impose order. Fearing for their own interests, the Spaniards mustered behind Gonzalo Pizarro, who marched into Lima in 1544 and was declared Governor of Peru. But unrest continued, and two years later the viceroy was killed in battle against Gonzalo's troops. When this news reached Spain, Pedro de la Gasca was sent to rule the troublesome colony. Gonzalo initially held his own but in 1548, deserted by his own men, he was forced to surrender, and was put to death, another victim of the greed and disorder that characterized the conquest.

The last Incas

While this in-fighting was going on, Manco Inca had maintained his court in Vitcos, teaching his troops Spanish military techniques in order to wage a guerrilla war. Manco's fatal mistake was to spare a group of pro-Almagro

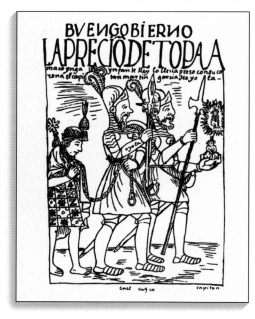

Spaniards who had fled to Vilcabamba. The refugees grew bored with exile and, believing they would be pardoned by the Pizarrist faction if they murdered the Inca, they fell on their host and stabbed him. They paid with their lives for their treachery, but the Inca leader was irreplaceable; with his death, any real resistance to the Spanish virtually collapsed.

As the Spaniards consolidated their rule, Manco Inca's son Titu Cusi maintained the Vilcabamba court. The Spanish understood that, as long as any legitimate royal figure stayed free, there would always be some faint hope for Amerindian freedom. Long negotiations were aimed at drawing the Inca out to live in Cusco, but to no avail. Then, in 1569, two Augustinian friars entered the secret Inca nation and attempted to convert the Inca to Christianity. In 1570, Friar Diego Ortiz became a close companion to Titu Cusi, and when Titu became ill, Friar Diego Ortiz prepared a healing potion which he hoped would save him. Unfortunately, the Inca died as soon as he drank it. His horrified troops, believing their leader had been poisoned, immediately killed Friar Diego Ortiz. The other was dragged along the ground for three days by a rope driven through a hole behind his jaw, before being dispatched by a blow to the skull from a mace.

This "martyrdom" gave the Spanish a pretext to invade Vilcabamba yet again. This time the conquistadors gathered an irresistible force. The new Inca, Tupac Amaru, put up a spirited defense against the invading column, but the Spaniards captured first Vitcos and then Vilcabamba.

Tupac Amaru tried to escape into the thick Amazon jungle, but his progress was slowed down by his wife, on the verge of giving birth, and a local chief betrayed the party's movements. Finally a pursuing team of Spaniards spotted a camp fire in the rainforest and pounced on the Inca, capturing him and bringing him back to Cusco with a golden chain around his neck.

The final humiliation of the ancient Inca Empire was at hand. Native generals were tried and hanged. Inca Tupac Amaru was put on trial for murdering the Spanish priest. Despite appeals from Spanish liberals and Inca nobles, Tupac Amaru was condemned to be beheaded. He was led through the streets of Cusco, riding a mule, his hands tied behind his back with a rope around his neck. On the scaffold, he appeared to recant his faith, telling his people that he had become a Christian and that the Inca religion was a sham. In 1572, nearly four decades after the Spanish arrived in Cajamarca, the last Inca had finally been killed.

With all resistance ended, and no leader to rally dissident spirits, the Spaniards were left in total control of the vast empire. But there was no time to rest on their laurels: they were already beginning to discover that governing the country was just as difficult a task as subduing it had been. ❏

LEFT: capture of Tupac Amaru (Huaman Poma de Ayala).

Looking for the Past

Ever since the first Europeans conquered parts of the Americas, and discovered the wealth of the Inca and Aztec empires, there has been an abiding belief in the existence of El Dorado, a hidden city stacked with gold. But it was not until the latter half of the 19th century that a revival of enthusiasm for American archeology brought explorers to Peru in search of Vilcabamba, "the lost city" to which the last Incas had retreated after the Spanish conquest.

It was this quest that brought Hiram Bingham to the Andes, where he discovered Machu Picchu in 1911, believing it to be Vilcabamba. He also stumbled across some ruins in Espíritu Pampa, but showed only a passing interest. In 1963 another American, Gene Savoy, who described himself as "a non-professional archeological explorer," and who had already made important discoveries of pre-Inca civilizations in the northern coastal valleys, turned his sights on the southern jungles, intent on disproving the widely held belief that Machu Picchu was the lost city.

Basing his work on his interpretations of the texts of the same Spanish chroniclers as used earlier by Bingham, Savoy took a closer look at Espíritu Pampa. It is a large site containing at least 60 buildings and some 300 houses, but unspectacular and overgrown with rainforest vegetation. With support from the University of Trujillo, he documented the site. The presence of colonial-style roof tiles, mentioned in Spanish chronicles, indicated that it was probably Vilcabamba. Subsequent research matched the location and size of the site and details of the remains to descriptions in the texts, and confirmed that it was indeed the lost city of the Incas.

Savoy made two more expeditions to the area, uncovering more Inca sites and remains of roads, then switched his attentions farther north in search of the ancient cities of the Chachapoyas, a pre-Inca tribe that ruled much of the northern Peruvian Andes (*circa* AD 1100–1400). In the remote Pajaten region, at the southern edge of the empire, he discovered a vast complex with large circular structures, decorated with stone reliefs depicting carved animal and human heads, suggesting that the site had ceremonial as well as defensive functions.

In the late 1960s Savoy explored many other known ruins in the Chachapoyas area, including Kuélap, an impressively defended fortress, perched on a mountain ridge high above the left bank of the River Utcubamba. He also publicized, for the first time, the existence of remains at Monte Peruvia (Purunllacta). He estimated that this site, some 155 sq. km (60 sq. miles) in extent and spread across more than 30 hill-tops linked by roadways, was one of the great cities of the Chachapoyas culture eventually conquered by Inca Tupac Yupanqui.

In 1969 Savoy changed direction again. Fascinated by the legend about the founder of the Chimu culture who arrived by sea, he hoped to prove that early Peruvians traded across the Pacific. To this end, he constructed a *totora* boat and sailed up the South American coast to Panama.

In the mid-1980s Savoy's adventures again hit the

headlines with the rediscovery of the Gran Vilaya (Congón) complex in a remote area east of Kuélap. Among the ruins he found a series of hieroglyphs, which he interpreted as signs of early ocean voyages. In 1997, although over 70 years old, he formed an expedition to put his theory to the test. Since then, he has sailed many times in a huge catamaran built according to designs on Moche ceramics (*circa* AD 100–600), to demonstrate that pre-Columbian inhabitants of Peru traded across the Pacific and as far afield as the Middle East and Africa.

Savoy, Bingham, Thor Heyerdahl, and Maria Reiche are just a few of the foreign explorers drawn to Peru, for there is something about its ancient cultures which continues to inspire the imagination today. ❑

RIGHT: early explorers were obsessed with El Dorado.

FROM COLONY TO REPUBLIC

From early colonial mismanagement, through the battles for independence, to 20th-century coups, Peru has known little stability

The chaotic years of early colonial administration were to change with the arrival in 1569 of Francisco de Toledo, Peru's fifth viceroy. A brutal but efficient ruler, Toledo consolidated Spain's command over the former Inca Empire. After finally crushing the rebel bastion of Vilcabamba and dealing with a revolt by dissatisfied conquistadors, he set about ordering every aspect of colonial life.

Spain's iron fist

The effects of Toledo's decrees were to alter the face of the Andes for ever. One of his most drastic measures was the establishment of *reducciones*, the forced resettlement of indigenous people into Spanish-style towns complete with a central plaza, church, townhall, and prison – the symbols of Spanish authority. *Reducciones* facilitated the collection of tribute from the Amerindians and their conversion to Christianity.

The new viceroy also formalized the *encomienda* system, whereby Amerindians provided labor and tribute to an *encomendero*, their Spanish landlord. The premise of the *encomienda* was completely alien to the Andean way of life, which was a system based on reciprocity and redistribution. In addition, the large tracts of land that formed the *encomiendas* ignored the Andean concept of verticality, whereby an ethnic group living near, say, Lake Titicaca, had access to land and produce – cotton, fish, and hot peppers – from the warm coastal valleys. Under the colonial order, distribution of goods went in only one direction: from tribute payer to local ethnic lord *(curaca)*, and thence to *encomendero*.

Because *encomenderos* rarely traveled outside the towns where they lived, it was usually the *curacas* who collected the tribute. Terrorized by the Spanish, they in turn terrorized the Amerindians into fulfilling their tribute obligations. They soon learned Spanish and borrowed

the trappings of colonial nobility, dressing in Spanish-style clothing, carrying firearms, and riding on horseback.

Squeezing Peru dry

The Spanish colonial economy was essentially based on coercion and plunder. The treasures

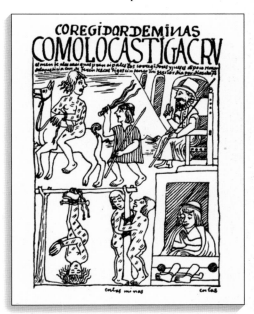

of Cusco had already been distributed, but there were other sources. In the north-coast city of Trujillo, named after Pizarro's birthplace in Spain, the Spanish crown granted licenses for the pillage of the ancient *huacas* (temples).

Once the Spanish had exhausted tombs to plunder, they turned to mines, a quest that led to the discovery in 1545 of Potosí. Today a bleak tin mining city in the Bolivian highlands, 4,070 meters (13,350 ft) above sea level, in its heyday in the 17th century Potosí was the richest and largest city in the world, with a population of 150,000 people. Potosí's silver filled the coffers of the Spanish Crown with the necessary cash to finance battles across Europe. The

LEFT: Amerindian nobles retained Inca trappings even in the 17th century. **RIGHT:** depredations of the Spanish (Huaman Poma de Ayala).

town's coat of arms read: "I am rich Potosí, treasure of the world and envy of Kings."

But the discovery of Potosí brought with it renewed hardship for the Amerindians. In 1574 Toledo legalized the *mita*, the traditional Inca system of enforced labor on a rotational basis. It was another example of an Andean institution twisted to suit Spanish needs; under the Incas the system had involved young people working in the service of the state for a limited period, depending on the task involved. In return, the transient workers had received hospitality from the local community as well as a look at the world outside their own village.

Under the Spanish version of the system, Amerindians were force-marched hundreds of miles to Potosí, where two out of every three died as a result of the appalling working conditions, since miners were forced to remain below ground for six-day stretches.

Even more horrific were the mercury mines in Huancavelica – one of which, Santa Barbara, soon became known as the "mine of death." Thousands of Amerindians from neighboring provinces died in the mines, asphyxiated by lethal fumes of cinnabar (sulphide of mercury), arsenic, and mercury.

The traditional chewing of coca leaves had initially been condemned by the Catholic Church until it was realized that the Amerindians could not survive the brutal mining *mita* without it. The leaf was soon touted by the Spanish as a cure-all to ward off hunger, thirst, and fatigue. The trade was organized and controlled: thousands of local highlanders, unadapted to life in the torrid jungle, died working the coca fields. Llama caravans carried coca leaves from Cusco, the center of production, to Potosí, 1,000 km (620 miles) away. The Church also reaped the benefits of the lucrative trade, collecting a tithe on each full basket.

Francisco de Toledo also initiated the *mita de obrajes*, or textile workshops. Working under harsh factory conditions, Amerindians were forced to weave for their Spanish masters, producing cloth for local consumption and export.

Toledo tried to limit the wealth of the *encomenderos* by ensuring that their land reverted to the Crown after a couple of generations, to be replaced with *corregimientos*. But this system had few advantages for the native peoples, as the *corregidores* (or co-regents) were also charged with collecting tribute and providing workers for the *obraje* and mining *mitas*.

Christians on the march

The early 1600s saw a far-flung campaign against idolatry, spurred on by a revival of native religion in 1565. The renewed religious zeal of the Catholic Church led to a push to stamp out native beliefs once and for all. At the same time, this crusade gave rise to valuable dictionaries and accounts that are still being studied by historians today. Priests visited outlying provinces, collecting information on cults and sometimes torturing villagers to reveal the whereabouts of idols and *huacas*.

THE FAT OF THE LAND

The *encomienda* system ensured a life of ease and luxury for the landowners. Contemporary records show that one group of tributaries in Conchucos in the north-central highlands were obliged to provide their *encomendero* annually with 2,500 pesos of gold or its equivalent in silver; the harvest of over 1,500 hectares (3,700 acres) in wheat, maize, barley, and potatoes; 30 sheep; 12 kilos (26 lbs) of candle wax; and 15 pairs of grouse every four months. In addition, they also had to give their master 20 eggs every Friday throughout the year and 25 donkey-loads of salt annually, 10 of which went to the viceroy.

In many ways, the Catholic campaign served to entrench native faiths; rather than taking over, Christianity formed a thin veneer over traditional cults and beliefs, many of which still exist today. This syncretism, in which traditional beliefs dominate, led to the replacement of Andean pilgrimage centers and festivals by superficially Catholic ones.

By the early 1700s the colonial system was firmly established throughout the Andes. At its height, the viceroyalty of Peru was 15 times the size of Spain and for two centuries ruled from Panama to Argentina. Colonists in Peru flourished. Under the prevailing system of

who reigned until Napoleon occupied Madrid in 1808. Efforts by various Bourbon monarchs to improve the colonial economy and stem corruption were to little avail.*

Amerindian uprising

During the 18th century, exploitation of the indigenous population sparked off various rebellions from Quito in present day Ecuador to La Paz (today's capitol city of Bolivia). The most serious of these was the uprising instigated by José Gabriel Condorcanqui, also known as Tupac Amaru II, as he claimed to be descended from the renegade Inca Emperor

mercantilism, which promoted exports and restricted imports and goods produced for local consumption, the elite grew rich, while the mass of people remained impoverished. Spain decreed that all trade from South America should pass through Lima, ensuring a massive influx of taxes. Lima, the opulent "City of Kings," was crammed with magnificent churches and mansions.

In Spain, meanwhile, the end of the War of the Spanish Succession (1700–13) saw the Habsburg dynasty replaced by the Bourbons,

LEFT: a colonial crucifix.
ABOVE: Simón de Bolívar takes on the Spanish forces.

THE DIABOLICAL HERB

Although some authorities tried to limit the production of coca, the "diabolical herb," too many fortunes were made from the trade. "There are those in Spain who became rich from this coca, buying it up and reselling it and trading it in the markets of the Indians," wrote Spanish chronicler and soldier Pedro Cieza de León, who traveled throughout Peru in the 1540s. "Without coca there would be no Peru," noted another contemporary observer. This terse statement on 16th-century coca production has a familiar ring some 460 years later, with the multi-billion dollar cocaine industry now threatening the stability of Andean nations.

killed in 1569 *(see page 54)*. Born in Tinta, south of Cusco, Tupac Amaru II studied in Cusco at a school for Amerindians of noble birth. It was not his intention to rid Peru of the Spanish yoke; rather, he fought against the tyranny of the *corregidores*, the miserable conditions at the *haciendas*, mines, *obrajes*, and coca plantations and the subsequent malnutrition and disease. Increasingly, he lobbied for Amerindian rights, demanding that the mine *mita* be lifted and the power of the *corregidores* limited.

In 1780 he had Tinta's hated *corregidor*, Antonio Arriaga, taken prisoner and hanged in

Charles III, who had come to the throne in 1759, ordered that commerce be opened up, allowing ports other than Lima to conduct trade. He banned the *repartimiento*, the forced sale of inferior goods to native peoples at inflated prices, and ended the *corregimiento* system. He also divided the viceroyalty into seven intendancies under royal rule, paving the way for the regionalism that would break South America into its present patchwork of republics.

Not all the Spanish Government and clergy exploited the Amerindians. One clergyman, Don Baltasar Jaime Martínez de Compañon y Bujanda, stands out. Appointed Bishop of Tru-

the public square. It was the start of a public revolt that spread throughout the Peruvian highlands. Spanish reinforcements were sent from Lima to quell the uprising. At a decisive battle in Checacupe, in 1781, the Spaniards dispersed Tupac Amaru's men and captured the rebel leader and his wife. Tupac Amaru was forced to witness the execution of his family before he was drawn and quartered, like his ancestor before him, in Cusco's public square.

As a result of the rebellion, the viceroy Teodoro de Croix (1784–90) began to institute long overdue reforms. He set up a special *audiencia*, or royal court, in Cusco to deal with Amerindian legal claims. Meanwhile in Spain,

jillo in 1779, he spent his years traveling around a vast diocese covering the northern third of Peru. In a letter to Charles III dated 1786 he described the "wretchedness" he encountered everywhere.

The push for independence

On the eve of Napoleon's march on the Iberian Peninsula, Spain's hold on its colonies was already waning. Despite the best endeavors of the authorities, news of the French Revolution (begun in 1788), as well as the United States' War of Independence from Britain (1775–83), had filtered through to the colonies – at least to the *criollos* or creoles (American-born

Peruvians of European descent) – and inspired hopes for self-determination. When Napoleon forced Charles IV to abdicate in 1808, and then placed his own brother Joseph on the Spanish throne, there were rebellions in many parts of South America. Declarations of independence in Upper Peru (now Bolivia) and Quito (Ecuador) in 1809 were followed by uprisings in the Peruvian cities of Huánuco and Cusco. But freedom from Spain was not so easily won: royalist troops regained control in many parts of the continent, and bloody wars were waged for the next 15 years.

There were many Peruvians who supported attacked Lima, dispersing royalist troops, who fled to the central and southern highlands. Meanwhile, the northern cities of Trujillo, Lambayeque, Piura, and Cajamarca declared their independence. General San Martín entered Lima in 1821, proclaiming independence for all Peru on July 28.

His first move was to abolish the Amerindian tribute, the mining *mita*, and the *corregimiento,* reforms which had been attempted earlier by Charles III. He even went so far as to ban the term "Indian" and proclaimed the descendants of the Incas to be citizens of Peru.

But Peru was not prepared for self-rule. San

the colonial system, since Lima was still its wealthy administrative capital. Peru became the strongest bastion of pro-Spanish feeling, and other newly independent countries could not feel secure until it, too, was liberated.

After Argentinian General José de San Martín's successful invasion of Chile in 1819, a rebel navy commanded by the British admiral Lord Cochrane sailed from the Chilean port of Valparaíso and landed in Paracas, on Peru's south coast. The following year the armada

LEFT: missionaries in the Amazon basin.
ABOVE: defending Lima from Chilean attack in the War of the Pacific.

THE PROGRESSIVE PRIEST

Fascinated by natural history and colonial life, as well as concerned about the welfare of the people, the Bishop of Trujillo, Martínez de Compañon, and his team of artists produced over 1,000 drawings, plans, and maps in ink and watercolor bound in nine volumes and covering antiquities, flora and fauna, customs, music, and costumes of northern Peru. The 18th-century cleric is also considered by many to be the grandfather of Peruvian archeology: he collected some 600 pieces of pre-Columbian textiles and ceramics for shipment to the Spanish king, who founded a "Cabinet of Natural History and Antiquities" in Madrid.

Martín opted for a new monarchy to replace Spanish rule and searched for a European prince to rule the former colony. In the subsequent tumultuous months, the monarchical plan was scuttled following the election of a parliament. The seven viceregal intendancies became departments headed by prefects, modeled on the French system of government.

Freedom and chaos

In 1822 San Martín sailed to Guayaquil (Ecuador), where he met Venezuelan statesman Simón de Bolívar, El Libertador. A far-sighted political thinker influenced by the ideas of the

Enlightenment, Bolívar had liberated his home country, and wanted San Martín's help to establish Gran Colombia, comprising Venezuela, Colombia and Ecuador (which lasted only from 1823 to 1830).

San Martín needed troops to root out the last Spanish royalist forces holed-up in the Andes and offered Peru's leadership to Bolívar. During his brief presidency (1824–26) Bolívar advocated republicanism. He commanded troops at the Battle of Junín in 1824, but it was not until the decisive Battle of Ayacucho later that year that rebels headed by Venezuelan General José de Sucre crushed the royalist troops.

Bolívar's departure for Colombia in 1826 created a power vacuum, and the congress elected José de la Mar as president. San Martín's promises to abolish the Amerindian tribute, *mita*, servitude, and even to recognize Quechua as an official language, were never followed through. The wars of independence had left the country ravaged, crops unattended, and food scarce. Instead of indigenous peoples being granted equal status as citizens of a republican Peru, an all-out assault on Amerindian landholdings began.

Between 1826 and 1865, 35 presidents, many of them military officers, governed Peru. Chaos reigned. Charles Darwin, who visited the capital during his journey of scientific discovery in the 1830s, recalled: "Lima, the city of Kings, must formerly have been a splendid town." But he found it in a "wretched state of decay; the streets are nearly unpaved, and heaps of filth are piled up in all directions, where the black *gallinazos* (vultures) pick up bits of carrion."

Rich pickings

By 1830 Peru had discovered a new resource that replaced minerals as the country's main export: guano. The rich piles of bird droppings deposited on Peru's offshore islands were much sought-after in Europe as fertilizer and fetched enormous prices.

The first guano contract was negotiated with a British company in 1840. Amerindians worked in appalling conditions at the guano stations, where ammonia fumes shriveled the skin and often caused blindness. By 1849, Peru's economy was almost entirely in the

---

RUBBER BARONS

The Peruvian economy also benefited from the rubber boom, which lasted from about 1880 to 1912. The existence of latex in the rubber trees of the Amazon was common knowledge, but it was only after Charles Goodyear discovered the process of vulcanization, which kept rubber firm in high temperatures, that its commercial possibilities were realized. The rubber barons of Iquitos in Peru and Manaus in Brazil lived in luxury for a few decades until an English adventurer smuggled the seeds from the Amazon to Asia (via Kew Gardens in England) and the monopoly came to an abrupt end.

hands of two foreign firms, one based in London, the other in Paris, which between them shared exclusive guano marketing rights.

There were a few other sources of income: large cotton and sugar estates had developed on the coast, and in 1849 Peru began to import Chinese labor to work the fields. In 1865 Spain, hoping to regain a foothold in its former colony, occupied the Chincha guano islands. A year later President Mariano Prado declared war on Spain and, after the Spanish navy bombarded the port of Callao, Peru decided to revamp its fleet, buying arms and munitions in Europe. Using the guano con-

War breaks out

In 1879 Chile declared war on Peru and Bolivia over a dispute concerning sodium nitrate and borax deposits in the province of Tarapaca. The War of the Pacific (1879–83) found the armed forces of Peru and Bolivia woefully unprepared. Chilean troops occupied southern Peru and then bombarded Callao, occupying Lima and cutting off the capital from the hinterland. Following the peace treaty of 1883, Peru ceded Tarapaca to Chile.

The war brought economic chaos. The Amerindian tribute was reinstated and a salt tax levied. In 1886, British bond-holders began nego-

cession as a guarantee for the vast sum of 20 million pesos, Peru acquired the *Huascar* and *Independencia* warships from Britain.

The guano boom also initiated an era of railroad construction in the 1870s. The US railroad entrepreneur, Henry Meiggs, won the bid for the Callao–La Oroya line, an engineering feat of tunnels and bridges that began at sea level and rose over 5,000 meters (16,400 ft) to the mining town of La Oroya. In 1877, unable to pay its British creditors, the Peruvian state became bankrupt. Worse was to come.

LEFT: the railroad comes to Peru. **ABOVE:** the 1956 inauguration of President Manuel Prado.

tiations: Peru's debt was cancelled in exchange for a 66-year control of the major railroads and 2 million tons of guano. The Peruvian Corporation was set up in 1890 to manage their interests.

By 1900, US interests were beginning to replace the British in controlling the Peruvian economy. Following the Spanish–American War over Cuba in 1898, US expansionists had begun to show an interest in Latin America. Many businessmen, seeing their domestic market as saturated, were looking for new outlets.

US investors set up the Cerro de Pasco Mining Company, which soon controlled all the mines in the central Sierra. In 1922 a smelter at La Oroya began belching fumes of arsenic, lead, and zinc into the atmosphere, ravaging the country; and fishmeal began to be exported from Peru's abundant anchovy plants.

Workers in the mines, coastal factories, and urban sweatshops began to form unions. But it was on the north coast, where laborers on the sugar *haciendas* began to organize, that a new class consciousness found political expression. In 1924, while exiled in Mexico, a popular activist named Victor Raúl Haya de la Torre formed the Alianza Popular Revolucionaria Americana (APRA), with a loose platform based on anti-imperialism and nationalization that attracted middle-class voters who felt neglected

by the oligarchical rule. Haya was allowed back to contest the 1931 elections, but was defeated in what *apristas* denounced as a fraud. Party members rebelled in Trujillo, killing 60 military officers. In reprisal, the military executed over 1,000 *apristas* in the ruins of Chan Chan.

Urban drift

For the next 50 years, APRA was kept out of power as Peru oscillated between conservative and military regimes. Manufacturing industry developed and thousands of *campesinos* (subsistence farmers) flocked into Lima. Pressure for land reform and some redistribution of wealth grew. The first government of Fernando

Belaunde (1963–68), who promised some cautious progressive measures, was a failure, and, after widespread disgust at tax concessions given to the International Petroleum Company (a subsidiary of Standard Oil of New Jersey), yet another coup occurred. Belaunde was marched out of the Presidential Palace in his pyjamas, and into exile. But General Juan Velasco, who headed the new junta, was not a typical military ruler, and went on to champion many of the radical APRA reforms.

Velasco's measures were drastic. They included sweeping agrarian reform, expropriating vast landholdings, and turning family-run estates into cooperatives. Petrol, mining, and fishing industries were nationalized at a stroke. Food for the urban population was subsidized by the state. And, in a profound symbolic gesture, Peru was recognized as a bilingual country, with Quechua as the second language.

A bloodless coup

Well-intentioned Velasco's measures may have been, but they were not backed by sound economic planning. The newly nationalized industries were badly managed and lacked the necessary finance, and the country was already slipping into economic chaos well before the 1973 international oil crisis. The military split into factions, and in 1975, Morales Bermúdez, heading an alliance of conservative and reformist officers, staged a bloodless coup against Velasco, who died soon afterwards.

The new military government soon proved incapable of running the country. Debt soared, and inflation ran out of control. A wave of industrial unrest culminated in a general strike in 1977, which marked a turning point. A constituent assembly was elected and its president, Haya de la Torre, lifted the last barrier to adult suffrage, giving 2 million illiterate adults the right to vote.

Peru returned to civilian rule in 1980, when President Belaunde was elected to a second period in office. Ironically, this also marked the emergence of the Sendero Luminoso (Shining Path) guerrilla group, when its members burned ballot boxes in Ayacucho. The following decade was marked by the single-minded violence of this group and the state's response to it. ❑

LEFT: General Juan Velasco.

The "Covered Ones"

Friction between Peru's Spanish-born residents and its upper-class *mestizos* did more than spark the independence revolution. It also bred rivalry between women from the two camps and gave Lima its most scandalous fashion. The Spanish women enticed men in traditional fashion, showing off their tiny waists and wafting elaborate fans. Not to be outdone, the *mestizas* created an alluring look of their own by covering their faces with Arab veils – except for one eye which peeked out. They were known as the *tapadas* or "covered ones."

Although veiled, the *tapadas* were far from modest. Their skirts were hiked shamelessly up to show feet tinier than those of their Spanish rivals, and necklines were lowered, while the fairer-skinned Spaniards remained covered under Lima's strong sun, this being long before the European craze for finding a suntan attractive.

When the European women squeezed their middles even more, the thicker-waisted *mestizas* scrimped on the fabric encircling their ample hips. As a result, skirts in the 1700s became so tight that their wearers could take only the tiniest of steps as they promenaded slowly down the street. But one part of the costume remained constant throughout these changes: the veil hiding all but one eye, with which a great deal could be said.

"This costume so alters a woman – even her voice since her mouth is covered – that unless she is very tall or very short, lame, hunchbacked or otherwise conspicuous, she is impossible to recognize," wrote early French feminist Flora Tristan. "I am sure it needs little imagination to appreciate the consequences of this time-honored practice which is sanctioned or at least tolerated by law."

The *tapadas* spent their afternoons strolling, and the "consequences" of their tantalizing fashion ranged from playful flirting to sinful trysts. Ironically, it was said that some of them even caught out their own husbands. So scandalous was the behavior the costume permitted that the archbishop attempted to condemn it, but the *tapadas* refused to serve their husbands, attend their families, or carry out church duties while the sanction was in effect.

Conspiracy was endemic in the early 19th century, and many *tapadas* used their afternoon walks to pass messages to organizers of the revolution, thus playing

RIGHT: the scandalous fashion of "the covered ones."

an important part in forming the nation. The site for this romantic and political intrigue was the Paseo de Aguas – a walkway of reflecting pools and gardens built for a woman who inspired one of South America's most famous romances.

By stealing a viceroy's heart, *mestiza* Micaela Villegas placed herself firmly in history and legend. Count Amat y Juniet built her Lima's finest house, bought her a gold and silver coach and, although in his sixties when they met, fathered her only child.

Villegas was known as "La Perrichola," Amat's mispronunciation of *perra chola*, literally "half-breed bitch," an epithet he threw at her during a heated argument. Despite the harshness of this name, Amat

adored the actress, who had first caught his eye on a Lima stage. Their love inspired Jacques Offenbach's 1868 opera *La Périchole*.

But the Perrichola story has a sad ending. Inconsolable when her aged lover was ordered back to Spain (where, in his eighties, he married one of his nieces), La Perrichola vowed that she would never love again. She gave her considerable wealth to the poor, and entered a convent.

On the site of the opulent mansion a Cristal beer factory now stands, but the Paseo de Aguas survives in the Rímac district north of the river, behind the Presidential Palace and next to the Convento de los Descalzos. The latter is worth a visit in itself for its collection of colonial paintings. ❑

DEMOCRACY AND CRISIS

*Peru has become a democracy, the battle against terrorism has been won,
and inflation is under control, but the rural–urban divide has still to be bridged*

Peruvian politics appeared to have turned full circle when Fernando Belaunde Terry was elected president for a second time in 1980. But he returned to a country that had changed a great deal after 12 years of military regimes, with a high level of popular frustration and the beginnings of violent armed opposition aimed at toppling the state. This threat grew throughout his four years in office, while at the same time international prices for Peru's raw materials fell, and the country, together with much of the rest of Latin America, was faced with a crisis of repayment of foreign debt.

After Belaunde, the APRA party and its leader Alan García came to power for the first time. But his administration's attempt to spend its way out of trouble led to huge inflation and institutionalized corruption. García also allowed the armed forces to embark on a counter-insurgency campaign that led to direct military rule over much of the country, and many human rights violations.

Peruvians were so disillusioned with the traditional political parties that in the next elections held at the end of 1989 they chose the outsider Alberto Fujimori, of Japanese descent, as their president. Fujimori installed an authoritarian regime that initially seemed justified when the leader of the Sendero Luminoso ("Shining Path") terror group was captured, and his movement defeated. Fujimori failed to bring the promised prosperity, and resorted to increasingly dishonest means to stay in power. But it was only after his controversial election for a third term in office in 2000 that public protests grew massively. Soon afterwards, video recordings of bribery, corruption, and other illegal dealings made by his unofficial intelligence chief Vladimiro Montesinos came to light. The scandal surrounding these videos led Fujimori to flee to Japan, and the congress stripped him of his office on the grounds of "moral incapacity". A caretaker administration organized free and fair elections in 2001 that

were won on a second round of voting by Alejandro Toledo, the first indigenous person to become elected president of modern-day Peru.

Buffeted by external forces

Belaunde brought with him a free market-oriented economic team that hastily undid some

of the Velasco legacy by returning some state companies to private control, and trying to increase competition and lower tariffs. They also turned their back on the experiment to kick-start a Peruvian industrial base, focusing instead on capitalizing on the country's rich natural resources.

External forces did much to disrupt their efforts. From 1982 raw material export prices slumped, while in 1983 a powerful El Niño current triggered flooding and natural disasters that devastated fishing and agriculture. Meanwhile, Belaunde, known for his high rhetoric, continued with expensive projects to build roads into the jungle and colonize eastern Peru, thus

LEFT: the people of Cusco in a celebratory mood.
RIGHT: supplicants waiting in the APRA office.

ensuring that public spending remained high. The Latin American debt crisis also undercut the economy, causing credit lines to dry up, leaving Peru faced with the choice of defaulting or strangling any hopes of economic advance.

The violent years

As popular discontent continued to grow, the Belaunde government became increasingly repressive, responding to strikes and protest marches with tear-gas and riot police. The government badly misjudged the Sendero Luminoso revolt in the Andes, ignoring early signs of activity, then allowing counter-insurgency forces to

limit its foreign debt payments to 10 percent of its export earnings, with the result that international bankers and lending agencies refused to offer any more credit to Peru.

The policy fanned domestic consumption and started a two-year spurt of growth. Yet this ran out of steam as foreign reserves tumbled and credit lines dried up. Inflation romped ahead and the value of wages slumped. The economy tumbled into chaos; inflation soaring at around 40 percent a month meant that people's savings were wiped out, and hardship and food shortages ensued. Shock austerity measures left many in poorer areas with no option but the *ollas comunes*

act with indiscriminate violence against the indigenous population. Tens of thousands of people are thought to have lost their lives in what was known as "the years of violence". Most of the victims lived in the Andean highland regions of Ayacucho or neighboring provinces.

Hopes dashed

The first-ever Peruvian president from the ranks of the mass APRA party, the youthful Alán García represented the country's hopes for unity and economic relief. García retreated from the previous government's ties with the IMF. In July 1985 he dropped a bombshell on the foreign banks, announcing that Peru would

(soup kitchens). Central bank coffers had been emptied by the chaotic early exchange-rate controls, followed by the raging inflation. The García administration ended its days amid allegations of widespread extortion and corruption.

García also failed to find a way of containing the growing threat from Sendero Luminoso and the smaller pro-Cuban Movimiento Revolucionario Tupac Amaru, with the former moving its attention from the Andes to the capital. His reputation as a man of the masses suffered as he appeared incapable of reining in the tactics of the military, who were determined to put down insurgency in the Andes. Thousands continued to be killed or "disappeared" by brutal attacks from rebels and the military. In Lima, the massacre of hundreds of rioting *senderistas* at two top-security prisons in July 1986 undermined García's human rights record. There was a growing sense of anarchy as a third of the country came under emergency rule.

One of García's legacies was the popular disgust with all traditional parties. That disillusion turned into a tidal wave of support for a former agricultural university rector, Alberto Fujimori, in the 1990 elections. At first, no one took any notice of the engineer of Japanese descent campaigning in shanty towns on the back of a tractor, but Fujimori began creeping up the opinion polls.

(the white elite), people turned to a candidate they related to more easily: Fujimori. The little-known candidate of the Cambio 90 party romped to victory against Vargas Llosa. The novelist left shortly afterwards and has taken up Spanish nationality, a move that has further alienated him from his home country.

The reign of Fujimori

No-one made a bigger impact on the Peru of the 1990s than Alberto Fujimori. He seized power with both hands and ruled with an instinctive sense of the popular mood, which he at first expertly manipulated. He began by breaking

The front-runner, well-known novelist Mario Vargas Llosa, made the crucial mistake of accepting an alliance with the old rightist parties, including Belaunde's AP (Popular Action Party), which sparked voters' concerns that he was a Trojan horse for the same old political elite. The popular perception of Vargas Llosa – who had lived much of his life in Europe – as a haughty intellectual, far removed from the grit of daily life in the shanty towns, also worked against him. Rejecting the *blanquitos*

FAR LEFT: former President Alán García.
LEFT: Abimael Guzmán, leader of Sendero Luminoso.
ABOVE: on the trail of the Shining Path.

electoral promises and adopting the economic shock programs championed by the defeated Vargas Llosa. The economic measures he introduced began with price rises and currency devaluation, which hit Peruvians hard. He combined these with a radical program of privatization, cutting tariffs, and simplifying taxes.

The Fujimori administration set its sights on returning to the international financial community, in order to win IMF approval. Gradually the economy appeared to recover, but the sale of state enterprises led to thousands of job losses, and workers' wage rates declined in real terms.

The main achievement of Fujimori's first term (1990–95) was not an economic one. In September 1992, the capture of the Sendero Luminoso leader, Abimael Guzmán, who had gained almost mythical status, dealt a fatal blow to the rebel organization. Shown to the press in a huge circus-size cage, dressed in a striped prison suit like those worn by cartoon burglars, the bearded, bespectacled Guzmán was seen to be just an aging man. Although Sendero remained active for a while, the capture of Guzmán and other top members destroyed its organization.

The arrest was one of the reasons for Peru's economy beginning to climb back out of a decade-long trough, as confidence returned to a community that had been shaken by bombings

being jailed for years on the say-so of others.

Yet Fujimori weathered international and domestic criticisms, and the election of a constituent assembly in 1993 persuaded the US government to lift a suspension on aid. The economy began to expand, and by 1993 Peru's growth rate was among the highest in the world.

The darker side of his authoritarian regime was seen in the killings of La Cantuta. A death squad of intelligence agents murdered nine students and a professor from the university and buried their bodies in sand dunes outside Lima. Several agents were tried and sentenced, but the Amnesty Law, passed in 1995, gave immu-

in the country and cities. Fujimori's autocratic style at first found an echo in a society that had been on the brink of chaos. Backed by army tanks, his decision in April 1992 to dissolve parliament and sack top judges met with majority support. He claimed he needed to take sole control of the government to bypass a corrupt parliament and judiciary. Further radical measures followed, with the decision to try alleged terrorists in "faceless" military courts, where the judge's identity was kept secret, and the repentance law that encouraged rebels to turn themselves in and receive pardon or lower sentences if they denounced others. In practice, that measure led to hundreds of innocent people

nity to members of security forces who had taken part in human rights abuses since 1980, and freed those convicted of the killings.

By the end of his first term, Fujimori was credited with almost eliminating the twin evils of the 1980s: inflation and terrorism. In gratitude, Peruvians not only voted him back in with a 64 percent majority in 1995, but also gave his Cambio 90–Nueva Mayoría alliance a majority in Congress. His main challenger, former UN Secretary-General Javier Pérez de Cuellar, lacked the popular touch.

Fujimori's resounding victory in what independent observers termed a generally fair and free election meant he recovered international political legitimacy. Yet hopes that he would relegate army and intelligence service to less important roles proved unfounded. The unofficial head of the intelligence services, Vladimiro Montesinos, became increasingly powerful. He used his position to buy off any corrupt politicians, members of the armed forces, the judiciary and the media, as well as to undermine many of Peru's democratic institutions.

Furthermore, Fujimori appeared to focus on finding a way to stand for a third term, even though the Constitution he had pushed through allowed only two consecutive terms of office. In many people's eyes, the business of government began to take second place to the push for re-election in the year 2000. The pro-Fujimori Congress suggested he could stand again, as his first election victory, in 1990, preceded the new Constitution. When three judges on the Constitutional Tribunal ruled that such a re-election was unconstitutional, Congress sacked them. The National Magistrates Council, charged with appointing and sacking judges, later resigned after its powers were cut. The apparent drive to achieve re-election created a crisis because of the lack of independent institutions to ensure guarantees for running the country according to law.

Equally, the privatization program that the Fujimori government embarked on began to falter in his second term. Public discontent with the cost of privatized services like telephones and electricity seemed to have sparked indecision on the part of policy-makers. In 1998, with Peru in the third year of an IMF program, the fund's team was expressing praise for the meeting of macroeconomic goals, and growth in 1997 had been a healthy 7.4 percent. Yet most Peruvians were perplexed that the figures were not reflected in an improvement in their standard of living. "If the economy is doing so well, why am I doing so badly?" was the front-cover headline of the weekly magazine *Caretas*, echoing the popular sentiment, with the main complaint being the shortage of properly paid jobs.

The siege

Fujimori's second term faced its greatest crisis at the end of 1996, when a group of masked and well-armed rebels of the Movimiento Revolucionario Tupac Amaru (MRTA) blasted their way into a reception at the Japanese ambassador's residence in Lima and took hundreds of guests hostage. The 126-day hostage crisis put massive international pressure on Fujimori's government because dignitaries of many nationalities were among the captives.

The siege came at a time when most Lima residents believed that terrorist attacks were a thing of the past. For the MRTA, an organization that grew out of far-left groups in the early 1980s, the siege was a last-ditch attempt to save the movement, whose support had dwindled to around 100 armed rebels, and to push for the release of hundreds of members then in prison.

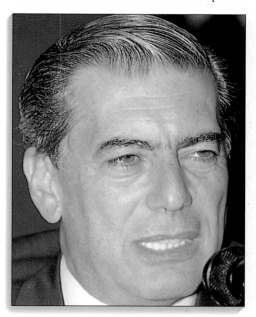

During the stand-off that ensued through the hot Lima summer, several groups of hostages were released from the besieged residence, until there remained a core group of 120, including Foreign Minister Francisco Tudela and Fujimori's brother, Pedro.

While the International Red Cross mediated, and talks to discuss the rebels' demands began, Fujimori took a gamble. Miners were drafted in to dig a warren of tunnels under the residence, and on April 22 1997, a special commando unit blasted its way in and rescued the hostages. One hostage, two commandos, and all 14 rebels were killed – according to some reports, after they had surrendered. Fujimori claimed he was personally

---

LEFT: casting a vote in the 2001 presidential election.
RIGHT: failed favorite Mario Vargas Llosa.

responsible for the successful rescue operation, and his popularity ratings immediately soared. But this success could not halt the growing discontent among many Peruvians, and their protests grew as Fujimori pushed for a third term in office in the 2000 elections. When he was declared the victor over his closest rival Alejandro Toledo, there were claims of widespread fraud and thousands protested during his inauguration in Lima.

Even so, Fujimori might have held onto power had it not been for the "Vladivideos". In September 2000, the first of hundreds of videos made by Montesinos in the intelligence headquarters came to light. These videos showed

how he and Fujimori had bribed politicians, judges, the police, media owners, and businessmen in order to cement their positions on power and to amass huge, illegal fortunes.

Fujimori and Montesinos fled the country. Fujimori took up residence in Japan, where his parents had been born, and faxed his resignation as president. The Peruvian congress stripped him of his office for "moral incapacity". He is still installed in a luxury apartment outside Tokyo, as Japan refuses all Peru's requests to extradite him.

Vladimiro Montesinos was less fortunate. After spending several months in hiding in neighboring Venezuela, he was captured and returned to Peru to stand trial. He faces charges

ranging from organizing death squads to involvement in illegal drugs trafficking, but it may be years before the full truth comes to light.

A caretaker government under the veteran politician Valentín Paniagua took over. They had three main tasks: to organize fresh elections, to guarantee continuity in economic affairs, and to investigate the massive corruption of the Fujimori regime and the human rights abuses committed in the struggle against the armed opposition groups over 20 years since 1980.

Truth and reconciliation

In 2001, the government set up the Truth and Reconciliation Commission, not only to look into the "years of violence" between 1980–2000, but to establish responsibilities, and also to pave the way for reparations. In its final report, presented in 2003, the commission concluded that some 69,000 people had died as a result of Sendero Luminoso and other extremist group attacks, the majority of them innocent peasants.

The Paniagua administration also established an independent electoral commission, which organized fresh presidential and congressional elections for April 2001. The front runners in the first round were center-left economist, Alejandro Toledo and former president Alan García. Despite only having returned to Peru a few months earlier, García and his APRA party made a surprisingly strong showing, but Toledo was the winner in a second round of voting.

Alejandro Toledo, who as a young man had been a shoe-shine boy but was later educated as an economist at Stanford and Harvard, took office in July 2001. Since then he has tried to restore faith in democratic rule. There have been attempts to renew the judiciary and the police. Many senior members of the armed forces are facing trial for alleged involvement in corruption. Elections for regional parliaments in 2002 also saw an attempt to try to change the economic and political balance away from the capital.

There is now complete press freedom and a much lower level of political violence than for many years. But increasingly, Peruvians are realizing that getting rid of Fujimori and Montesinos was only the start of a long and difficult process of building a real democracy. ❑

LEFT: President Alejandro Toledo waves after Peru's annual military parade in Lima.
RIGHT: protesting Fujimori's bid for a third term.

SOCIETY

Peruvian society represents a blending of cultures, each of which has left an indelible mark on the national identity

Since pre-Columbian times Peruvians have been divided by geography. There are three main geographical regions: the arid *costa* (coastal strip); the Andean Sierra or highlands, and to the east of the mountains, the Amazon basin. Almost half of Peruvians live in the coastal region, some 8 million of them in the capital, Lima. It is a city of extremes, with the richest and most Europeanized Peruvians living not far from the poorest shanty towns, where *mestizo* migrants from the provinces have come in search of work or to escape the violence that marked Peru in recent years.

From the arid deserts of the coast, the Andean Sierra rises up to more than 6,000 meters (19,700 ft) above sea level. The highlands comprise about a quarter of Peru's territory, but are home to about half the population. For the modern nation state, this mountain mass poses major problems for development and integration into a single society. The huge natural barrier severely limits the penetration of motorized transport and telecommunications, while frequent earthquakes and landslides further complicate the already arduous terrain.

The result is dramatic regional diversity, and considerable inequalities in services and living standards. Health, education, and law enforcement programs are unevenly distributed across Peru. About a third of the country has no conventional medical services: people rely on the *curanderos* – healers who use a variety of natural and spiritual remedies. Social anthropologist John Murra described the Andes as an archipelago, a series of island-like pockets of isolated communities. It is an apt description.

Many worlds

Over the past 470 years, there has been a long process of inter-cultural mixing, creating the *mestizo* – a mixture of Amerindian and European heritage. Today the majority of Peruvians

PRECEDING PAGES: young sandboard enthusiasts.
LEFT: a *chiclayo* flower seller.
RIGHT: rider on Peruvian pacing horse *(caballo de paso).*

fall into this category, and it is possible to become *mestizo* by choice as well as by birth. Anyone assuming Western dress in the rural highlands is usually referred to as *mestizo* or sometimes *cholo*. Peruvian social divisions are culturally, as much as racially, defined.

There are two large ethno-linguistic groups in

the Andes: the larger of the two speaks Quechua, the language of the Inca Empire; the smaller group speaks Aymara and is settled around Lake Titicaca and in neighboring Bolivia. The Quechua language is far from uniform, and someone speaking the dialect of Huancayo might not be fully understood by a Quechua-speaker from Cusco.

Beyond these broad distinctions, other complexities arise. There are "white" ethnic groups, like the Morochucos of Pampa Cangallo (Ayacucho) who have light-colored eyes and hair, speak Quechua, and see themselves as *campesinos* (subsistence farmers). The *misti*, the dominant social class in the Andes, speak

Quechua and share other cultural traits but enjoy access to education and some of the luxuries of modern life. To the east, the Andes mountains fall away to the River Amazon system. The *selva alta* (higher slopes) were colonized by *campesinos* only in the second half of the 20th century. Some of the valleys here are where most of Peru's coca crops are grown. The lower foothills of the Andes gradually give way to the vast Amazon river system and its *selva baja* (low-lying jungle). It is here that the 53 ethno-linguistic indigenous groups (some 5 percent of Peru's population) live, although their lands are increasingly being encroached upon by settlers.

run by *chinos* (who, like the former president Fujimori, could in fact be Japanese) and cheap Chinese restaurants or *chifas* are to be found everywhere. Lima has a strong Anglo community, while in the high jungle, around Oxapampa, there are descendants of German and Austrian immigrants, mainly coffee growers, who still retain firm links with their countries of origin.

The urban–rural divide

Peruvian culture is sharply divided between indigenous and colonial societies, between the mountains and the city. There are elite white *criollos*, most of whom live in Lima,

Until the trade was banned in the 19th century, landowners brought in black Africans to serve as slaves on their *haciendas* and frequently used them to repress the local Amerindians. Black influence on the music and dance of Peru has been extensive *(see page 112)* and has also made an impact on the country's cuisine. Today, Afro-Peruvians are prominent in sport and noticeably absent in political life, and still suffer discrimination.

Between 1850 and 1930, Chinese and Japanese workers were brought into Peru. They helped build the railways, worked on cotton and sugar plantations, and set up small businesses in the towns and cities. Many corner stores are

who trace their bloodlines back to the Spanish Conquest of 1536. They are joined by incomers from Italy, Spain, and other European countries. A surprising number of politicians have Arabic surnames, as there was an influx of Palestinian refugees to Peru after 1948. The *criollos* and other "gringos" enjoy the cultural legacy of colonialism, and their eyes are firmly fixed on Europe and the United States.

North American mass culture, from Reebok to Disneyland, is an integral part of their children's upbringing, and shopping trips to Miami for clothes and consumer goodies are quite common. Most of these products can now be found in the mega shopping centers of Lima, but they still cost a lot more. A visitor from Europe, or the USA will feel a comfortable familiarity in Lima's cafes, department stores, and supermarkets.

Rural communities now also aspire to ownership of televisions and jeans, but this comes into conflict with their traditional values. Heirs to awe-inspiring pre-Columbian cultures, the people of the Andes are maintaining the traditional practices of their ancestors in a rapidly changing world. Their livelihood continues to be based on family-owned fields, or *chacras*, which are farmed by hand or with the help of draft animals.

The social organization of communities in

communal meals and plentiful supplies of *chicha* (homemade corn beer).

The Quechua- and Aymara-speaking peoples of Peru inhabit some 5,000 peasant communities located throughout the Andean Sierra. These communities are based on an agricultural economy, but families frequently supplement their incomes with labor-intensive cottage industries in which they produce the distinctive handicrafts found on the tourist trail, in addition to foodstuffs such as bread, cheese, and honey.

A large majority of highland people live a marginal and impoverished existence. While retain-

the Andes differs greatly from that of Europeanized *criollo* culture. Work, marriage, and land ownership are centered around a complex extended family organization – called the *ayllu* in Quechua – which dates back at least to Inca times. One of the main functions of *ayllus* is to organize reciprocal work exchanges. These often take the form of group projects like roof-raising or potato harvesting, which are usually made more festive and enjoyable by

FAR LEFT: stately *marinera* dancers in Trujillo.
LEFT: praying in a cemetery.
ABOVE: pipe-playing on Taquile Island.
ABOVE RIGHT: soccer fan in a Lima shanty town.

RECLAIMING THE LAND

The Cusicacha Trust, a British-funded charity for research and development, has recently completed projects in the Cusicacha and Patacancha valleys, which focused on redeveloping and restoring Inca irrigation and terracing, bringing land back into cultivation and people back into the areas.

The trust has worked with Peru's indigenous peoples to improve water systems, to establish vegetable gardens and worm pits, to set up local markets, and to encourage women to take control of the household economy. New projects are planned for Ayacucho and Apurimac, areas severely affected in the past by terrorist activity.

ing a fierce loyalty to their ancestral heritage, the poor of the Andes are nevertheless eager to share in the benefits of a modern lifestyle, which include educational opportunities, electricity, sewage systems, and clean water.

Growth of a monster

Many Andean communities suffered greatly during the 20th century, and between the 1960s and the 1980s Lima seemed like a promised land to the rural poor. Thousands of migrants from as far afield as Ayaviri, Bambamarca, and Huaraz gradually filled the city with a huge Andean population. Added to

was no place within the city for all these people to go *(see page 163)*. A symbol of this cultural influx is the vibrant *chicha* music of Lima, which mixes the traditions of Andean and creole music to express the melancholic realities of urban life.

With the end of rural violence, migration to the capital has slowed. But Lima still receives a huge proportion of Peru's resources and services, and has the greatest population mix of the entire country, with groups from the interior often concentrated in their own neighborhoods.

Under Fujimori, regional poles of development such as those centered in the cities of Trujillo,

endemic poverty in the highlands, there were various other reasons for the influx: President Velasco's agrarian reform in the early 1970s was unsuccessful, as the *campesinos* did not know how best to work the land they were allotted, while in the 1980s and early 1990s Sendero Luminoso guerrillas terrorized the rural poor, the very people in whose interests they claimed to be fighting. For many, war between the *senderistas* and the military made life in the central Sierra impossible.

Urban authorities were unable to satisfy the basic needs of these migrants, and thus the multitude of *pueblos jovenes,* or shanty towns, surrounding Lima came into being, as there simply

Cusco, and Iquitos were increasingly centralized as the ex-president tightened his grip on power, sucking the life out of the provinces. Attempts to reverse this trend under President Toledo have yet to prove effective, as many Peruvians argue that local politicians and political leaders are just as corrupt as those in Lima.

Many people in recent years have returned to their villages, with help from a state repopulation program. But when the state aid runs out, some trickle back to the cities before they can reap a harvest, and their children, used to a degree of urban living, find it difficult to settle in the inhospitable *puna*. It is unlikely that the trend to move to the cities will be reversed.

Middle-class Peru

The most difficult social area to define is that of the middle classes. Until the 1960s, it was the poor cousin of the oligarchy, providing clerks, merchants, and civil servants. Once modernization started in earnest in the 1970s, the middle class came into its own, both in Lima and in provincial cities. This was due to the diversification of the economy and to the expansion of the Peruvian State, both as a purveyor of public services and as an employer.

However, middle-class prosperity was short-lived, as these were the very same people who suffered most under García in the 1980s, when

Roads penetrating into the Sierra and the Amazon Basin started to link up the hinterland with Lima and with important coastal markets. Mass communication began to reach out to new audiences. In 1970, the Peruvian football team's participation in the World Cup, which was broadcast nationally on radio and television, promoted a sense of nationalism even in the most remote communities.

These social changes were matched by political ones. A military regime under the indigenous-born General Velasco caused many upheavals. He stripped the traditional political elites of their power, and encouraged *mestizo*

hyper-inflation wiped out their savings and diminished the buying power of their salaries. Many professionals, teachers among them, were forced to eke out a hand-to-mouth existence. Their situation is somewhat better now, but, as recent history has demonstrated, the middle class is vulnerable because it depends for its lifestyle on a disposable income.

Decade of change

In the 1970s, several trends began to break down the isolation of much of the country.

LEFT: *chicha* and onions for lunch.
ABOVE: off to market along the Panamericana Highway.

grassroots organizations. His government took over many big estates, and distributed land to the *campesinos*. He nationalized foreign companies, including US oil firms, and increased the state sector enormously *(see page 64)*. Although this approach was ill thought-out and badly managed, and soon resulted in economic chaos, it did mark an important change in attitudes, as *campesinos* and shanty-town residents began to challenge *criollo* leadership.

The change in attitudes was also due in part to the explosion of public education in the latter half of the 20th century. *Campesinos* and their recently migrated cousins in the cities struggled and sacrificed a great deal to get an education so that they could gain access to status and income. But schooling represents a great lifestyle change for rural people, as children traditionally work on the farms and tend the livestock.

It also represents a new expense. Thousands of poor Andean communities have built one-room schools with dirt floors, benches, and painted blackboards. The communities bore the costs and performed the labor which constructed and maintained these schools, and they also pay the wages of the teachers. In the Río Tambo area, too, dedicated young teachers are working in one-room schools in remote rain-

Haphazard development

Westerners often take for granted the progress achieved in the 20th century. In Peru, material progress has caused many problems in a poor, mainly rural society. It is only in the past 25 years that many remote regions have come into contact with the outside world, with the building of roads, the spread of electricity, and the modernization of agriculture.

The state is still regarded with suspicion and fear by many rural Peruvians, who cling to their traditional social structures and practices. The idea of democratic rule is recent – it was only in the 1980 elections that some 2 million Peruvians

forest villages, largely funded by local communities. These added expenses, together with the loss of child labor on the farms, obviously complicate rural education programs. Although the Fujimori government made building new schools a priority, there are still about one million school-age children in Peru who receive no state education.

But progress is being made, and in many villages the sharpest students are sent off to the cities to finish their schooling, as their parents realize that learning to read and write can mean gaining full citizenship. Education is opening up new horizons, but for many families it requires determination and sacrifice.

who could not read or write were given the vote.

Even the Roman Catholic church, a pillar of the old order, has changed tremendously in recent decades, with consequences for Peru's predominantly Catholic population. Since the late 1960s, there has been increasing tension between the conservative Catholic church hierarchy and the so-called "liberation theologists" who argue that the church must fight to reduce poverty and injustice in this world. They have encouraged Masses in Quechua, Aymara, and other languages, and helped lead social protest movements. But the Lima archbishop and other dignitaries have insisted that the church in Peru should concentrate on its spiritual message. In recent years there has also been a big increase in evangelical sects, particularly among the groups newly arrived in the cities from the country areas.

A woman's place

The shake-up of Peruvian society that came with the terror of the Sendero Luminoso years in the 1980s brought a sudden change in the role of women. Although in pre-Conquest Andean Peru women had rights and obligations on a more equal footing than in the colonial era, that standing had gradually been eroded in a society best described as *machista,* where women generally took traditional wife-

madres (mothers' clubs). The community soup-kitchens the women organized were vital to feed their families, and the work of organization brought forward many female community leaders at a time when other popular organizations like trade unions and local political parties were falling apart because of rebel and military threats.

Divorce is not uncommon, but can be hard to obtain. Many married men openly take lovers, and in this predominantly *machista* society this is accepted without much fuss. In many rural communities the attitude toward women is still extremely traditional: in societies like that of

and-mother roles. In many ways, the 1980s marked a shift. In the Andes, and later in the Amazon, the disruption of normal life by Shining Path attacks and migrations often left the women in charge of reorganizing life; some 78 percent of migrant families had a woman head of household at one point. In Lima shanty towns, where economic chaos left many impoverished, it was women who were the backbone of daily life, holding the family together with the *vaso de leche* (glass of milk) breakfast clubs and the ubiquitous *clubes de*

the Ashaninka in the central Amazon jungle men still take two or more wives. Women do most of the work in the fields, while men restrict themselves to hunting and fishing. In rural Peru illiteracy rates are much higher among women (43 percent) than among men (30 percent). In urban Peru, women are starting to shake off the restrictions of the *machista* society, with the numbers of students going to university now almost equal between the genders, and women starting to have a presence in professional ranks as judges, academics, and bankers.

The wide-reaching family-planning program given priority by Fujimori in the early 1990s has meant a decline in births, with population growth

LEFT: neighbors in Villa El Salvador, Lima.
ABOVE: enjoying a beer in Lima's Cordano bar.

now down to around 1.8 percent a year. That same program came in for some serious criticism, including allegations that many thousands of poor uneducated women were being sterilized without sufficient information or after-care. Large numbers of them died as a result – an indication of the disregard for the well-being of rural peasant women. A lack of health services in many parts of Peru means that maternal mortality is still high, with 261 deaths of mothers for every 100,000 births. Life in Peru still revolves largely around the family. For economic reasons young people usually live with their families until they marry, and many continue to do so afterwards.

THE MOTHER OF INVENTION

Now that most of the *ambulantes* are off the streets of Lima, vendors tend to be the more desperate and most needy people, wandering the city streets with bags of chewing gum, sunglasses, hairclips, or trinkets. Among the more inventive people working in the informal economy these days are those who set up stalls outside the prisons and hire out the long skirts and low-heeled shoes that female visitors are required to wear; and those who wait at traffic lights, not to clean your windshield as you might expect, but to waft a herb called *ruda* over your car, to bring you good luck in exchange for a small sum of money.

Law and order

Terrorism has been almost eradicated, apart from a few incidents in the remote Andes. Although there are reports of assaults and muggings in the larger cities, pickpocketing or bag-snatching is the most commonly encountered crime.

The power of the military has been greatly diminished following the revelations of their involvement in the corrupt Fujimori regime. Several generals are in jail awaiting trial. The Toledo government has made efforts to cut the military budget, and has also begun a reform of the police in an attempt to clean up the institution. However, bribery still occurs frequently. The judicial system was also compromised because of its collusion with Fujimori and Montesinos; once again, the new government is making efforts to establish a more transparent system.

As a sign of Peruvians' renewed confidence after the fear of the 1990s, there have been many street protests against government measures. Most of these have been quickly brought under control by the police, although there was considerable violence during of demonstrations in the southern city of Arequipa in 2002.

The black economy

One striking feature of contemporary society is the massive scale of the informal or black economy, in which some 40 percent of the nation's population are involved. However, the *ambulantes* (street vendors) who once crammed the streets of Lima have been swept away, and many of the vendors have now been reorganized in markets and given tax ID numbers.

The informal sector is epitomized by the so-called *combi-culture*, a result of large-scale government lay-offs which led to an explosion of independent *combi* (minibus) and taxi drivers attempting to replace jobs lost in the state sector. Cars and *combis* would be bought with severance pay and launched into direct competition with existing transport services.

Such examples are common, and are not confined to the poorest sectors. As full-time jobs and careers have become scarce, more and more middle-class and professional Peruvians also work at two or three jobs in order to survive. Everyone is looking for a *chamba* – a way to make money and stay afloat in an uncertain world. ❏

LEFT: smiles all round.
RIGHT: having fun on the streets.

DAILY LIFE IN THE ANDES

Traditional hospitality and hard work remain the norm in Andean villages
where life has changed little over the centuries

The route to most villages in the Andes is a narrow, graded-earth road, in the dry season baked concrete-solid under the fierce sun, in the wet season awash with torrents of rain, slick with mud, narrowed or closed by rock-slides. These roads wind tortuously through the mountains, making complicated switchbacks up and down their flanks or following deep river valleys.

The vehicles that ply the roads, the means of transportation readily available and affordable to most of the village inhabitants, may be small, rattle-trap buses, retired from service on proper roads somewhere else and consigned to end their days traveling perilous mountain routes. More often they are heavy trucks, with wooden sides and a gate and ladder at the back, which carry everything from grains and potatoes destined for markets in the cities, to livestock and people.

Harsh agricultural world

The villages at the ends of these roads in the Peruvian Andes are inhabited for the most part by Quechua-speaking people, descendants of the groups once ruled by the Incas. In the ensuing centuries, these resilient people have adapted to the superimposed cultures, adopting elements that were forced upon them, like the ardent, albeit flexible, Catholicism of their conquerors, as well as those which were useful to them, like the livestock and crops that the Spanish colonists introduced to the Americas.

They took the European dress of the period of the Conquest which, in most places and in a derivative form, is still worn to this day. And more recently they have accepted such amenities as running water, electricity, aluminum pots and pans, radios, stereos, and flashlights.

Nevertheless, the fundamental outlines of life in the Andes remain very much as they were in the 16th century, resembling life in a medieval European village far more than any

LEFT: a colorful Andean market.
RIGHT: a son of the Sierra.

way of life with which we might be familiar.

Life in the village is simple and hard, based on subsistence agriculture and pastoralism. Most villages are only marginally connected to the national cash economy through the production of some crops for sale in city markets, and so, as has been done since the inception of ag-

riculture in the Andes, each family must produce the food it will live on for the entire year – and enough to sustain it through a bad year if the crops should fail.

Only the larger communities have electricity, or even generators. Some villages now have a system of drinkable water, so there may be taps outside houses or at points in the village supplying cold mountain water (which spares people walking several times a day to a spring or stream).

Village houses are made of adobe bricks or, in some places, of stone, with packed-earth floors and thatched or tiled roofs. The open rafters inside are always blackened and sooty from years of smoke from the cooking fire in a hearth in the corner.

There is no furniture except perhaps a couple of rudimentary stools, though a more affluent family may have a bed, or a table. Women sit, or more often, squat, on the floor – a characteristic posture for a Quechua woman – while the men sit on earthen benches built against the walls of the house.

The family's possessions consist of their clothing, their cooking and eating utensils, some simple agricultural implements, a few other tools, and their house, lands, and animals. Their most prized possession may be a radio, often

trols. For a village in the high *puna*, the economy consists mainly of the cultivation of potatoes and high-altitude grains, and of herding – mainly of llamas, sheep, a few goats, and perhaps some cattle. There is little arable land to be conserved, and it might be widely dispersed among various settlements of small houses. These dwellings have one or two rooms, sometimes with a second-story storeroom, often built of stone and roofed with a heavy thatch of *puna* grasses. Among the houses might be corrals for the animals, ringed by fences of stacked stone. Around the perimeter of the village will be small potato fields, their ridges

their sole connection to the rest of the world.

The Quechua-speaking peoples inhabit the entire range of altitudes that will sustain human life in the complex vertical ecology of the Andes, from the lush, subtropical river valleys to the high, desolate *puna*. Each village exists within a sort of micro-climate that allows it to produce a certain range of crops – perhaps lemons, limes, oranges, avocados, and chilis, and a variety of vegetables, both familiar and exotic.

High-altitude living

The character of each village is in large part determined by the potential of the land it con-

and furrows giving them the appearance of corduroy patches on the smooth fabric of short, tough *puna* grasses.

Other towns in the highlands reveal a markedly different plan. These were the *reducciones* (settlements) created by the Spanish in the 1570s as they gathered together the native population living in scattered communities throughout a particular region. It made life much easier for the conquerors if their subject people were brought together in such settlements: the control of rebellious elements, the collection of taxes and tithes, and forced conversion to Catholicism were all far more easily achieved.

The populations of many *reducciones* are today much smaller than they were at the time of their initial settlement, for many of the inhabitants drifted back to their native communities and land. But the straight, roughly cobbled streets remain, as do the public plazas or main squares. And sometimes, in some little town in the middle of nowhere, you will find a magnificent, rambling, adobe church, its tiled roof sagging, its gloomy interior still brightened by a great altar of tarnished silver or flaking gilt, its walls still adorned by enormous paintings, their ornate frames warped and their images darkened to obscurity over the years.

fallowed fields is turned in preparation for the coming year's crops, often under most unpleasant conditions – in rain, hail, and mud. In May, when the rains have ended, the potatoes are harvested.

The village's communally held potato lands lie in the *puna*, often two or three hours' walk from the village, and the harvest is a tedious and time-consuming labor, so each family packs up the essentials of its household – food, pots, serving and eating utensils, bedding – and, leaving behind someone, an older child perhaps, to pasture the sheep and cows, moves to the fields until the harvest is completed. The families live

The Andean cycle

Family activities are determined throughout the year by the needs of the crops. In the highland region, the agricultural cycle begins in August and September, when the Andean winter – a succession of warm, cloudless days and stunningly clear and frigid nights – begins to draw to a close. The crops are generally planted from low altitude to high altitude, and harvested in reverse order. Summer, the growing season, is also the rainy season. During these months, the fields are hoed and weeded, and the earth of

LEFT: grinding corn on the Uros Islands.
ABOVE: a highland wedding ceremony.

during that time in tiny, temporary huts, in a manner that is much like a form of camping.

The grains and beans are then cut and allowed to dry for threshing; the corn is harvested in June. After the grain is threshed, the community turns to the dry-season activities of weaving and building and repairing the damage done by the rains, and to the whole-hearted celebration of the numerous Catholic religious festivals that fall during these months.

Twenty-four hours in the village

In order to appreciate what Andean village life is like, imagine yourself spending a full day

task is to stir up the embers of yesterday's fire in the hearth and add a few sticks of firewood, to fetch water and put on a kettle for *mate*, a heavily sugared herbal tea. Breakfast, eaten at or before dawn, consists of *mate* with bread or with *mote* – boiled dried corn, one of the basic dishes of Quechua cuisine. While the family eats this simple meal, the woman begins to prepare the next: *almuerzo*, or lunch, which will be taken at an hour when most people would be having breakfast.

Almuerzo – usually a rich soup of vegetables and rice, served with boiled potatoes and perhaps a hot pepper sauce and a glass of

with a family. That day would begin in the darkness well before the first cock-crow, when someone stirs and turns on the radio. In the south central highlands around Cusco it will be tuned to Radio Tawantinsuyu, a station based in that city whose disc-jockeys broadcast their programs in Quechua and Quechua-Spanish. In the dark the day's first strains of *wayno* and *marinera*, the country music of Peru, are heard.

The woman of the family rises from her bed, a pallet of heavy, handwoven woolen blankets laid over a pile of sheepskins on the earthen floor of the adobe hut, or, in more fortunate households, on a wooden bed-frame with a mattress fashioned of bundles of reeds. Her first

THE CUP THAT CHEERS

The fermented corn beer called *chicha* plays an important role in Andean life, and if you were spending a day in a village you might feel obliged to try it. It doesn't look very appetizing, being a thick, off-white substance, more like soup than beer in appearance, and the taste is definitely an acquired one.

As a tourist you are most likely to come across *chicha* at festivals, where it flows generously throughout the day and night, and drinkers get progressively more inebriated. The effect seems to be a soporific one: you rarely see anyone spoiling for a fight – but you do see lots of people falling asleep.

chicha, a homemade corn beer – is eaten before the men set out for their day's work. The man of the household is assisted by his sons and grandsons, and by neighbors – often *compadres*, the godfathers of his children – who may owe him a day's work in exchange for one he has spent helping in their fields. The entire complement of laborers gathers in the kitchen to be fortified with bowls of soup and glasses of *chicha*.

After this, they will work steadily all day, in the hope of completing the job before nightfall, pausing only occasionally to refresh themselves with beer, and once for a meal,

fields, she may be assisted by the wives of the men working with her husband, or perhaps only by her daughters and small children.

At midday, she packs the meal into a carrying cloth with plates and spoons, and sometimes a bottle or two of cane liquor *(trago)* for the men, and sets out for the fields, sometimes accompanied by other women carrying a share of the burden, sometimes trailing small children.

The men pause in their work to eat, and to drink *chicha* and a few tiny glasses of *trago*. As the men plow or hoe the last rows of the field, the women may help, though more often they sit and watch, talking among themselves

which the woman will bring to the fields.

As they leave the house, the woman will begin cooking the third meal of the day, one considerably more complex in its preparation, comprising two or three dishes, with meat and potatoes and *mote*. This meal is a gesture of gratitude toward the men assisting her husband. At the same time, she tends to the children and animals, feeding children, chickens, and pigs, and milking the cow before it is led to pasture by one of the children, along with the sheep. Depending on the task being performed in the

and sipping *chicha*. At the end of the day, everything is gathered up and they begin the walk home. The group meets up in the deepening shadows with the children driving home the cattle and herds of sheep and goats. At home, the small children drowse in their parents' or their siblings' laps as the adults have another glass of *chicha* warmed over the fire, or maybe only a cup of *mate*. Eventually the fire is allowed to die, the pallets are laid out, and everyone settles down for a well-deserved night's sleep.

Days of celebration

But on other days, the villagers' primary obligation will be not work but the celebra-

LEFT: villagers from Huilloc enjoying a fiesta.
ABOVE: celebrating the sun god at Sacsayhuamán.

tion of one of the numerous Catholic religious festivals that occur throughout the year. Each village celebrates a series of Catholic saints' days – that of its patron saint and those of other saints significant to the village for one reason or another – as well as certain other dates in the religious calendar: Christmas, (pre-Lent) Carnival, Easter, All Souls' Day, the Day of the Dead. Those which fall during the months of the dry season, when the most critical and urgent work of the year – the work upon which simple survival depends – is done, are approached with special abandon.

The basic religious formulas pertaining to

these holidays are generally observed in some fashion. Masses are attended, vigils kept, and the processions bearing the images of saints are followed piously through the streets of the village. But each of these festivals has taken on a distinctly Quechua flavor. Around each a separate complex ceremony has developed which has little to do with Catholicism, and much more to do with ancient Andean traditions of worship and religious observance.

Every public festival – as well as private ones such as birthdays, weddings, and christenings – is also celebrated by characteristic, overwhelming Andean hospitality: the serving of great quantities of rich food and copious sup-

plies of alcohol, all of which fuels the revelry. Guests are expected to get drunk and to dance – to the consternation of any representative of the church hierarchy who may be present.

Cultural mix

In short, contemporary Quechua culture is a result of syncretism, a thorough blending of the ideologies of two very different cultures. While pictures of saints may adorn the walls of adobe huts, and nearly everyone in the villages has learned and may remember at least some of the words of common Catholic prayers in the Quechua language, people pay homage to the traditional powers of the Andes – the mountains and the earth – and more often turn to them for guidance and healing.

One ironic example of the intimate coexistence of Quechua and Catholic custom exists in the contemporary rituals of marriage. The ultimate goal of the process is a proper Catholic wedding in a church, registered in the parish log-books, but local people take a distinctly un-Catholic route to get there.

An alliance between a young couple is arranged by their parents, based on the expressed interest of the two young people. The couple then enter a period called *sirvinakuy* – which means "to serve each other" – during which they help their potential in-laws with the household work, a test of their suitability and readiness for marriage. During this time the young couple sleep together under the roof of one or other set of parents.

The couple will not marry until a child is conceived, demonstrating the reproductive viability of the union, and may not do so even then. A wedding, to be sponsored by the couple's parents and godparents, is an elaborate and expensive affair, and may be put off for years, although the couple must be officially married before their children can be baptized. Although this system of cohabitation is commonly known, the issue is generally avoided when the couple finally arrive at church, often with several children in tow, to be legally married.

How to celebrate

A major festival might include a variety of events. A village might play host to the visiting images of patron saints from the churches of other villages, and might hold daily Masses and stage processions, led by a priest, throughout the week-long celebration. The mix of Catholicism and pagan religions is ever present in these colorful festivals.

Some holidays are celebrated until the *octavo*, the "eighth day," though the celebration may wane before then as the will to drink and dance falters from exhaustion. There may be bullfights, and soccer matches between rival village teams, all performed in the shadows of enormous altars erected in the plaza, made of eucalyptus poles and adorned with complex configurations of painted wooden panels, banners, and small mirrored boxes containing the miniature images of saints.

At many festivals, there are bands of musicians, local or hired from the nearest town, playing instruments ranging from brass, accordions, and drums to local-style flutes; violins, the little Andean mandolin, the *charango*, the body of which is the shell of an armadillo; and the 36-string Andean harp with its great half-conical sounding box.

Or the music may be provided by scratchy 45-rpm records of *waynos* and *marineras*, played on little, portable, battery-operated phonographs, the words of the songs and even the tunes rendered unrecognizable by distortion. There may be troupes of dancers in elaborate costumes (sometimes involving several different layers of skirts) which transform their wearers into characters ranging from the white-stockinged-masked jesters called *ukukus*, or Andean spectacled bears, to soldiers and *sanitarios* (rural doctors).

Open-air market

At night there may be bonfires in the plaza, tended for the duration as people dance in their light, with music giving the night an unaccustomed life, and *chicha* flowing freely until the celebrants stagger home to collapse into bed. The festival might also attract vendors from the cities and other nearby towns who set up their stalls to offer for sale everything from clothing to candy to small manufactured goods such as *barrettes* (hairslides), sewing needles, toys, and balloons.

The villagers themselves may claim spaces among the vendors at the edges of the plaza to sell *chicha* and prepared food and produce, so

that the local economy briefly enjoys the benefits of its own open-air market.

Feasting, drinking, and dancing also go on in the households – especially those of the *carguyugs*, the men who have accepted and fulfilled responsibility for some element of the celebrations. The hospitality of the host family is another ritual gesture of gratitude for the part others have played.

During these days the village is transformed into a riot of color and high energy. Work is temporarily abandoned, and everyone revels in a brief respite from the responsibilities of everyday life. ❑

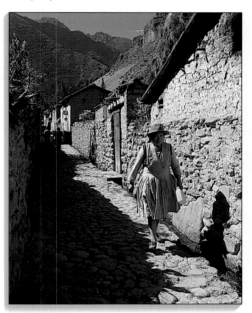

LEFT: looking after the llamas.
RIGHT: a street in Ollantaytambo.

PEOPLES OF THE AMAZON

Amazon peoples are facing threats to their traditional ways of life:
change is inevitable, but cultures must be protected

The indigenous peoples of the Amazon have long played a part in Peruvian history. According to Inca oral history, hordes of Amerindians were said to have climbed over the Andes and sacked the Inca capital of Cusco several times. The Inca fortress of Pisac is thought to have been an outpost protecting the capital from attack by jungle tribes to the east. The Incas referred to the eastern quarter of their 4,500 km- (2,800 mile-) long empire as Antisuyo, and to the Amerindians who inhabited its jungles as the Antis – from which the name Andes derives.

When the Incas and the Antis were not warring, trade was carried out between them, the former trading cloths, manufactured goods, and bronze axes in return for gold, feathers, exotic fruits, woods, and other jungle products.

The lure of gold

After the collapse of the Inca empire, the Spaniards concentrated on mining wealth from the Andes and on the coast, and generally left the indigenous people alone. The few expeditions mounted into the jungle generally met with disaster. In some cases, such as among the Jivaro Amerindians then living in northern Peru, the Spaniards did establish towns and attempt to tax the Amerindians' increasing quantities of gold. In 1599, however, the Jivaro staged a massive revolt, burning and sacking the cities and slaughtering thousands of people. They then captured the Spanish governor who was on a tax-collecting mission.

"They stripped him naked, tied his hands and feet and while some amused themselves with him, delivering a thousand castigations and jests, the others set up a large forge in the courtyard, where they melted the gold. When it was ready in the crucibles, they opened his mouth with a bone, saying that they wanted to see if for once he had enough gold. They poured it little by little, and then forced it down

LEFT: a Yagua Amerindian from the Iquitos region.
RIGHT: a woman prepares the family meal.

with another bone; and bursting his bowels with the torture, all raised a clamor and laughter," wrote one colonial chronicler.

The indigenous peoples had few such victories. As elsewhere, their greatest nemesis was not so much Spanish military force as the introduction of European diseases: their immune

systems were totally unprepared for European pathogens. In the Inca empire there are thought to have been about 7 million *indígenas* at the time of the Spanish conquest, but 50 years later there were fewer than 2 million. The same pattern was repeated in the jungle, beginning in the zone of greatest contact – the Amazon and its major tributaries – and gradually working its way into deeper parts of the forest.

Slave-raiding, which started on Brazil's coast in the 16th century, gradually worked its way further into the Upper Amazon and Peru. Within 100 years of Orellana's first descent *(see box on page 96)*, the "teeming Indians" who had once thronged the Amazon's banks were nowhere to be seen. Tribes that hadn't been captured or wiped out by disease simply retreated further into the interior of the jungle.

The biggest incursion into Peru's Amazon, however, didn't occur until the rubber boom in the late 19th century. Almost overnight, the most isolated jungle rivers and streams were overrun by rubber tappers who carried the latest Winchester carbines. Rubber trees were few and far between – hence rubber-tapping demanded intensive labor. Entire villages were sacked to capture indigenous people for slave labor. In the case of especially hostile tribes, *correrías*, or armed raids, were carried out in which villages were surrounded and their inhabitants slaughtered by the employees of the great rubber barons. Whole areas of the Amazon were thus wiped clear of native populations in a matter of decades. But in 1912 the rubber market began to collapse and, almost overnight, the rubber tappers withdrew. The remaining tribes were left alone except for occasional visits by missionaries.

The bulldozers arrive

In the 1960s, Peru's government became concerned about the numbers of peasants moving from the Sierra to the coastal cities, yet was

unwilling to enact the land reforms which might have kept them in their villages. It therefore chose the easier alternative, encouraging these people to move into the vast, unsettled Amazon that makes up two-thirds of the country. A north–south highway was partially bulldozed through the jungle to encourage settlement, and soon impoverished Peruvians began to pour in. New communities, some of them organized by religious sects anxious to make new converts, were established.

The systematic extraction of hardwood trees – mahogany, cedar, and caoba – repeated the pattern of the rubber boom as day laborers bankrolled by wealthy patrons moved into the

FIRST CONTACT

The first of the conquistadors to get close to Peru's Amazon Amerindians was Francisco Orellana, who was part of Gonzalo Pizarro's expedition which left Quito in 1540 in search of El Dorado. He later recalled: "We saw coming up the river a great many canoes, all equipped for fighting, gaily colored, and the men with their shields on, which are made out of the shell-like skins of lizards and the hides of manatees and of tapirs... they were coming on with a great yell, playing on many drums and wooden trumpets, threatening us as if they were going to devour us." Orellana survived, and even learned enough words to talk to the Amerindians.

virgin forest looking for quickly extractable wealth. Gradually, one by one, isolated tribes were contacted by missionaries, woodworkers, or oil-drillers. Although there were some 40 uncontacted tribes in the Peruvian Amazon at the start of the 20th century, there are now only two or three such tribes left (all living in the southeastern jungle). Today most of Peru's 200,000 native Amazon peoples exist in varying stages of acculturation.

Amerindian cultures

In the 16th century there was considerable discussion in Europe as to whether the New

and game animals which, while diverse, are few and far between.

As a result, Amazon villages on the *terra firma* – the immense areas of land between the large rivers – are typically small (25 to 100 people), mobile and widely spaced due to the jungle's low bioproductivity and the rapid exhaustion of the soil. In addition, these tribes almost universally practiced contraception techniques or infanticide in order to keep their populations down. Thus, the Jivaro penchant for head-shrinking was simply a variation on trophy head-taking and warfare patterns widely practiced throughout the Amazon.

World Amerindians were "the sons of Adam and Eve," and hence deserving of the rights of real human beings. Finally in 1512 a Papal Bull decreed that Amazonian Indians did, indeed, possess souls.

Alexander von Humboldt (1769–1859) was the most famous of the scientists who made exploratory trips into the Amazon; and eventually anthropologists began living among different tribes and recording a bewildering variety of cultures. The Amazon jungle is characterized as having extremely poor soils,

But tribes on the *varzea* – the more limited floodplain areas where the soil is renewed annually – did not fight among themselves, and instead had permanent villages running into thousands of inhabitants. Although battles were sometimes fought with the *terra firma* tribes in order to take slaves for work in *varzea* fields, population control did not exist. The necessity for carefully monitoring seasonal planting patterns and river fluctuations gave rise to an infrastructure which eventually came to include temples and priests, as well as complex systems of rules and food storage. And although the *varzea* tribes were the first to be hit by European contact and disease, Orel-

LEFT: Yaminahua Amerindians in Parque Nacional Manu.
ABOVE: preparing for a ritual in the south-east.

lana's men, back in the mid-16th century, reported numerous *varzea* tribes living in towns with temples and roads leading off into the interior.

As a result of their similar habitats, the Amazon tribes had other features in common. Almost invariably, they viewed their forest and the animals in it as sacred and imbued with spirits. Most Peruvian tribes took one or more hallucinogenic drugs such as *ayahuasca*, the "vine of death," which allowed them to see and interact with the powerful spiritual world. The forest was their provider – their mother – and was not to be abused.

Even today, most scientists concede that no one understands the jungle better than the remaining Amerindians. For thousands of years they have lived there harmoniously, and while they do not possess our own far more powerful technology, they have an understanding of and reverence for this most complex habitat on earth which the rest of the world lacks.

A people left in limbo

Currently there are some 200,000 native Amerindians in the Peruvian Amazon, who are divided into 53 different ethnic groups, speaking languages from 12 different linguistic families. Some groups, such as the Toyeri in south-eastern Peru, were said to number several thousand at the turn of the 20th century but are composed of only a couple of individuals today. Others, such as the Machiguenga and Campa, living in the jungles north and east of Machu Picchu, number tens of thousands.

Unlike Brazil, which has a governmental entity (FUNAI) to regulate indigenous affairs, jungle Amerindians in Peru have little governmental support. Legislation allowing Amerindian communities to possess land was only finally passed in 1974. Over 30 native organizations have sprung up in the past two decades as different indigenous groups have gradually realized that only if they put aside historical enmities and organize themselves can their rights be defended or secured.

Despite increasing organization, Peru's Amazon peoples continue to exist in a social and legal limbo. At best they are seen as a hindrance to a government whose goal is to "develop" the Amazon. The native peoples' limited territorial rights have not been helped by the government's threat to sell off state land that it considers "uncultivated." Amerindians have been encouraged to reject their own culture and become, in effect, rootless Peruvian citizens. Because of the Peruvian government's lack of interest in its people's history, foreign missionary groups have taken on the job of contacting and integrating Peru's jungle Amerindians into the national culture.

A US Protestant missionary group, the Summer Institute of Linguistics (SIL), has worked with dozens of tribes over the past 50 years, giving their languages a written form into which they hope to translate the Bible. Although SIL has nursed a number of tribes through contact-induced epidemics, it has been widely criticized for contributing to the destruction of cultural identities, and it now has a much lower profile.

Some cultures seem to withstand or assimilate acculturation better than others. The Shipibo people living along the River Ucayali have, despite long historical contact, maintained much of their traditional culture. They operate their own cooperative store (Maroti Shobo), where they sell and export their exceptionally high-quality weavings and pottery decorated with striking geometric designs using traditional materials and methods. In 1990 the Ashaninka Amerindians living on the Ene river retaliated fiercely against Shining Path guerrillas who had killed their chief. Other tribes, however, have less resistance to change and have lost their cultures within a very few generations.

Contemporary problems

The greatest new pressure on indigenous groups comes from oil and gas exploration. Reserves in the northern jungles, which have been exploited for over three decades, are declining, and the Peruvian government has begun auctioning off new prospecting blocks along the eastern flanks of the Andes, including the Upper Amazon basin.

In Madre de Dios, a consortium headed by Mobil Oil has attracted strong international criticism for entering the remote Las Piedras region, home to uncontacted native groups.

Encouraged by pressure groups, Mobil has taken some measures to minimize risks should contact occur. Nevertheless, hundreds of kilometers of seismic lines have been carved though the forest, small camps cleared and supplies flown in by helicopter during the exploration phase alone – all against the wishes of the Federation of Native Peoples of Madre de Dios (FENAMAD). Mobil is also exploring the Candamo Valley, one of the most biodiverse areas known on earth, and the Karene Communal Reserve between Tambopata and Manu.

In preparation for this invasion, FENAMAD secured international funding to visit most of the native communities likely to be affected in order to explain the potential impacts of oil exploration. Subsequently, it organized a conference in Puerto Maldonado so that local viewpoints could be aired more publicly.

To the west of the Parque Nacional Manu, where uncontacted Machiguenga and Yaminahua indigenous groups live, lies the enormous Camisea natural gas deposit. The pipelines that would run to the Peruvian coast, and possibly across to Brazil, could also prove to be a potential source of conflict with indigenous communities.

In northern Peru the Achuar, a Jivaro-speaking group, have maintained their reputation as a fiercely independent people and refused to allow oil workers into their territory. Despite government threats and new laws stating that indigenous lands no longer belong to them by right, the impasse remains.

One notable success for local people was the exclusion of oil companies from the Pacaya-Samiria protected area. Native representative groups are having to learn fast how to deal with multinationals and persuade them to respect their lands and offer fair compensation.

Biological prospecting is another threat to indigenous knowledge and lifestyles. Several

multinational pharmaceutical companies have visited the region in recent years to assess the biological possibilities. Due to one of their discoveries, huge quantities of *uña de gato* (cat's claw), known to alleviate some symptoms of cancer and Aids, have been harvested in an uncontrolled manner and sold to outsiders.

On a more positive note, the land titling program for indigenous communities proceeds apace, especially in central and northern Peru, with several million hectares titled in recent years.

Change is inevitable, but it must be handled carefully, in partnership with the indigenous peoples, so that their culture is protected. ❏

LEFT: Yagua children.
RIGHT: two generations of Amazon women.

HOW CRAFTS HAVE ADAPTED

Many of Peru's crafts have pre-Columbian origins yet have incorporated modern designs and contemporary images

Long before the Incas, Peru was a land of craftspeople. Fine weaving found in the funeral bundles at Paracas, gold pieces worked by the Chimu Amerindians in northern Peru, and startlingly realistic Moche ceramics pay testimony to a people for whom work done with the hands was always important. In the Inca Empire, specially chosen women dedicated their lives to such tasks as weaving delicate capes from the feathers of exotic birds. And metallurgy was a high-status occupation long before the Spaniards arrived in the New World.

Fortunately, these artistic traditions were not obliterated by the European conquest, and today there are few places in Peru where handicrafts – some little changed from those of centuries ago, others modified for the tourist market – cannot be found.

Ancient artifacts

Handicrafts played multiple roles in indigenous cultures that had no written language. Moche ceremonial cups were not simply for drinking: they told stories – depicting everything from festivities to daily events. Through these finely detailed ceramics archeologists have identified diseases afflicting the Moche people, discovered that the Amerindians punished thieves by amputating their hands (then fitted the reformed criminals with prosthetic limbs), and determined that they practiced rudimentary birth control. Likewise, the patterns on clothes woven in the highlands have unraveled some of the secrets of how the Aymara Amerindians lived.

The designs used in some clothes depicted the status of the wearer; other garments were used only for special fiestas, and still others had woven into them motifs that were important to the community. (Nowadays the designs include airplanes and other modern inventions). After

the Spanish conquest, handicrafts began to fuse the old and new ways as Amerindian wood-carvers whittled statues of the Virgin Mary dressed like a *campesina*, or angels with Amerindian faces.

Some handicrafts are found all over the country, but in different colors and designs,

such as the popular wall-hangings displayed in outdoor markets. Other items come from only one community or region. The decorative gilt-edged mirrors sold in Peru generally originate in Cajamarca; authentic ceramic Pucara bulls are crafted in Pupuja, near Puno; real Yagua Amerindian jewelry comes only from the jungle area near Iquitos; but artisanal items from all over the country can be picked up in Lima.

The biggest selection of handicrafts in Lima is available at the **Mercado Artesanal**, a group of markets on Avenida La Marina on the way to the airport. Some of these goods, such as the Christmas tree ornaments and *arpilleras* –

PRECEDING PAGES: weavings from the Nazca culture.
LEFT: a modern view on an ancient craft.
RIGHT: traditional weaving techniques are still employed.

embroided and appliquéd scenes – are produced by women's cooperatives in Lima's shanty towns. At these markets, visitors can find gold- and silver-rimmed goblets, carved leather bags, woolen goods of all kinds, jungle blowpipes, ceramics carrying both modern and antique designs, and a wealth of jewelry. Bargaining is traditional here, and prices may be comparable with those in Cusco or the jungle.

Lima's Miraflores neighborhood is full of handicraft boutiques. Hand-knitted llama- and alpaca-wool sweaters and ponchos in modern styles, as well as carved wood and leather furniture, grace the store windows. This is also the best place to buy indigenous paintings, jewelry, and traditional gold and silver items.

Gold and silver

Chile has its lapis lazuli and Colombia its emeralds, but the item most associated with Peru is gold, with silver and copper running close seconds. The 16th-century chronicles of Garcilaso de la Vega tell of the Europeans' first glimpse into the courtyard of Coricancha, the Temple of the Sun, in Cusco. Before them was a lifesize scene in blindingly brilliant gold, perfect in detail down to the tiniest butterfly. Worked in gold were llamas, corn stalks, flow-

HANDMADE GOODS

Throughout the city of Lima, artisan shops stock a variety of handmade items of the highest quality, including finely displayed collections of woven goods, colorful woodcarvings of toucans, pewter mugs, and delicate silver and turquoise jewelry *(for listings see the Travel Tips section)*.

The handicrafts sold in these well laid out arcades of small shops come from every geographical and cultural region of Peru: jungle, coast, and highlands.

Arrangements can be made for shipping articles overseas and the prices, although not negotiable, are quite attractive.

ers, birds. What remains in the Lima museums and the Museo Brüning in Lambayeque is but a fraction of the treasure that once existed. Today, gold and silver items, ranging from silver-rimmed crystal glasses to fruit bowls and candelabras, are available from a large number of boutiques in Lima *(see page 161)*.

The Spanish conquerors also found skilled craftsmen working gold and silver into finely turned jewelry and adornments. This tradition has not been lost, as evidenced by the intricate gold filigree produced in Catacaos outside Piura in the northern desert. These complicated pieces, which try an artist's patience and imagination, dangle from the ears of the townswomen who claim that gold shines even brighter under the desert sun. These are the big, drooping earrings that women dancing the *marinera* wear. In San Jerónimo, near Huancayo in the central highlands, silver filigree is tooled into peacocks, fighting cocks, and doves.

Jewelry made from out-of-circulation coins is sold in the Plaza San Martín in Lima and around the Plaza de Armas in Cusco. Popular items are earrings, necklaces, and bracelets made from leather and *sol* coins bearing the image of a llama. Informal jewelry-makers also sell jewelry made from Peruvian turquoise and hand-painted ceramic. But Peru's best-quality hand-painted ceramic jewelry is designed by the Association of Artisans of **Pisac Virgen del Carmen** in Pisac, about an hour outside Cusco.

Woven tales

Although much of today's *artesanía* is more practical than illustrative and is geared toward tourists, some items still tell stories. Delicately woven belts sold in the Sunday market at Huancayo carry designs of trains, a tribute to the metal monster that connected that isolated highland city to the rest of the country. The wide belts are worn both for decoration and for support by the women who trudge the highlands with their children on their backs. Colors in the textiles and knitted goods on Taquile, the distinctive weavers' island in Lake Titicaca, can indicate the wearer's marital status or community standing. Some colors are used only on certain holidays.

Everywhere you go on Taquile Island you will see men knitting the distinctive woolen hats which they habitually wear. Legend has it that the rainbow Kuyichi, angered by the Taquile Amerindians, took away their color and left them in a world of grays and browns, but the people used their fingers to weave color back into their lives.

Taquile goods can be purchased from the cooperative on the island. Knitted items are available from a number of shops in Cusco, and some of the best bargains (although the quality is hit and miss) come from the women selling their wares in the arcade around the Plaza de Armas in that city. Be wary of assurances by these unlicensed vendors as to whether the item

is made of wool from sheep, llama, or alpaca, as they are likely to upgrade the fiber to ensure a sale. Stop at some of the upmarket shops and feel the difference between wools from the three animals before starting your shopping.

Woolen cloth which is purported to be antique usually is not. The damp highland climate does not allow wool to last indefinitely, and many weavers now use dark colors and ancient designs to give the impression that the textile has been around for centuries. Such cloth is no more antique than are the rustic-looking dolls that some sellers claim have come from ancient graves.

Knitted and woven goods are definitely the purchases most popular with visitors. Highland markets – including the big Sunday market in Pisac outside Cusco – abound with alpaca sweaters, llama rugs, small woolen bags called *chuspas* that are used to carry coca for chewing, blankets, and cotton cloth. In Cajamarca, Amerindian women in layered skirts called *polleras* walk down the streets with drop spindles dangling from their fingers.

The quality of woven items ranges from those made with crude wools still embedded with flecks of thistle, to the fine yarns and modern designs found in Lima's boutiques. Brilliant dyes made from seeds, herbs, and

LEFT: tapestries for sale at Pisac.
RIGHT: elaborate woodcarving techniques.

vegetables are often used to produce the typical vivid colors. Cloth may come from the Andean highlands, particularly Cusco, Puno, and Cajamarca, or from the jungle where the Conibo and Shipibo peoples weave cotton with designs incorporating serpents and Christian crosses.

Crafts from the Amazon region can be obtained in the Lima suburb of Miraflores, at the **Antisuyo** store, or from the South American Explorers' Club *(see page 125).*

Basketware

From frigid Puno to the hot desert near Chiclayo, Peru is proud of its basket weavers. On

Lake Titicaca, *totora* reed baskets and miniature boat souvenirs are produced by the indigenous people, who live in reed huts on reed islands. In the port of Huanchaco, on Peru's northern coast, the fishing boats themselves are woven from reed; tourists can purchase miniature versions. This coastal region is also known for its finely woven straw hats, similar to Panamas, and known as *jipijapas*. These hats, and white cotton *ponchos*, make up the traditional dress of the northern cowboys, or *chalanes*.

Religious scenes

A very different kind of handicraft are the colorful *retablos*, originally made in Ayacucho,

which derive from the small portable shrines brought to Peru by the conquistadors. Usually smaller nowadays, and tucked into decorated wooden boxes or the hollow of a reed, these depict busy scenes that may be solemn or comical in mood, depending on the artist's inclination. The subject matter used always to be religious, and often still is, but even the scenes showing religious processions are turned into rollicking fiestas, overflowing with figures made of wood, plaster, papier-mâché, or clay, which may include a snoozing drunk, disruptive children, and wayward animals, or even artisans making hats or weaving cloth. Superb *retablos* fashioned of hollow gourds are still a specialty in Ayacucho, as well as the traditional wooden ones, some tiny, some as much as a meter (3 ft) high. Wooden *retablos* may be found in most outdoor markets, but the most delicate ones – carved from the white-and-gray Huamanga stone some call Peru's marble – are found only in boutiques and cooperatives such as Artesanías del Peru. Actually a type of soapstone, Huamanga is carved into anything from matchbook-sized nativity scenes to oversized chess sets – with figures of Incas and llamas replacing traditional kings and knights. Incidentally, much of what appears to be marble in Peru's churches is actually Huamanga stone.

Outside Lima and Cusco, the best places to purchase crafts are usually cooperatives or outdoor markets. In markets you are usually expected to bargain, and you generally get a good price. Depending on the size and vitality of the town, the markets may last only from pre-dawn to mid-morning once a week, or they may go on for days at a time. ❑

FORBIDDEN GOODS

Beware of unscrupulous merchants. Some claim to be selling antiques from grave sites: they are almost certainly fakes, and if they are genuine, remember that it is illegal to buy or take pre-Columbian antiques out of the country. Much the same goes for those who might offer you anything made from vicuña. It is almost certain to be untrue and, if the item really does contain vicuña fibers, it has been made in violation of international law. And don't even consider buying anything made from the feathers, skins, or shells of rainforest creatures, many of which are endangered species; this trade wouldn't flourish if people refused to buy the goods.

Pottery culture

The ancient civilizations of Peru produced fine pottery in many different styles, and museums throughout the country give some idea of their achievements. The earliest examples are thought to date from 1500 BC, but the first major center of pottery production is the Chavín culture in the central Andean region from around 1000 BC to 300 BC. The pots they produced are often in the shape of images of the jaguar god and other mythical animals. Others show that the Chavín potters were masters in the use of subtle colors, producing geometric patterns in reds and browns. It was this early group which had already begun to make the typical "stirrup-spout" pottery, where handles from twin vessels rise to form one central spout.

From a similar period on the south coast comes the wares produced by the Paracas culture. Here geometric designs predominate, and the colors used are much more vivid, with patterns made from incisions into the fired clay. Other pots show a wide range of fruits, vegetables, and plants that are of use to humans, suggesting they were symbolic food for the dead.

But the most astounding Peruvian pottery belongs to the Moche people, who thrived on the northern coast from AD 100 to AD 700. Many beautiful examples have been found in tombs excavated in recent years. Moche pottery is extraordinarily realist, especially in the pots known as "portrait-head effigies," which display individual characteristics, emotions, and sometimes even diseases.

The most popular Moche pottery takes realism to even greater lengths in its *huacos eróticos* (erotic vessels) showing every combination of the sexual act. The Rafael Larco Herrera Museum in Lima (www.museolarco.perucultural.org.pe) has a particularly good collection *(see page 161)*. So realistic are these pots that they are also used by anthropologists to study the sexual behavior of the ancient Peruvians, and they are thought to be ceremonial rather than pornographic in intent. The Moche were also the first group in Peru to mass-produce their pottery thanks to the use of molds. The Mochica artisans also portrayed scenes from their mythology onto their pots, as well as accurately portraying detailed scenes of everyday life. A very different style of pottery was produced to the south, along

the coastal strip, by the Nazca people. They were master potters, producing highly colored vessels with stylized geometric forms. They preferred to paint figures on their pots rather than making sculptures of them as the Moche did.

Farther inland, the harsh mountain conditions often meant that the pottery traditions were not so developed. But the Huari people near Lake Titicaca produced some pots with remarkably realist portraits and highly skilled ceremonial ware.

The Chimu people (who thrived from about AD 100 to their conquest by the Incas in the 15th century) learned the secret of making black pottery by reducing the oxygen during firing. Once again, they used

molds to produce many versions of the same pot. These were often burnished after firing to give them a characteristic silver sheen.

Inca pottery production was similar to that of the Chimu, mass produced and less distinguished. As with many things in their empire, utility was the most important factor, so their most typical pottery is the large water containers or *aryballos* that could be strapped onto people's backs. The arrival of the Spaniards meant that much of this production was smashed, particularly anything considered idolatrous, and the old traditions and culture were lost. But for the tourist, some of the colonial wares with their green and brown glazes and Moorish influence are also very beautiful pieces, to be appreciated in their own right. ❑

LEFT: a master goldworker displays his craft.
RIGHT: Nazca pot depicting a feline god.

THE SOUND OF MUSIC

The traditional sounds of the Andes are joined in a musical melting pot
by African rhythms of the coast, and salsa in the cities

Whether we are aware of it or not, many of us became acquainted with Andean music in the late 1960s when Paul Simon and Art Garfunkel released a recording called *El Cóndor Pasa*, accompanied by a group called Los Incas. Its English lyrics were new, but the melody was ancient, a traditional Andean folksong of haunting native tonalities. Los Incas, who later called themselves Urubamba, were in the vanguard of a movement to preserve the indigenous culture of the Andes, to present it proudly to the world beyond the borders of its native countries. Now this music is played by *conjuntos folklóricos* in settings – dimly lit restaurants and European theaters – which would be inconceivable to the indigenous peoples for whom it is simply a part of daily life.

The music can also be heard on the street corners, played by native musicians who depend on their talents – sometimes extraordinary – and other people's appreciation of them to gain a meager living. And it can be heard, far from the nightlife of the cities, in villages, where a less well-rehearsed group of musicians may accompany the private celebration of a wedding or a public dance performance during a festival, or where a lone shepherd might play a melancholy song to keep himself company on the mountainside.

Ancient tradition

The instruments, the forms of the songs, and the lyrics have constituted a linked tradition of oral poetry in a culture that until recently had no written language. Its roots lie deep in Peru's pre-Columbian history. In the ruins and ancient graveyards on the Peruvian coast you can still find small broken clay panpipes and whistle-like flutes which produce pentatonic or diatonic scales, and sometimes other exotic scales that defy description by Western musical notation. They are tossed aside by

huaqueros (grave robbers) in search of the fine textiles and pottery buried in the tombs. The Incas inherited an astonishing variety of wind instruments, including flutes and panpipes of all types and sizes. Inca musicians also played conch-shell trumpets, and drums made from the skin of the Andean puma.

Quenas are notched end-blown flutes with a fingering style similar to that of a recorder. *Quenas* were often made of llama bone, but are now usually carved of wood. They produce a pentatonic scale which, to ears trained to a European musical tradition, has a distinctly melancholy tone to it. *Quenas* vary in size and pitch, so that each has its own reedy voice.

The panpipes, called *antaras* or *zampoñas*, also vary in size, and there may be one set of four or five pipes, or three or four joined sets of eight or ten pipes, each of a different octave, to be played by a single musician with astonishing dexterity. *Antaras* or *zampoñas* are played by blowing across the end of the pipes, a tech-

---

LEFT: musician at a Cusco *fiesta*.
RIGHT: open-air performance in the southern mountains.

nique which gives a breathy sound which may be as high-pitched as a bird call or almost as deep as a bassoon. They are often played in complex duets, with musicians alternating single notes of a quick, smooth-flowing melody, never missing a beat.

Hispanic influence

To this ensemble the Spanish introduced strings, which native musicians readily adopted, inventing new, uniquely Andean instruments such as the *charango* (a small mandolin, scarcely the size of a violin, the body made from the shell of an armadillo), and the Andean harp

provided by a simple, deep-voiced frame drum – a *tambor* or a *bombo* – played with a stick with a soft, hide-covered head, or by an even simpler instrument called the *caja*, which, as its name implies, is a wooden box with a sound hole for reverberation, upon which the player sits to thump out a rhythm with the hands.

These, essentially, are the instruments which are played today – joined occasionally by a violin or accordion – though the drums now are more likely to be covered with goat skin than puma skin, and the eerie, wind-like call of the conch-shell trumpet may be heard only in the most traditional highland villages. There is also

with its great, boat-like, half-conical sounding-box. The instruments melded together perfectly; an ensemble of *quenas* and *zampoñas* weaves a rich tapestry of windy pentatonic harmony, and into this fabric are woven, like golden threads, the bright, quick sound of the *charango* – which may be strummed or plucked – and the voice of the harp.

The Andean harp has 36 strings spanning five octaves of the diatonic scale, though it is usually played in a pentatonic mode. Its deep sounding-box gives it a full, rich sound and a powerful bass voice, so that a bass line is usually played by the left hand while a melody or harmony is plucked by the right. Percussion is

an element of improvization – the composition of a village group may depend on who is available at the time.

The effect is magical, utterly characteristic of the Andes, evocative of high, windy passes, of the breeze blowing through the reeds of Lake Titicaca, of the dwarfing immensity of the mountains on a clear, bright, winter day.

The indigenous chronicler Felipe Huaman Poma de Ayala, in his massive descriptive history of life under both Inca and Spanish rule (*Nueva Crónica y Buen Gobierno*, written between 1576 and 1615), listed the names of a number of song forms, which are the ancestors of contemporary Andean music: the *yaravi*, the *taqui*, the *llamaya*, the *pachaca harahuayo*, the *aimarana*, the *huanca*, the *cachiva*, and the *huauco*.

Many of these he attributed to particular characters or activities – a shepherd's song (the *llamaya*), a song for victory in war, or for a successful harvest, or to accompany work in the fields. Of these names only the *yaravi* (or *haravi*) seems to have survived in common usage, but the lineage of contemporary Andean music can be traced back to at least the 17th century, and probably to pre-Columbian origins, perhaps the very songs named by Huaman Poma.

become household names, and their careers are followed attentively, especially by the young. They come into fashion, then disappear, like groups anywhere in the world.

The primary form of popular music which has evolved from those traditional forms is the *wayno* (or *huayno* in its Spanish spelling, and pronounced "wino" in both), which constitutes a rich complex of poetry, music, and dance. The *wayno* is a rural music, like bluegrass, for example, and each region has developed its own characteristic variation.

Music accompanies most aspects of Quechua life – from the most mundane activ-

Popular revival

But music never stands still. The traditional music, which has survived in relatively pristine form among native musicians, and in the past few decades enjoyed a renaissance as folklore, has also evolved a parallel, popular form. Today this is not only performed in the *chicherías* or *cantinas* frequented by both urban and rural Quechua speakers, but is also recorded in sound studios on records, cassette tapes and CDs, and played on the radio. The recording artists, like pop musicians and vocalists everywhere,

LEFT: twirling to the rhythm.
ABOVE: an Andean harpist.

SORROWFUL LAMENT

The 16th-century chronicler Huaman Poma offered the words of a song which he called a *huanca*:

"You were a lie and an illusion, like everything which is reflected in the waters… Perhaps, if God approves, we shall one day meet and be together forever. Remembering your smiling eyes, I feel faint; remembering your playful eyes, I am near death…"

These lyrics, which were translated by Christopher Dilke in *Letter to a King* (E.P. Dutton, 1978), are typical of the genre. Huaman Poma's example of the *yaravi* reveals much the same universal themes of love, loss, and loneliness.

ities to the most solemn rituals and the most abandoned celebrations. The Quechua people seem to live to dance: all new clothing is said to be "for dancing," and the *wayno* is fundamentally dance music. It is typically played in 2/4 time with an insistent, infectious rhythm; the dance is usually performed by couples, their hands joined, with much stamping of the feet to cries of "*Más fuerza! Más fuerza!*" ("Harder! Harder!").

But the *wayno* is also a literary form, representing a tradition of oral poetry which goes back at least to the time of the Incas. The *wayno* is essentially a love song, but a melancholy and

festivals in every village of the Peruvian Sierra.

The *wayno* will certainly continue to evolve; today an urbanized form of this fundamentally rural music is developing, in which the traditional naturalistic motifs are being replaced by abstract, more universal terms. But, in the light of its long history, it seems pretty safe to guess that this music will survive for nearly as long as the Andes themselves.

Música criolla

Peruvian music cannot be fully understood without looking at the contributions made by the country's black population. The first black

melodramatic one: a song of love found and lost or rejected, a song of rivalry and abandonment, and of separation and wandering in strange lands far from home. The modern *wayno* is clearly a direct descendant of the songs of Huaman Poma's day.

Melodramatic as they may be, however, anthologies of lyrics disclose a sophistication of poetic form and poetic voice, ranging from tragic to ironic to comic, which is remarkable in a completely oral tradition. *Waynos* to this day are learned and preserved within a social context, transmitted informally and usually anonymously, from musician to musician, in the setting of private celebrations or great religious

SALSA FEVER

Alongside all the traditional music it must be remembered that Peru, like any other country, does have a pop culture as well, although most of it is imported. Rock, pop, and reggae – sometimes original versions by US, British, or Spanish singers sometimes translated and sung by local vocalists – will be heard on the radio and in clubs, bars, and discos.

Most popular of all, though, is *salsa*, originating in Colombia but now heard throughout the continent – and beyond. Go to one of the crowded *salsatecas* and watch Peruvians dancing to this infectious music, or shed your inhibitions and try it for yourself.

people to arrive in the Americas came on Christopher Columbus's first voyage, in 1492. They were brought to the New World as servants of the conquistadors and at first enjoyed a measure of liberty. But by the end of the 16th century, shiploads of blacks were being brought in from various regions of Africa as slave labor.

In Peru – where slavery was not as pervasive as it was in some other parts of Latin America – Africans were brought in to raise the *plantaciones* (crops) of cotton, sugar cane, and grapes grown on the central coast. They were concentrated mainly in places like Lima, Chincha, and Cañete, where there are still significant black populations today.

Their masters, not content with working them for punishingly long hours in the fields, made their slaves entertain them at parties and other social occasions, by playing instruments or dancing. Because the slaves came from different parts of Africa, their music thus became a mixture of these different regional forms, gradually blended with Andean and Spanish rhythms, to emerge as *música criolla*.

Slavery in Peru lasted until the republican period, in the mid-19th century, when President Ramón Castilla granted slaves their freedom. But although they were legally free, blacks were still marginalized. They lived in what were known as *palenques* (an Antillan name which means "an inaccessible place"): isolated villages which became focuses of resistance to the abuse that their people still suffered. But although geographically isolated, the *palenques* were linked to the city markets, establishing interaction between the outcasts and society.

This interaction helped the Afro-Andean population to develop a musical culture. Their music was a way of expressing resistance, and asserting themselves in a situation where they were otherwise dominated and suppressed. Music was also the practice of an art and, no less important, a way of having fun.

The *panalivio*, or "bread relief", was a musical form with a lamenting tone, in the vein of the black music of the southern United States, which reflected the social conditions under which the blacks of the time lived, and which ended in an upbeat tempo. From this music arose other rhythmical variations such as the *festejo* and the *resbalosa*.

Dance variety

Dance, naturally, grew up alongside Afro-Peruvian music. The *zamacueca* stands out as the unmistakable precursor of the stately and elegant *marinera*, which has become the national dance, with *limeña* and *norteña* versions. In and around Trujillo, you may well stumble across one of the frequent *marinera* dance competitions. The Festival de la Marinera in January is the biggest one.

Varieties of black music and *zapateo* (a form of rhythmic tapping) can often be seen and

heard in various parts of Lima and in Chincha, where it is especially popular. (Chincha's Fiesta Negra in February is a good time to hear all kinds of Afro-Peruvian music.) The guitar, the *cajón* or *caja* (described earlier), sometimes a donkey's jawbone and other instruments combine to create rhythms that accompany the *zamacueca* and the *festejo*.

Another typical dance is *El Alcatraz*, in which dancers holding lighted candles attempt to inflame their partners. A *conjunto* called Peru Negro is one of the most popular dance groups in the country, while black singers such as Susana Baca and Eva Ayllón have gained numerous fans since the 1990s. ❏

LEFT: Afro-Peruvian dancers in Cañete.
RIGHT: putting on the style.

FESTIVALS AND FUSION

Peru's numerous festivals are a fusion of Catholic, Inca, and early agricultural rites, celebrated with high spirits and a fitting sense of drama

In any Andean community at any time of the year, you may stumble on a village *fiesta*. These local events are colorful occasions, always accompanied by music, dance, vivid dress, and large quantities of food and *chicha*. Coastal festivals can also be lively, especially in Chincha, where the black population stages the Fiesta Negra in February with Afro-Peruvian music and dance.

Major festivals, like the Fiestas Patrias in the last days of July, commemorating Peru's Independence, are celebrated nationwide. Others are specific to one location, like Lima's celebration of El Señor de los Milagros, which sees thousands of people following a procession headed by a black figure of Christ on the Cross.

A blending of cultures

One of the reasons Peru's festivals are so exciting is that they blend the rites of the Catholic Church with those which go back much farther – to Inca times or the veneration of Pacha Mama, Mother Earth. A good example of this is the Inti Raymi celebration in Cusco. The Festival of the Sun had been a huge event under the Incas, and Catholic leaders, realizing it could not be stamped out, nudged it to June 24, the day of John the Baptist, and everyone was happy. Pre-Lent Carnival, which was grafted onto pagan celebrations in Europe, is widely celebrated, very noisily, with lots of water hurling. La Virgen de la Candelaria (Candlemas), in February, is another event where Catholic and pre-Columbian rites mingle, particularly in Puno, where the *diablada*, a devil dance involving grotesque masks, is the main event.

▷ **INTI RAYMI**
Musicians accompany the Inti Raymi festivities, which are celebrated in Cusco and Sacsayhuamán on June 24. The Inca Festival of the Sun is the most important event in the Cusco calendar.

△ **THE LORD OF THE MIRACLES**
The figure of a black Christ is carried through the streets of Lima each October, accompanied by purple-robed penitents.

△ **THE THREE KINGS**
The festival of Los Tres Reyes on January 6 in Ollantaytambo is a mixture of Christian and indigenous rites.

▷**THE INCA'S ARRIVAL**
The Inca is carried on a litter during the winter solstice celebrations at Sacsayhuamán, the culmination of the Inti Raymi festival.

LORD OF THE EARTHQUAKES

Celebrated on the Monday of Holy Week, this is a major event in Cusco. Our Lord of the Earthquakes (Nuestro Señor de los Temblores), the image of Christ on the Cross which hangs in the cathedral, is credited with saving the city from destruction during a major earthquake in 1650. The statue is carried through the streets on an ornate silver litter. Red flower petals, symbolizing the blood of Christ, are scattered in its path and thousands of *cusqueños* join the procession, along with civic leaders, priests, nuns, and military representatives.

When a severe earthquake rocked the city in 1950, the image was set up in the Plaza de Armas, while townspeople begged the Lord to stop the tremors.

Like many other festivals, this is a mixture of superstition, genuine religious feeling, and enjoyment of ritual for its own sake, and it is a splendid occasion.

▽ **VIRGEN DEL CARMEN**
Virgen del Carmen revelers in Paucartambo, near Cusco, which stages the most colorful celebration of this festival on July 16.

A WORLD OF TASTE

*From the fish-based cuisine of the coast to the substantial, spicy dishes of the
highlands and the fruits of the jungle, Peruvian cooking offers a world of delights*

Peru's different geographical regions, its varied climates, and its mixture of peoples combine to provide a cuisine that is among the most extensive and interesting in South America. This food appears not only on dining tables but is also immortalized in pre-Hispanic pottery which sometimes takes surprisingly realistic forms of fruits and vegetables, in the centuries-old weavings found in many of the burial grounds that have been excavated, and in wall paintings. Some of the smartest restaurants in Lima have researched these discoveries, and offer menus based on what they believe the pre-Hispanic Peruvians ate – although all the food is fresh.

Fruits of the sea

Understandably, the best dishes in Lima and other coastal cities are based on the abundant seafood available off the coast. The collision of the Humboldt and other currents means the Peruvian sea is full of the plankton that larger fish eat, providing fishermen and cooks with a great variety to choose from.

The most typically Peruvian dish is *ceviche*, a plate of raw white fish in a spicy marinade of lemon juice, onion, and hot peppers. Each restaurant has its own marinade recipe, and when the fish is freshly caught, *ceviche* can be delicious. Tourists should avoid buying the cheaper versions sold in the street, and perhaps wait a few days until they give it a try. *Ceviche* is traditionally served with corn, yucca, or potatoes, and there are many variations on the basic formula, often with the addition of shellfish in *ceviche mixto.*

Among the best shellfish are *camarones* (shrimp), *calamares* (squid), and *choros* (mussels), all of which are prepared in a number of ways. Any dish listed as *a lo macho* means it comes with a shellfish sauce. The Paracas area and the Ballestas islands are the best places in all Peru for shellfish brought straight from the

water. This is the place to ask for a *chupe de camarones,* a thick shrimp stew, or *tacu tacu,* an invigorating mix of different shellfish with rice and beans.

Another cold fish recipe is *escabeche de pescado,* cold fried fish in a sauce of onions, hot peppers, and garlic, adorned with olives and

hard-boiled eggs. The king of fresh sea fish is the *corvina* or white sea bass, together with another excellent white fish, the *chita,* and the *lenguado* or sole. These are usually served *a la plancha* (grilled) or with any number of sauces.

In Cusco and other towns of the highlands, *trucha* or rainbow trout is very plentiful, as they are farmed in many rivers and lakes. Less common but more distinctive is *pejerrey* or kingfish, served steamed with potatoes and yucca.

In the jungle region, the central ingredient of many dishes are the fish caught in the Amazon and its tributaries. The most succulent is perhaps the pre-historic looking *paiche* fish, with its abundant soft white flesh. Broiled or grilled,

LEFT: taking seafood seriously. **RIGHT:** peppers spread out to dry in the Cordillera Blanca.

it may be accompanied by *palmito* (strips of soft palm heart that look deceptively like ribbons of pasta), yucca, and fried bananas; or it may be wrapped in banana leaves and then baked on coals to make a dish known as *patarashca*. Other fish worth trying in the jungle region are the *zúngaro* and even the *piranha*, which despite their vicious reputation are soft and tender on the plate.

Desert dishes

As well as the seafood, the cities and towns of the coastal desert region offer hearty dishes with chicken, duck, or goat. A favorite on the

northern coast is *seco de cabrito* (roasted kid goat), often cooked with fermented *chicha* and served with beans and rice. A similar recipe is used to cook lamb, which becomes *seco de cordero*. A popular way of serving chicken is *ají de gallina,* a rich concoction of creamed chicken and a touch of hot peppers served on boiled potatoes.

In Lima, especially during the gray winter months, the *limeños* often prepare a thick vegetable stew or *sancochado* served with meat: a dish guaranteed to lift the spirits. Another hearty meal common in the capital is *cau cau*, tripe cooked with beans and potaotes and served with rice.

Many of the fertile coastal valleys have developed the production of fruit and vegetables: Ica and Trujillo are centers of asparagus and artichoke production, while Piura exports delicious mangoes. These are used to accompany and enrich many local dishes.

Spicy peppers

Hot peppers are grown all over the country and are used to add spice to everything from fish to stews. On the north coast, where fish is an important part of the diet, sauces of hot peppers and onions are heaped on top of the main dish or offered as accompaniment in small side bowls. In the Amazon, where the food tends to be less spicy, people dip jungle vegetables and yucca into fiery pepper sauces.

But it is in the highland region where *picante* (as the hot, spicy taste of peppers is known) reaches an art form. The degree of spiciness depends on the type of *ají* or chile pepper used. These can vary from the moderately sharp taste that novices can tolerate, and increase to the screamingly hot *rocoto* peppers whose fire-engine red is not only decorative but a warning signal. And tourists beware: as in Mexico, locals love to confuse newcomers with the strength of the *picante*, which can destroy your tastebuds for the rest of the day.

It is thought that early farmers in Peru grew about five species of hot peppers, which were transported over the years to Central America, the Caribbean, and Mexico. Christopher Columbus, who was searching for the black pepper of the eastern isles when he came upon hot chiles in the Caribbean, may be responsible for their English name. "There is much *axí,*

GOLDEN GRAINS

An Amerindian tale describes the dismemberment of the god Pachacámac. His teeth, it is said, were changed into grains of corn, and his genitals into yucca and sweet potatoes, thus providing the earth with food, so that his people would not go hungry. Another popular legend tells the story of an Inca noble who fell into a well while walking. His father, the sun god, looked down sadly on his imprisoned son, but could not intervene to save him. The tears of gold that fell from the father's eyes reached the earth, irrigated it, and made the fields flourish. The grains of corn that grew were said to be the golden tears of the sun god.

which is their pepper, and it is stronger than pepper, and the people won't eat without it for they find it very wholesome," he wrote in his journal in 1493. The hot peppers he brought back were an immediate success in Spain and the rest of Europe.

Contrary to popular belief, researchers have found that hot spices are not all that hard on the stomach. And, ounce for ounce, peppers contain double the vitamin C of oranges. The restaurants in Arequipa vie with each other to serve their version of *rocoto relleno* (stuffed peppers), which are delicious with fresh local cheese. But tourists unaccustomed to hot spices

climate around Puno and Lake Titicaca. These potatoes can be stored for up to four years. In some areas around the lake, the Aymara still ritually stuff potatoes with coca leaves and bury them as a tribute to the earth mother, Pacha Mama, in the hope of a bountiful next harvest.

Potatoes are an essential part of most of the filling one-pot dishes common in highland cuisine. A famous dish named after them is *papas a la huancaína,* a creamy concoction of potatoes, peppers, and boiled eggs. Or they can be served with a peanut sauce in *papa ocopa,* or simply stuffed with meat, onions, boiled eggs, and raisins for *papa rellena*. They also take

should beware: eating too much *picante* can cause a kind of diarrhea known as *jaloproctitis*; this is why Peruvians do not serve it to small children, nursing mothers, or the infirm.

A world staple

The small subsistence farms of the Peruvian highlands are home to a vegetable now found all over the world: the humble *papa* or potato. Several hundred varieties are cultivated, including the yellow *limeña*, the small purple potato, and the dried *chuño* which is frozen in the harsh

LEFT: *ceviche* street stall. **ABOVE:** *anticuchos*, beef heart brochettes of Afro-Peruvian origin.

their place in *estofado* (a stew of chicken, corn, carrots, and tomatoes) as well as the ever-present *lomo saltado* (strips of beef with onions, tomatoes, and fried potatoes. The *papa amarilla* (yellow potato) is considered the best.

Peru's highland soil also produces other tubers that form part of the national cuisine. There is the *olluco* vegetable, which can range in colour from red to orange, and has a taste like new potatoes. It is often shredded and served with dried llama meat or *charquí* (beef jerky) in a stew. And in a few places you may find *oca* or *arracacha* served instead of the usual potato. The sweet potato or *camote* is also plentiful and full of taste.

Ritual food

Corn was introduced to Peru from Central America many hundreds of years ago. It was the most sacred food for many of its peoples before the Spanish invasion, and is found in nearly as many colors and varieties as the potato. Corn was regarded as the first gift of the gods to man, and was used not only as food but as a commodity for barter. The fermented corn drink *chicha* is made into a cloudy and extremely strong beer that is ceremoniously poured onto the ground during planting and harvest festivals, and then drunk in enormous quantities. Purple corn is converted into a

refreshing non-alcoholic drink known as *chicha morada*, and turned into the purple dessert called *mazamorra morada.*

Corn is cooked and presented in many ways. *Choclo*, boiled large-grained ears of corn, are sold on every street corner, usually with slices of cheese and *picante* sauce. Corn kernels are also part of stews such as *chicharrón con mote,* with pork and tomatoes. And fried corn kernels called *cancha* are a common snack served before meals, or to nibble with beer or *pisco*.

Before the arrival of the Spaniards, the different highland civilizations in Peru cultivated many other grains. Some of them, including

the purple-flowered *kiwicha* and the golden quinoa – both kinds of amaranth – were banned by the Vatican on religious grounds, and disappeared from the Peruvian diet for several centuries. They are now being rediscovered as healthier variants to the potato, and are being used once more in breads, cookies, soups, and salads.

Jungle fare

As well as the plentiful fish of the Amazon and other tropical rivers in Peru, the jungle area offers many other culinary delights. There is *jabalí* or wild boar, and other game. There are the *juanes* – a kind of *tamale* stuffed with chicken and rice, and turtle soup. In the Amazon, bananas replace potatoes as the staple, with many different kinds for frying, boiling, or eating fresh. The other staple is yucca, which accompanies most meals, and is also fermented to make a strong alcoholic drink called *masato*.

Acquired tastes

There are two dishes served throughout Peru which are very popular, although visitors are often taken aback when offered them. Every street corner and many restaurants offer *anticuchos* – skewers of meat which were originally grilled cattle and pig hearts, but can now include even pieces of fish and vegetables. If you are invited to a Peruvian barbecue, this is more than likely what you will be served. And around Cusco, a choice delicacy is the *cuy* or guinea pig. This is often presented deep-fried like Southern chicken, and the taste is somewhere between chicken and rabbit.

RESTORATIVE DISH

Fish is traditionally believed to have rejuvenating powers, and *aguadito* – a thick rice and fish soup (which is also sometimes prepared with chicken) – was traditionally served to all-night revelers after the three-day wedding celebrations once common along the coast. An *aguadito* may also be served to those guests who just won't go home after a party that continues into the wee hours of the morning.

At vendors' kiosks in working-class areas of Lima, a sign promising *aguadito para recuperar energía* (*aguadito* to recuperate energy) can be found over many of the food booths.

Sweet teeth

Peruvians love to finish a meal with a sweet dessert. Often this will be something that is part of the culinary tradition brought over from Spain. Favorites include *manjar blanco*, a kind of fudge made from boiled milk and sugar; *cocadas* (coconut macaroons); or the typically Spanish *churros*, pastry dough similar to donuts fried and eaten with honey or chocolate.

During the October celebrations honoring the Lord of Miracles (El Señor de los Milagros) another Spanish delicacy, *turrones,* are sold everywhere. In the summer months, cones of crushed ice *(paletas)* flavored with fruit syrups (and optionally topped with condensed milk) are sold on street corners – but be careful with them, as the water used to make the ice may upset travelers' stomachs.

Other common sweets include *yuquitas*, deep-fried yucca-dough balls rolled in sugar; *picarones*, donuts coated in honey; and *tejas,* a sweet biscuit filled with *manjar blanco*. One of the oldest traditional desserts is the crunchy cookie known as *revolución caliente*, which dates from the independence era in the early 19th century. Street sellers call out: *"Revolución caliente, música para los dientes."* ("Hot revolution, music for the teeth.")

As well as these sweet concoctions, Peru has a wonderful variety of fruit, served fresh or as juices *(jugos)*. Passion fruit or *maracuyá* is perhaps best as a juice, but the jungle region also provides mangos, papaya, and other tropical fruit. *Lúcuma,* a small brown fruit only found in Peru, has a strong, nutty exotic taste, and is used in ice creams and sorbets. Produce from the highlands include *chirimoyas* or custard apples, which are well worth the effort needed to peel and chew them, and the *tuna*, the fruit of the desert cactus, which can be eaten alone or as part of a salad.

Thirst-quenchers

As with other Latin American countries, it was the Spanish missionaries who first established vineyards in Peru. But until recently the Peruvian wine industry has not been as developed as those of Argentina and Chile, and only a few of the vineyards around Ica – the Tacama, Vista Alegre, Catador, and Ocu-

caje labels for example – are of any note. Most of the grapes are used instead for making *pisco*, which in turn is the basic ingredient for the Peruvian national drink, *pisco sour*. This cocktail is a mixture of *pisco,* egg whites, lemon juice and sugar, plus a few drops of bitters. The result seems innocuous, but can be explosive. So important is *pisco* to national identity, that in 1988 the Peruvian Government declared it to be part of the "cultural heritage of the nation".

Mate de coca tea made from coca leaves is served in hotels and restaurants throughout the highland region as an antidote to altitude

sickness. *Manzanilla* or camomile tea is also a popular way to finish a meal. When coffee is requested, even some expensive restaurants will place a jar of instant coffee on the table: although a small amount of fine coffee is produced in Peru, almost all of it is exported. Ask for *café chancamayo,* after the region where it is produced.

Carbonated drinks are called *gaseosas*, and the extremely popular local one is known as *Inka Kola*. There are many lager-type beers *(cerveza)*, including brands such as Pilsen, Cristal, Arequipeña, or Cusqueña – the latter generally considered by connoisseurs to be the best in Peru. ❑

LEFT: spoilt for choice.
RIGHT: selected fruit and vegetables.

ADVENTURE IN THE ANDES

The Peruvian Andes offer superb opportunities for trekking, mountaineering, and river-rafting, with excursions to suit both novices and experts

The great Andes mountain chain stretches the length of the South American continent, and is made up of dozens of individual mountain groups called *cordilleras*. In Peru, these snow-capped peaks have been the source of superstition, frustration, and inspiration to mankind for thousands of years.

Pre-Columbian cultures worshiped individual mountains and made ritual offerings to the relevant deities. Mountain worship, in remote areas, is still practiced by Amerindian groups under a thin veil of Christianity.

The conquistadors, led by Francisco Pizarro, found the Andes daunting. Hernando Pizarro, Francisco's brother, wrote: "We had to climb another stupendous mountainside. Looking up at it from below, it seemed impossible for birds to scale it by flying through the air, let alone men on horseback climbing by land."

Long after the Spanish Conquest, a new breed of conquerors came seeking victory, this time over high altitudes rather than indigenous cultures. In the early 1900s, mountaineers discovered the Andes of Peru and began the assault, which still continues, on the highest tropical mountain range in the world. More than 30 majestic peaks rise well over 6,000 meters (20,000 ft).

Modern-day outdoor enthusiasts have also found that walking around mountains can be as much of a thrill as climbing them. For these trekkers, Peru is a paradise.

Mountain cultures

Except for the most remote and rugged areas, the Peruvian Andes offer little in the way of untouched wilderness. Only 23 percent of Peru's land is arable, and every fertile meter is farmed. For most trekkers, "getting away" means leaving behind the 21st century and becoming acquainted with an indigenous life style which is centuries old.

The formidable Peruvian Sierra was tamed

by the Incas, whose terraced system of agriculture enabled large areas of steep yet fertile land to be cultivated. This efficient but arduous system is still employed in some areas, and the remains of ancient terracing give an insight into the productivity achieved by this civilization.

Campesinos (subsistence farmers) today cul-

tivate numerous small plots of ancestral land. During the growing season the hillsides are plowed in a variety of geometric shapes and, as crops begin to mature, the mountains are carpeted in colors ranging from deep green to warm gold. Trekkers wander along ancient paths, occasionally pausing to allow a herd of llamas, to scramble by, crossing high Andean passes at altitudes of 4,000 meters (13,000 ft), and marveling at the glacier-covered peaks that serve as a spectacular backdrop.

One of the best things about trekking in Peru is the opportunity to stop and try to communicate with local people, although many of the older *campesinos*, especially the women, speak

LEFT: camping in the Sierra.
RIGHT: almost there.

very little Spanish – Quechua, the language of the Incas, is most often heard. Highland people are typically reticent with strangers, but curious children or bolder adults may initiate a conversation, wanting to know where you're from, what your name is, or – most important to the children – if you have any candy.

Passing remote, populated areas is like stepping back into the past. One- or two-room huts constructed of crude mud bricks and topped with *ichu* grass have changed little in design since Inca times. There is no electricity, and fresh running water is taken from nearby streams. Small courtyards house chickens and

sphere, this does not mean that the seasons are the opposite of those in the northern hemisphere. Being so close to the equator, Peru experiences only two climate changes – rainy and dry. Knowing *when* to trek is as important as knowing where.

Technically called winter, the months from May through October are the finest for trekking because the weather is clear and dry. During the rainy season, from November through April, when skies are often cloudy and rain frequent, travel can often mean long delays due to washed-out roads, and trekking takes on the characteristics of a long mud slog.

cuy, or guinea pig (considered a delicacy in the Sierra), and corn, along with other grains, can often be seen drying in the midday sun.

Preparing for a trek

Trekking differs from mountain climbing in that it requires little technical skill and the routes are more lateral than vertical. Most treks in the Peruvian Andes are simply extended walks along often steep paths and can be attempted by any reasonably fit and healthy person. Local porters or *arrieros* (donkey drivers) can be hired to help carry heavy loads.

The first thing to realize before setting out is that, although Peru is in the southern hemi-

Most treks wander through the Andean highlands at an altitude of 3,000 to 5,000 meters (10,000 to 16,500 ft). Winter days are usually sunny, with temperatures of 18–24°C (65–75°F). The equatorial sun is strong, and the frequent application of sunscreen is necessary. Nights can feel bitterly cold, especially at higher altitudes, so lightweight thermal underwear, a few layers of warm clothes, and a fleece jacket are necessary. A tent and a good sleeping bag are also essential, as well as a dependable multi-fuel cooker. White gas, called *bencina*, is usually available, but is often of low-grade quality, which can clog up a temperamental cooker. Kerosene and leaded petrol can also be used in a multi-fuel stove and are essential supplies since there is no wood for fires at higher altitudes, and using up the scarce reserves at lower levels only exacerbates the problem of soil erosion that plagues the area.

Lightweight hiking boots are suitable for the majority of trails. The best equipment will be available in your home country, but if the idea of lugging around an assortment of gear does not appeal to you, most necessities can be hired in the major trekking centers of Huaraz and Cusco for only a few dollars a day. But the quality of hired clothes and equipment can vary widely; be sure to check that it is at least ade-

foods in the first few days, and drinking plenty of liquid, you will minimize the effects of altitude. Drinking *mate de coca*, tea made from the coca leaf available in most highland cafes, also helps reduce symptoms.

Food for treks can be bought easily in the larger villages, but the freeze-dried variety is harder to find. Packet soups and dried pastas, as well as dried fruits and grains, are readily available in the markets. Favorite spices brought from home take up little room in your luggage and add flavor. Take as much food as will be needed for the duration of the trek, since it is unlikely that anything will be available on the way other than

quate for your needs. Stoves have been known to fail suddenly just a few miles into the trek.

Thin mountain air

Before setting off, spend a few days becoming acclimatized to the altitude with short hikes around the area. The thin, high-altitude air can quickly exhaust the unaccustomed and cause physical discomfort. Headaches, mild nausea, shortness of breath, and sleeplessness are some of the common symptoms of high-altitude sickness, or *soroche*. By avoiding alcohol and fatty

LEFT: mule transport is available.
ABOVE: climbing Mount Alpamayo.

SOUTH AMERICAN EXPLORERS' CLUB

When you are planning a trek, one of the best places to start is in Lima at the South American Explorers' Club, a non-profit information network. The clubhouse, at Av. República de Portugal 146, in Lima's Breña district, has an invaluable stock of maps, guidebooks, and trail reports. The staff are friendly and more than willing to give advice both to beginners and experts.

If you join the club (membership currently US$50 annually; US$80 for couples) you get its quarterly magazine, use of the library, and many other perks, including gear-storage facilities. For information, write to Casilla 3714, Lima 100 or log on to www.samexplo.org.

the occasional piece of bread or fruit in the most populated areas. All drinking water should be treated by using purification tablets, iodine solution, or a filtering pump. Iodine works better than chlorine-based purifiers because it kills more bacteria. Treated water is not especially palatable, but drink-flavoring powder can be bought in most shops, and not only hides the chemical taste but also adds energy-boosting sugar.

The Cordillera Blanca

Eight hours by bus north of Lima, or eight hours south from Chimbote, is one of the most popular trekking areas in Peru. For its diversity and

buying souvenirs is easy. A number of good restaurants (which can seem excellent after a long hike) serve a variety of food, and there are a couple of lively *peñas*, featuring groups playing the traditional music of the Andes, which provide a place to loosen up before or after a strenuous four days' trekking. More details of treks in the region can be found in the chapter on the Callejón de Huaylas *(see page 196)*.

Trekking around Cusco

The best-known trek in the vicinity of Cusco is the Inca Trail to Machu Picchu *(see page 285)*,

large number of mountain peaks clustered so conveniently in one central area, the **Cordillera Blanca** is a trekkers' dream.

The small town of **Huaraz** *(see page 194)* is the hub for all hiking activity, and frequent rural buses transport enthusiasts to a variety of trailheads. A *Casa de Guías*, located just off the main street, will provide the latest information about routes and mountain conditions, and can provide trekkers with a list of porters and *arrieros*. Along the main street of Luzuriaga, colorful billboard signs lend distinction to an otherwise dull facade of shopfronts. Most of these promote tourism in some form, so finding a comfortable day tour, renting hiking gear, or

RECLAIMING THE PATHS

In the late 1980s and early 1990s much of the central highlands, including the Huaraz area, was subject to a degree of control by Sendero Luminoso (Shining Path) terrorists. Particularly affected was the beautiful circuit around the Cordillera Huayhuash, some 50 km (30 miles) to the southeast of the Cordillera Blanca, which was closed to visitors.

Since the arrest of Sendero's leader, Abimael Guzmán, and a number of other leading lights in 1992, the movement has lost most of its power and influence, and the area is now considered safe for trekkers and climbers.

but the whole area is rich in superb trekking possibilities. Routes around the high mountains of Salcantay and Soray originate from the small village of Mollepata and provide some exquisite views of the Cordillera Vilcabamba.

The **Ausangate Loop** route around Nevado Ausangate (6,270 meters/20,700 ft) is considered by many to be one of the finest hiking areas. A truck from Cusco is the usual form of transport, and the village of Tinqui the destination for the start of this five-day trek. The eight-hour ride is hot and dusty by day, and bitterly cold at night.

The route meanders up and down, through one valley after another, each divided by passes

Vicuña, a cameloid cousin to the llama, are elusive creatures valued for their fine wool. Herds of these skittish beasts may be seen, but only from a distance. Their domesticated relatives, llamas and alpacas, also graze along the route, usually tended by traditionally dressed *campesino* children. The Andean condor, with a wing span up to 3 meters (10 ft), may be sighted soaring on air currents high above.

Mountaineering

For the more adventurous and technically minded mountain enthusiast, the Cordillera Blanca is unrivaled for the pursuit of moun-

nearing altitudes of 5,000 meters (16,000 ft). Soothing hot springs welcome the hiker on the first day. Huge moraines (rock and silt deposits left behind by the Ice Age) and glacial lakes, each a stunning yet different shade of blue, provide plenty of visual feasts for the days ahead.

Close-up views of Ausangate are spectacular. At one point the tongue of a glacier extends down within walking distance. A little exploration will reveal a huge ice cave within. It's easy to break the icicles concealing the entrance and roam through the numerous chambers.

LEFT: on the right trail.
ABOVE: abseiling in the Cordillera Blanca.

taineering. With glacier-covered peaks varying in altitude from 5,500 meters (18,000 ft) to 6,800 meters (20,000 ft), and technical levels from very easy to extremely difficult, there is something for everyone. But because all climbing here is at high altitude, and any glacier travel requires technical knowledge, climbing in the Cordillera Blanca should be attempted only by those with experience. Beside the usual trekking equipment, a rope, an ice ax, crampons, and ice stakes or screws are necessary.

Trekkers generally don't experience anything more than *soroche*, or mild altitude sickness, but at higher altitudes serious complications can arise. Pulmonary edema occurs when the lungs begin to fill with fluid. Early symptoms include a dry, incessant cough, a rattling sound, and tightness in the chest. Cerebral edema occurs when fluid collects in the brain. Symptoms include loss of coordination, incoherent speech, confusion, and loss of energy. Both of these illnesses are extremely serious and can be fatal. The only cure is immediate descent to a significantly lower altitude. The victim is usually the last one aware of the problem, so it's essential that each person in the group keeps an eye out for symptoms in the others.

A more common high-altitude problem is hypothermia, or exposure. This occurs when

the body loses more heat than it can replace. The symptoms begin with uncontrolled shivering that will eventually cease, though the body is still cold. Lack of coordination, confusion, drowsiness, and even a feeling of warmth are other symptoms.

A victim suffering from hypothermia will need to be dried-off immediately, placed in a warm sleeping bag, and given warm liquid to drink. Never give a hypothermia victim alcohol, whatever you may have heard about the restorative qualities of a sip of brandy. And don't try to warm the extremities, as this draws blood away from the core area of the body. In advanced cases, victims won't be able to gen-

erate any body heat and will need the warmth of other bodies, skin-to-skin in a sleeping bag, to get the temperature back to normal.

Hypothermia is prevented by staying warm and dry. Wearing wool or a synthetic insulating material next to the skin will help hold in warmth, even when wet. Cotton has no insulating properties and will actually draw off body heat when wet. Layering clothes is an effective way to regulate body temperature during times of exertion and rest. Food also helps stoke up the internal generators: eating quickly assimilated food like chocolate will help keep the system functioning. Try not to get over-tired, as fatigue makes you more vulnerable.

Many climbers feel that acclimatization comes with activity – getting the legs in shape for the more demanding climbs is as important as having the lungs working at capacity. To this end, several short warm-up climbs are favored. **Nevado Pisco**, just over 5,800 meters (19,000 ft), is popular for its steep yet rapid ascent, and the views from the saddle are some of the finest anywhere in the Cordillera Blanca.

The approach to the base camp begins just above the Llanganuco lakes. The 5-km (3-mile) hike follows a footpath along the crest of a lateral moraine and gains 750 meters (2,460 ft) in altitude. Camping is on a flat, grassy area below an incredibly steep moraine, which you know must be negotiated the next day.

Some groups choose to continue on past the base camp, tackle the difficult moraine on the same day, and carry on up to the high camp just below the glacier. An early-morning start from here allows climbers to make the summit and be back in camp for afternoon tea. The next day's descent is quick, and climbers are usually back in Huaraz by the evening.

Mountain biking

Mountain biking is a newish activity in Peru but is fast gaining popularity, particularly around Cusco and Huaraz. From Cusco you can make one-day trips, or longer ones if you know where to go, or employ a guide. In Huaraz, the *Mountain Bike Adventure* agency runs its own tours. Bicycles can be rented cheaply in both towns; they aren't as good as you would get at home, but the quality should improve as the sport becomes more widespread. ❑

LEFT: scaling the heights.

Riding the Rapids

High in the Peruvian Sierra, where icy waters churn over huge boulders and rush through narrow canyons, river travel has never been practical. Not, at least, until white-water rafting was introduced. With the astonishing number of rivers in Peru – the Andes having been at work for thousands of years forcing new waterways to carry their glacial melt-off – the choices for river adventures are many and varied.

The Cusco area is well-suited for river-rafting. The Río Urubamba winds through the Sacred Valley of the Incas, and floating along its waters gives a different perspective on one of the most culturally rich areas in all of Peru. Remains of ancient terracing are evident on the hillsides, and simple mud huts with thatched roofs dot the riverbank. Women can be seen washing clothes in the shallows, children herding cattle and sheep, and men working the fields – all of whom will pause to watch with mild surprise as the floating rubber dinghy makes it way downriver, before carrying on with their work. The tranquility lulls you into a peaceful daydream – until the next set of rapids brings you to life and starts you paddling for all you're worth.

Trips, lasting between half a day and two days, can be arranged with several reputable agencies in Cusco (*see Travel Tips, page 342*). They are mostly suitable for beginners, and the longer ones usually combine visits to some of the nearby Inca ruins.

Trips on the Río Apurimac, just a few hours from Cusco, are for the more experienced rafter who is looking for a longer and rougher ride. Most trips, which should also be arranged in Cusco, take about five days and are only possible between June and October. Superb white water is found in a spectacular, mile-deep tropical canyon on this source river of the Amazon. When not occupied with immediate survival in the challenging rapids, rafters have time to enjoy steep waterfalls cascading down the canyon walls, and to search for wildlife including otters, deer, pumas, and the Andean condor.

Afternoons are usually spent relaxing in camp on a sandy beach, perhaps trying a hand at fishing, or hiking along goat trails. The last remaining Inca bridge stretches across the Río Apurimac just above the common take-out point.

Several hours from Arequipa is the spectacular Cañón del Colca, vying with nearby Cotahuasi Canyon for world's deepest canyon status, with the crystalline waters of the Río Colca snaking along its bottom. At Cabanaconde, toward the western end of the canyon, the river runs some 2,200 meters (7,218 ft) above sea level, while not far to the south, the volcano peak of Nevado Ampato rises to 6,314 meters (20,715 ft).

It wasn't until 1981 that a complete exploration of the Río Colca was undertaken, by the CanoAndes Polish Expedition. Many sections of the river are technically difficult – enough to test the limits of experts. This, along with a setting devoid of vegetation, a lunar landscape of rocks and volcanic lava, makes a trip along the Colca one of the most impressive you can imagine. Excursions to this zone are only for those who really know what they are doing, and must be ar-

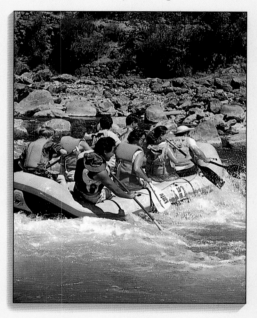

ranged in advance in Arequipa. Runs of varying degrees of difficulty can be done on the nearby Río Majes – also arranged through an agency in Arequipa.

Nearer the coast, to the south of Lima, the Río Cañete can be run from December through March. Rafting and kayaking trips through the stark desert landscape start from the village of Lunahuaná. There are several local operators, in nearby San Jerónimo and Paullo, or book in advance in Lima.

The best option for river-rafting otherwise is the Río Santo in the Huaraz area. It's a relatively easy run, best done between December and March when the river is at its highest. Trips can be arranged in Huaraz. (*For details of outfitters and agencies see Travel Tips on pages 341–3.*) ❏

RIGHT: tackling the Río Urubamba.

WILDLIFE OF THE SIERRA

From cameloids to condors, the Peruvian Andes and the cloudforest
have a stunning variety of wildlife

The Andes of Peru have been heavily populated by wildlife for thousands of years. In Inca times all types of Andean wildlife enjoyed a form of protection, and although periodic hunts occurred, these were few, and the privilege of the ruling class. After the Spanish Conquest and the breakdown of the Inca infrastructure, wild animals were hunted indiscriminately and consequently suffered a population decline that was further advanced by the cutting of high Andean woodlands, which provide essential cover for many animals.

Today the persecution of wild animals continues, in some cases because of damage caused by animals to crops, in most cases because of misconceptions. The careful observer, however, can still find a wide variety of Peruvian fauna while traveling in the Andes.

Endangered species

The most conspicuous animals encountered by a visitor to the Peruvian Andes are the cameloids. There are two wild cameloids in the country: the vicuña and the guanaco. The vicuña, reputed to have the finest wool of any animal, has been brought back from the verge of extinction through concerted conservation efforts. Special areas have been established for the species, such as the Pampas Galeras reserve in south-central Peru.

They are now to be found in quite large numbers in many areas but are still considered vulnerable. In Inca times, vicuña wool was obtained by running the animal to the ground, picking its fleece by hand and then releasing it. This not only assured a regular supply of wool each year but also maintained population levels.

The modern illegal hunter resorts to firearms, the primary cause of the vicuña's demise. Prosecution is rare, however, since the people who possess guns are often influential, and therefore immune to prosecution.

The other wild cameloid, the guanaco, reaches its northernmost limit in the highlands of central Peru, and from here extends down the Andean chain to the southern tip of South America – Tierra del Fuego. In Peru the guanaco is most likely to be seen in the departments of Tacna, Moquegua, Arequipa, and

Puno, and is to be found in isolated rocky ravines with bunch grass. Guanacos are wild relatives of the llama and alpaca, but they are instantly distinguishable from their domesticated cousins by their bright tawny coloration, similar to that of the vicuña.

The precise relationship between the domestic llamas and alpacas and the wild guanacos and vicuñas is not entirely clear. All possible crosses of the four cameloids have been accomplished, and the offspring of all crosses are fertile. Most taxonomists now agree that the domestic llamas and alpacas are a product of the cross-breeding of guanacos and vicuñas. Whatever the exact relationships, the domes-

LEFT: the flight of the condor.
RIGHT: the puma is rarely encountered.

ticated cameloids are to be found throughout the Peruvian highlands.

The only natural enemy of the cameloids is the puma or mountain lion. This large, tawny, unspotted cat was much revered by the Incas as a symbol of power and elegance.

Unfortunately, after the Conquest, Andean people lost the conservationist outlook of the Incas, and the puma has suffered dramatically as a result of indiscriminate hunting. The puma's habit of picking off an unwary llama has not endeared it to the local people, and these days it is possible only to catch a fleeting glimpse of this magnificent cat as it crosses

this species can be seen at the snow line nearly 5,000 meters (16,000 ft) above sea level, but for the short-term visitor to the Andes an encounter with any of the Peruvian wild cats is a rare event indeed.

Woodland creatures

More conspicuous, and more commonly seen by backpackers in the highlands, are the two species of deer. Both species were once more common than they are now, and the principal causes of their demise are hunting and the cutting of the high Andean woodlands that provide essential cover. The white-tailed deer is

remote Andean valleys or stalks mountain viz-cachas – sturdily built, burrowing members of the rodent family.

Two smaller members of the cat family are also to be found in the high Andes. Both species are shy, and little is known of their status and habits. The pampas cat *(Felis colocolo)* is typically an animal of the intermontane Andean valleys, although it does occur close to the coast in northern Peru and in the high cloudforest of the eastern slopes of the Andes. The Andean cat *(Felis jacobita)* is rarer still and in Peru is limited to the southern highlands. This is a high-altitude species, mostly nocturnal, and seems to prey on mountain vizcachas. Tracks of

PRECIOUS FIBERS

Vicuña wool is the finest, and the most expensive, in the world. This is partly because the animals are so rare, and partly because each one produces only a very small amount of wool. Unlike sheep, vicuña cannot be shorn annually, but only about every third year. Hence, they are a protected species, and their wool is not commercially produced. A UN agreement is in the pipeline, by which vicuña wool may be woven and sold under strict guidelines. Alpacas – which are far more numerous – can only be shorn on alternate years, but the wool yield is much greater. It is softer than that of the lowly sheep, and much finer than that of the llama.

still relatively abundant in more remote areas where hunting pressure is low, since this species shows a remarkable adaptability to various habitat types. It occurs from the coastal plain (in zones of sufficient vegetation) to 4,000 meters (13,000 ft) above sea level, and then into the cloudforest of the eastern slopes of the Andes, down almost to the Amazon basin at 600 meters (2,000 ft). It is quite common for a hiker in the Andes to encounter this animal.

Its much rarer relative, the Andean huemul (or *taruka* as it is known in Peru), is harder to see. The *taruka* is a species in danger of extinction and is found at extremely high altitudes. Its

highlands of Peru are the rodents and omnivores. The Andean fox is ubiquitous in all parts of the Andean region, and can be found at all altitudes up to 4,500 meters (14,800 ft). This species of fox is larger and longer legged than its North American and European counterparts and commonly investigates any empty cans or leftover food outside tents. The Andean fox is everywhere regarded as a dangerous stock killer, especially of sheep. The stomachs of these animals often contain quantities of vicuña wool, but it is not known whether it is a predator of this species or only a carrion eater. Whenever possible, the Andean fox is killed by the

presence is governed by the availability of cover, mostly small isolated patches of woodland. This type of woodland is disappearing at an alarming rate, as it is a primary source of fuel at high altitudes. Consequently, the barrel-chested, short-legged *taruka* is on the decline. If encountered, it is easily distinguished from the white-tailed deer by its two-pronged antlers (the white-tailed deer has one prong only). It is still possible to find this species on the Inca trail to Machu Picchu.

Easiest of all to see while hiking through the

local people, yet it remains common.

While walking along stream banks or drystone walls, the observant hiker will notice a large number of small rodents, ranging from the typical house-mouse type familiar to all of us, to mice with a striking color combination of chocolate-brown and white. It is not that there are a greater number of mice-like creatures in the Andes, but simply that, because of very low temperatures at night, most Andean rodents are diurnal. They are also the principal food source of a variety of predators including the Andean weasel (*Mustela frenata*), a vicious mustelid that will tackle prey twice its size. The abundance of diurnal rodents also

LEFT: a flock of shy vicuña.
ABOVE: Andean white-tailed deer in mid-flight.

accounts for the high density of birds of prey, such as the red-backed and puna hawks, the cinereous harrier, the black-chested buzzard-eagle, and the aplomado falcon.

The guinea pig, or *cuy* as it is known in Peru, is domesticated extensively in the Andes, and wild ones are also fairly common along stony banks and dry-stone walls, where they live in colonies. Any Quechua household will have its colony of guinea pigs living in the kitchen area, as the animal is regarded as a delicacy.

The last two conspicuous animals of the Andes are the hog-nosed skunk and the mountain vizcacha. The former, which may be famil-

tinues from 3,600 meters (11,800 ft) down to the tropical rainforest of the Amazon basin. The type of forest above 2,500 meters (8,200 ft) is commonly known as "cloudforest," a name derived from the fact that for most of the year the trees are shrouded in mist. Indeed, most of the moisture needed by the forest is captured from the enveloping clouds. The cloudforest grades into high grassland at about 3,400 meters (11,200 ft) and harbors some exotic animals that will not be forgotten if once glimpsed.

The spectacled bear is perhaps the most impressive animal of the zone, with a total body length of up to 183cm (6 feet). This animal is a

iar to visitors from North America, is mostly nocturnal and can often be picked up in car headlights. The latter is a sociable creature commonly found in rock screes and boulder fields. Very well camouflaged, it often betrays its presence with a high-pitched whistle. Looking like a cross between a chinchilla and a rabbit, the mountain vizcacha (the prey of large carnivores) can be seen sunning itself on boulders in the early morning and late afternoon.

The cloudforest

On the eastern slope of the Andes the environment is dominated by humid temperate forest. Where left undisturbed by man, the forest con-

true omnivore, eating a wide variety of foods such as fruits and berries, large insects, succulent plants and, at high elevations, the lush hearts of terrestrial bromeliads. The spectacled bear will also eat small mammals and rodents when given the opportunity.

Other shy inhabitants of the cloudforest include two species of small deer. The larger of the two is the dwarf brocket deer. About half the size of the white-tailed deer, it is found to a height of 3,300 meters (10,800 ft) in the departments of Puno and Cusco. The other is the pudu, the size of a small dog, difficult to see and mostly nocturnal. It is relentlessly hunted with guns and dogs and must be considered vulnerable at present. Occupying the same habitat as the pudu is the wooly monkey, found in small family groups where hunting pressure is low and can still be found in cloudforest beyond Paucartambo in the department of Cusco.

Diversity of birdlife

The Andes are not just the home of mammals: southeast Peru has a greater diversity of birdlife than any other area on the planet. The majority of these species occur in the cloudforests and lowland rainforests of the eastern Andean slopes, but a wide variety can be seen right up to the snowline.

drop of ice-capped Andean peaks is one that will not be forgotten quickly.

The condor is still a common sight for hikers through the high country, but far more commonly seen are the smaller songbirds such as sierra finches, cinclodes, miners, and seed-snipes. Once one reaches the limit of the cloud-forest, the number of species increases dramatically, and the birds are much more brightly colored. Anyone taking a stroll here in the morning will notice mixed-species flocks of colorful mountain-tanagers and flycatchers, as well as various species of hummingbird, flitting between the moss-festooned branches. ❏

The bird that first comes to mind when one is writing of the Andean peaks is the Andean condor. This huge member of the vulture family is a carrion feeder, but is not averse to starting its meal a little prematurely. The condor is not a hunter and is incapable of grasping or carrying prey, having feet not unlike those of a chicken. (Sensational reports in newspapers of condors carrying off unattended babies must therefore be dismissed.) The sight of a condor sailing effortlessly against the back-

LEFT: the spectacled bear, a true omnivore.
ABOVE: an eagle soars in the sun.
ABOVE RIGHT: a llama in need of a haircut.

CONFLICT OVER CONSERVATION

The spectacled bear is a good example of the conflict between conservation and, for the poor, self-preservation. Although an important animal in Andean folklore, the bear has a very poor reputation among small farmers due to its habit of raiding maize crops at the edge of hill forests. Farmers also complain that spectacled bears kill their livestock, though in reality they do not.

Unfortunately for the bear, its fat is much sought-after and its body parts have medicinal uses. None of this bodes well for the bear's survival, and it is being hunted to the extent where population levels are becoming dangerously low.

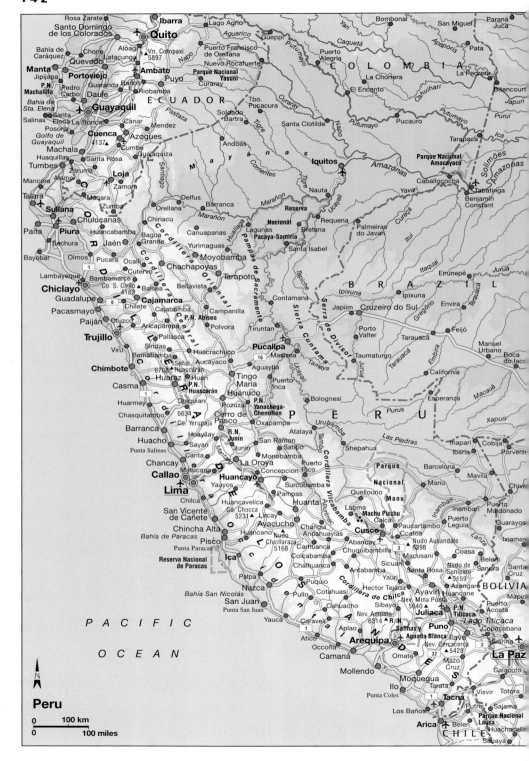

Peru

Rosa Zarate · Ibarra · Lago Agrio · Bombonal · Paraná · Juca · Paraná · San Miguel · Pata

Santo Domingo de los Colorados · Quito · Aguarico · Gueppí · Caquetá · Apaporis · COLOMBIA

Bahía de Caráquez · Chone · Aloag · Vn. Cotopaxi 5897 · Puerto Francisco de Orellana · Puerto Alegría · La Chorrera · La Pedrera · Bitencourt

Manta · Quevedo · Latacunga · Napo · Nuevo Rocafuerte · El Encanto · Cahuihari · Vapuri

Jipijapa · Portoviejo · Ambato · Puyo · Parque Nacional Yasuní · Putumayo · Pucauro · Purui

P.N. Machalilla · Guaranda · Baños · Curaray · Tbo. Pucacura · Santa Clotilde · Napo · Pucaro · Putumayo · Ica

Bahía de Sta. Elena · Pedro Carbo · Daule · Riobamba · ECUADOR · Tigre · Marañón · Caballococha · Tarapaca

Guayaquil · Canar · Mendez · Pastaza · Soldado Bartra · Corrientes · Iquitos · Amazonas · Parque Nacional Amacayacu · Solimões · Amazonas

Salinas · Santa Elena · La Troncal · Cuenca 4137 · Azogues · Andoas · M a y n a s · Nauta · Yavari · Tabatinga · Benjamín Constant

Golfo de Guayaquil · Machala · Cumbe · Gualaquiza · Delfus · Barranca · Reserva Nacional Pacaya-Samiria · Requena · Curaca · Itui

Huaquillas · Sarita Rosa · Santiago · Orellana · Marañón · Lagunas · Bretaña · Palmeiras do Javari

Tumbes · Zaruma · Loja · Zamora · Chiriaco · Marañón · Huallaga · Santa Isabel · Ipixuna · Eirúnepé · Juruá

Mancora · Alamor · Macara · Zumba · Canuapanas · Yurimaguas · Contamana · Ipixuna · Envira · Itaquai

Talara · Sullana · Chulucanas · Huancabamba · Bagua Grande · Moyobamba · Japiim · Cruzeiro do Sul · Gregório · Feijó · Jurúa

Paita · Piura · Sechura · Jaén · Chachapoyas · Tarapoto · B R A Z I L

Bayobar · Olmos · Pucara · Ocalli · Cuervo · Bellavista · Contamana · Porto Valter · Tarauacá · Feijó · Manuel Urbano · Boca do Iacc

Lambayeque · Bambamarca · Cajabamba · Campanilla · Serra de Divisor · Taumaturgo · Tarauacá · Embira · California · Macauã

Chiclayo · Co. S. Cristo 4183 · Balsea · Cajamarca · P.N. Abiseo · Polvora · Tiruntan · Ucayali · Macuã · Esperanza · Xapuri

Guadalupe · Chilete · Cajabamba · Pallasca · Huacrachuco · Pucallpa · Masisea · Sierra Contama · Purus · PERU

Pacasmayo · Otuzco · Sindas · Aucayaco · Tingo María · Puerto Inca · Aguaytia · Iñapari · Cobija

Paiján · Viru · Pomabamba · Señal 6768 Huascarán · Huari · Huánuco · Bolognesi · Iberia · Porvenir

Trujillo · Chimbote · Huaraz · P.N. Huascarán · Chiquian · P.N. Yanachaga-Chemillén · Tambo · Las Piedras · Ihapari · Barcelona · Mavila · Chive

Casma · Huarmey · Chasquitambo · 6634 · Ce. Yerupaja · Cerro de Pasco · Oxapampa · Atalaya · Uruamba · Shepahua · Manu · Puerto Maldonado · Guarayos

Barranca · Huacho · Huayllay · R.N. Junín · San Ramón · Satipo · Monobamba · Puerto Rico · Cordillera Vilcabamba · Parque Nacional Manu · Quellouno · Inambari · Puerto Leguia · Ixiamas

Punta Salinas · Sayán · Canta · Junín · Concepcion · Surcubamba · Huanta · Lucma · Machu Picchu · Calca · Paucartambo · Coasa · Belen · Santa Cruz

Chancay · Matucana · Huancayo · Yauyos · Pampas · Cusco · Ccatca · Nudo Ausandate 6398 · Macusani · BOLIVIA

Callao · Lima · Chilca · Huancavelica · Co. Chocca 5231 · Lircay · Ayacucho · Chungui · Andahuaylas · Abancay · Chuquibambilla · Sicuani · Santa Rosa · Yauri · Nudo de Sunipata 5159 · Azángaro · Huandane · Mapiri

San Vicente de Cañete · Huancano · Nudo Chiclaraza 5168 · Carhuanca · Colcabamba · Chalhuanca · Antabamba · Hector Tejada · Ayaviri · Nev. Mina Punta · P.N. Titicaca · Puerto Acosta

Chincha Alta · Pisco · Bahía de Paracas · Ica · Palpa · Puquio · Cotahuasi · Cahuacho · Nev. Ampato 6314 · R.N. Salinas y Aguada Blanca · Juliaca · Puno · Ilave · Copacabana

Reserva Nacional de Paracas · Punta Paracas · Nazca · Pullo · Yauca · Caraveli · Aplao · Nev. Cercacerca 5428 · Huarina · La Paz

Bahía San Nicolás · San Juan · Punta San Juan · Camaná · Arequipa · Omate · Mazo Cruz · Calacoto

PACIFIC OCEAN · Atico · Occoña · Mollendo · Moquegua · Tarata · Visvir · Totora

N · Ilo · Punta Coles · Los Baños · Tacna · Putre · Sajama · Parque Nacional Lauca

Peru · Arica · Belen · CHILE · Huachacalle · Sabaya

0 100 km
0 100 miles

PLACES

*A detailed guide to the entire country, with principal sites
clearly cross-referenced by number to the maps*

Mapping out an itinerary for Peru might seem a daunting prospect. The country is three times as large as California, and many times more varied, with the Andean mountain range and Amazon jungle creating some imposing barriers to travel. Yet journeys that were all but impossible 50 years ago are now every-day events: each of Peru's major cities is linked by safe, modern jet flights; regular long-distance bus services run to lesser urban centers; and even tiny mountain villages can be reached on a rattling ancient bus or in the back of one of the ubiquitous Peruvian trucks that are an informal mode of public transport. These days, too, the threat from Sendero Luminoso (Shining Path) guerrillas has receded, and few areas are now regarded as unsafe.

Most travelers to Peru begin their journeys in Lima. As the former center of Spanish South America, it retains some fine colonial archi-tecture, and treasures from all over the country can be found in its impressive museums. The Panamericana highway runs the length of the coast: to the north of Lima, it leads to the ancient Chimu site at Chan Chan, and relaxed coastal cities like Trujillo, from where you can turn inland to the beautiful Andean market town of Cajamarca. To the south, the Panamericana takes you to Nazca, whose plains are etched with gigantic drawings made by a mysterious pre-Inca culture, and only visible from the air.

For many people the mountainous Inca capital, Cusco, is the high-light of their visit. A 40-minute flight from Lima – one of the most spectacular on earth – takes travelers straight into the heart of the Andes. Apart from its own attractions, Cusco also serves as a base to visit the Urubamba Valley and the most famous site on the conti-nent: Machu Picchu. No matter how many times you have seen these ruins in photographs, nothing will quite prepare you for the reality.

Less than two hours from the coast, yet nestled high in the Andes, Arequipa is one of Peru's most elegant colonial cities, set in the shadow of the snow-capped Volcán Misti, and renowned for its intel-lectual life. From Cusco and Arequipa, many travelers fly or take a lengthy but popular railway journey to Puno, by the shores of Lake Titicaca. The world's highest navigable lake is populated by fasci-nating indigenous communities, who still ply its waters in *totora* reed canoes.

Increasing numbers of travelers are visiting an area that takes up over half of Peru's landmass: the Amazon basin. In the northern Amazon, the city of Iquitos is the traditional center from which to begin a tour. And in the south there is the Parque Nacional Manu, possibly the purest section of rainforest in South America. ❑

PRECEDING PAGES: sand dunes, Pasamayo; salt terraces at Moray;
a slow afternoon on Taquile Island.

Lima

0   1 km

0   1 mile

N

Aeropuerto Internacional
Jorge Chávez

Rimac

Av. del Ensor

Av. Elmer J. Faucett

Av. C. Peru

Av. Morales Duarez

Av. Morales Duarez

Av. Maquinarias

Terminal
Marítima

Av. de Mayo

Pl.
Fanning

CALLAO

Av. República Argentina

Av. Panamá

Guardia Chalaca

Av. Saenz Peña

Av. Benavides

Fuerte Real Felipe

Constitución

Playa Chucuito

Buenos Aires

Playa Cantolao

Jr. Canera

Loreto

LA PUNTA

Av. Bolognesi

Escuela
Naval

Av. Grau

Playa
Carpayo

LA PERLA

Av. Costanera

Ovalo
Saloom

Av. República de Venezuela

Av. de la Marina

Centro
Médico
Naval

Universidad
Nacional de
San Marcos

Playa
Malecón

Av. de los Precursores

**PARQUE
DE LAS
LEYENDAS**

Santa Rosa

Av. la Paz

SAN MIGUEL

Colegio Militar
Leancio Prado

Av. Libertad

Av. de los Patriotas

Manco II

Av.

Av. Libertad

**Feria Internaciona
del Pacífico**

MAGDALENA

Miraflores

0   200 m

0   200 yds

N

Av. Comandante Espinar

Habich

Arica

**PARQUE
TAHUANTINSUYO**

Larco Herrera

Tarapaca

Petit Thouars

Elias

Tanca

Av. Angamos Oeste

Av. Av. Angamos Este

Chiclayo

Atahualpa

Arequipa

Chiclayo

Vidal

Piura

Pl.
República

Piura

Teatro
Marsano

Paseo de la República

Palacios

Independencia

Borgoño

Palacios

Gonzales Prada

2 de Mayo
Hospital

2 de Mayo

Tanca

Cofina

Av. Jose Pardo

Bolognesi

Libertad

Berlin

**Cinema
El Pacífico**

Av. R. Palma

Av. J. Chávez

Galvez

Bonilla

Esperanza

Colegio
Champagnat

**PARQUE
CENTRAL**
**La Virgen
Milagrosa**

Cantuarias

Francia

**PARQUE
KENNEDY**

Municipalidad

Madrid

Schell

Diez

Canseco

Italia

Av. A. Benavides

Av. A. Benavides

Mc Cisneros

Tripoli

Venecia

San Martin

Colon

Bolivar

La Paz

Bolivar

Lavalle

Mc 28 de Julio

Manco Capac

Av. 28 de Julio

San Martin

Buenos Aires

Av. 28 de Julio

Gonzales

Manco Capac

Fanning

Ferre

Gonzales

P   A   C   I   F   I   C   O   O

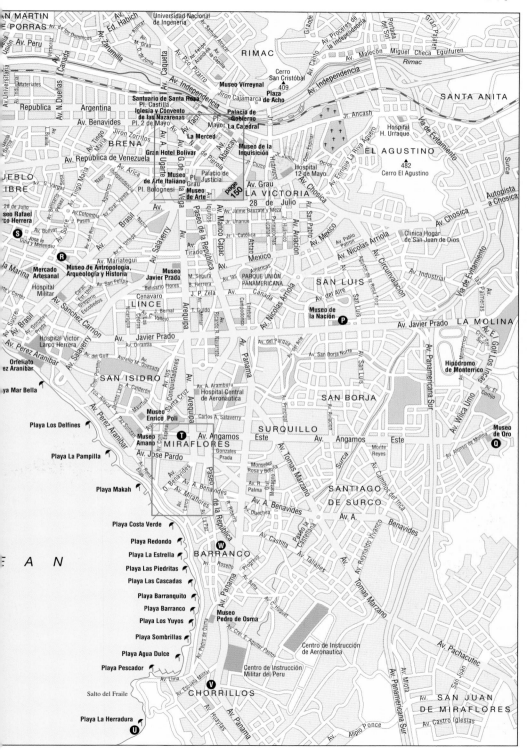

LIMA

Major urban renewal schemes have given Lima back some of its former splendor. But it remains a sprawling city with many different faces, from the old colonial heart to modern Miraflores

Maps on pages 146 & 150

Lima

H erman Melville (the 19th-century American author of *Moby Dick*) called Lima ❶ "the saddest city on earth." Many visitors have agreed with him, while some residents have been even less complimentary – "Lima the horrible" was how writer Sebastián Salazar Bondy described his native city in the 1960s. But tourists who take such descriptions – and their own first impressions – at face value risk missing out on a city of rare fascination and unexpected pleasures.

While locals may gripe, most have an enduring love-hate relationship with their paradoxical city. Lima has both decaying colonial splendor and the teeming vitality of an Oriental bazaar; melancholy cloudy winters and warm breezy summers; impoverished urban sprawl and quiet, elegant corners among ancient buildings where the night air is scented with jasmine.

The City of Kings

Lima was founded by the Spanish conquistador Francisco Pizarro on January 18, 1535. The foundation was planned for January 6 – Epiphany, or the Day of the Kings – and despite the delay the capital was still known as La Ciudad de los Reyes or "The City of Kings." Pizarro traced a grid of 13 streets by nine to form 117 city blocks on the site of an existing indigenous settlement beside the southern bank of the Río Rimac (from which the name Lima was derived). But he had no great army of workers: the city's first inhabitants numbered fewer than 100.

Pizarro had originally made his capital at Jauja, in the Andes. The rapid switch was determined by a strategic need to be close to his ships – his only lifeline in a rebellious, still largely unconquered country. The Rimac Valley provides the best line of communication through the Andean peaks to the interior of central Peru, while the rivers Chillón and Lurín also reach the sea within the present-day boundaries of the city, making the site one of the best-watered in the coastal desert. Several *huacas*, or funeral mounds, along with other pre-Columbian ruins, survive in greater Lima as testimony that the area was populated before the Conquest. The most important pre-Inca religious site in coastal Peru was nearby at Pachacámac.

The only drawback was the future city's microclimate. Because of a meteorological phenomenon known as thermal inversion, Lima is often draped in a damp blanket of low cloud – the *garúa* – from May through October, although the summer months can be agreeable. And though the visitor may often forget the fact, seeing exuberant gardens of yellow amancaes or purple bougainvillaea (the product of careful irrigation), rainfall rarely amounts to more than a few nights of drizzle, insufficient to wash the desert dust from the facades of buildings that require frequent repainting.

PRECEDING PAGES:
Plaza Mayor.
LEFT: guarding the Archbishop's Palace.
BELOW: colonial balconies.

Capital of the New World

For two centuries after its foundation, Lima was the political, commercial, and ecclesiastical capital of Spanish South America, and the seat of the Inquisition as well as of the viceroys. But its beginnings were modest, and gave little clue to its later splendor. The *mestizo* chronicler Garcilaso de la Vega described it as having "very broad and very straight streets, so that from any of its crossroads the countryside can be seen in all four directions," adding that the houses were roofed with reeds rather than tiles.

But by the early 17th century, Lima's population had risen to about 25,000, the majority of them indigenous peoples working as servants or artisans, and African slaves. In the 1680s a protective wall with 12 gateways was built around the city, because of fears of raids by English privateers. The wall was demolished in the 1870s, although fragments can still be seen beside the railway line in the Barrios Altos. Despite being frequently damaged by earthquakes, the city was rich as well as powerful. The most powerful earthquake, in 1746, destroyed

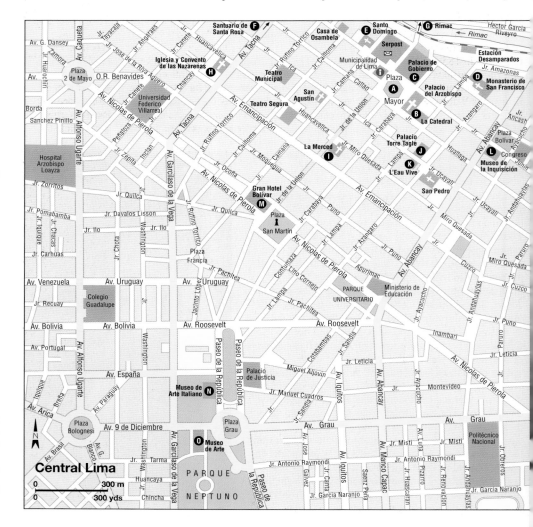

Central Lima

much of the city, and the palaces, churches, mansions, and monasteries we see today were subsequently rebuilt and expanded. Across the Río Rimac, pleasure gardens for the aristocracy were carefully laid out.

Lima's gradual decline from pre-eminence began in the late 18th century, as new viceroyalties were created in Bogotá and Buenos Aires, and the city's monopoly on trade between Europe and South America was broken. As would be expected of a royalist city, independence from Spain was initiated from outside. Expeditionary forces, first from Argentina under General José de San Martín and then from Colombia under Venezuelan Simón de Bolívar, "the Liberator," occupied the city. Installed as republican Peru's first president in the suburb of Magdalena, even the austere Bolívar was affected by Lima's sybaritic elegance. It was at a ball in the city that he met and fell in love with Manuela Saenz, the Ecuadorean wife of a British doctor, who was to become his lifelong companion. Bolívar's presidency lasted only from 1824 to 1826, and when he left for Colombia a period of political instability and economic chaos ensued.

Bursting its boundaries

After an initial turbulent period, the city's development resumed in the mid-19th century. The first railway in South America opened between Lima and its port of Callao in 1854, followed swiftly by further lines to connect the city with the growing coastal villages of Miraflores and Chorrillos. But setbacks followed, as Lima was occupied and partially sacked by Chilean troops in 1881 during the disastrous War of the Pacific. It was only in the early 20th century that the city burst its 17th-century Spanish limits and embarked on a process of change and growth that has lasted to the present day, the product of both massive migration

Map on pages 146–7

Simón Bolívar, Liberator.

LEFT: an ornate colonial doorway.
RIGHT: a richly gilded altar.

*Cathedral door
knocker.*

from the Andean hinterland and the decline of the upper classes as Peru moved falteringly toward democracy. The outline of the modern city dates from the beginning of this period. Industry began to spread westward along the Callao railway, and up the central highway to Vitarte in the east.

The building of Paseo Colón and Avenida Nicolas de Piérola or La Colmena (begun in 1898) and of Plaza San Martín (1921), created new arteries and a new central focus to the south of Pizarro's Plaza de Armas, which was revamped in 1997 and renamed the Plaza Mayor. The rising urban upper-middle class moved away from the crowded center to the spacious south, toward Miraflores and the new district of San Isidro, laid out as a leafy garden suburb. Working-class suburbs sprang up over the river in Rimac, in El Agustino to the east, and in La Victoria to the southeast. By 1931, Lima's population had reached 280,000, having doubled in little more than two decades.

In the years since then, two trends have given Lima its present urban structure. Infill development of middle-class suburbs has completed a triangle enclosing the area between the city center, Callao, and Chorrillos. Outside this triangle, Andean migrants made their homes in sprawling, self-built shanty towns stretching north, south, and northeast, occupying the vacant desert sands in the shadow of the Andean foothills. The shanty towns now contain half the city's estimated population of nearly 8 million. They started as squatter settlements of rush-matting huts, but decades of hard work have turned some into pleasant districts. Many others remain desperately poor, lacking electricity, piped water, or paved streets. But the migrants and their children have changed the character of the city irrevocably. Many of them came to Lima during the 1980s, when the violence of the Sendero Luminoso movement and the military, of which

BELOW: city portrait artist.

campesinos (subsistence farmers) were often the innocent victims, made rural life intolerable. As the city swelled with rural migrants, the old downtown area fell into decay, and businesses and hotels took flight, re-establishing themselves in better-run districts like San Isidro, Miraflores, and La Molina. Street vendors, drug-pushers, prostitutes, and pick-pockets took over the city center. But in the past few years things have been looking up: successive mayors embarked on a clean-up campaign which moved the street vendors – *ambulantes* – from the historic center. This was accompanied by a certain amount of strife, but has proved successful. Many of the vendors are now operating in organized markets, and have found that the move has also brought commercial success.

The colonial heart

A major program of urban renewal is in progress in the historic center of the city. Under the auspices of UNESCO it has been declared part of "the Cultural Heritage of Mankind," and there have been spectacular changes in both architectural restoration and street cleanliness and security. The usual starting point for exploring Lima is **Plaza Mayor Ⓐ** (formerly Plaza de Armas), which has benefited greatly from recent renovation. Stand in the middle of this handsome square, by the 17th-century bronze fountain, and you are at the city's historic heart. Look out for the Angel of Fame on the fountain: it's a copy of the original which, it is said, flew away in 1900. Most of the buildings are 18th-century reconstructions, but the spirit of the conquistadors permeates the square.

The eastern side of the square is dominated by the **Catedral Ⓑ** (open Mon–Sat 10am–4.30pm; entrance charge) on a site chosen by Francisco Pizarro, but reconstructed several times after earthquakes. The present building was

Map on page 150

BELOW: Plaza Mayor.

begun in the 18th century, after the almost complete devastation of the previous one in the 1746 earthquake. Much of the exterior has been painted in yellow-ochre, as part of a successful policy to brighten up dusty facades with colors used in the colonial period.

Inside, the cathedral is large and unusually austere. Notable are the 17th-century wooden choir stalls. To the right of the entrance is a small side-chapel dedicated to Pizarro, where his skeleton lies in a sealed wooden coffin. Found in 1977 during excavations in the cathedral crypt and put on display in 1985, to mark Lima's 450th anniversary, it replaced the remains of an anonymous conquistador, long mistakenly thought to have been Pizarro.

Next door to the cathedral is the **Palacio del Arzobispo** (Archbishop's Palace), rebuilt in the 1920s with an impressive wooden balcony. Opposite stands the **Municipalidad de Lima** (City Hall), built in the 1940s after fire destroyed its predecessor. The pleasant interior includes a fine library. Next to it on the square is the headquarters of the **Club de la Unión**, a lunchtime haunt of politicians and professionals. Between them at the mouth of Pasaje Santa Rosa is a monument, in the form of a large chunk of rough-hewn stone, to Taulichusco El Viejo, the last *cacique* (chief) of pre-Conquest Lima, which was unveiled in 1985 as a belated antidote to the ghost of Pizarro.

On the north side of the plaza is the **Palacio de Gobierno** ⓒ Government Palace (open Mon–Fri 10.30am–12.30pm; free admission; or a free two-hour guided tour – take a copy of your passport at least one day before, 2–5pm), built on the site of Pizarro's palace, where he was assassinated in 1541 – the first Latin-American coup d'état. The present building was completed in 1938, and suffers from the taste for grandiose French baroque which afflicted dictatorial

The Central Post Office building is now regarded as a national monument, and is under the auspices of the Instituto Nacional de Cultura.

BELOW: changing the Guard at the Presidential Palace.

leaders of the time. Much of the ground plan at the rear of the building remains the same as in Pizarro's day. At noon, every day except Sunday, you can catch the Changing of the Guard, performed in the front courtyard by goose-stepping troops from the Hussares de Junín regiment, dressed in the red-and-blue ceremonial uniforms and ornamental helmets of the independence period. To arrange a guided tour of the palace go to the office of Relaciones Públicas in the same building to make an appointment, or tel: 427-6732, ext. 451.

In a small side square, between the palace and the Municipalidad, stands an equestrian statue of the ubiquitous Pizarro, somewhat disregarded these days, although a plan to have him removed altogether was unsuccessful. Behind him, the building topped with antennae houses an office of Peru's National Intelligence Service. To the left is the Café Conquistador, with tables on the pavement – a good place for a coffee and a rest while sightseeing. Nearby stands the Central Post Office, now called **Serpost**, its offices grouped around a handsome open-air neo-classical arcade, recently restored.

Farther up toward the river are a couple of splendid old hat shops, where you can acquire a felt stetson or a Panama for around US$12–15. This is where the booming contraband market of **Polvos Azules** used to be, but the street vendors and shop-owners have been moved to the old industrial area just outside the center. Thieves abound here and in the city center generally, and visitors should take great care of their valuables while exploring the streets of Lima. Until you become accustomed to the city, you would also be best advised not to wander alone in the center by night.

Doubling back into Plaza Mayor again, on a charming street corner (the intersection of Jirón Carabaya and Jirón Junín) you will find the oldest building in

Map on page 150

Santa Rosa medallion.

BELOW: Lima street vendor, and child.

the square, La Casa del Oidor. Dating from the early 18th century, it has the wooden balconies in the form of enclosed galleries projecting from the first floor that were colonial Lima's most graceful feature. Farther up Carabaya, past several shoe shops (hand-stitched cowboy boots made to measure), is the **Desamparados Station**, a neo-classical building dating from 1908. This was the terminal for the journey to Huancayo, along the highest rail track in the world (via Ticlio, at 4,800 meters/14,000 ft above sea level). The service was reintroduced briefly in 1998 but was closed again in mid-1999. With the removal of the street vendors, a new promenade, the Paseo Chabuca Granda, has been created behind the Presidential Palace on the southern bank of the Río Rimac. Many limeños (the people of Lima) like to stroll here at the weekends, and the municipality organizes concerts and theater performances in specially constructed arenas.

If you are wondering why some street names include the word "Jirón," they are the major thoroughfares, made up of several blocks. Each individual block may have a different name.

Books and bones

Turn right along Jirón Ancash and you will come to the **Monasterio de San Francisco** , the jewel of colonial Lima. Even if you are not a fan of colonial churches, don't miss this one. The church faces a small paved square, full of pigeons and portrait photographers. The outside is attractively painted in colonial yellow, but it is the interior that is fascinating; much of it is decorated in the geometrical *Mudéjar* (Andalusian Moorish) style. Established soon after the foundation of Lima, it has suffered earthquake damage over the years but has been sensitively restored in the original style. Its outstanding features include the 17th-century library, with 25,000 leather-bound volumes and 6,000 parchments dating from the 15th to the 18th century. The cupola has a superb *Mudéjar* carved wooden ceiling of Panamanian cedar, dating from 1625. In a gallery above the nave of the church are 130 choir stalls and 71 panels with carvings of Franciscan saints, made of the same wood. Recent work has exposed (under eight layers of paint) 17th-century murals in the cloister and adjacent chambers (open Mon–Sun 9.30am–5.30pm, guided tours; entrance fee).

BELOW:
steps lead up to the Monasterio de San Francisco.

The monastery's collection of religious art includes paintings from the workshops of Rubens and Zurbaran and, in the refectory, a *Last Supper* painted in 1697 by a Flemish Jesuit priest. San Francisco has probably survived more recent earthquakes because of the solid base provided by its catacombs, which were used as Lima's cemetery until 1810. A network of underground chambers, which are open to the public, contains hundreds of skulls and bones, stored in racks according to type. A secret passage (now bricked up) led from here to the Government Palace.

There are many other colonial churches in the center. To reach the **Iglesia de Santo Domingo** (open Mon–Sat 9am–noon and 3–6pm, Sun 9am–noon; entrance charge) retrace your steps along Ancash, past the Post Office, to the corner of Jirón Camana. The church, which has a pleasant cloister with tiling from Seville, contains the tomb of San Martín de Porres, a black saint who lived and died in Lima and is venerated throughout Latin America. There is also an urn here which holds the ashes of Santa Rosa de Lima, the patron saint of the New

World and the Philippines as well as the city of Lima. To reach the **Santuario de Santa Rosa** ❻ continue along Conde Superunda and turn right on Avenida Tacna. The sanctuary, a modest hut built in the 16th century on the site of the saint's birthplace and now set in a pleasant garden, contains relics of Santa Rosa (daily 8am–noon and 3–6pm; free admission).

As you walked along Conde Superunda, between Santo Domingo and the Santuario, you may have noticed that this is one of several streets in the center with good colonial balconies. Since the city council's "Adopt a Balcony" campaign many balconies – previously in a sad state of decay – have been restored by private investors. The **Casa de Osambela** is open to the public and well worth visiting. A late 18th-century mansion with an ornamental cupola, beautifully restored in the 1980s, it houses a small art gallery and the offices of various cultural institutions (open Mon–Fri 9am–4pm; free admission).

Across the river

At this point, make a small detour. You could cross the Puente Santa Rosa here or, better, return to the little bridge behind the Palacio de Gobierno, the **Puente de Piedra** (Stone Bridge), built in Roman style in 1610 (its mortar reputedly bound with thousands of egg whites for strength), which leads over the river to **Rimac** ❼, once the playground of the aristocracy and now a lively working-class district. The Hatuchay Peña (a nightclub with Peruvian music and dancing), popular with both tourists and locals, is in Jirón Trujillo, as soon as you cross the bridge.

Turn right and you will come to **Plaza de Acho**, the oldest bullring in the Americas. The **Museo Taurino** (open Mon–Fri 10am–6pm, Sat 9am–6pm, Sundays by appointment only; tel: 01-48 23360) has a collection of bullfighting memorabilia and, notably, some Goya engravings. There is a panoramic view of the city from Cerro San Cristóbal. Organized tours visit the Rimac district and this hill several times a day. Buses leave from the main plaza and the tour includes a visit to the bullfighting museum. At the foot of the hill is the **Alameda de los Descalzos**, laid out in 1610 as a pleasure garden with statues and wrought-iron railings, but now rather run-down. It leads to the **Monasterio de los Descalzos** (Monastery of the Barefoot Friars; open daily 9.30am–1pm; entrance fee), recently restored and well worth the walk to get there. To the right is the **Paseo de Aguas**, another pleasure garden created in the 18th century by Viceroy Amat for his famous mistress, La Perrichola *(see page 65)*, but also sadly in need of repair.

Churches and miracles

On the south side of the River Rimac, on the corner of Avenida Tacna and Huancavelica, stands the **Iglesia y Convento de las Nazarenas** ❽, which houses the image of El Señor de los Milagros (The Lord of Miracles), the black Christ painted by a freed African slave that has become the most important focus of popular religious feeling in Lima. The miracle was that the wall on which the painting appeared was the only part of a 17th-century shanty town to survive an

Map on page 150

BELOW: decorative ceiling in the Convento de San Francisco.

earthquake. In October the image is borne around the city center for several days (October 18, 19, and 28) by teams of men wearing the purple robes of the brotherhood of El Señor de los Milagros. Hundreds of thousands of people turn out to accompany the image in what is one of the largest public gatherings in South America. The church can be visited (open Mon–Sat 6.30am–noon and 4.30–8.30pm; free admission) but the convent is a closed order.

Leaving Las Nazarenas, go to the next corner and turn left down Avenida Emancipación for four blocks, then left again on Jirón de la Unión, which brings you to the **Iglesia de la Merced ❶**. This church, which, like most in Lima, suffered severe earthquake damage and was rebuilt in the late 18th century, is built on the site of the first Catholic Mass celebrated in the city, in 1534 (open daily 9am–noon and 4–7pm; free admission).

Leaving La Merced, go down Jirón Quesada, then turn left on Jirón Azangaro and you will reach the **Iglesia de San Pedro** (open Mon–Fri 9am–noon and 2–4pm; free admission), another baroque church with *Mudéjar* influences, which was consecrated in 1638.

Colonial mansions

The city center contains several fine examples of secular colonial architecture. Outstanding is one on Jirón Ucayali, close to San Pedro: the **Palacio Torre Tagle ❿** was completed in 1735 and gives a good idea of the opulence of Lima in its colonial prime. It now houses the Foreign Ministry, but visits are allowed to the courtyard, from where you can see the finely carved wooden balconies. Opposite Torre Tagle, in another colonial mansion, is **L'Eau Vive Restaurant ⓚ** (open for lunch Mon–Sat 12.30–3pm; for supper 7.30–9.30pm), run by French-

BELOW: the opulent Palacio Torre Tagle.

speaking nuns. They serve excellent, reasonably priced French food. Customers are encouraged to join them in singing the Ave María at 3pm and 9pm.

From here make a slight detour to the **Museo de la Inquisición** ⓛ (Museum of the Inquisition), on Jirón Junín. This is the building where generations of alleged heretics were tortured and tried. You can visit the main hall (with a fine 18th-century wooden ceiling) and the sinister, underground dungeons and torture chambers. The stocks are original, and there are mock-ups of other torture techniques. Between here and the river is a huge daily market, and an archway proclaiming that this is Lima's **Chinatown** (open Mon–Sun 9am–5pm; free admission).

Republican Lima

South of the Plaza Mayor, the largest square is the **Plaza San Martín**, the hub of the modern city center. If you approach the square from Plaza Mayor, you should take the pedestrianized **Jirón de la Unión**, once Lima's most elegant shopping street. As recently as the 1940s it was considered scandalous for women to stroll along Jirón de la Unión without wearing a hat. Now it is a teeming mass of shoppers and fast-food joints. Street vendors, who used to lay out their goods all over the sidewalks, have been sent packing under the recent clean-up campaign.

The colonnaded Plaza San Martín, recently restored and repainted and brightly lit, is an important gathering place for political meetings. In the center is an equestrian statue of General José de San Martín, Peru's Argentinian independence hero. On its west side is the **Gran Hotel Bolívar** ⓜ, built in the 1920s. Though now it often seems to have more elderly waiters and bellboys than

Map on page 150

A presidential guard.

BELOW: the Bridge of Sighs, Barranco.

guests, the hotel retains much of its former atmosphere. A Palm Court trio serenades people drinking afternoon tea in the domed lobby, and its giant *pisco sours* (called *catedrales*) remain justly famous. Even if you are not staying here, the Bolívar is the perfect place to stop and rest during a city tour; the decor and ambience make the high price of the drinks worthwhile.

Next to the Bolívar is **Jirón Ocoña**, the center of Lima's street foreign exchange market, where money-changers buy or sell dollars round the clock. The market is sophisticated and in times of high inflation, rates change hourly. Across La Colmena from the Bolívar is the **Club Nacional**. Though it is no longer the watering-hole of Peru's once all-powerful oligarchy, it has recently taken on a new lease of life, with the revamping of the city center. The clients now are a blend of old-money families and prominent members of the business community.

Touring the museums

Lima has a wealth of museums, some of them displaying the best of the pre-Columbian treasures unearthed from sites around the country. It is a very large city and the museums are scattered around it, but transport is not hard to find. The Tourist Office will be able to help you find the best routes between places of interest. Taxis are inexpensive and there is no shortage of them. They come in all shapes and sizes, some smart, some very dilapidated, and they don't have meters, so try to fix a price in advance. Then, armed with a map, you can pick and choose among Lima's cultural offerings.

Leaving Plaza San Martín, head south down Unión (which becomes Belén) to the Paseo de la República and the **Museo de Arte Italiano** (open Tues–Fri 9am–7pm, Sat–Sun 11am–5pm; entrance fee). There is a good selection of Italian and other European paintings from the early 20th century, and the neo-classical building itself is worth seeing for its fine mosaics.

On the other side of Avenida 9 de Diciembre (usually called Paseo de Colón) is the **Museo de Arte** (open daily except Wed 10am–5pm; free on Mon) containing an extensive collection of Peruvian art from the Conquest to the present. The Filmoteca here is a cinema club that shows films for a low admission price. It has two auditoriums where concerts are given, and is surrounded by a very pleasant public park.

From the museum, take the Avenida 28 de Julio, then turn right down Avenida Aviación to the San Luis district. Here, on Avenida Javier Prado Este in San Borja, you will find the **Museo de la Nación** (National Museum; open Tues–Sun 9am–5pm; entrance fee), which has a wonderful collection of artifacts from the Chavín culture, including an ingenious replica of Chavín stela, woven articles found at Paracas, and ceramics from Nazca, among other things, making it one of the best museums in the city.

In 1998 it was discovered that a large proportion of the exhibits at the **Museo de Oro** (Gold Museum; open daily noon–7pm; entrance fee) were modern replicas. However, the museum also has a collection of genuine textiles, stone carvings, and ceramics on display.

The next stop on the museum tour is the **Museo de**

The plethora of oddly assorted taxis in Lima is a sign of the 1980s' so-called combi-culture, when hyperinflation hit jobs and salaries, and many professional people took to driving taxis and minibuses.

BELOW: La Rosa Náutica restaurant, Costa Verde.

Antropología, **Arqueología y Historia ®** (Museum of Anthropology, Archeology and History), in (another) Plaza Bolívar in the suburb of Pueblo Libre. Although some of the exhibits have been moved to the Museo de la Nación, it is still one of the most interesting museums in the country, with a superb collection of pottery and textiles from all the main cultures of ancient Peru. It is well laid out, in chronological order, and the curators have resisted the temptation to swamp visitors with too many exhibits (open Tues–Sun 9am–4.30pm; entrance fee).

Close by on Avenida Bolívar is the **Museo Rafael Larco Herrera ❺** (open Mon–Sun 9am–6pm; entrance fee), which has a vast collection of pre-Columbian ceramics, gold and silver objects, and some interesting textiles. A small annex holds a fascinating collection of erotic pottery from the Moche period. Few of the exhibits are labeled, but they are impressive for their fine quality.

The modern capital

It's time now to leave museums behind for a while and have a look at modern Lima. Two main arteries, the Avenida Arequipa and the Paseo de la República expressway, link the city center with the business district of **San Isidro**, where you might take a look at another museum: a very special private collection called the **Enrico Poli** (Lord Cochrane 446; open Mon–Sun, tel: 447-7100 for an appointment, call one or two days before; admission fee). It's well worth a stop to see the School of Cusco paintings and silver and gold work from colonial and pre-Columbian times.

These two long avenues also lead to **Miraflores ❼**, the main area for restaurants, cafes, nightlife, and some shopping. Avenida Larco used to be the main shopping area, but in recent years new commercial centers like Centro Comercial Larcomar, Caminos del Inca, and Jockey Plaza Shopping Mall have become the places for those born to shop. Good but expensive handicrafts are sold in Avenida La Paz (the handicraft markets on Avenida Petit Thouars in Miraflores, or on Avenida La Marina, on the way to the airport, are cheaper). Miraflores is really a place for the here and now, but there is one museum worth a look, the **Museo Amano** (Retiro 160, 11th block of Avenida Angamos; tours Mon–Fri at 3, 4 and 5pm; tel: 222-5827 – call two or three days before for an appointment; free admission, donations welcome). The museum displays a beautiful collection of textiles, mostly from the Chancay culture.

Close to Avenida Arequipa is the massive pre-Inca adobe pyramid site called the **Huaca Pucllana**. This has been cleared in recent years, and there are frequent guided tours (open Mon, Wed–Sun 9am–1pm and 2.30–5pm; entrance fee). There is also a small museum, and an excellent bar and restaurant.

At the top end of Larco is the **Parque Kennedy**, where artists sell paintings at the weekend. Here, next to the Pacífico Cinema, is the Café Haiti, a prime spot for people-watching. Round the corner, in Ricardo Palma, is the more up-market Vivaldi Café. Walking down Diagonal you will find great export-quality Peruvian coffee in the trendy Café Café or the Café Olé, and a little farther on, a pedestrianized side street crammed with pizzerias with open-air tables. Contin-

Map on pages 146–7

BELOW: high-rise architecture in Miraflores.

Map on pages 146–7

A cultural museum in Villa El Salvador tells the history of the nearby pre-Columbian ruin of Pachacamac as well as that of the settlement itself.

BELOW: Museo Pedro de Osma, Barranco.

ue down the Diagonal and you reach the cliffs overlooking the Pacific, laid out with gardens – a lovely place to watch the sunset. A cobbled road leads down a gully to the sweep of beaches called the **Costa Verde**. *Limeños* flock here in their thousands to bathe on summer Sundays, but the sea is polluted. The resorts to the south of the city are better for swimming.

But the Costa Verde is an attractive place, for the coast road sweeps on round (with fine views of the city) to the isolated beach of **La Herradura** , a popular spot to eat *ceviche* (fish marinaded in lemon juice with onion and hot peppers) while watching the Pacific breakers. Closer to Miraflores are two superb fish restaurants (with international prices) – the Costa Verde on the beach, and the traditional Rosa Náutica, built on a pier surrounded by the ocean.

From Playa La Herradura, the road doubles back through a tunnel, leading to **Chorrillos** , an area of mixed social composition, high on the sandy cliffs. Down on the beach is a fishing wharf, where small boats can be hired.

The road now loops back toward Miraflores and takes you to **Barranco** , a beautiful district of colonial and 19th-century housing, much of which has been recently restored. This romantic neighborhood is the home of many bohemians, writers, and artists, and is celebrated in Peruvian waltzes. It has become the center of the city's nightlife, with a score or more of *peñas* (folk clubs) and bars where music of all kinds is played. The bar La Noche (Avenida Bolognesi 307) is where young people go for a beer, and it's recommended for a night out in Barranco. For a more traditional evening, go to Juanito's, an old Italian-run bar on the plaza and a popular haunt of generations of *barranquiños*.

Opposite the attractive main square is the wooden **Puente de Los Suspiros** or Bridge of Sighs, a traditional meeting place for lovers, set among gardens overlooking the Pacific. Cross the bridge, follow the path by the church, and you'll find several small bars where *anticuchos* (marinated beef-heart kebabs) are served. From the bars right at the end you have a good view of the Costa Verde. On Saturday evening you can sample *anticuchos* the traditional way, from the stalls that are set up outside the church. For a touch of culture among the food, romance, and nightlife of Barranco, visit the **Museo Pedro de Osma**, a private museum containing colonial art (Pedro de Osma 423; open Tues–Sun 10am–1pm and 2.30–6pm; admission fee).

The Pacific port

Now joined to Lima, the port of **Callao** was originally a settlement apart, some 15 km (9 miles) west of the city on a low-lying bay. Though Callao is poor and run-down, it has several points of interest. The **La Punta** area is one of them. There the Club Universitario restaurant, the Rana Verde (the Green Frog; Plaza Gálvez) is open to visitors at lunchtime. Permission is required to enter the docks, but from the neighboring wharf launches take passengers for trips round the bay. Nearby stands the 18th-century **Real Felipe Fort**, the last royalist redoubt in Peru. It was captured by Bolívar's forces in 1826 after a year-long siege. It now contains a military museum – the **Museo Militar** (open Mon–Fri 9.30am–4pm). ❑

Oasis of Hope

Villa El Salvador is more than just another shanty town formed by aspiring Andean migrants. Tucked behind sand dunes not far from the Inca shrine of Pachacámac, about 30 km (20 miles) south of Lima, it was founded in 1971 by an initial wave of 10,000 migrants who had fled from the mountain areas around Huaraz in the wake of an earthquake. Today it is home to around 350,000 people, and is a prototype of self-determination by Peru's marginalized Andean majority.

The settlement's success has brought international recognition. It has been nominated for the Nobel Peace Prize, won Spain's prestigious Prince of Asturias award for social achievement, and been designated by the United Nations as a Messenger of Peace. Its key factor is the Andean tradition of community organization centered on the family unit.

Each block of houses, or *manzana*, comprises 24 families; 16 blocks make up a residential group, and 22 of these form a sector. Health centers, communal kitchens, and sports grounds bond the groups together. Education is prioritized, and illiteracy in Villa El Salvador is minimal, unlike in other similar shanty towns. Most of the houses are built of adobe bricks or concrete, and have drainage, mains water, and electricity. The community is crisscrossed by roads and dotted generously with shady poplar, eucalyptus, pomegranate, and banana trees.

Clever irrigation, worthy of the residents' Inca forebears, has converted hundreds of hectares of sandy desert into arable land, using the community's own treated sewage. Fruit and cotton are grown in the fields, as are corn and fodder crops for the thousands of privately and communally owned cattle whose milk and cheese are sold locally.

Villa El Salvador's first martyr was Edilberto Ramos, who was killed resisting police attempts to expel the original settlers. It was his death that forced the government to hand over the land. But the powerful sense of local identity, forged by such bravery and collective action in combating poverty, was shaken by terrorist infiltration during the early 1990s.

In 1992, popular community leader and deputy mayor María Elena Moyano was shot dead in front of her children by Sendero Luminoso guerrillas. Later that same year the mayor of Villa El Salvador was wounded in a terrorist attack after criticizing Moyano's killers. These deaths helped to strengthen the sense of community in Villa El Salvador, and to reinforce local political development.

The town's libraries, community radio station, and written bulletins demonstrate the determination to communicate, and the belief that education genuinely brings self advancement and change. The industrial park, created in 1987, provides much-needed local employment and exports products to many parts of the world.

The community continues to flourish despite enormous problems of malnutrition and continuing underemployment. It is an oasis that has tapped a spring of hope from beneath the desert floor. ❑

RIGHT: a boy with hope for the future.

THE NORTH

*The colonial city of Trujillo, a wealth of archeological digs,
Peru's best beaches, and a witchcraft market can
all be found along the north coast*

Maps
on pages
168 & 170

The north coast of Peru is not visited as much as the area farther south, but it has much to offer, including a wealth of archeological sites, the colonial city of Trujillo, and the port of Chiclayo. Regular buses ply the Panamericana north from **Lima ❶** to the border with Ecuador. The first stop after Lima for most people is **Sechín ❷**, an ancient archeological site decorated with extraordinary wall carvings showing bellicose warriors and their hapless, dismembered victims. The first excavation work here was done in the 1930s by the eminent Peruvian archeologist J.C. Tello. The site is still under excavation, but much of it can be seen, and there is an informative museum on the site (open daily 9am–5pm; entrance charge). The site is believed to date to the end of the Initial Period (*circa* 1000 BC), but nothing is known about the people who built it. You can get to Sechín by taking one of the frequent buses from Lima (about 350 km/220 miles) to the small town of Casma, from where you can get a taxi or a *colectivo* to the ruins.

The next stop is at **Trujillo ❸**, Peru's most important northern city (and the second largest in the country, with a population of 1.2 million). Charming, formal, and simple, this is the perfect spot from which to explore Peru's gentle but fiercely patriotic north. Founded in 1535 and named after Francisco Pizarro's birthplace in Spain, Trujillo was the resting place for Spaniards journeying between Lima and Quito. It soon merited the title "Lordliest City," and its well-preserved colonial homes with intricate wooden Andalusian-style balconies and window grilles pay testimony to an elegant past.

Political passions

Although European ways were firmly planted here, Trujillanos eschewed blind loyalty to the Spanish crown. In December 1820, it became the first Peruvian city to proclaim its independence from Spain, and liberator Simón de Bolívar, moving down the coast from Ecuador, set the seat of his revolutionary government here. From Trujillo he prepared his campaigns for the decisive battles of Junín, Pichincha, and Ayacucho. At the latter battle, on the plain bearing the same name, soldiers under Mariscal José de Sucre turned back the royalist troops once and for all.

A century later, political fervor coursed through Trujillo when the city gave birth to the progressive political party APRA, the American Popular Revolutionary Alliance. But the ideas of its founder, Victor Raúl Haya de la Torre, were too radical for the government of the day; the party was outlawed and forced to operate in secret. Government repression and torture of *apristas* (as APRA party members were called) culminated in 1932 in the brutal "Trujillo Massacre".

PRECEDING PAGES:
a *Caballo de Paso*
and his rider.
LEFT: fisherman
from a north-
coast fleet.
BELOW: a carved
figure at Sechín.

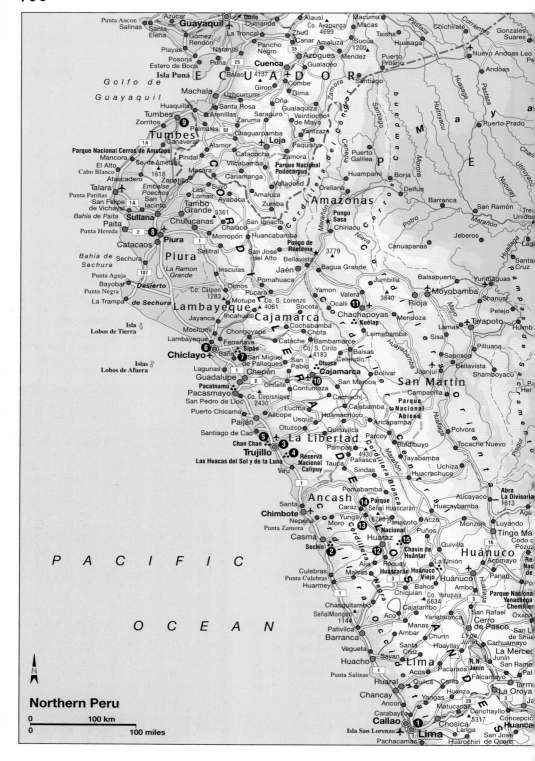

Northern Peru

0   100 km

0   100 miles

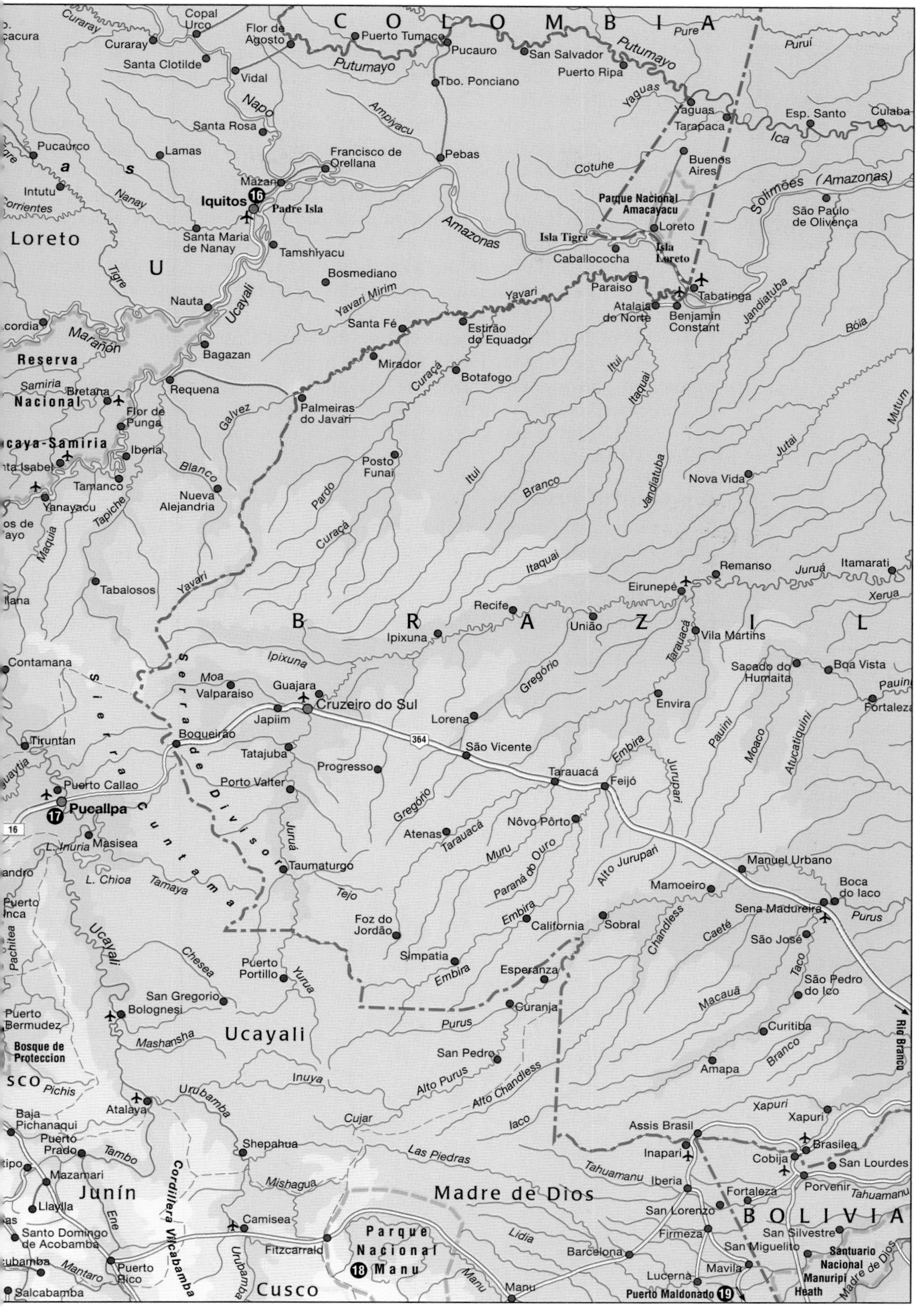

COLOMBIA
Copal Urco
Curaray
Flor de Agosto
Puerto Tumaco
Pucauro
San Salvador
Putumayo
Pure
Puruí
Santa Clotilde
Vidal
Tbo. Ponciano
Puerto Ripa
Yaguas
Tarapaca
Esp. Santo
Culaba
Ica
Napo
Ampiyacu
Santa Rosa
Pucaurco
Lamas
Francisco de Orellana
Pebas
Buenos Aires
Cotuhe
Solimões (Amazonas)
Intutu
Mazan
Iquitos
16
Padre Isla
Nanay
Corrientes
Parque Nacional Amacayacu
São Paulo de Olivença
Loreto
Santa Maria de Nanay
Tamshiyacu
Amazonas
Isla Tigre
Caballococha
Isla Loreto
Tigre
Bosmediano
Paraiso
Tabatinga
Nauta
Ucayali
Yavari Mirim
Yavari
Atalaia do Norte
Benjamin Constant
Jandiatuba
Santa Fé
Estirão do Equador
Marañón
Bagazan
Mirador
Bóia
Reserva
Samiria
Bretana
Nacional
Requena
Botafogo
Curaçá
Ituí
Itaquaí
Flor de Punga
Galvez
Palmeiras do Javari
Mutum
Pacaya-Samiria
Iberia
Posto Funai
Jutaí
Santa Isabel
Blanco
Nova Vida
Tamanco
Nueva Alejandria
Branco
Jandiatuba
Yanayacu
Tapiche
Pardo
Maquia
Itaquai
Remanso
Juruá
Itamarati
Tabalosos
Yavari
Eirunepé
Xerua
Recife
BRAZIL
Ipixuna
União
Tarauacá
Vila Martins
Contamana
Ipixuna
Sacado do Humaita
Boa Vista
Serra de Divisor
Sierra Cuntamana
Moa
Valparaiso
Guajara
Gregório
Pauini
Cruzeiro do Sul
Envira
Fortaleza
Japiim
Lorena
Tiruntan
Boqueirão
364
São Vicente
Tatajuba
Embira
Moaco
Atucatiquini
Progresso
Jurupari
Tarauacá
Feijó
Puerto Callao
Porto Valter
Pucallpa
17
16
Gregório
Nôvo Pôrto
Masisea
L. Inuria
Juruá
Atenas
Muru
Alto Jurupari
Manuel Urbano
Taumaturgo
Paraná do Ouro
Mamoeiro
L. Chioa
Tamaya
Tejo
Boca do Iaco
Puerto Inca
Sena Madureira
Purus
Caeté
Ucayali
Foz do Jordão
Embira
California
Sobral
Chandless
São José
Pachitea
Chesea
Simpatia
Puerto Portillo
Yurua
Esperanza
Embira
Taco
São Pedro do Ico
Macauã
San Gregorio
Curanja
Puerto Bermudez
Bolognesi
Purus
Rio Branco
Curitiba
Ucayali
Bosque de Proteccion
Mashansha
San Pedro
Branco
Amapa
Pichis
Inuya
Alto Purus
Alto Chandless
Atalaya
Urubamba
Xapuri
Xapuri
Baja Pichanaqui
Cujar
Iaco
Assis Brasil
Puerto Prado
Tambo
Shepahua
Las Piedras
Brasilea
Inapari
Cobija
Mazamari
Cordillera Vilcabamba
Mishagua
Tahuamanu
Iberia
San Lourdes
Junín
Madre de Dios
Fortaleza
Porvenir
Tahuamanu
Llaylla
Ene
San Lorenzo
BOLIVIA
Camisea
Santo Domingo de Acobamba
Parque Nacional Manu
18
Lidia
Firmeza
San Silvestre
Fitzcarrald
San Miguelito
Santuario Nacional Manuripi Heath
Barcelona
Mantaro
Puerto Rico
Urubamba
Manu
Mavila
Madre de Dios
Lucerna
Salcabamba
Cusco
Manu
Puerto Maldonado
19

*A wall carving at
Sechín.*

After a rebellious crowd of party followers attacked an army post and killed the officers in charge, one thousand people were executed by military firing squads among the adobe walls of Chan Chan.

Over the following decades, the *apristas* were the most strident opposition party, but never came to power. In 1962, Haya de la Torre, by then aged 67, won the elections for APRA, only for the military to refuse to recognize his victory. It was not until 1985 when Alan García won a landslide that APRA finally governed Peru – but Haya de la Torre himself had been dead for six years. Even today, on the anniversaries of Haya de la Torre's birth and death, his grave with its eternal torch and inscription "Here Lies the Light" is piled high with flowers. And the mention of his name sparks perhaps more outpourings of love – and hatred – than that of any other Peruvian.

Another of Trujillo's militant *apristas*, the writer Ciro Alegría, was exiled to Chile, where he published the first of the trilogy, based on his childhood and *campesino* (subsistence farmers) life, that made him one of the continent's most acclaimed authors. He won literary attention with *La Serpiente de Oro (The Serpent of Gold)*, but is best known for *El Mundo Es Ancho y Ajeno (The World is Wide and Foreign)*.

A peaceful present

These tumultuous days of exile and bloodshed seem distant now in Trujillo, where formality and turn-of-the-20th-century charm hang in the air. The best way to see this city is on foot, and the best place to start is the huge **Plaza de Armas Ⓐ**, at the center of which is a statue of a running winged figure – Liberty, whose face closely resembles Simón Bolívar's – holding a torch. This land-

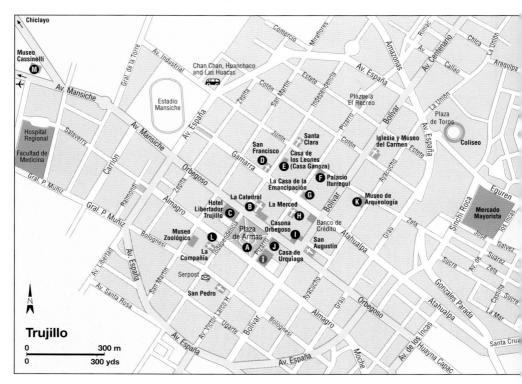

Trujillo

0   300 m
0   300 yds

mark stands on disproportionately short legs, designed to appease officials who feared the monument would end up taller than the cathedral facing it.

The plaza is dominated by the newly renovated **Catedral ⑬** (open daily 6.30am–noon and 4–8pm), dating from the mid-18th century. The cathedral once had elaborate metal adornments and railings, like many of the colonial houses, but they were melted down for armaments during the War of Independence. The **Hotel Libertador Trujillo ⑭**, housed in a beautiful colonial-style building, stands on the northwest corner of the square. Even if you are not staying in the hotel (it's about the most expensive in Trujillo), try to have breakfast or lunch in its small-windowed dining room looking out onto the plaza. From this vantage point one can see the comings and goings of the city's elderly men who stake out shady benches to read their morning newspapers, the young mothers carrying their market baskets with toddlers in tow, or uniformed school-girls huddled together sharing secrets.

Two blocks from the square, on Avenida Independencia, is the colonial **Iglesia San Francisco ⑮** (open daily 6.30am–noon and 4–8pm). Almost opposite stands the attractive **Casa de los Leones ⑯** (open Mon–Fri 9am–1pm and 2–6pm, Sat 9am–1pm), also known as the Casa Ganoza Chopitea, which houses a small art gallery as well as an office of the Policía de Turismo. It got its name from the statues of lions that guard the front door. Most of Trujillo's mansions have been elegantly restored by national banks or other private enterprises, and are well worth visiting if you can get inside. If not, you must be content with the view from outside of the detailed window grilles and intricately carved wooden balconies, which are synonymous with this city. The window grilles are purely decorative; over the centuries their simple designs became increasingly elabo-

Map on page 170

BELOW: Trujillo's Plaza de Armas.

*The enlightened
18th-century Bishop
of Trujillo.*

BELOW: the ruins at
Chan Chan.

rate as the colonial Trujillanos tried to outdo one another. The balconies, on the other hand, had a practical purpose: they allowed upper-class women to look down onto the street, but prevented interested menfolk from looking in.

From Casa de los Leones, turn right on Junín, then right again on Jirón Pizarro, to see the **Palacio Iturregui** ❻ (open 8–11am; free admission), a neo-colonial building where Trujillo's unilateral independence from Spain was declared in 1820. It is now the home of the rather smart Club Central, which runs a small ceramics museum (open daily 11am–6pm; entrance charge). Rather oddly, it is not this building but another one nearby that is called **La Casa de la Emancipación** ❼ (House of the Emancipation; open Mon–Sat 10am–6pm). This mansion is typical of those constructed in the 16th and 17th centuries, and is one of the few containing its original furniture. Like many of Peru's most elegant colonial mansions, this is now the property of a bank, the Banco Continental, and the staff are happy to show visitors where earthquakes and remodeling over the centuries have changed the building's original lines. Back towards the Plaza Mayor you will find the **Iglesia de La Merced** ❽, where a small crowd of visitors can often be found peering upward at the intricately carved dome. The next stop, on the corner of Orbegoso and Bolívar, is the **Casona Orbegoso** ❾ (open Mon–Fri 9am–1pm and 2–8pm, Sat 9am–1pm; entrance fee), which is also a bank as well as a museum of early republican furniture and silver. Almost opposite is the Iglesia de San Agustín, the oldest church in the city.

Back on the Plaza de Armas is the elegant colonial **Casa de Urquiaga** ❿, which belongs to the Banco de la Nación (open Mon–Sat 9am–1pm; free admission), said to be where the liberator Simón Bolívar stayed when in Trujillo.

A block away from the Plaza de Armas, on Jirón Pizarro, lies the **Museo de**

Arqueología , the museum of the National University of Trujillo (open Mon–Fri 9.30am–1pm; entrance fee). Among the artifacts here are fine pieces of Moche and Chimu pottery and copies of some of the wall paintings found at La Huaca de la Luna *(see below)*. Turn left into the square (along Almagro) and you'll come to **La Compañía** , another notable colonial church. Close to the church is the Museo Zoológico (again, ask at the tourist office for opening hours) but the stuffed exhibits are not very exciting. For an interesting experience you could then get a taxi to the western outskirts of the city, in the direction of Chiclayo, to one of the most unusual museums you are likely to find. The **Museo Cassinelli** (open Mon–Sat 8.30–11.30am and 3–5.30pm; entrance charge) is housed in the basement of the Cassinelli gas station and holds a fascinating private collection of Moche and Chimu ceramics.

Maps:
Area 168
City 170

Horses' hooves and bare feet

Trujillanos are proud of their *caballos de paso*, a fine breed of horses with a tripping gait that has made them known worldwide. Another legacy of the Conquest, since there were no horses on the continent before the arrival of the Spaniards, these horses have been immortalized in Peruvian waltzes. In particular, composer Chabuca Granda, for whom a monument is erected in the bohemian neighborhood of Barranco in Lima, wrote of the *chalanes* or riders in their *jipijapa* sombreros upon their honey-colored mounts. These riders still compete in their own form of the *marinera* dance – smoothly guiding their horses through the steps. The best of these trotters are bred in and around Trujillo, and buyers from around the world congregate to see them shown at the annual Spring Festival – *Festival de la Primavera*. Don't forget, though, that Peru's spring is the northern hemisphere's fall, and this festival takes place in September.

BELOW: examining a rainbow carving at Chan Chan.

   The *Festival de la Marinera* is celebrated in the last week of January, when dancers from all over the country compete for the title of *Campeones de la Marinera*. It's a spectacular show, and the whole town has a party atmosphere, particularly during the finals on the last weekend. The *marinera* is a graceful dance rooted in African and Spanish rhythms; some say its steps mimic the strutting of a rooster courting a hen. Women in ruffled lace skirts seductively flit toward white-garbed men in ponchos before quickly pulling away. The men attempt to win back their attention, tossing up hats and catching them in mid-fall.

A journey to the past

About 10 km (6 miles) southeast of Trujillo lie **Las Huacas del Sol y de la Luna** (the Temples of the Sun and the Moon) . You can get there by minibus from Trujillo, or go with a guide on an organized tour. These two pyramidal temples were built by the Moche people (100 BC–AD 850) over several generations. The Huaca del Sol (arguably the largest pre-Columbian building in the Americas) is currently being excavated, but at the smaller Huaca de la Luna, years of archeological work have begun to unveil a series of temples superimposed on one another to form a pyramid covered in beautiful, brightly colored murals (open daily 9am–4pm; entrance fee).

To the northwest of Trujillo (take one of the frequent minibuses or *colectivos* from Trujillo) are the ruins of **Chan Chan ❺**, possibly the world's largest adobe city. Perched on 20 sq. km (7½ sq. miles) just 600 metres/yards from the ocean, its seven citadels are enclosed by a massive adobe wall. Chan Chan was the capital of the Chimu Empire. Its people fished and farmed, worshiped the moon and had no written records – leaving it to archeologists to unravel their secrets. An echoing silence surrounds visitors to this ancient city, whose walls bear carvings of fish, seabirds, fishing nets, and moons, recently restored and coated with polyvinyl acetate to try to prevent the structures from crumbling.

Aided by sophisticated aqueduct and irrigation systems, the Chimu turned the arid wasteland around them into fertile fields of grain, fruits, and vegetables supporting a population that may have reached 35,000. When conquered by the Incas, the Chimu were not forced to change their ways – except for the addition of the sun to their collection of gods. Rather, Inca teachers were sent to study their farming and irrigation systems and Chimu goldsmiths were sent to Cusco. It wasn't until the Incas, under Tupac Yupanqui, sabotaged the aqueducts after repeated attempts to invade Chan Chan that the fearless Chimu left the protection of the city – and were conquered.

An entrance ticket to Chan Chan also allows visitors to see **La Huaca del Dragón** – also known as La Huaca Arco Iris (the Rainbow Temple) – with its beautifully restored wall carvings, and the ruins of **Huaca La Esmeralda** nearby. Licensed guides can be hired at the ticket office. Tourists are advised to begin their visit in the morning and avoid going alone; the tourism police at Chan Chan frequently go home in mid-afternoon, and there have been a number of robberies at the isolated site. Visitors should also steer clear of vendors hawking what they claim is antique pottery. Most pieces are fakes, and genuine items can be confiscated and the holder fined or jailed for trying to take them out of Peru.

Archeology enthusiasts should also visit the Huaca el Brujo, a recently discovered site a few hours outside Trujillo in the Chicama Valley. Ask at the Tourist Information Office for details.

BELOW: Chiclayo's Mercado de Brujos.

Sugar and surf

Before you set off north, another short trip (about 15 km/10 miles) from Trujillo is to the seaside village of **Huanchaco**. Two centuries ago, when Huanchaco residents paid taxes to the Spanish crown, it was a quiet village of men who fished and women who wove baskets in the sunshine. Today Huanchaco is a popular destination for surfers and beach lovers, although it still retains a village air. Sun-bronzed fishermen head out each morning with their nets tucked into *caballitos de totora*, literally "little horses" woven from *totora* reed. The design of these peapod-shaped boats is not very different from that of the craft used by pre-Inca people, and the *caballitos* contrast startlingly with the brightly colored surfboards that now share the Pacific waves.

Some 40 km (25 miles) north of Trujillo (there are buses) are vestiges of one of the sources of Trujillo's past wealth: sugar. Owing to its gentle climate, the Chicama Valley region produces most of Peru's sugar crop, an important product in a country where three spoonfuls go into every cup of coffee and all children seem to be born with a sweet tooth. Land reform, begun in the late 1960s, turned most of the great *haciendas* into cooperatives, but the opulence of the past is still evident. The most impressive are Casa Grande and Hacienda Cartavio, now large-scale agro-industrial projects; the latter is where the sugar is used to make Cartavio rum.

Map on pages 168–9

Magic stalls and Moche finds

The next stop north is the busy port of **Chiclayo** ❻ some 200 km (125 miles) up the Panamericana – there are regular bus services as well as frequent flights from Lima and Trujillo. This bustling city is a major commercial hub for northern Peru, and is a lively and friendly spot with few pretensions. This vitality is reflected in the architecture of the city center, in which the modern happily co-exists with the colonial in the winding streets.

One unmissable sight within the city is the extensive **Mercado de Brujos** (Witchcraft Market), also known as the Mercado Modelo, one of the most comprehensive in South America. Here is an overwhelming choice of herbal medicines, potions, charms, and San Pedro cacti, from which a hallucinogenic drug is extracted and used by *curanderos* (healers) in traditional shamanic healing rituals.

A short distance away is the coastal resort of **La Pimentel**, with a good sandy beach – an excellent place to try the local specialty of *pescado seco*, a kind of rayfish known as *la guitarra*, which can often be found hanging out to dry in the sun in Chiclayo's market. Just south of Pimentel is **Santa Rosa**, where beautiful fishing boats can be seen drawn up on the beach.

Chiclayo is, of course, the starting point for visits to two of the continent's most exciting archeological digs. The greatest attention has been lavished on the Moche burial area at **Sipán** ❼ (open daily 9am–6pm; entrance charge; guided tours available), about 30 km (18 miles) south of the city. Here, Peru's best documented grave, known as the tomb of El Señor de Sipán, was uncovered in the late 1980s, originally by *huaqueros* (grave robbers), before the excavation was taken over by Dr Walter Alva *(see page 179)*. The site is well worth visiting, but to see the stunning gold, silver and ceramic artifacts taken from it (when they're not touring the world's museums) you must visit the **Museo Brüning** (open daily 9am–6pm; entrance charge), which is in Lambayeque, about 17 km (10 miles) from Chiclayo.

From Lambayeque you can go on to the huge site at **Túcume**, with its numerous pyramids. The excavation here was originally directed by Norwegian Thor Heyerdahl *(see page 34)*.

Travel north from Chiclayo through the great coastal desert, sometimes turned green by the heavy rains induced by El Niño. **Piura** ❽ is a hot commercial city best known for its folk dance, the *tondero*, a more rustic version of Trujillo's *marinera*, and the black magic still practiced by the descendants of slaves. The *tondero* is a lively barefoot Afro-Peruvian dance accompanied by strong rhythmic music and sashaying dancers in multicolored outfits. But many Peruvian visitors come to see more than the dancers. There are Lima business executives who travel here annually to consult the area's *brujos* –

A stamp depicts marinera *dancing.*

BELOW: carrying a reed boat.

witch doctors and folk healers who use herbs and potions to cure patients.

Nearly as famous as its esoteric pursuits is Piura's cuisine, with its sharp flavors and elaborate preparation. The best dishes include *seco de chavelo* (mashed plantains with fried pork), *majado de yucca con chicharrón* (mashed manioc with fried pork), fried plantain *(chifles)*, and the molasses called *natilla* made from goat's milk and sugar cane; it is washed down with *chicha de jora*, a drink made from fermented corn.

Piura has a proud history, beginning with its foundation by the Spanish in 1532 – three years before Lima – and continuing through the War of the Pacific with Chile (1879–83). That war's most famous Peruvian hero was Admiral Miguel Grau, and his home on Jirón Tacna across from the Centro Cívico has been converted into a museum, the **Museo Naval Miguel Grau** (opening hours vary; free admission). Of interest there is the scale model of the British-built *Huascar*, the largest Peruvian warship in that conflict. Grau was commander of the vessel and used it to keep the invading Chilean forces at bay until he was forced to scuttle his ship in the Battle of Angamos, an event still remembered every year on October 8.

Admiral Grau was known as "Gentleman Grau" because of his attempts to get more supplies for his men, and his determination to rescue the Chilean sailors who were left floundering in the water after each battle.

Hemingway's marlin

North of Piura, on the way to the Ecuadorian border, lies **Talara**, a desert oasis and petroleum-producing center. Closer still to the northern border are some of the best and most fashionable beaches in Peru: **Máncora**, **Punta Sal**, and **Playa La Pena**. **Cabo Blanco** (south of Máncora) is a popular spot for marlin fishing, once frequented by Ernest Hemingway, but experts say the marlin have now been carried south by the Humboldt Current to Máncora. Several beachside seafood restaurants in Máncora are recommended, for obvious reasons. Peru's

BELOW: a northern fishing fleet.

Map
on pages
168–9

coast has some of the world's most spectacular waves, and Máncora is frequently the site of international surfing competitions.

Talara is as unattractive as any oil town, and travelers are recommended to seek accommodations in the above-mentioned beach resorts. Camping is permitted at Cabo Blanco and other nearby beaches. South of Talara are the **Brea Tarpits** where the Spanish boiled tar to caulk their ships.

Frontier town

About 140 km (85 miles) north of Talara is **Tumbes ❾**, a frontier town with a military post and immigration offices, although it is about 30 km (18 miles) from the Ecuadorian border. Although there has been an ongoing effort to give this city a facelift, there continues to be a problem with theft – particularly affecting tourists, often occuring near the bus offices or at the colorful outdoor market. A few miles outside the city, at the actual border, known as **Aguas Verdes** on the Peruvian side, travelers are barraged by unscrupulous money-changers, porters, and over-friendly individuals with dubious motives. Police corruption is notorious here, although that is something which affects Peruvians far more than outsiders, and focuses on the widespread cross-border trafficking in contraband items.

Tumbes is also within spitting distance of the few Peruvian beaches that offer white sand and warm water for swimming year round. **Caleta La Cruz**, which has an attractive fishing fleet, can be reached by taxi, in *colectivos*, or by combis heading north from Máncora, as can **Zorritos**, a larger fishing village with a couple of hotels. **Puerto Pizarro** has intriguing mangrove swamps around the village with some interesting birdlife. In the port, boat tours can be arranged with fishermen. It is a spot that is becoming popular among deep-sea fishing enthusiasts. ❑

BELOW: riding a Pacific wave.

UNEARTHING BURIED TREASURES

Excavations of grave sites in Peru have revealed fascinating evidence of rich and varied cultures that flourished long before the Inca empire

The architectural remains of the Inca Empire are so awe-inspiring that it is easy to forget that a number of earlier civilizations flourished in Peru. They left no written records, so much of the information that has been gleaned about them comes from grave sites.

The best-known are at Sipán and Sicán, both in northern Peru. Originally unearthed by grave robbers in 1987, the tomb of the Lord of Sipán, believed to be a ruler of the Moche period (*circa* 100–700), yielded unimaginable riches: gold masks, turquoise and lapis lazuli jewelry, copper headdresses, ceramic pots, and domestic implements provided archeologists with vital information about the Moche way of life.

Sacrifice and ceramics

At Sicán, the first site to be excavated using radar, similar riches were discovered, including golden death masks, a copper crown, and a beaded cloak. The Sicán era spanned the 9th and 10th centuries, the period between the Moche and the Chimu. At both sites, there is evidence of what appears to be human sacrifice: at Sicán the bodies of young women were buried with that of their lord, and at Sipán servants or soldiers accompanied their master to the grave. The Sicán site museum is at Ferreñafe, north of Chiclayo.

In the southern desert, at the Paracas Necropolis (*circa* 1st century AD), excavations in the 1920s by archeologist J.C. Tello yielded hundreds of mummified bundles, wrapped in intricately embroidered cloth. Examples of these textiles can be seen in the Museo de la Nación in Lima. At the Chauchilla Cemetery, farther south, remains of the Nazca culture (*circa* 200–800) were discovered in the early 1900s. Designs on the pottery buried with the dead gave important clues about their daily lives.

▽ **EYES OF BLUE**
A golden mask with huge eyes of lapis lazuli, its opulence denoting the status and importance of the wearer during his earthly life.

◁ **FINE JEWELRY**
Exquisite gold and turquoise earrings which were part of the treasure trove at the Sipán site.

◁ GILDED GLORY
A gilded copper mask with conch-shell fangs found at the site which has become known as the tomb of the Lord of Sipán. Like most of the important Sipán finds, the mask has now been placed in the Museo Brüning in Lambayeque.

DISTURBING THE DEAD

▽ EARTHLY COMFORTS
The bodies of servants and soldiers were buried with the Lord of Sipán, as well as jewelry, utensils, and ceramic pots to make him comfortable in the afterlife.

△ KEEPING IT SAFE
Archeologist Dr Walter Alva, curator of the Brüning Museum, displays a golden peanut, found among the treasure excavated from the Sipán site.

The smuggling of antiquities is a multi-million-dollar international trade, so it's little wonder that ancient grave sites have attracted looters.

Around the Cemetery of Chauchilla, near Nazca, the desert is strewn with bones and skulls unearthed by *huaqueros* (looters), stripped of valuables, and left to bleach in the sun. Priceless treasures have been lifted from graves all over Peru and sold to collectors.

It was the *huaqueros'* discovery of the Sipán tomb that provoked a clamp-down. Initiated by Dr Walter Alva, curator of the Museo Brüning, a government-backed program targets looters, rewards informers, and uses education campaigns in an attempt to end the lucrative trade. At a local level, it is having a measure of success.

Aerial surveillance is vital to the program. Archeologists board air-force flights over the Lambayeque Valley to chart mounds that may conceal ancient complexes and sites where human destruction is obvious.

△ PRESERVED PAIR
Two mummies from Chauchilla. Fragments of skin and bone have been preserved, as well as the wrapping cloths.

NORTHERN SIERRA

*Journeys in the highlands are long and the roads are poor,
but the rewards are friendly towns, breathtaking scenery,
and some spectacular ruins*

Map
on pages
168–9

Lima

Across the dusty desert into the Andean highlands, lies **Cajamarca** .
Now dotted with cattle herds and dairy farms, where Peru's best cheese is
made, this was one of the largest cities in the Inca empire and marks the
site where the indigenous Amerindians and the Spaniards had their first showdown. According to Spanish chronicles, it was in Cajamarca that the Inca
Atahuallpa was kidnapped and later executed.

Pizarro had sent envoys to the Inca, camped in the valley with his huge army,
telling him that "he loved him dearly," and wished to meet him in Cajamarca.
But Atahuallpa walked into an ambush: in the Plaza de Armas the heavily armed
Spaniards massacred thousands of Amerindians who were futilely trying to protect their leader. Despite the Spaniards' numerical disadvantage, their audacity
in kidnapping the Inca threw an already divided kingdom into confusion.

A demand went out across the Inca Empire to assemble an outrageous ransom
for Atahuallpa's release. Leading llamas laden down by riches, Amerindians from
as far away as Cusco began the journey to Cajamarca, filling the "Ransom Room"
with some of the kingdom's most valuable treasures – which the Spanish promptly
melted down into bullion. The Ransom Room is still there; a red line on one wall
shows where the tall and powerful Atahuallpa allegedly drew a mark, agreeing to
have his subjects fill the room to that line twice with
silver and once with gold. But once the majority of the
ransom had been collected, the conquistadors, afraid
that the Inca would serve as a focal point for rebellion as
long as he remained alive, had him garrotted after he
had been baptized with Pizarro's own name – Francisco.

LEFT: dawn over
the Sierra.
BELOW: deep in
conversation by
Cajamarca's
cathedral.

Coming to Cajamarca

Cajamarca can be reached by daily flights from Lima,
by bus from Trujillo, which takes about nine hours, or
Chiclayo (about seven hours), or on a better, faster
road that turns off the Panamericana near Pacasmayo
(about five hours).

The hub of this slow-paced city of some 120,000
inhabitants, built on the banks of the Río San Lucas,
is the **Plaza de Armas**, the spot where Atahuallpa
was executed. It is still sometimes said that the pink
grain on a stone slab, where the Inca was allegedly
killed, is the indelible mark of his blood. The massive Inca palaces that stood here are gone, and the
plaza is now ringed by colonial buildings, the cathedral, and the lovely San Francisco church.

The center of the square is graced by an imposing
stone fountain, frequented every evening by locals
stopping for a chat with friends, and all day long by
birds dipping down for a drink.

The **Catedral**, founded in 1776, is the most noteworthy building on the plaza. Its carved wooden altars

are covered in gold leaf, and its facade of intricately carved volcanic rock is impressive. But something is conspicuously absent – its belfries. The bell towers were deliberately left unfinished because the tax that Spain imposed on churches only became payable when a building was completed.

On the opposite side of the plaza is the **Iglesia San Francisco** (Church of San Francisco), older and more ornate than the cathedral, and home to the **Museo de Arte Religioso** (Museum of Religious Art; open Mon–Fri 2–5pm; entrance charge), which is filled with colonial-era paintings and statues, often portraying violent and bloody subjects. A guided tour of the museum, which is a veritable storehouse of silver candelabras, gold altar vessels, jeweled vestments, and portraits of saints, includes entrance to the church's eerie catacombs – precursor to the present city cemetery.

Situated next door to the cathedral stands the Hotel Sierra Galana a better-than-average lodging house with rooms furnished with heavy wooden antiques. There are a number of reasonable places to stay in Cajamarca, located in and around the Plaza de Armas, and a handful of inexpensive restaurants. One of them (in the plaza itself) is the family-run Restaurante Salas, described by one *cajamarquino* (the name by which the city's citizens are known) as the "city's nerve center." Here locals catch up on the news and gossip while downing the city's best, and most economical, home cooking: anything from crisp salads and thick *chupe verde* (potato and vegetable soup) to hearty beef ribs and spicy *cuy* (guinea pig) stew. No meal is complete without *panqueque con manjar blanco*, a sweet, rich dessert consisting of a thick crêpe bathed in a condensed milk sauce. Hung on the restaurant's walls are paintings by local artist Andrés Zevallos, one of the founding fathers of Cajamarca's longstanding community

BELOW: Cajamarca.

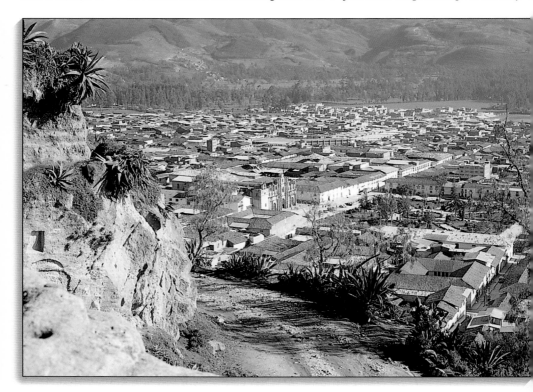

Map on pages 168–9

of poets, writers, painters, and musicians. Most notable of these was Mario Urteaga, the only Peruvian artist to have his work in the permanent collection at New York's Metropolitan Museum of Art, and a person so much loved in his hometown that the procession at his funeral in 1957 lasted into the night. Urteaga's oils depict *campesinos* (subsistence farmers), simple yet human, and the Cajamarca countryside was his studio. Today, local photographer Victor Campos Río captures the beauty of the country and its people in photographs and documentary films.

A king's ransom

A few blocks from the main plaza, on Avenida Amalia Puga, is **El Cuarto del Rescate** (The Ransom Room; open daily 9am–noon and 3–5pm; entrance charge, which also gives admission to the Complejo Belén and the Ethnographic Museum). This is the sole surviving Inca structure in the city, and there is some debate about whether it was where Atahuallpa was imprisoned, or where the treasure collected from across the empire was to be stored. As *rescate* means both "ransom" and "rescue" in Spanish, it could be either; whichever it was, it forges a very real link with a past that sometimes seems almost mythical.

Also close to the plaza, on Apurímac, is the **Teatro Municipal**, now known as the **Teatro Cajamarca**, rescued by this culture-loving city after being used first as a movie theater and then as a storehouse for industrial cleaners. Built by a wealthy German merchant, the theater has an impressive stamped metal ceiling, and its seating almost exactly duplicates that in the original plans. Ticket prices are kept low to entice students and less affluent *cajamarquinos*, but unfortunately performances are not staged on a regular basis.

Brand name.

BELOW: window in the Complejo Belén church.

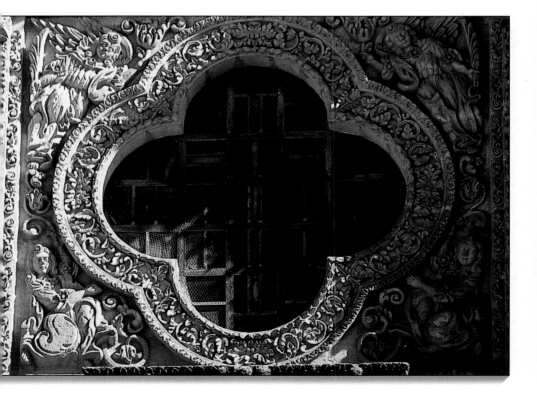

The Complejo Belén

Heading east along Junín from the theater you will come to the **Complejo Belén** (open daily 9am–noon and 3–5pm) housing the Institute of Culture, Cajamarca's most picturesque chapel, a museum, and an art gallery. The 17th-century Belén church is undoubtedly the city's loveliest, with elaborately carved stone and woodwork and brightly colored statues and side altars. The small white carved dove suspended over the pulpit represents the Holy Spirit and allegedly gives those who stand under it the power of eloquence. The chapel's cupola and altar depict the three levels of life: on the ground level are the common people, in an intermediary area the saints and priests, and on the top level – heaven – God and the Virgin Mary, represented by the sky-blue dome of the cupola. Many visitors are fooled by the brilliantly painted details on the upper walls and ceiling of the church; these saints and cherubs are not made of painted wood or plaster, they are intricately carved stone. More carving is found on the massive wooden doors in the church, most of them solid pieces of Nicaraguan cedar.

Connected to the church is the **Pinacoteca**, a gallery of local artists' work in what was once the kitchen of a hospital for men. Off the Pinacoteca is the former hospital ward, a room with alcoves along its side walls. The alcoves were the patients' "bedrooms," and the images of saints originally painted above them corresponded to their illnesses. The sickest were bedded closest to the altar, conveniently located near the door to the cemetery. An example of an alcove with blankets and its painted saint can be seen across the street at the **Museo Etnográfico y de Arqueología** (Ethnographic and Archeological Museum; open daily 9am–noon and 3–5pm), which was once a maternity hospital. The only difference between the two hospitals was that from the tops of the women's alcoves dangled long scarves, which the patients pulled to help them when giving birth.

Cajamarca enjoys festivals. The pre-Lent carnival is a riotous celebration, lasting four days, which includes music, processions, masks, and the inevitable water fights.

BELOW: modern and traditional dress in Cajamarca.

The museum has a collection of ceramics from Amerindian cultures that dominated this region of Peru, samples of local handicrafts, and costumes used during the annual carnival celebrations – the most raucous in the country. Across the street at the **Instituto Cultural**, Spanish-language books and the area's best postcards are on sale. The Institute has details of ongoing archeological digs that can be visited from October to May, before the highland's rainy season begins. Excavations include the Huacaloma and Kuntur Wasi digs sponsored by the University of Tokyo.

Cajamarca by night

There's not a lot to do in Cajamarca after sunset. The town rolls up its sidewalks early, as befits a farming community where work begins at sunrise. But nocturnal souls can listen, and dance, to boisterous local music at the Emperador, or join the camaraderie at the Sitio Bar connected to the Hostal Cajamarca behind the Complejo Belén. Here local people meet to sing, drink, and play their music, ranging from *boleros* to the *huaynos* of the Andean highlands; however, it has got a bit expensive of late, and the food isn't as good as the music. There is also live music at the Peña Usha Usha, on Amalia Puga.

Scaling the heights

For the physically fit, the best way to delight in Cajamarca's charms is from above. That means climbing steep **Cerro Apolonia**. Stone steps take climbers as far as a little chapel – a miniature version of Nôtre Dame Cathedral, about halfway up the hillside – and the rest of the journey is on a curvy road bordered by cacti, flowers, and benches for the fatigued. Near the top is the **Silla del Inca** (the Inca's Chair), a rock cut into the shape of a throne where, it is said, the Inca Atahuallpa sat and looked out over his kingdom. A bronze statue of the Inca, and parking for those who arrive by taxi or car, top the hill.

The view is of green, rain-fed fields, red-tiled-roofs, and whitewashed houses. At night, the Cajamarca skies – which in daytime may switch in minutes from brilliant blue to stormy gray – are usually clear and star-studded. Early risers are in for a special treat: sunrises in these highlands are beautiful, and the show is a long one. It can take the sun up to 45 minutes to switch from a silhouetting blue-black to a brilliant red-orange before lightening to a hazy yellow.

An equally spectacular view of the city can be found at Hacienda San Vicente, the most intriguing hotel in town. A charming country inn perched on a steep rocky hill at the edge of Cajamarca, this lodge was constructed using Inca techniques, with a few modern twists. The walls are made of packed earth painted with ocher and vegetable dyes. Skylights give illumination, fireplaces heat common areas after nightfall, and guest rooms are decorated with local handicrafts. San Vicente was built on the site where a colonial estate house once stood; its original chapel remains next door, and on San Vicente's day local farmers still take up their musical instruments and bouquets of flowers and parade to the tiny church.

Map on pages 168–9

BELOW: agricultural work is tough.

A highland piper.

Inca bathing place

If you look from the Cerro Apolonia by day, you may see a white mist hovering over the edge of the city. This is the steam rising from the **Baños del Inca**, said to be the Inca's favorite bathing spot. A sign over a huge stone tub at the bubbling mineral springs claims that it was here that Atahuallpa bathed with his family. The springs are so hot at their source that local Amerindians use them to boil eggs. Whether or not they are curative, as the locals believe, they merit a visit – you can get a bus or a *colectivo* (a taxi which takes a number of different people) from the center of town. The city has channeled the water from the springs into a lukewarm Olympic-sized outdoor pool, and built rustic *cabañas* where families or groups of friends can splash privately, and modern "tourist baths" where one or two people can soak in tiled hot tubs. There is a minimal entrance fee for the use of these facilities.

At the springs, several tourist hostels have sprung up, all of them with bathtubs or swimming pools fed by the springs. The best-known and most impressive, despite its rustic appearance, is the Laguna Seca, a converted *hacienda* (farm estate), which has a pool, a pungent sauna where eucalyptus is steamed on hot coals, a weight-lifting room, and – something you don't find every day – a small bullfighting ring and a cockfighting arena, as well as "Baños del Inca" water running into the deep bathtubs of every room.

Ceramic traditions

BELOW:

contestants for a country cockfight.

Cajamarca and its environs are good places for buying ceramics. The Complejo Belén artisan shop and others near the Plaza de Armas are filled with pottery, as well as good-quality knitted sweaters, baskets, leather goods, and the

Map on pages 168–9

gilt-framed mirrors popular in this northern region. But the most fascinating – and least-expensive – spot to buy ceramics is a few kilometers to the south of the city at the village of **Aylambo**, where there is a series of ecologically balanced workshops. Sewage at the workshops is processed into natural gas, which used to generate heat and light, and, rather than buying expensive fuel and imported heat-resistant bricks, the students who learn their skills at the workshops collect kindling from the hillside and make their own heat-tolerating kiln tiles – in much the same way as their Amerindian ancestors did.

Products here range from plates bearing traditional Amerindian motifs to teapots with modern glazes – designed and concocted by the students – and the proceeds from pottery sales go to the people who work in the studios. Aylambo artisans, who range in age from children to the elderly, are not charged a fee to learn the crafts, but economic necessity would force them to leave the workshop and find paid jobs if study stipends were not available. The long-term goal of the project is to inspire a series of environmentally sound workshops providing jobs, reclaiming ancient pottery designs, preventing further deforestation of the hills, and keeping *cajamarquinos* living in the countryside.

Beyond the city

There are many possible excursions outside Cajamarca, all of which are best organized through a travel agency which can arrange transportation to the isolated area, there are several agencies in Cajamarca that provide these services. From here it is possible to visit the puzzling **Ventanillas de Otuzco** (about 8 km/5 miles from town), the cliffside "windows" that served as ancient Amerindian burial grounds. Anthropologists and archeologists still have not

BELOW: highland transportation.

Map
on pages
168–9

Traveling anywhere even slightly off the beaten track in Peru is often done by pick-up truck. Even those who at first find it an odd form of public transport soon come to accept it as the norm.

BELOW: colonial church tower.

unraveled the mystery of how the pre-Inca people were able to open the burial holes on the sides of sheer cliffs, but they have counted the openings to get an idea of the population – and importance – of the area before the conquistadors' arrival.

Equally astonishing is **Cumbemayo**, about 24 km (15 miles) from Cajamarca, a valley cut by an Inca irrigation ditch of carved rock. The sophistication and precision of the ditch's angles – hewn by stone tools – leave modern-day hydraulic engineers marveling. Sharp turns in the ditch prevent the water from rushing too fast, as do imperceptible inclines. In the same valley are Los Frailones (The Friars), huge rocks that have eroded into the shape of hooded monks – sparking a number of local legends – as well as some primitive petroglyphs and caves once used as places of worship.

Those who start their countryside ramblings early may have time to reach the dairy farm called **Hacienda La Colpa** before cow-calling time. Every day, just before 2pm, the cows at this cooperative are called by name – to the delight of the crowd that gathers to watch. The animals respond by sauntering up to the milking areas bearing their names. Colpa is an example of the many cooperative dairies outside Cajamarca, famous for its butter, cheese, and *manjar blanco* – a milky dessert. A hostel offers travelers a pastoral spot to spend the night, although most people, after admiring the nearby, pretty village of Llacanora, head back to Cajamarca.

Toward the Amazon

There is a rough but scenic route from Cajamarca, via Celendín, to **Chachapoyas** ⓫, heart of the pre-Inca culture of the same name. Very little is known about the Chachapoyas period, which was roughly contemporary with the Chimu (*circa* 1000–1400), but its people were certainly good at building cities and, judging by their fortifications, must have felt themselves under threat. There are buses to Celendín (about 120 km/75 miles from Cajamarca) on a slow road, but from there on the usual method of transport is by truck. If your time is limited, or you visit during the rainy season when the road gets washed away, it's advisable to access Chachapoyas from Chiclayo. This road is in much better condition and there are more buses. There are also flights from Lima to Chachapoyas.

Chachapoyas alone, although pleasant, would not be worth the long journey, but the spectacular surrounding area, the sense of visiting a spot which still sees few tourists, and the opportunity to visit the area's many hilltop ruins make it a trip worth taking.

The best of the sites is **Kuélap**, a great pre-Inca walled city perched high above the Río Utcubamba. Minibuses leave in the morning for the village of **Tingo**, from where a road goes to within 15 minutes' walk of the ruins. Discoveries are still being made in this area. In 1997, 219 mummies were uncovered in a cliff tomb up by a lake near Leimebamba (near Celendín), where they are now housed. Vilaya Tours (tel:044 777 506) offer visits to these areas, or ask a local guide to accompany you. ❑

Huallaga

I n *la ceja de la selva* (the eyebrow of the jungle), where the mountain flanks meet the Amazon basin, lies the broad tropical valley of the Río Huallaga. Maize and rice are grown on a large scale in the fertile valley, but it is known for another product – coca.

In the Andean highlands of both Peru and Bolivia, coca has been a part of the traditional culture for more than 4,000 years. The leaves are for sale in any mountain market. Ask at a cafe for *mate de coca* and you will get a cup of coca-leaf tea, a drink that is the best prevention and treatment of the symptoms of *soroche* – altitude sickness.

Coca gives energy, and dulls the senses against cold, hunger, and exhaustion. The biggest consumers have always been miners, who use up to half a kilo a day each, but it is used at many other times. Before giving birth, a woman chews the leaves to hasten labor and ease the pain. When a young man wants to marry a girl, he offers coca to her father. And when somebody dies, *mate de coca* is drunk at the wake and a small pile of leaves placed in the coffin.

Coca was first cultivated in the Andes around 2000 BC. Centuries later the Incas turned its production into a monopoly, as a means of controlling subject populations. Its use was restricted to royalty, priests, doctors, and the message runners, known to travel vast distances on the energy gained from chewing the leaves. The Incas had relaxed their monopoly by the time the Spanish arrived, but the Catholic Church tried to ban the leaf, denouncing it as "the delusion of the devil." However, it changed its tune, and established a monopoly of its own, when it found that the Amerindians needed the leaf to survive the brutal conditions in the mines and plantations.

Back in Europe and the United States, coca was almost unheard of until the mid-1800s, when a Parisian chemist, Angelo Mariani, marketed a wine made from the leaf that became immensely popular. This Vin Mariani inspired American soft-drink companies to produce other coca-based drinks, such as Coca-Cola. At the same time, cocaine was being developed, and was quickly taken up by such luminaries as Sigmund Freud, who called it a "magical substance."

In the 1970s, the drug became more popular, particularly in the United States. Much of the crop grown in the Andes is crushed by foot in chemicals, turned into a gummy paste and flown to Colombia. After being refined into powder, the cocaine is then smuggled into North American and European cities.

Cocaine has brought violence to the Huallaga Valley, in the shape of a complex conflict between the Peruvian drug squad – backed by US Drug Enforcement agents – and Colombian cocaine traffickers, left-wing guerrillas, and the coca farmers themselves. More than 40 light aircraft used by drug-traffickers to transport the paste to Colombia have been shot down over Peruvian airspace in an ongoing anti-drug offensive.

Although the Huallaga Valley is an area of great natural beauty, and around the fringes there are places, such as Tingo María, that can be visited safely, only the most foolhardy tourist will venture into the heart of the valley. ❑

RIGHT: coca leaves, the Huallaga Valley crop.

CALLEJÓN DE HUAYLAS

Spectacular scenery and the challenge of climbing Peru's highest mountain are among the attractions of this remote area

Stretching for 160 km (255 miles) and ranging in altitude from a mere 1,800 meters (5,900 ft) to 4,080 meters (13,380 ft), the valley known as the **Callejón de Huaylas** rates as one of the finest areas in all of South America for its superb mountain vistas and a wealth of opportunities for outdoor pursuits. Many dedicated enthusiasts arrive prepared for sports ranging from trekking and climbing to snowboarding, paraskiing, and skiing, while others are content to spend their days relaxing in a spectacular mountain setting and exploring the villages that sprawl along the hillsides.

The Callejón de Huaylas is bordered on the east by the Cordillera Blanca (White Mountains) – a mountain range with the greatest number of 6,000-meter (20,000-ft) peaks outside the Himalayas – and on the west by the lower range known as the Cordillera Negra (Black Mountains) for their sparseness of vegetation and complete lack of snow. To the north, the valley terminates with the Cañon del Pato, a narrow gorge of a canyon with sheer rock walls, steep precipices, and a dirt road winding its way through numerous crudely constructed tunnels down toward the coast. There are daily bus services from Chimbote to Huaraz – go by day for the exciting views. The hair-raising narrow road has been widened, and is now known as the Carretera de Huallanca, which is good news for those approaching Huaraz from the north. The 40 km- (25 mile-) wide Callejón de Huaylas is renowned not only for its breathtaking scenery but also for Inca and pre-Inca history, unusual flora and fauna, lively markets and traditional villages.

Disaster area

The Callejón de Huaylas is also well known for a history of natural disasters. Earthquakes and alluvions – the name given to floods of water combined with avalanches and landslides – have caused considerable damage over the past 300 recorded years. The capital city of Huaraz was severely damaged by an alluvion in 1941 when an avalanche caused Laguna Calcacocha to overflow. Much of the central district was destroyed, and nearly 5,000 lives were lost. The most tragic disaster occurred in 1970, when an earthquake measuring 7.7 on the Richter scale devastated the entire region and was responsible for more than 80,000 deaths.

More than 30,000 people died in Huaraz, and over 80 percent of the city was flattened, but hardest hit was the village of Yungay. The entire town and most of its inhabitants completely disappeared under a massive avalanche of rock and snow when part of the Huascarán massif broke loose and plunged down the valley.

In the aftermath of these catastrophes many of the towns and villages have been almost completely rebuilt, mainly with uninspiring concrete structures.

PRECEDING PAGES: the Cordillera Blanca. **LEFT:** a village nestles beneath snowy peaks. **BELOW:** flowers on the mountain slopes.

*Mending shoes in
Carhuaz.*

Understandably, the need to rehouse people was given priority, and little
thought was given to preserving an architectural heritage. The colonial charm
encountered in other highland areas has been all but lost. Sadly, these natural
disasters also took a heavy toll on the archeology of the region. Notably lacking are many ancient remains, primarily from the Inca empire, which did not
survive the calamities.

Mountain retreat

The center of most commercial activity and the common destination for visitors
to the Callejón de Huaylas is the city of **Huaraz ⑫**. There is an airport just outside the town, but flights from Lima are very unreliable, so most people get
here by bus, from either Lima or Chimbote – both journeys take about eight
hours on a paved road. There are frequent services, and the more expensive
buses are quite comfortable. As the capital of the department of Ancash, and
with a population of more than 80,000 inhabitants, Huaraz is well-suited to
support the demands of tourism. At first glance, it appears to be little more than
a one-horse town, but a closer look proves that all necessities are readily available. Scores of low-cost hostels offer accommodations of varying kinds, some
very basic, others quite comfortable, and there are a few higher-priced hotels for
those who would like a bit more comfort during their mountain retreat.

Before departing for remote regions, or after a long trek in the mountains,
you'll find plenty of activity in the bustling town of Huaraz. Along the main
street of Luzuriaga, vendors sell a wide selection of woolen goods, pan flutes,
and ceramic replicas of the Chavín temple. Other traditionally dressed highlanders sell regional food specialties from wooden carts. Andean cheeses, rich

BELOW: electronic
sounds for sale.

honey, and *manjar blanco* (a sweet, milky concoction used as a dessert or filling) are a few tasty edibles that are worth trying. Store-front tour companies set out brightly colored billboards promoting day trips to popular tourist sites and advertize an assortment of climbing and trekking gear for hire. A wide range of restaurants caters to international tastes: pizzerias, Chinese food and hamburgers are found alongside more typical dishes such as *lomo saltado* (strips of beef with potatoes), *pollos a la brasa* (griddled chicken), and *cuy* (roasted guinea pig).

Worth a visit is the **Museo Arqueológico** (open Tues–Sun 9am–1pm and 3–7pm), off Ancash on the **Plaza de Armas**. It is a humble affair, yet considered noteworthy for its collection of stone monoliths from the Recuay culture, which date from 400 BC to AD 600. Also on display are mummies, ceramics, and household utensils dating from the same period.

Huaraz nightlife, too, has plenty to offer. There are several cinemas showing recent US films in English with Spanish subtitles, although the sound system frequently leaves something to be desired. *Peñas*, or folklore nightclubs, entertain with traditional Andean musical groups in the early evening, and switch to disco later on for serious high-altitude dancing. Tambo Taverna and Amadeus Taberna are the most popular and are packed to capacity on weekends and during high season.

The outlying area of Huaraz offers numerous opportunities for day excursions. Footpaths lead to a number of small villages and agricultural areas within walking distance of the city center. Rataquenua, Unchus, Marían and Pitec are just a few of the *pueblos* that can be visited in a few hours.

About an hour by local bus south of Huaraz lies the small town of Catac, often visited by those keen to see the giant *Puya Raimondi*. This unusual plant

Map on pages 168–9

BELOW: the bustling streets of Huaraz.

TIP

Be well prepared for
your trek. In recent
years Huaraz has
become geared up to
the influx of outward-
bound visitors and is
able to cater for most
needs. The Casa de
Guías in the Plaza
Ginebra can supply
the names of
recommended
mountain guides,
and a lot of other
information.

Below: Lagunas
de Llanganuco.

is often referred to as a cactus, but is actually the largest member of the brome-liad family. It is a rare species, considered to be one of the oldest in the world, and is found in only a few isolated areas of the Andes. At its base, the *Puya Rai-mondi* forms a huge rosette of long, spiked, waxy leaves – often reaching a diameter of 2 meters (6 ft). As it begins to flower, a process that takes its entire lifespan which is estimated to approach 100 years, it sends up a phallic spike that can reach a height of 12 meters (39 ft).

As the final flowering begins, usually in the month of May, the spike is cov-ered in flowers – as many as 20,000 blooms on a single plant. During this sea-son, if you are incredibly lucky, groups of *Puya Raimondi* may bloom together, creating an unbelievable picture set against the backdrop of the snowy peaks of the Cordillera Blanca.

Trekking

The Huaraz area is a trekker's paradise. Just above the city is **El Mirador**, a scenic lookout marked by a huge white cross. The route heads uphill east along city streets, which eventually turn into a footpath beside an irrigation canal lined with eucalyptus trees. Fields of wheat ripening in the sun add a serene, pastoral feel. At the top, the highest mountain in Peru, **Huascarán** (6768 meters/22,200 ft), dominates the northern horizon; the lower Vallu-naraju (5,680 meters/18,600 ft) peeks out over the foothills to the east, and the city of Huaraz sprawls below.

Another popular choice is the **Pitec Trail to Laguna Churup**. There is no public transportation to this small village 10 km (6 miles) from the center of Huaraz, but often a taxi driver or someone driving a pick-up truck can be found

at *el puente* (the bridge) at Huaraz who will navigate the rough road to Pitec. Walking is an option – it takes around two hours at a slowish pace – but it's nicer to be fresh at the trailhead and then walk back down to Huaraz afterwards.

The trail begins at the parking lot before the vil-lage of Pitec is reached. A well-worn footpath heads north up a ridgeline, and the Churup massif rises just above 5,495 meters (18,000 ft) in the distance. At the base of this mountain is the destination of the hike, Laguna Churup, fed by glacial melt-off and sur-rounded by huge boulders. A picnic lunch and a mid-day siesta in the warm sun reward the effort of getting here. A leisurely hike back to Huaraz follows a cob-bled road through *campesino* homesteads.

Ancient remains

About 8 km (5 miles) north of Huaraz, and easily reached on foot, is the small pre-Inca ruin of **Wil-cahuan**. Little is known about this three-storied struc-ture which stands in the middle of an agricultural valley, but, because of the typical masonry style, it is thought to date from the Expansionist Period of the Huari-Tiahuanaco culture (200–700). The window-less inner chambers can be explored with a flashlight, or with candles proffered by any one of the hordes of schoolboys who haunt the site and offer their services as guides, for a small fee. Most of the rooms within

Map on pages 168–9

the construction are inaccessible from the debris of centuries, but a few of them have been opened up to reveal a sophisticated ventilation system and skillful stone craftsmanship.

Longer excursions to the surrounding country are as simple to arrange as locating the proper rural bus to take you there. A major road stretches the length of the Callejón de Huaylas, running alongside the Río Santa, and local transportation is readily available to a variety of villages situated along the route. It is also very easy to negotiate a mini-bus tour with one of various agencies in the center of town.

The village of **Monterrey**, just 5 km (3 miles) outside Huaraz, is worth a visit for its *baños termales* (hot springs). Two swimming pools of warm water, and private baths of the steaming variety, are extremely inviting, especially after a rigorous trek in the mountains. About 35 km (22 miles) farther up the valley is **Chancos**, which claims to have its own Fountain of Youth – more thermal baths with natural saunas and pools of flowing hot water.

Buses frequently leave Huaraz, loaded with an assortment of *campesinos*, their chickens, *cuyes* (guinea pigs), and children, heading for the small village of **Yungay** ⓭, which lies north down the valley. This is the village described earlier in this chapter that was completely destroyed by the 1970 earthquake. During the most recent rebuilding of Yungay, the village site was shifted a few kilometers north of its original location in the hope that it would now be out of the way of any future natural disasters. All that remains of the abandoned Yungay, now known as Campo Santo, is a solitary monument dedicated to those whose lives were lost, and a few battered palm trees that once lined the charming Plaza de Armas.

The Llanganuco to Santa Cruz Loop

Yungay is the turn-off point for the popular two-hour ride up to the **Lagunas de Llanganuco**. *Camionetas*, small pick-up trucks, wait in the plaza to transport hikers and sightseers up the valley to the dazzling, glacier-fed lakes. It is also one of the starting points for the **Llanganuco to Santa Cruz Loop**. One of the most frequently hiked trails in the region, this five-day route passes under a dozen peaks over 5,800 meters (19,000 ft), and panoramic views abound. The following route assumes that you are beginning the loop here at the Lagunas de Llanganuco, but if you are hoping to use donkey transport for your baggage it is recommended that you do it the other way round, because donkeys and their drivers are easier to find in the village of Cashapampa.

The trailhead lies a few kilometers above the lakes, near the **Portachuelo** (high pass) of Llanganuco, and the trek begins with a descent toward the village of **Colcabamba**. Immediately the steep face of **Chopicalqui** (6,350 meters/20,800 ft) towers over the trail like a sentinel, and soon a few thatched-roofed houses come into view. A sampling of local cuisine may be possible here.

At this point, the trail begins a steady ascent up the **Huaripampa Quebrada** (Narrow Valley). The snow-capped peaks of **Chacraraju** (6,110 meters/20,000 ft)

BELOW: a hut in Huascarán National Park.

and **Pirámide** (5,880 meters/19,285 ft) provide splendid photo opportunities, and a chance to rest, as the trekker labors up the steepening trail toward the high pass of **Punta Unión**. In the last hour before sunset, as camp is set up, the mountains are cast in the silver and pink of "alpenglow."

At over 4,750 meters (15,500 ft), Punta Unión becomes both literally and figuratively the high point of this journey. **Taulliraju**, over 5,830 meters (19,000 ft), glistens in the midday sun, and a number of glacial lakes lie like scattered jewels in the distance. The valley below opens up to reveal a wide stretch of snow-capped peaks, a mere hint of the magnitude of the Cordillera Blanca, and huge Andean condors can often be seen soaring high above the pass.

As the trail descends toward the village of **Cashapampa** (this is the village where donkeys can be hired) the scenery changes from dramatic mountain vistas to open, marshy pastureland where herds of llamas and goats graze. Farther along, the trail narrows as it begins to wind through forests of stunted trees and follows the easy meandering of a small stream.

Caraz ⓮ is the end point of this loop, a pretty town that was fortunate enough to survive several recent earthquakes with relatively little damage. Fields of flowers line the road as you approach, and at the other side of town groves of orange trees sit beneath snowy mountain peaks. There are several small hotels and a few basic restaurants around the Plaza de Armas. If you choose to start, rather than finish, your trek here, you can get a bus from Huaraz, which is only about 65 km (40 miles) away. From Caraz you can take gentle walks in the nearby hills, or visit the stunning turquoise-blue **Lago Parón**, some 30 km (18 miles) up a rugged, winding road. It's a magnificent all-day hike, or a relatively inexpensive trip by taxi.

BELOW:
growing up in the
Cordillera Blanca.

Reserve in the Sierra

Much of the Cordillera Blanca above 4,000 meters (13,000 ft) and the area around Huascarán mountain fall within the confines of **Parque Nacional Huascarán**. The park is easily visited from Huaraz, and its office, where you can get information before your visit, is located there. Established in 1972, the park marked Peru as a frontrunner in Latin America in the area of conservation. Huascarán National Park was formed to protect the indigenous wildlife, archeological sites, geology, and natural beauty of an area threatened by mining and other commercial interests. An entrance fee is charged to help offset the cost of providing park guardians and preserving trails.

Of the more interesting wildlife that you can possibly see, with a little patience and a bit of luck, is the vizcacha, a small, elusive rabbit-like animal with characteristics similar to the North American marmot; the vicuña, a cameloid cousin to the llama; and the stealthy puma.

Daily life in the Andes

Throughout the Callejón de Huaylas, a lifestyle dating back centuries continues to thrive. The traditional dress of the villagers has not changed radically in many years. The women, especially, hold on to their heritage, wearing layers of colorful woolen skirts and embroidered blouses which developed during colonial times. In addition, each wears a hat whose style may vary significantly from village to village. The custom of hat-wearing can also be used to indicate marital status, as in the village of Carhuaz. There, a woman wearing a black band round her fedora is a widow, while a rose-colored band is worn by single women, and a white one shows that the wearer is married.

Map on pages 168–9

A cactus in bloom.

BELOW: approach to Chopicalqui, Cordillera Blanca.

Agriculture, the mainstay of the valley, has also seen little change over the centuries in either methods or crop variety. Double-yoked oxen still drag crude wooden plows through the black, fertile soil. Honey-colored wheat can be seen ripening throughout the valley, and maturing quinoa plants, a high-altitude grain rich in protein, are easily recognized by the rich colors of burnt orange, fiery red, and deep purple that blaze along the hillsides.

Corn – the sacred crop of the Incas and one of the earliest foods, which took man from hunter-gatherer to farmer – is grown in abundance and is the staple of life along with the ever-present potato. From it, a thick, slightly fermented corn beer called *chicha* is made. *Chicha* is drunk in great quantities in the highlands, especially during festivals. It was originally the royal drink, considered suitable only for consumption by the ruling Inca and his courtiers.

Festivals play a large part in the lifestyle of the indigenous people who inhabit the Callejón de Huaylas. They provide a way to break out of the monotony of the day-to-day existence and reaffirm the traditions that give continuity to life in the Andes. Since the Spanish Conquest, festivals have assumed a religious veneer and coincide with Catholic feast days, but underneath still lies a strong thread of meaning left behind by ancient cultures. The Catholic Church, which has always been good at assimilating pre-existing customs, is well aware of this, but has wisely decided to turn a blind eye.

Every month of the year sees a celebration, or several, in full swing. Some are particular to one village, while others are observed throughout the whole area. The major festivals of San Juan (St John on June 24) and San Pedro and San Pablo (St Peter and St Paul on June 29), celebrated all over the region as in many other parts of the continent, are particularly lively, especially since they fall at the same time as the national day that has been set aside to honor the *campesino* (subsiststence farmer).

On the eve of San Juan, fires are lit throughout the valley, burning the chaff from the harvest and the wild *ichu* grass on the hillsides, and having absolutely nothing to do with John the Baptist. From a high mountain camp, the fires look like starlight brought to earth, and the next day the valley is thick with smoke.

Semana Santa, or Easter, is another widely celebrated festival. Many villages have their own special traditions, but the celebrations are always colorful and abundant. Processions of finely adorned religious figures carried on litters, scenes of the Resurrection sculpted in flower petals on the ground, and folkloric bands playing music throughout the village are common events during the festivities of Holy Week.

Temples of the jaguar-worshipers

Many visitors to the Callejón de Huaylas come not only for the majestic mountains and typical highland life but also to see one of the oldest archeological sites designed by one of the most influential cultures in the Americas. At the temple complex of **Chavín de Huantar** ⓯ (open daily; entrance charge) lie the remains of one of the most important pre-Inca cultures. Dating from around 1300 to 400 BC, the Chavín culture was typified by a highly developed artistic style and a cult whose influence lasted longer than

The first Spaniards were considered liberators of sorts, and the daughter of Kuntar Guacho, the lord of Huaylas, was given as mistress to the conquistador Francisco Pizarro himself.

BELOW:
an icy precipice.

that of the Roman Empire, and was so widespread that archeologists have termed this formation period "the Chavín Horizon." Recently some archeologists have come to believe that this culture culminated at Chavín, rather than originating there, but as yet there is no firm evidence either way. The Huaylas culture, which once occupied this valley, was briefly dominated by this more sophisticated civilization.

Map on pages 168–9

The site is actually located across the mountains in the next valley to the east, near the village of Chavín, but is most accessible from Huaraz. There are regular buses, and the journey takes about five hours. Tours of the site can also be arranged in Huaraz, where there are several agencies. If you go under your own steam you will find guides to show you around, but they may not speak much, if any, English.

Archeologists have been able to learn very little about the culture because it left no written records, so much of what is suggested is based on pure supposition. But it is widely accepted that, at the time the Chavín culture was emerging, mankind was moving from a hunter-gatherer way of life to a society based on agriculture, which gave people new-found leisure time to devote to cultural pursuits. The theories that have been put forward about this mysterious culture are mostly based on the study of this 7-hectare (17-acre) site containing a temple, plazas, and a multitude of stone carvings and drawings. The temple of Chavín de Huantar is thought to have been a major ceremonial center, and felines, principally the jaguar, were the most important deities of the cult. It is also believed that the Chavín people were not warlike: their influence on the architecture and sculpture of the northern coast and central highlands appears to have been spread by peaceful means.

BELOW:
a Chavín noble.

What first strikes most visitors upon their arrival at Chavín de Huantar is the quality of the stonework found in the temple walls and the plaza stairways. The dry-stone masonry construction reflects a sophistication not expected from a culture that flourished more than 3,000 years ago. Added to this are huge stone slabs with highly stylized carvings of jaguars, eagles, and anacondas; the designs are intricate and fluid.

The temple sits above a large, sunken plaza where it is believed pilgrims came to worship during certain seasons. On one side sits a large granite slab with seven hewn-out indentations that must have served as an altar stone for group rituals. Two 3 meter- (10 ft-) high stone portals overlook the plaza and represent the entry way into the interior of the temple. Finely etched bird-like figures, one male and one female, face each other across a stairway, symbolically divided into two halves – one painted black and the other white.

Niches set around the outside of the temple walls originally held protruding sculpted stone heads, human in shape but with the snarling grin of a jaguar. Some theories suggest that the eyes were originally inset with crystals, which would reflect the light of the moon and ward off evildoers. Only one of these so-called keystones remains in place; a few have been stolen over the years, and the rest are safely stored within the temple.

Map on pages 168–9

TIP

Don't forget the usual health precautions when climbing: altitude sickness can be a problem if you are not acclimatized; guard against hypothermia by bringing the right clothes and being aware of early symptoms – see page 128.

BELOW:
a carved head at
Chavín de Huantar.

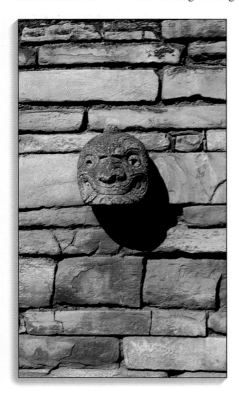

The interior of the temple is a subterranean labyrinth of passages and galleries set on at least three levels which are connected by a series of ramps and stairs. Though there are no windows, a highly engineered ventilation system allows the continuous flow of fresh air throughout – another marvel produced by an ancient civilization. Some of the rooms contain the remains of the sculpted heads and intricately carved slabs that portray a variety of Amazonian and highland animals.

Granite god

At the heart of the underground complex two narrow passageways cross, and at their junction stands the crowning glory of the Chavín religion – the Lanzón de Chavín. This 4 meter- (13 ft-) high granite monolith is thought to be the principal god-image worshiped by this cult. Its Spanish name comes from the lance or dagger-like shape of the monolith, which appears to be stuck in the ground. A mythological image emerges from the elaborate stone carving, and its demeanor is in keeping with most of the terrifying god images created by the Chavín people.

The large head of the monolith is square and human-like, yet definite feline characteristics are noted in the grinning mouth, which has a long fang protruding from each corner. The nose has two big holes for nostrils, and an arm and a leg are visible on each side. Round earrings dangle from the creature's ears, and long flowing hair is made up of intricately carved serpents. Carved into the top of the head are thin, grooved channels, and some speculate that animals, or even humans, may have been sacrificed to this god.

Above the god image there was once an opening in the ceiling, now closed to preserve the figure from exposure to the elements. Here, many believe, a sacrificial rock may have been positioned and, as animals or people were slaughtered, the blood would flow through the opening in the ceiling and would run down through the channel in the figure. However, some other archeologists disclaim the sacrificial theory and suggest instead that the Lanzón was merely the dominant figure for worship.

Two other monoliths are considered important in the Chavín cult, but both are now housed in the **Museo de la Nación** in Lima *(see page 160)*. The 1.8-meter (6-ft) stone called the stela Raimondi is named after the archeologist Antonio Raimondi (who also gave his name to the *Puya Raimondi* cactus described on page 195); he moved the stele to the Museum of Anthropology and Archeology in Lima at the end of the 19th century after it had been used as a table by a *campesino* (peasant) who had discovered it in 1840. It depicts a monstrous feline anthropomorphic god, with widespread arms, claw-like feet, and a tangle of serpents representing its hair.

The second major piece is the Tello obelisk, which was discovered by archeologist Julio C. Tello. This towering, intricately carved piece also depicts feline images, as well as a caiman – a creature not normally associated with highland culture. The significance of this, as of much that we see at the temple, is a mystery, but the experience is unforgettable. ❑

The highest mountain

Huascarán is Peru's highest mountain. There are two huge summits: the south one, at 6,768 meters (22,200 ft), is 113 meters (370 ft) higher than its more frequently climbed northern sister. Some regard the nearby Alpamayo (5,945 meters/19,500 ft) as the world's most beautiful mountain.

The hike begins at the village of Musho, where *arrieros* (muleteers) can be hired to carry the heavy load of climbing gear and food provisions to the first camp. The trail wanders through farmland and eucalyptus groves for a few hours, and then a sharp ascent above the treeline leads to a flat, grassy area known as Huascarán base camp.

Another two hours up a steep ridge lies the moraine camp. The donkeys can't make it up here, so it means donning the heavy weight yourself. It's on the second or third day that most climbers pack up at moraine camp and head for Camp One on the glacier.

From there, the route will often be "wanded" with small flags placed by previous climbers for an easy descent and to avoid getting lost on the glacier during a "whiteout" when clouds obscure everything. The climb is unforgettable. Wide crevasses, icy cracks, and massive pillars of tumbled ice are constant reminders that glaciers are anything but static piles of snow.

Camp One at 5,200 meters (17,000 ft) is a welcome relief after five to seven hours of traversing the lower glacier, but the pleasure is short-lived as the sun goes down and temperatures drop well below freezing. It is in this bone-chilling cold that climbers rise early the next day and prepare to set off for the final high camp at La Garganta (The Throat) at 5,790 meters (19,000 ft), the most interesting part of the entire climb. About an hour after you leave camp and cross a wide crevasse, the first technical part of the route appears. A 100-meter (300-ft), 70-degree ice wall must be climbed, and quickly because it is a natural avalanche chute.

Early morning is the best time as the snow pack is still frozen and likely to stay in place. Above the chute, the route remains steep and prone to avalanche activity. It's important to move as quickly as possible, despite the aching lungs and reeling head.

At La Garganta Camp, after another cold night, climbers prepare for the summit attempt. A small blessing is that the heavy equipment can be left behind in camp. All that's needed are spare warm clothes, food, water, and a camera. The summit route heads up across the saddle between the two peaks of Huascarán, and the climber is treated to a view of distant mountains set ablaze in the early-morning sun. The climb ascends several steep snow slopes, and the first few hours involve zig-zag traverses.

Rather than one long slope to the summit, you encounter a series of gentle inclines. From the high point of one, all that is seen is another. Breathing is so labored that three breaths are needed for each step, but keep going and soon the summit of Peru's highest mountain will be conquered. ❑

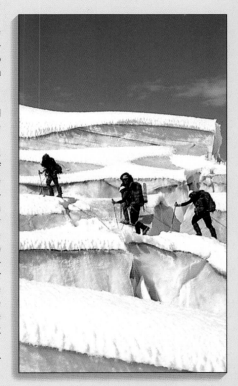

RIGHT: scaling the highest peak.

THE NORTHERN AMAZON

Travel by river boat through the Amazon region and discover the huge diversity of flora and fauna – but don't expect to keep to a schedule, for time means little here

Map on pages 168–9

Lima

Viewed from the air, Peru's Amazon looks like an endless sea of lumpy green sponges, stretching in all directions to the horizon. It is this thick umbrella of trees – the jungle's equivalent of an enormous housing project – that creates the millions of homes below in which animals and specialized plants live. If you were able to enter the upper canopy slowly from the top you would soon discover that the first layer is virtually a desert. The crowns of the trees are exposed both to the fierce tropical sun and to winds that frequently snap and topple the tallest of trees. To reduce evaporation, the leaves at this level are quite small. Many of the epiphytes – plants that live on top of other plants – actually take the form of cacti, to reduce their loss of water.

As you descended through the upper canopy, however, you would immediately begin to enter a different world of reduced light. Protected from direct sun and wind, the leaves are thus larger in size than those above, and the fierce struggle for light has begun. Traveling farther down toward the jungle floor, you would see that leafy plants are much less abundant. Although explorers traveling by river often reported thick and impenetrable jungle, under the canopy away from the rivers one can move about quite easily as most branches and leaves are well off the floor.

The air here is calm even in strong storms, and at times completely still. The sound of insects is overpowering as millions of unseen little creatures call to one another. At the bottom-most level the leaves are very large; less than 5 percent of the sun's light actually reaches the jungle's floor.

It is this enormous variation of light, wind, and temperature that, together with the thousands of different species of plants, affords millions of different homes for animal and plant species. Whole communities of insects, birds, and other animals are specialized and adapted to different levels of the rainforest, so it is not surprising that it contains the highest species diversity in the world.

Parque Nacional Manu in southeastern Peru, for example, covering an area roughly half the size of Switzerland, houses over 800 bird species (approximately the same number as is found in the whole of North America), 20 percent of all the plant species found in South America, and more than 1,200 species of butterfly (Europe has 400). A recent study by the Smithsonian Institution of the insects in Manu's upper canopy has increased the total number of the world's estimated animal species by 30 million.

Push toward conservation

Jungles have existed for hundreds of millions of years, but it is only within the past 100 years that they have

PRECEDING PAGES: a jaguar in the wild. **LEFT:** jungle waterfall. **BELOW:** tagging a baby caiman.

been on the decline. The trend is in direct relation to the population of human beings. In the course of the past century humans have destroyed half of the world's rainforests. At the present rate of destruction, most experts agree, the majority of the remaining rainforests will have disappeared within the next 20 years.

Tampering with the jungles is not a modern phenomenon, of course. Europeans have long viewed the Amazon as a storehouse of raw materials. The 16th- and 17th-century search for gold was replaced by quests for other valuable commodities native to the Amazon jungle and found nowhere else in the world: quinine (which allowed British troops to conquer India without succumbing to malaria), cocoa (the basis of the world's huge chocolate industry), mahogany, vanilla, and others. No product made a bigger impact, however, than that which naturally exudes from three species of Amazonian tree: the sticky-white latex called rubber.

In 1743 the French scientist Charles-Marie de la Condamine used rubber latex to waterproof his instruments, and was the first European to introduce the substance to the Old World.

The rubber boom

The commodity had been known about for a very long time – Columbus reported Amerindians using strange "elastic" balls in their games – but its commercial use was limited due to the fact that natural rubber grew soft and sticky in hot weather and brittle and hard in cold. In 1844, however, Charles Goodyear invented the process of vulcanization, which allowed rubber to stay tough and firm at all temperatures. This revolutionized the rubber industry. With John Boyd Dunlop's later invention of the pneumatic tire, suddenly an enormous demand was created, which only the Amazon could satisfy.

The ensuing rubber boom was short-lived – it lasted from approximately 1880

BELOW: giant water lilies.

to 1912 – but it completely transformed the Amazon's economy. Rubber trees in the most remote regions were soon being tapped, the latex gathered in cups, then coagulated into large balls that were cured over a fire. The tappers themselves were bankrolled by entrepreneurs who amassed enormous wealth and lived in luxury in newly burgeoning jungle cities such as Manaus in Brazil and Iquitos in Peru.

In the midst of the boom, however, an English adventurer named Henry Wickham quietly collected 70,000 rubber seeds and smuggled them out of the Amazon. First planted in Kew Gardens in England, and then transplanted to tropical Asia where they were safe from indigenous diseases, the seeds flourished. By 1912 the Amazon rubber boom was at an end.

In the latter half of the 20th century the largest destructive force on the Peruvian Amazon was the unmanaged influx of peasants from the Andes and the coast. Since the 1960s, successive governments, both military and civilian, have viewed the eastern Andean slopes and the Amazon basin as regions of unexploited natural resources, believing that their development would provide a politically painless solution to several urgent problems: land hunger in the Andes, the migration of masses of the rural poor to coastal cities, and the need to populate remote border regions in order to defend national sovereignty.

As a result the Belaunde government financed the construction of a "marginal highway," a road paralleling the Andes to the east, which it was hoped would help open up the area to colonization and industry. But the idea of settling the Amazon ignored reality: less than 5 percent of the Peruvian Amazon's soil is suitable for agriculture, and much of the region supports populations of indigenous peoples and settlers that are already large in relation to the exploitable resources. As a consequence, agriculture that began on a few relatively fertile

Map on pages 168–9

BELOW: a cautious young puma.

*An Amerindian
family in Satipo.*

BELOW: morning
calm in the jungle.

terraces in the eastern Andes has now spread to land ill-suited to continuous exploitation. With inadequate knowledge of better practices, many farmers work the land too long, allowing no time for it to renew itself. Once the soil has been drained of nutrients, poor farmers, unable to buy fertilizer, have no alternative but to move on, carving yet another plot from the forest.

The result has been extensive deforestation of Peru's cloudforest, where an estimated 50 percent of all neotropical plant species are found. Thus far over 70,000 sq. km (27,000 sq. miles) of the Peruvian Amazon have been deforested; 300,000 hectares (741,300 acres) are deforested every year.

An additional impact on Peru's rainforest was the illegal cocaine industry, mostly concentrated in the north-central jungle's Huallaga Valley *(see page 189)*. Hundreds of thousands of hectares of virgin rainforest were destroyed in order to grow illegal plantations of coca shrubs – all to support the drug habits of North Americans and Europeans. The US Government pressurized Peru to use a major defoliant – Spike – on coca plantations, but protests by local and international conservationists about the effect such a chemical could have on the surrounding jungle prevented its use. In recent years, however, many hectares of coca-leaf plantations have been turned over to legal cash crops such as cocoa, coffee, or corn, and a government program has been initiated to help farmers find markets for their new crops.

System of protection

In spite of increasing rainforest destruction, however, a number of encouraging developments have taken place. Peru currently has roughly 5 percent of its territory protected by a system of around 50 national parks, reserves, sanctuaries,

and other designated areas, a process that has thrived since it was begun in the 1960s. During the past few decades considerable ecological awareness has developed and, as a consequence, there has been a proliferation of conservation organizations. In 1990 a giant 1.5 million-hectare (3.75 million-acre) "reserved zone" was declared in the Madre de Dios region – Peru's southernmost department, which contains some of the richest rainforest found anywhere in the world. This area – including almost the entire watershed of the Río Tambopata – is currently at the forefront of tropical rainforest conservation.

Map on pages 168–9

Eco-tourism develops

The idea is to convert the zone not into a park but rather an "extractive reserve," which means an area of rainforest where renewable yearly harvests of Brazil nuts, rubber, and other rainforest products will create more revenue, in the long run, than the permanent destruction caused by unmanaged farming, logging, and cattle-ranching. The scheme was pioneered by the Brazilian rubber tapper Chico Méndez (who was murdered in 1988 by Brazilian cattle-ranchers, and whose story has been made into a film by David Puttnam), but it remains to be seen how such ideas fare.

The practice of so-called eco-tourism has also developed over the past three decades. This new "green" tourism is based on the belief that the rich natural rainforest can not only be preserved, by using it as an extractive reserve, but can also attract tourist dollars. If the eco-tourism industry is managed responsibly, the income it generates, pumped into local economies and national-park infrastructures, may well prove to be one of the few counter-destructive economic forces currently available for preserving the jungle. The more people

BELOW: a caiman in close-up.

who travel to virgin rainforest areas, the more people will become involved in the international fight to save them. Just as importantly, tourism can prove the monetary value of intact rainforests to the many hard-pressed, developing nations that can't afford the luxury of the industrialized West's "untouchable" parks and reserves.

The northern jungle

Some 3,200 km (1,990 miles) upriver from the Amazon's mouth lies the jungle-locked city of **Iquitos** . The capital of the department of Loreto, it has a population of 400,000, and is linked to the exterior world only by air and river boats. At one time the clearing-house for the millions of tons of rubber shipped to Europe, Iquitos still displays the vestiges of its former status as one of the most important rubber capitals in the world. Houses both near the main plaza and the river are still faced with *azulejos* (glazed tiles), which at the height of the rubber boom were originally shipped from Italy and Portugal along with other luxury goods such as early 20th-century ironwork from England, glass chandeliers, caviar, and fine wines.

On the **Plaza de Armas** stands the Casa de Fierro, or Iron House, which was designed by Gustav Eiffel for the Paris exhibition in 1898. It is said to be the first prefabricated house in the Americas and was transported unassembled from Paris by a local rubber baron. It is entirely constructed of iron trusses and bolted iron sheets. This sounds more impressive than it looks, and is more interesting as a symbol of the town's short-lived affluence than as a piece of architecture. Also on the plaza is the house of Carlos Fitzcarraldo, the Peruvian rubber baron who dragged a steamship over the pass that bears his name, thus opening up the

TIP

You can do your bit for conservation by refusing to buy anything made from animal products. If local people see that tourists would rather look at the live creatures than buy articles made of shell or feather, the trade will become much less attractive.

BELOW: a river boat near Iquitos.

department of Madre de Dios. The German director Werner Herzog shot part of his film *Fitzcarraldo* here, and several of the refurbished steamships that he used are still in port. Hundreds of *iquiteños* were used as extras in the movie, which created a brief mini-boom of its own.

Iquitos today is a colorful, friendly city that seems to have a monopoly not on rubber but on three-wheeled taxis (charging approximately 50 cents a ride); motor scooters, with the consequent din as they are continually revved up; Amazon views; and a very special atmosphere. It is located some 80 km (50 miles) downriver from where the **Marañon** and **Ucayali** rivers join to create the River Amazon.

The local dish is *paiche a la loretana*, a fillet of a huge primitive fish, served with fried manioc and vegetables. Exotic fruit juices are sold on the street corners, as are ice creams that are flavored with mango, papaya, *granadilla* (passion fruit), guanabana, and many other fruits.

You can take a taxi or simply walk down from the main plaza to the picturesque waterfront district of **Belén**, to the southeast of the town, where the houses float on rafts in the water. A Venetian-style labyrinth of canals, canoes, and stores, Belén is the center for an incredible variety of Amazon products: exotic fruits, fish, turtles, edible frogs, herbal medicines, and waterfowl. Plowing the waterways are a plethora of small canoe-taxis paddled by *iquiteños*, some as young as five years old. A canoe tour of one of the most unusual waterfronts in the world costs just a few dollars.

Some 15 km (9 miles) south of the city is the beautiful **Lago Quistaocha**, set in lush tropical jungle, which can be reached by bus. There is a small zoo, the Parque Zoológico de Quistaocha (closed Monday; entrance charge), where

Map
on pages
168–9

BELOW: paddling near the Belén market, Iquitos.

jaguars, ocelots, parrots, and anacondas can be seen, as well as the giant paiche fish – the one that features in the local dish – which are bred here in hatcheries.

Jungle lodges

The delicious paiche fish grows to a length of 2 meters (6 ft) and can weigh more than 80 kilos (176 lbs).

Iquitos has long been a center for excursions into the surrounding jungle. It should be remembered, however, that because there are a lot of people in this area, and the Amazon here is a main waterway, you must travel well beyond a 60-km (37-mile) radius of the city to see wildlife such as caiman, monkeys, macaws, or pink dolphins – in fact, the latter are found only on remote tributaries of the upper Amazon and Orinoco rivers.

A good way to become acquainted quickly with the jungle is to visit one of a number of lodges that have been set up on nearby rivers. Although many of the two- or three-day lodge tours can be booked through a travel agent in Lima, they are much cheaper if arranged in Iquitos. Avoid the numerous individuals in the airport and the city trying to set up a "jungle lodge tour." Since these men are paid on a commission basis, you can buy the same package deal more cheaply by simply walking into a lodge's downtown office, most of which are clustered around Jirón Putumayo near the Plaza de Armas *(see page 223 for details of jungle lodges).*

Explorama Tours is one of the largest companies with five different lodges, all of them well-run and efficient. One of the advantages of booking into one of the Explorama lodges is that they also provide access to the canopy walkway at the Amazon Center for Environmental Education and Research. First opened in 1992, it is now around 500 meters (1,640 ft) in length, and reaching a height of up to 37 meters (120 ft) it offers breathtaking views for birdwatching from a

BELOW: shady river transport.

unique perspective. One of the most beautiful sights is that of mixed flocks of birds feeding in the early morning and late afternoon. Sloths, marmosets, and monkeys can also be spotted.

Other lodges in the area offer river trips to the beautiful Río Yarapa, where river dolphins can be seen, and interesting shamanic tours for the more esoterically minded travelers.

Slow boats

A commercial river boat traveling either upriver toward Pucallpa or downriver toward Brazil is a great way to experience the Amazon. Although not much will be seen in the way of wildlife along the way (boats traveling upstream hug the banks, those in the opposite direction travel down the center of the river), the traveler will still see how people live along the Amazon and also enjoy beautiful sunsets and magnificent scenery.

Be warned that life along the Amazon is slow and leisurely – you should never travel by river boat if you are in a hurry or have an inflexible schedule. Boats break down, linger sometimes for days in port, and are generally unpredictable. Even so, it is an unforgettable way to travel, and well recommended. The best place to look for boats in Iquitos is by going down to the docks and asking around, or by visiting one of the river boat offices.

The price for a seven-day trip to Pucallpa will include food (generally rice, meat, and beans cooked in river water – which might prompt you to bring tins and fruits of your own), and deck-space for your hammock (you can buy one in Iquitos for around US$10); you can get a cabin ticket if you want a berth. Traveling to Manaus in Brazil takes around ten days and requires a boat change at

Map on pages 168–9

BELOW: the unpopular piranha.

Map
on pages
168–9

the border. The *Clive, Monteiro,* and *Juliana* all make this journey; they are clean and have reasonable food. There are two operators: Expreso Turístico and Expreso Ucayali. But if you want to make the trip in style the best boats are run by two foreign companies, International Expeditions, and Abercrombie & Kent International. You should make reservations directly with the companies as they cannot be made in Lima or Iquitos.

Another way to see the Amazon, and one highly recommended for those who have a little more time and want to get off the beaten path, is to hire a small boat and guide of your own. In every Amazon port there are boat-owners who are willing to rent you their services at only a fraction of the cost paid at a typical jungle lodge. If you make up a small group, it is even more economical. As with the commercial river boats, the best way to locate a small boat and guide in Iquitos is simply to ask about on the wharves. With a boat, the entire Amazon suddenly opens up for your exploration.

Only 100 km (62 miles) from Iquitos, for example, is the biggest national park in Peru, the 2-million-hectare (5-million-acre) **Reserva Nacional Pacaya-Samiria**, a wildlife-packed lowland jungle area that can only be reached by hiring a boat and a guide, in either Iquitos or the village of Lagunas, and staging your own expedition.

The central jungle

Seven days' travel upriver from Iquitos on the Río Ucayali is **Pucallpa** ⑰, a rapidly growing city of 200,000 that can be reached from Lima by air – there are several flights daily – or on a 24-hour bus journey. Most people arriving in the city prefer to stay at Puerto Callao on the nearby **Lago Yarinacocha**, a 20-minute bus ride from the city, which is the main tourist attraction of the area. Based here are the **Hospital Albert Schweitzer**, which serves the local Amerindians, and the **Summer Institute of Linguistics**, a non-denominational missionary organization studying many of Peru's jungle Amerindian languages with the intention of concocting an alphabet so that the Bible can be translated into these hitherto unwritten languages. The latter organization, which can be visited by appointment only, has attracted a great deal of criticism from those who believe that through its influence indigenous peoples are in danger of losing their own culture and tribal identity.

In Puerto Callao you can visit the fascinating artisanal cooperative **Maroti Shobo**, where high-quality ceramics and weavings made by the Shipibo Amerindians from the surrounding villages are displayed and sold, and are sent to museums all over the world. The Shipibo people have inhabited the area for at least the past 1,000 years, and trips can be arranged to some of their villages. There are a couple of lodges on the lake, and more wildlife than you might expect, considering the nearby population. The lodges will also organize jungle excursions, and private excursions by motor canoe into the surrounding jungle and canals are easy to arrange from Puerto Callao. While traveling on the canals, you may see numerous piranhas, caiman, and the occasional monkey. ❑

BELOW: enjoying a riverside lunch break.
RIGHT: an expert at tree climbing.

MANU TO MALDONADO

*One of the truly pristine areas of the tropics,
a birdwatcher's paradise, can be reached from the
gold-boom town of Maldonado*

Map
on pages
168–9

Lima

The traditional hopping-off point for Peru's little-explored southern jungle is the city of Cusco *(see map on pages 230–1)*, where a variety of tours is available, along with a wealth of information on some of the national parks in the southern region, but the area has been included in this section of the book to offer continuity to readers who are interested in all aspects of travel in the Peruvian Amazon.

The adventurous traveler can go from Cusco by rail and truck to **Quillabamba** and **Kiteni** and from there hire a boat through the **Pongo de Manique**, a narrow gorge surrounded by lush jungle and waterfalls on the upper **Río Urubamba**, a journey described in Peter Matthiesson's 1962 classic, *Cloud Forest*. It must be emphasized that transport is infrequent in this area, and you should be extremely flexible. There is a government air service that operates from the mission town of **Sepahua** (lower down on the Urubamba) to Pucallpa and then to Lima, but the flights are extremely unreliable. If you are highly adventurous and self-sufficient – only very basic food is available – you may find a boat to take you all the way to Pucallpa.

LEFT: red, green, and scarlet macaws.
BELOW: jabirú storks, Manu National Park.

Parque Nacional Manu

Also accessible from Cusco is what has been called the most bio-diverse rainforest park in the world, located in Peru's southernmost jungle department of **Madre de Dios**. At 1.8 million hectares (4½ million acres), the **Parque Nacional Manu** , one of the few truly pristine regions of the tropics, is perhaps the best area in the Amazon rainforest for watching wildlife. In many other jungle areas, because of the proximity of humans, you may be lucky to see anything other than birds, insects, or an occasional large animal, but in Manu you will see so many monkeys (there are 13 different species) that you may grow tired of them. Besides an abundance of turtles, you'll have a great opportunity to see giant otters, peccaries, capybaras, tapirs, and even the occasional jaguar.

Manu is also an unparalleled place for birdwatching. Founded in 1973, the park was declared a Biosphere Reserve in 1977, and a World Natural Heritage Site ten years later. It harbors over 1,000 species of bird – 300 more species than are found in the United States and Canada combined. The world record for the number of species seen and heard in one day was set in Manu in 1982, when 331 species were recorded in just a few square miles of forest.

The only lodge located in the Reserve Zone is **Manu Lodge** *(see page 223)*, which overlooks a tranquil rainforest lagoon, and its expanding trail system provides access to seasonally flooded forest, high-ground forest, and patches of bamboo. There are also experienced guides to help visitors find shy bird species. Large, rare game-birds such as razor-billed curassows and piping-guans have been hunted out of most areas, but are easy to see at Manu Lodge. Also seen are macaws, pale-winged trumpeters, the tall jabiru storks, roseate spoonbills, and five species of large eagle including the majestic harpy eagle. New species are continually being discovered. The extremely rare rufous-fronted ant-thrush, for example, was previously known from only one location but has now also been found at Manu Lodge.

By far the easiest way to visit Manu is with one of the local tour operators such as **Manu Nature Tours** or **Expediciones Manu** *(see page 223)*, since all preparations for the trip must be made in advance and permits are required for entry into the reserve (although you don't need a permit for the Cultural Zone). The tour operator arranges all permits, transport, equipment, gasoline, and food supplies for the trip. It can take two days to reach this isolated area by traveling overland from Cusco, down through the cloudforest and later transferring to a boat – an unforgettable experience. There is also the option of chartering a small plane, which can fly to the junction of the Madre de Dios and Manu rivers. This is much more expensive, but a good idea if your time is limited. Prices depend on the number of passengers.

Reserva Nacional Tambopata Candamo

There are yet more chances to see birds in the second-largest reserve: the **Reserva Nacional Tambopata Candamo**. Created by the Peruvian Government in 1989, this 1.5 million-hectare (3.8 million-acre) zone has been set up both as an extractive reserve (for rubber, Brazil nuts, and other products) and for

A non-profit group dedicated to preserving these virgin forests is Pronaturaleza, Av. Los Rosales 255, San Isidro, Lima. E-mail: fpcn@mail. cosapidata.com.pe.

BELOW: beware of the poison-dart frog.

eco-tourism. The reserve encompasses the entire watershed of the **Río Tambopata**, one of the most beautiful and least-disturbed areas in Peru. The river begins high in the Andean department of Puno; several tour companies lead kayak expeditions down the Tambopata, which offers a spectacular transition from the Andes to the low jungle. The reserve protects the largest macaw lick in South America, the Colpa de Guacamayos. Here birdwatchers can view one of the world's phenomenal avian spectacles, as hundreds of red, blue, and green parrots and macaws gather at the lick daily. Squawking raucously, they wheel through the air before landing together on the river bank to eat clay. This breathtaking display can only be seen where there is undisturbed rainforest with healthy populations of wild macaws, as in southeast Peru.

Trails around the macaw lick offer birding in both floodplain and high ground forest. Orinoco geese and large horned screamers can also be seen along clear streams near the Andean foothills. Comfortable accommodation is provided at the macaw lick by **Tambopata Research Center Lodge**, run by Rainforest Tours. The only lodge in the uninhabited area of the reserve, it is about six hours from Puerto Maldonado in a speedboat, but twice that in one of the river boats known locally as *pequepeques*. Rainforest Expeditions, in conjunction with the Ese'ejas community, also runs Posada Amazonas, near Lago Chinbadas, where giant river otters and harpy eagles can be seen, and where mammals such as peccaries, tapirs, and a rodent known as a pacarana congregate at a nocturnal salt lick.

Also in the Tambopata Reserve is the **Explorers' Inn** lodge, around which some 500 bird species can be seen. These include quetzals, manakins, and many antbirds. The lodge trails also provide good access to patches of

Map on pages 168–9

A wise old owl.

BELOW: scanning the sky for rare birds.

Map
on pages
168–9

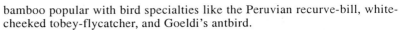

TIP

If you are on a low budget and can't afford the packages offered by the lodges, try staying with a local family. Arrangements can be made with contacts at Puerto Maldonado airport.

BELOW: birdlife photographers.

bamboo popular with bird specialties like the Peruvian recurve-bill, white-cheeked tobey-flycatcher, and Goeldi's antbird.

The forests of southeast Peru offer the finest birdwatching experience. However, identifying all the different species, and finding elusive birds in the forest undergrowth, can prove overwhelming for an ornithologist inexperienced in tropical forests, which is why an expert guide familiar with the rainforest and its birdlife is invaluable. Such birdwatching tours also help to support many local families, who will conserve rainforest birds as if their livelihoods depend on it. Local people won't hunt macaws for trade or feathers if they can make more money by taking visitors to see the birds at clay licks. By choosing such tours, visitors can make a positive conservation impact while enjoying the spectacular birdlife. However, the birds can't survive without the pristine rainforests in which they live, and conservation organizations and indigenous peoples are joining the battle to preserve them.

Boom town of the south

From Cusco you can reach **Puerto Maldonado** ⓳, the capital of the Peruvian department of Madre de Dios, either by air or along the 500-km (310-mile) road, a trip that takes two and a half days; it's a bit uncomfortable, but worth it for the scenery. Long cut off from the rest of the world both by rapids on the **Río Madeira** and by the Andes, Puerto Maldonado, a thriving rubber town at the turn of the 20th century, lapsed into anonymity again until the discovery of gold in the 1970s and the building of an airport in the early 1980s turned the city into a gold-rush boom town.

Set on a bluff overlooking the Madre de Dios and Tambopata rivers, Puerto Maldonado has a pleasant **Plaza de Armas**, and numerous hotels for miners on brief trips to town, but not much to see or do. In 1897 the rubber baron Carlos Fitzcarraldo traveled through here after having dragged his steamship, with the help of hundreds of Amerindians, over the Fitzcarraldo pass and down the Manu and Madre de Dios rivers on his way to Iquitos via Brazil *(see page 213)*. You can make an excursion, about half an hour from the city, to the site where locals will tell you Fitzcarraldo's steamship is located, beached a little way inland. Actually, this isn't his boat at all; it is the remains of a German hospital ship which plowed the Madre de Dios.

Buy a bag or two of Brazil nuts while you're here. These rich, abundant, and inexpensive nuts will help encourage the preservation of Madre de Dios' rainforest, where 30 percent of the population is involved in nut extraction.

Only an hour south of Puerto Maldonado is **Lago Sandoval**, a beautiful jungle lake that can be reached by boat from Puerto Maldonado's port. Three hours farther downriver, and well worth an overnight fishing expedition, is **Lago Valencia**, which is quite remote and relatively free of tourists. A several-day expedition can be mounted to the 100,000-hectare (250,000-acre) **Reserva Nacional Pampas de Río Heath**, a wild area of plains and swamps located on the Río Heath bordering Bolivia. ❏

Jungle Lodges

Jungle lodges are the usual form of accommodations in the Amazon, and bookings can be arranged in Lima before you start your trip, or in Cusco or Iquitos.

There are various tour companies, some of whom run their own lodges, who will make the arrangements for you. In Iquitos, Explorama Tours (Av. La Marina 340, tel: 252 526 or 252 530; fax: 252 533; email: amazon@explorama.com), one of the largest and most reliable companies, has three lodges, all well-run and efficient: Explorama Inn, 40 km (25 miles) from Iquitos, has comfortable bungalows, hot water, good food, and attractive jungle walks. Explorama Lodge, 60 km (40 miles) from Iquitos at Yanamono, is a little more basic: there's no hot water or electricity, but it's perfectly adequate and runs good jungle hikes. The third lodge is the Explornapo, 140 km (90 miles) from Iquitos on the Río Napo, the most rustic of all, but facilities are good and you get a chance to explore primary forest, plus access to the canopy walkway at the Amazon Center for Environmental Education and Research.

Among other northern jungle lodges is the Anaconda Lara Lodge (Fenix Viajes, Pevas 210, tel: 239 147 or 233 430; fax 232 978). Some 40 km (25 miles), upstream from Iquitos on the Río Momón, it offers trips to the beautiful Río Yarapa where river dolphins can be seen. Amazon Camp Tourist Service (Requena 336, tel: 23 3931; fax: 231 265) runs a lodge on the Río Momón and organizes river cruises.

There are numerous lodges in the southern jungle, including three in the Cultural Zone of Parque Nacional Manu, for which you don't need a permit. These are the Manu Cloud Forest Lodge, near the Río Unin; the Amazon Lodge at Río Alto Madre de Dios; and the Albergue Pantiacolla Lodge. The only accommodation in the Manu Reserve Zone is the comfortable Manu Lodge. Overlooking a rainforest lagoon, it has both an expanding trail system and experienced (English-speaking) guides to help you spot the rarer bird species.

There are two very good agencies in Cusco who will organize trips to the Manu lodges:

the first is Manu Nature Tours (Av. Pardo 1046; tel: 252 721; fax: 234 793; information office: Plaza de Armas Portal Comercio 137, tel: 252 536), which also runs all-inclusive tours to Colpa Lodge, on the Río Tambopata, where macaws can be watched close up. The other is Expediciones Manu (Av Pardo 895; tel: 226 671; email: manuexpe@amauta.rcp.net.pe), run by English ornithologist Barry Walker. He specializes in camping trips but will organize visits to most of the above lodges.

The best-known lodge in the Reserva Nacional Tambopata Candamo is Explorers' Inn (Plateros 365, Cusco, tel: 23 5342; website: www.peruviansafaris.com), 60 km (38 miles) from Maldonado. Many new lodges have opened in Tambopata: Rainforest Expeditions (Av Arambaru 166, 4B, Miraflores, Lima; tel: 421 8347), and the Ese'ejas community run Posada Amazonas *(see page 221)*. Cusco Amazónico Lodge (Julio C. Tello C13, Urb Santa Monica; tel: 245 314) and Tambopata Jungle Lodge (Pardo 705, tel: 22 5701) offer good service and reasonably priced packages. ❑

RIGHT: afternoon tea at Manu Lodge.

BIRDS OF THE AMAZON

For the keen amateur ornithologist, seeking out some of Peru's exotic birds may turn out to be the experience of a lifetime

Nowhere in the world is there such a plethora of birdlife as in the Amazon rainforest. The Parque Nacional Manu alone is home to over 1,000 different species. Their names are often as exotic as their appearance: from golden-headed quetzals to yellow-rumped caciques, roseate spoonbills to pale-winged trumpeters, they represent a birdwatcher's dream. Who wouldn't think their trip worthwhile if they spotted a paradise tanager, known as the *siete colores* because of its seven-colored plumage? Or a jabirú stork, one of the largest flying birds in the Americas, up to 1.4 meters (4½ ft) in length?

VARIOUS FEATHERS FLOCK TOGETHER

Many species fly in mixed flocks: insectivorous birds, such as woodcreepers and antbirds, will flock together, sometimes as many as 100 of them traveling in a great cloud. This makes individuals difficult to distinguish on first sighting, but they tend to stick to the same feeding areas so, if you identify their territory, you will have a great opportunity to spot a variety of species together.

The same applies to the mixed flocks of fruit-eaters, which include tanagers, fruitcrows, and parrots. Once you identify a food source you have an excellent chance of seeing a large number of birds. Not that rainforest birds are always easy for the uninitiated to spot, which is why an experienced guide is invaluable, and one usually accompanies visitors on organized tours.

The oxbow lakes of the Amazon are the habitat of herons, hoatzins, egrets, and wattled jacanas, species not difficult to spot as they forage for food on the shores. Raptors, flying high above the canopy, can present more of a problem, but the harpy eagle and the crested eagle, among other majestic creatures, can be spotted from vantage points at clearings or on riverbanks.

▷ **HOATZINS**
These can manage only short, clumsy flights. They form mating groups, and share the rearing of their offspring. The young have clawed wing bends, to help them clamber about in trees.

△ **BLACK-NECKED RED COTINGA**
A solitary and elusive bird, the cotinga belongs to the same family *(cotingidae)* as the cock-of-the-rock and the fruit crow. It feeds on fruit and insects, which it finds in the treetops.

◁ **RUFESCENT TIGER HERON**
These elegant, reddish-colored birds are frequently spotted in and around the lakes and streams of Parque Nacional Manu. They can also be spotted flying over clearings.

STAMPING OUT THE BIRD TRADE

One of the most spectacular sights in the Peruvian Amazon is that of macaws gathered at the huge salt licks in the Reserva Nacional Tambopata Candamo. But some people still regard exotic birds as interesting pets, and the macaws and parrots that inhabit the same part of the rainforest can be trapped, exported, and sold on the international market.

Although the Convention on Trade in Endangered Species (CITES), signed in Washington DC in 1972, protects the species that are most under threat, it is not strictly adhered to, and doesn't affect birds whose numbers are high. The influx of tourists has helped to create an alternative source of revenue, making the trade less economically attractive to local trappers.

◁ **YELLOW-RIDGED TOUCAN**
These gregarious birds usually fly in pairs. Their bills may be one-third of the total length.

▷ **WIRE-TAILED MANAKIN**
This manakin has a long filament in the tail which the male uses to strike his partner during the courtship ritual.

◁ **WATTLED JACANA**
Foraging at the edge of an oxbow lake in Parque Nacional Manu, the wattled jacana is unusual in that the female takes more than one mate, lays several clutches of eggs, and leaves the males to rear the young.

SOUTHERN PERU

The cryptic Nazca lines attract many people to the southern coast.
For others, wildlife, sandsurfing, and Afro-Peruvian music
have an appeal that isn't at all mysterious

Map
on pages
230–1

Peru's southern desert coast, although inhospitable at first glance, is a historical and geographical encyclopedia of a handful of highly developed pre-Inca cultures known for their masterful pottery, fine weaving, and medical advances, and for the enormous and mysterious drawings they left on the desert plain at Nazca.

The south coast is also where ancient indigenous peoples proved once again that they could at least adapt to the harsh physical reality of their environment even if they could not tame it. This time it was not the imposing Andean mountain chain that separated the different tribes, made agriculture difficult, and left the people subject to the subtle changes in climate. Rather it was the parched and desolate desert, often compared to the deserts of North Africa, that proved to be the obstacle.

Captivating women

Starting your southward journey from **Lima ❶**, the first place of any interest you will come to is **Pachacamac**, some 32 km (20 miles) south of the capital and normally visited on a day trip from the city. Although the more recent Inca culture has overshadowed much of the earlier development of this site, the artisan work left by the pre-Inca civilizations proves that they were more sophisticated in terms of both ceramics and textiles. The ruins of the original settlement occupy a vast site on a low sand-hill overlooking the ocean. There is also a reconstruction of the Inca Templo de las Vírgenes (House of the Chosen Women), also known as *mamaconas*.

Heading south for another 35 km (22 miles) you will come to **Pucusana ❷**. This coastal resort town, very popular with *limeños*, is also a charming fishing village with panoramic views from its cliffs and good seafood in several of its restaurants. During the Peruvian summer, from January to April, the beaches at Pucusana, La Isla, Las Ninfas, and Naplo can get crowded on weekends. If you want peace and quiet, go on a weekday, when Pucusana reverts to being a fishing town and vacationers are fewer. Also, local fishermen ferry passengers around the island in the bay, and to other beaches, so you may be able to negotiate a ride to one of the more isolated stretches of sand, such as Naplo, first arranging to be picked up later in the day.

You may want to take a trip past the **Boquerón del Diablo**, literally the Devil's Big Mouth, which is a tunnel carved in the rock. If you decide to tempt fate by entering the tunnel either on foot or in a boat, do not be surprised if the astonishing din, described as "the groans of a thousand devils," makes you wonder if you will ever come out alive.

PRECEDING PAGES:
the barren coastal
desert.
LEFT: sea lions on
the Islas Ballestas.
BELOW: the Nazca
lines, seen from
the air.

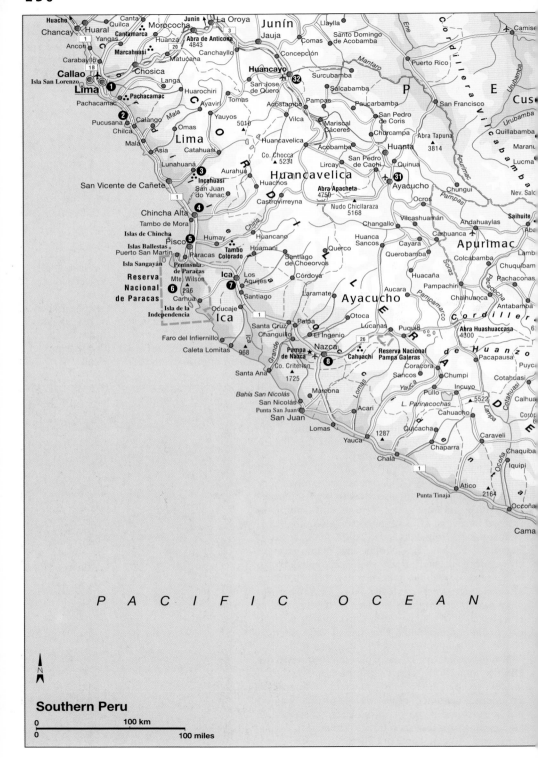

Southern Peru

0   100 km

0   100 miles

TIP

If you want to try river-running on the Río Cañete you must organize it in advance in Lima. The trips are suitable for novices.

Some 75 km (47 miles) down the coast is Cañete, from where a road goes inland to **Lunahuaná** ❸, a pretty village that has begun to attract *limeños* and foreign visitors. The village is set in a wine growing valley; there are a couple of wineries that can be visited, and a wine festival – the *Fiesta de la Vendimia* – in March. The Incawasi ruins lie just outside the village, and river-rafting trips on the Río Cañete during the rainy season have become popular.

Back on the coast, about 55 km (34 miles) south of Cañete, lies **Chincha** ❹, a city known for wine, fine-quality cotton, excellent athletes, and ferocious fighting cocks. Its name may be derived from *chinchay* – the Yauyo Amerindians' word for feline – although when the Spanish named it in 1571 it was more pompously called Pueblo Alto de Santo Domingo. Grapes and cotton flourish here, thanks to an elaborate system of irrigation and the re-routing of the Cochas River.

The city's fairly modern coliseum pays tribute to the long sporting tradition here. Chincha has turned out a number of the country's sports stars, principally in the fields of soccer (football) and boxing. The great Peruvian boxer Mauro Mina came from Chincha, and defeated a number of North Americans, including Floyd Patterson, before a detached retina prevented him from going for the middleweight world title. Another distinguished Chincha athlete, Fernando Acevedo, was a Pan-American running champion in 100- and 200-meter events. His nickname was "The Harpoon of Chincha."

This town is home to much of Peru's black population, descendants of slaves brought here to work on coastal plantations. As such, it is the center for Afro-Peruvian dances, including the energetic and amusing *El Alcatraz* in which a gyrating male dancer with a lighted candle in his hand attempts to ignite the cloth tail hanging from his partner's brightly colored skirt. Many of these dances

BELOW: the Plaza de Chincha in Ica.

are accompanied by rhythms supplied by the *cajón*, which is simply a hollow box pounded by open-palmed drummers to produce a reverberating rhythm. The *Fiesta Negra* in February and *Fiestas Patrias* in late July are the best and most atmospheric times to see and hear Afro-Peruvian music.

Map on pages 230–1

Pisco

Continuing south on the Panamericana you come to **Pisco ❺**, a port city that gave its name to the clear white-grape alcohol that is Peru's national drink, and is used to make the cocktail called a *pisco sour* which consists of *pisco*, lemon juice, egg white, and sugar syrup, whipped and served with a dash of Angostura bitters. The invention of *pisco* is believed to have been a mistake made by the Spaniards when they were introducing grapes and wine production into the dry coastal area of the New World. But it seems that once they tried this smooth yet potent version of brandy they decided it had merit of its own – and many Peruvians have gone on thinking so ever since.

The city of Pisco (pop: 90,000) joined the bandwagon when revolutionary fever overtook the continent in the early 1800s. Half a block from the town's **Plaza de Armas** is the **Club Social Pisco**, used as the headquarters for liberation leader General José de San Martín while he was fighting the Spaniards. A statue to this Argentinian hero of the Independence War is found on the main plaza. Originally, Pisco stood on another spot not far away, but an earthquake in 1687 and subsequent pirate attacks badly damaged many of the structures in the city, prompting the viceroy, Count de la Monclova, to order it to be moved to a safer spot. Construction of the opulent baroque **Catedral** started shortly afterwards, and was only completed in 1723.

There's not a lot to do in Pisco itself, but it makes an ideal base for visits to the Paracas Peninsula National Reserve and the Islas Ballestas *(see page 235)*. There are a couple of tour agencies in town around the Plaza where these can be arranged. There are also a number of hotels in Pisco and a few reasonable restaurants.

Pisco's small military airport serves as the emergency landing strip when heavy fog prevents planes from descending in Lima; passengers are then bussed to the capital or have to wait until the weather clears before completing their journey. From 1960 to 1970, small propeller planes of the foreign-owned Consorcio Ballenero buzzed the waters offshore in a now defunct project to locate and count groups of whales that regularly visit this coast.

Then, in late 1988, Peruvian scientists, in conjunction with experts from the Natural History Museum at the Smithsonian Institution in the United States, announced the appearance of a new whale species. One of these mammals, named the Mesoplodon Peruvianus, was inadvertently picked up by fishermen working the waters between Pucusana and Pisco. The 4 meter- (13 ft-) long sea mammal is one of the smallest members of the whale family.

Peru's Galápagos

Some 15 km (9 miles) down the coast lie the bay and peninsula of Paracas which, together with the Islas

BELOW: taking the donkey for a drink.

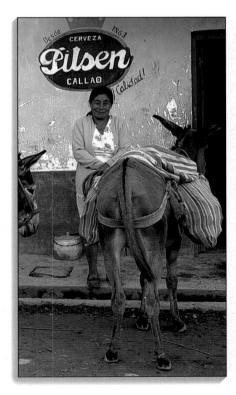

Ballestas, comprise the **Reserva Nacional de Paracas ❻**. The area, named after the Paracas winds – blustery sand storms that sweep the coast – has a wide variety of sea mammals and exotic birds, among them the red-and-white flamingos that allegedly inspired General San Martín to design the red-and-white independence flag for the newly liberated country. A monument marks the spot where San Martín set foot in Peru on September 8, 1820, after liberating Argentina. (A law passed by the National Congress has made September 9 a provincial holiday.)

Not long after San Martín's arrival, a shipload of British troops under the command of Lord Cochrane dropped anchor in the same bay and headed to shore to help him plan his strategy against the Spanish. The British motivation was not to liberate a struggling people from their colonial masters, but to break Spain's monopoly on trade in the region.

The beach here is lovely, although craggy for swimming, and the waters contain jellyfish – some of them enormous and with a very unpleasant sting. There are a number of good jellyfish-free beaches around the isthmus: La Mina, Mendieta, La Catedral, and Atenas, the latter very popular for windsurfing. The famous **Candelabro**, a candelabra-shaped drawing scratched onto the highest point of a cliffside overlooking the bay, can be seen from the beach, although it is best viewed from a boat. Some scientists link the drawing to the Southern Cross constellation; others say it is actually a stylized drawing of a cactus – a symbol of power from the Chavín culture, which flourished farther north but whose influence has been found at great distances from its seat of power. The magic associated with the cactus is related to both its hallucinogenic powers and its use by high priests in ancient indigenous cultures.

The Humboldt penguin is one of the few species that lives far from the cold Austral southern zone. There are about 1,500 of them in and around Paracas.

BELOW: colonial church in Pisco.

Map on pages 230–1

A visit to the **Islas Ballestas** is highly recommended, and should be organized in Pisco, as you have to go with a tour group. Most of the trips start off quite early in the morning. You can arrange a trip from the Hotel Paracas, on the bay itself, but it will be more expensive. For reasons of conservation visitors are not allowed to land on the island, but boats will take you close enough for a good view of the wildlife. Here sea lions, seals, penguins, guano-producing birds, and turtles rarely found at this latitude converge before photo-taking tourists. Dozens of bird species thrive here, among them albatrosses, pelicans, boobies, cormorants, and seagulls. Also worth a visit in a fishing-boat or launch is **Punta Pejerrey**, nearly at the northernmost point of the isthmus and the best spot for seeing the Candelabro. During the 19th century, this region was important for its guano – mineral-rich bird-droppings used as fertilizer in Europe – and guano collection still continues today, though on a smaller scale.

On the exact opposite side of the isthmus is **Punta Arquillo** and the *Mirador de Los Lobos*, or sea-lion lookout point. This rough and rocky place can be reached by an hour's trek on foot, but take care, because the sun is very strong. It is far better to go by car, and if you are with a tour group transport may be provided. Looking down on the sea lion refuge you will find yourself almost face to face with a congregation of noisy sea mammals.

On lucky days, a look skyward is rewarded by the sight of a pair of condors soaring above. These majestic birds sweep down on sea lion carcasses, looking particularly for the seal's afterbirth during the breeding season, then use the intense coastal winds to wing themselves up to the high altitudes they normally frequent. So well-known was the birds' presence at Paracas that, when the nature reserve was being named, one scientist pushed for the name Parque Nacional de los Condores (Condor National Park), but was unsuccessful.

Extensive exploration of the peninsula is best done with the help of a guide, as paths are not clearly marked and it is easy to become lost. In June and August, Paracas is foggy – a reaction to the heat and extremely sparse precipitation combined with the water-laden ocean winds that caress the coast. A meteorological office here recorded only 36.7 mm (1½ inches) of precipitation during a 20-year period, although the effects of the particularly harsh 1998 El Niño brought heavy rain to the area, and turned the desert green for a while.

Desert burial grounds

Paracas is the name not only of the area but also of the ancient Amerindian civilization founded here over 3,000 years ago, a pre-Columbian (and pre-Inca) culture that was uncovered in 1925 when Peruvian archeologist Julio C. Tello found burial sites under the dunes. The sand and the extreme dryness of the desert protected the finely woven textiles around and inside the funeral bundles, which were buried when the Paracas culture thrived from 1300 BC to AD 200. The best examples of textiles and funeral bundles, and information about how the burial pits were arranged, can be found in several museums in Lima. Recommended are the Museo de la Nación, the Museo Nacional de Antropología y

BELOW: the famous Candelabro in the Paracas desert.

San Martín, who created the Peruvian flag, had his headquarters in Pisco.

Arqueología in Pueblo Libre, and the private Museo Amano collection of textiles in Miraflores, and also the Museo Regional in Ica. The **Museo Julio C. Tello** (opening times vary – check with tour agencies; entrance charge), near the necropolis on the isthmus joining the Paracas peninsula to the mainland, has exhibits of artifacts discovered during the archeological dig, and although much of the collection was lost in a robbery it is well worth a visit.

The discovery of hundreds of so-called "funeral fards" – or burial cocoons – gave anthropologists and archeologists yet another small insight into this civilization. The fine weavings in both cotton and wool, with intricate and highly detailed embroidered designs, still astound modern-day textile experts, particularly those who are interested in how the Amerindians were able to develop permanent dyes with such brilliant tones.

The elaborately wrapped funeral bundles show that the Paracas culture performed skull trepanation, crude "brain surgery" designed to treat fractures and tumors, common injuries among a people whose battles were fought using stone-headed clubs and slingshots. The Paracas also practiced the intentional deformation or molding of infants' skulls for esthetic reasons. The results, akin to a conehead shape, were not only considered attractive but also clearly identified an individual's clan, since the molding differed significantly from tribe to tribe.

Heading some 48 km (30 miles) inland from Pisco you will come to remains dating from another culture: **Tambo Colorado**. This adobe settlement, called *colorado* (colored) because of the red paint on many of the walls, is among the best Inca ruins on Peru's southern coast. Among the buildings still standing at this complex is one that is believed to have been a temple.

BELOW:
a *bodega* near Ica.

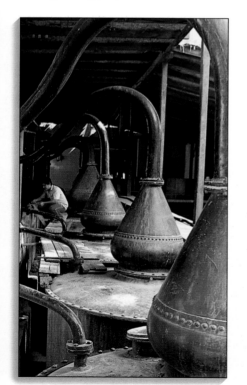

Treading the grapes

About 80 km (50 miles) farther south along the coast is **Ica ❼**, a bustling oasis amid one of the continent's driest deserts, and Peru's richest wine-growing region. Ica was hit quite badly by the El Niño flooding in 1998, but thanks to rapid clean-up and reconstruction work life got back to normal fairly fast. Vineyards and wineries can be explored all year round, but there is most to see during the grape harvest, from February to early April. The **Bodega El Carmelo** *pisco* distillery, open to the public, has an ancient grape press made from a tree trunk. Tours (in Spanish) can be taken at the **Vista Alegre** wine and *pisco* distillery in Ica, and there is a good shop. Peruvian wines tend to be very sweet, although the best ones, Ocucaje and Tacama, and Tabernero, are finer and drier. It is difficult to arrange to visit these vineyards, which are some distance from town, but the wines can be bought all over the country.

Every March, the city goes all out with its annual wine festival, featuring grape-treading beauty queens and a flow of home-made wine that the locals swear is better than anything available for sale. The week-long event, called the *Fiesta Internacional de la Vendimia*, is punctuated by sports contests, cock fights, music, drinking, religious ceremonies, and general merrymaking.

The wine festival is accompanied by an abundance of dancing, including the energetic *yunza*. Hatchet-carrying men and skirt-flouncing women dance around a tree, drinking the wine derived from newly fermented grapes and stopping at intervals to take swings at the unlucky tree. The dance continues until the tree falls; the couple responsible for the felling are promised a year of good luck. In addition, if the woman is unmarried, she can expect to find a partner soon.

Although the festival is the most riotous time of year to investigate the area's wine heritage, it is also a tricky time for accommodations. There are a number of reasonably priced hotels in town, offering quite good accommodations, but they fill up fast at *fiesta* time, and the rates tend to rise steeply as well. The same accommodations problem arises during the week-long celebration of the town's foundation in mid-June, and at the festival of El Señor de Luren, on Maundy Thursday, when all-night processions take place in which an image of the crucified Christ is paraded around the city. A second procession in honor of the city's patron saint takes place on the third Monday in October.

The statue is believed to have arrived in Ica more than four centuries ago, carried to shore on a wave, then transported to the town. Records from the San Francisco monastery in Lima show that the image was purchased by a friar in 1570. A storm at sea, and the fear that the ship in which the statue was being transported would sink, apparently prompted the ship's captain to toss much of the cargo – including the wooden box containing the statue – overboard. Religious Ica residents took the icon's intact arrival as a miracle.

Disasters and revolutions

Although Ica was founded by the Spanish in 1536, European attempts to control the city were constantly fraught with problems. The city residents resisted the Spanish presence, and Ica was never granted a coat of arms, owing to its

Map on pages 230–1

BELOW: penguins on the Islas Ballestas.

Detail of a Paracas necropolis textile.

repudiation of attempts to make it a colonial center. Local residents remain proud of that rebellious image. The town has also suffered natural disasters: strong earth tremors caused damage in 1568 and 1571, and a devastating earthquake in 1664 completely leveled it, leaving 500 people dead – a phenomenal toll in those days.

Almost 300 years later, in 1963, floods seriously damaged much of the town, which explains why most of its colonial buildings have been replaced by more modern structures. Still, the city center retains its square-block layout, based on a chessboard design.

Churches worth visiting are **La Merced**, just off the Plaza de Armas, with its delicately carved wooden altars; **San Francisco** (on the corner of Municipalidad and San Martín) with some admirable stained-glass windows; and, to the southeast of the town, the church of **El Señor de Luren**, home of the image that arrived by sea. Competing with the Christian importance of Ica is the city's widespread reputation for witchcraft, for which it is well-known across the country.

One of the city's most famous sons was José de la Torre Ugarte, author of Peru's national anthem. He was born in Ica in 1786 and served as a local judge until he joined the revolutionary troops under General San Martín. After Peru's independence, he turned to politics but found an even more dangerous line of work than being a freedom fighter: in a power struggle between factions in the congress, he was condemned to death. When spared by the colonel commissioned to execute him, Torre Ugarte returned to a career in law.

BELOW: Laguna de Huacachina, an oasis resort.

The first civilian president of Peru was also from Ica, although Domingo Elass's tenure in office was short-lived owing to political upheaval in the newly

independent country. His attempt in 1854 to start a revolution of his own failed, although he was initially able to take control of Arequipa before fleeing to exile in Chile.

Knotted strings

Today, just a 20-minute walk or a short bus ride from Ica's center, this region's role in the revolution is traced in a room at the **Museo Regional** (Av. Ayabaca block 8; open Mon–Fri 9am–6pm, Sat 8.30am–6.30pm, Sun 9am–1pm; entrance charge), one of Peru's most interesting small regional museums. But even more interesting are exhibits of mummies, ceramics, and skulls from the Paracas, Nazca, and Inca cultures. On display are a number of *quipus* (also spelled *kipus*), the mysterious knotted strings believed to have been used to keep calculations, records, and historical notes for the Incas, who had no system of writing.

Since only selected members of the Inca civilization were permitted to "read" the *quipus*, the meaning of these knotted strings has been lost in intervening centuries, although some experts maintain that they were a sophisticated accounting system in which colored strings represented commodities and knots showed quantities. It is thought that the *quipus* may have been crucial in keeping food inventories in the Inca empire.

The regional museum also has an excellent collection of Paracas textiles and feather weavings. And most visitors find their curiosity piqued by the rehydrated mummy hand on exhibition – a must for those who think they have seen everything. Placed in a saline solution after being buried for centuries on the desert coast, this hand was part of an experiment by scientists who hoped that rehydration would provide medical information about the deceased individual.

Map on pages 230–1

BELOW: Nazca's desert hummingbird.

On the **Plaza de Armas** is the **Museo Cabrera** (Bolívar 178; closed Sunday; entrance charge), intriguing for the number (over 10,000) and variety of stones it contains, but the scientific community has pooh-poohed its owner's theories that they come from a technologically advanced Stone Age civilization. Despite this, Dr Javier Cabrera, descendant of one of the city's founders, is a charismatic and amusing man, always happy to have an audience for his theories, and is very good value.

Ica suffered badly from flooding due to heavy rains produced by the ferocious El Niño current in 1998, but the government threw its weight behind emergency salvage and rebuilding work.

Consuls and healers

Outside Ica is **Las Dunas**, a full-scale resort and the most luxurious hotel complex of the area. With a restaurant, swimming pool, sand surfing, horses to hire for riding, and its own airstrip for flights over Nazca, this hotel regularly attracts diplomats and was featured in the US television series "Lifestyles of the Rich and Famous." It is said that some foreign diplomats make annual pilgrimages to Ica, staying at Las Dunas and consulting with *curanderos* or healers and occult practitioners, but this may be a local myth.

Las Dunas was in the forefront of the sand-surfing frenzy that recently overtook this dune-covered coastal area. Principally attracting European sports fans, especially from Italy and France, the hotel has sponsored competitive sand-surfing events on Cerro Blanco – a massive dune some 14 km (8 miles) north of the town of Nazca, purportedly the world's biggest sand dune.

Also on the outskirts of Ica is **Laguna de Huacachina**, a green lagoon of sulfur waters that Peruvians claim has medicinal value. Since Angela Perotti, an Italian living in Ica, began espousing the curative properties of the waters in the 1930s, this spot has become a favorite pilgrimage center for people suffering from rheumatism and skin problems. This peaceful setting just 5 km (3 miles) outside Ica, also draws those just looking for sun, solitude, and sandsurfing beside the palm trees and dunes that ring the lagoon. The Hotel Mossone, a pleasant, colonial-style hotel, is an idyllic place to stay. Next door, the Hotel Salvatierra offers a cheaper alternative.

BELOW: remains of a mummy at Chauchilla.

The Nazca lines

Thanks to irrigation, cotton fields and ribbons of orange trees mark the landscape on the voyage farther south along the coast to **Nazca ❽**, the home of the mysterious lined drawings that have prompted theories ranging from the fanciful to the scientific.

Sixty years ago Nazca was like any other small Peruvian town with no special claim to fame, except that it was necessary to cross one of the world's driest deserts to reach it from Lima. But it is that desert – a sketch-pad for ancient Amerindians – that has since drawn thousands to this sun-bleached colonial town of 30,000 and made the *pampa*, or plain, north of the city one of the greatest scientific mysteries in the New World.

The Nazca lines are a series of drawings of animals, geometrical figures, and birds ranging up to 300 meters (1,000 ft) in size, scratched onto the arid crust of the desert and preserved for about 2,000 years (it is estimated) owing to a complete lack of rain and winds

Map
on pages
230–1

that cleaned – but did not erase – the surface of the *pampa*. The drawings were made by removing surface stones and piling them beside the lighter soil that was revealed beneath.

It wasn't until 1939 that Paul Kosok, a North American scientist flying over the dry coast in a small plane, noticed the lines, then believed to be part of a pre-Inca irrigation system. A specialist in irrigation, he quickly concluded that this had nothing to do with water systems. By chance, the day of the flight coincided with the summer solstice and, making a second pass over the area, Kosok discovered that the lines of the sunset ran tandem to the direction of one of the bird drawings. He immediately dubbed the Nazca *pampa* "the biggest astronomy book in the world."

But it was not Kosok but a young German mathematician who became the expert on the lines and put the backwater on the map. Maria Reiche was 35 years old when she met Kosok, serving as his translator at a seminar on the lines. After giving his speech the scientist encouraged her to study the *pampa*, and she dedicated the next half century to the task.

Reiche concluded that the sketches corresponded to the constellations, and thought they were part of an astronomical calendar made by the people of the Nazca culture, and designed to send messages to the gods. She speculated that her favorite drawing, the monkey, was the ancient symbol for the Big Dipper, the constellation that was linked to rain. When rain was overdue – a common thing in this plain – the Nazca people sketched the monkey to remind the gods that the earth was parched.

There are, of course, many people who do not accept Reiche's theories, denying that the ancient people would have drawn something that they themselves could not see. Because the drawings can only be seen from the air, the International Explorers' Club set out in 1975 to prove a theory that the Nazca Amerindians had used balloons. The Explorers' Club made a cloth-and-reed hot-air balloon, the Condor I, and flew it for 60 seconds, reaching an altitude of 100 meters (330 ft). But the flight, 14 minutes shorter than planned, hardly resolved the issue. It simply added another, rather wacky, theory to the many that surround the Nazca lines.

Writing from the planets?

One well-known theory about the lines came in 1968 when Erich von Daniken published his book *Chariots of the Gods*, in which he argued that the *pampa* was part of an extra-terrestrial landing strip – an idea that Reiche discarded impatiently and which has been given little credence by scientists. The book drew thousands of visitors to the lines, but the newcomers set out across the *pampa* in search of the drawings on motorcycles, four-wheel drive vehicles, and even horses – leaving ineradicable marks of their visits. Now it is illegal to walk or drive on the *pampa*, and Reiche used the profits from sales of her book, *Mystery on the Desert*, to pay guards to patrol the plain.

Other theorists say that the lines marked tracks for running competitions; that they were enlarged designs used in weaving and textiles; or that they are actually

BELOW: a spider etched in the sand.

an enormous map of the Tiahuanaco civilization that once flourished near Lake Titicaca. But the idea that the drawings were some kind of message to the gods, appealing to them to send rain, is one that has recently been given backing by new scientific research, and in this barren landscape it is certainly a believable theory. Another idea that has gained a good many sensible adherents is that the lines were walkways linking sacred sites, and were kept clear for many years by the frequent passage of footsteps.

Maria Reiche used to live at the Hotel Nazca Lines (then called the Hotel Turistas) where she gave an hour-long talk on the lines every evening, until increasing age and infirmity made it impossible. Her last trip to the *pampa* was with Phyllis Pitluga, a US astronomer, whose initial computer-based research on the Nazca lines appeared to support their link to the constellations. Other researchers have pointed to the vividly painted Nazca pottery, with its clock-shaped pieces and elaborate solar calendars, as further evidence of close links with the movement of the heavenly bodies. Reiche died in June 1998. Children waving German and Peruvian flags joined the crowds that thronged the streets on the day of her funeral.

Some 20 km (12 miles) north of Nazca, just off the Panamericana, there is a *mirador* (observation tower), although the only lines that can be seen clearly from here are the *arbol* (tree) and the *manos* (hands). The best way to capture the impact of the lines is to fly over them in small propeller planes. Aero Cóndor offers flights from Lima, Ica, and the small airport in Nazca. Lunch and a stop in the archeological museum in downtown Nazca are included in the day-long Lima package, but it is the most expensive of those on offer. Other flights can be taken from Ica or Nazca. The Nazca flight, the cheapest of the options, takes about 30 minutes, and the best time to go is mid-morning. Earlier in the day there is sometimes a haze over the *pampa*; later on, the winds that buffet the plane leave observers more concerned about their stomachs than about the spectacle spread out beneath them.

Unless visitors take the Aero Cóndor flight from Lima, the only way to reach Nazca is by bus. The trip can take up to eight hours from the capital, along the Panamericana, but it's quite an impressive trip through the vast coastal desert. If you are approaching Nazca from the other direction, there are also regular buses from Arequipa and Cusco. For several years there have been discussions about building an international airport at Nazca, but the project has never gone farther than the drawing board.

Red dot in the desert sky

Occasionally, Nazca is deluged with astronomers who find the desert plain an optimal spot for viewing some rare cosmic happenings. On September 23, 1989, the autumn equinox, scientists went to Nazca to view Mars – which appeared as a red light in the desert sky for a 12-hour period. Laden down with telescopes, the astronomers said that the unusual phenomena would not present itself again until 2005.

Although the perplexing Nazca lines are what draw tourists to this area, they are by no means the only thing to see. Some 30 km (18 miles) from Nazca is the

BELOW: Maria Reiche in old age.

fascinating **Cementerio de Chauchilla** (Chauchilla Cemetery) where sun-whitened bones and skulls, pottery shards, and mummies litter the plain, although some have recently been reburied. The cemetery otherwise remains as it was, in part to avoid further desecration of the area (most of the mummies were unearthed during tomb looting) and in part because there is not sufficient money available to fund proper storage or exhibition of the mummies and grave artifacts. Grave-robbers, or *huaqueros*, are a major nuisance at all the archeological sites in Peru, despite a major crackdown by the authorities *(see page 179).*

Local tours to the cemetery usually also stop at the **Paredones Ruins** in the grounds of the Hacienda Cantalloc beside the **Cantalloc Aqueducts**, an immense and complicated system built by the Incas and still supplying water to irrigate fields nearby, where cotton is grown.

Following the Panamericana

The Panamericana continues down the coast from Nazca to **Camaná** ❾ (about 220 km/135 miles), which has some good beaches and is a popular summer resort for Arequipa residents as well as being the hometown of Peru's chess grand master, Julio Granda Zuñiga. Buses from the town center head to La Punta (about 5 km/3 miles) and the fine, although undeveloped, beach area. Camaná was, in colonial times, the unloading point for cargo headed to Arequipa and then on to the silver mines in Potosí in Bolivia.

From Camaña the highway goes inland, and after about 130 km (80 miles) it divides, going farther inland to Arequipa *(see page 249),* toward Moquegua and Tacna and the Chilean border, or back to the coast to **Mollendo** ❿. Mollendo and its sister resort, Mejía, 15 km (10 miles) farther south, are popular with

Map on pages 230–1

BELOW: a house of reeds near the Panamericana.

upper-class *arequipeños*. Mollendo was a principal port before being replaced by **Matarani**, 14 km (8 miles) to the northwest. Now its attractions are three sandy beaches and its closeness to the **Santuario Nacional Lagunas de Mejía**, a nature reserve that is home to a great variety of coastal birds and the stopping-off place for many migratory species. You can get a bus from the town to the reserve and to the agricultural lands of the Río Tambo valley, where an ambitious irrigation project means that rice and sugar can be grown. Mejía used to be a fishing village, and a few old fishermen's cottages still remain. There are no hotels, but *arequipeños* spend part of the summer in their holiday homes here.

The road from the valley rejoins the Panamericana, which continues south to **Moquegua** ⓫, a parched and dusty town on the banks of the Río Moquegua, at the spot where the Peruvian coastal desert reaches its driest point. Buildings here – even the cathedral – are roofed with sugar-cane stalks daubed with mud. Its streets are cobblestones, and its residents' topiary skills are evident on the **Plaza de Armas** where most of the bushes are trimmed into the form of llamas. Wine and avocados are shipped out of this city, and both are worth sampling.

Peru's southernmost coastal city is **Tacna** ⓬, separated from Chile only by a mined stretch of desert that marks the border between the two nations. The Atacama Desert region from Tacna as far as Antofagasta once belonged to Peru and Bolivia, but the nitrate-rich territory was lost to Chile in 1880 during the War of the Pacific. The treaty of Ancón in 1929 returned the land to Peru, and in the 1980s it was one of the main spots in the country for contraband activity. Government-subsidized milk and medicines were smuggled into Chile, while less expensive clothing and imported cosmetics were brought back into Peru.

Unlike other border cities on the continent, Tacna is fairly well-developed and

BELOW: the Costa de Mollendo.

Map on pages 230–1

has some of Peru's best schools and medical facilities – perhaps owing to its importance as a military base. The downtown area has been refurbished, and its main boulevard is cut by an attractive flower-and-tree-studded promenade. A pedestrian mall passes by the shops, and here ice cream, or cold drinks such as *horchata*, the popular icy cinnamon-laced soy-milk beverage, help offset the intense heat during the Tacna summer. The tree-shaded **Plaza de Armas** is a welcome relief from the unrelenting sun.

The centerpiece of the plaza is the huge arch that was built as a monument to the heroes of the War of the Pacific. The bronze fountain nearby is the work of Gustave Eiffel, who designed the Eiffel Tower. He also designed Tacna's cathedral, with its onyx high altar and interesting stained-glass windows.

The **Museo Ferroviario** (Railway Museum; open Mon–Fri 9am–5.30pm; entrance charge) at the railway station has train engines from the turn of the 20th century when the British began constructing the complicated and, in some cases, rather reckless railway system in Peru. There is also a collection of railway-theme stamps.

Where tourists are targets

If you are in Tacna at all, it will be because you are on your way to or from Chile, and as Latin American border towns go, it's a very pleasant one. Even so, visitors should be on the alert in the train and bus station areas, and in the evening should avoid entirely the street where the bus companies are. Pickpockets and thieves work these areas, and tourists are an easy target. It would be a shame to leave Peru on a bad note. You can cross the border from Tacna to Arica by bus, train, or taxi, although the train service is slow and notoriously unreliable. ❑

A Humboldt penguin crossing the road.

BELOW: a beautiful coastal *mestiza*.

AREQUIPA

Arequipa, the intellectual capital of modern Peru, is a proud and prosperous city with some of the most beautiful colonial architecture in the country

ar from Lima, isolated in a fertile valley tucked between desert and mountains and crowned by turquoise skies, **Arequipa** ⓭ was a key stop on the cargo route linking the abundant silver mines of Bolivia to the coast. Built from the white sillar rock that spewed out from **Volcán Misti**, one of a trio of imposing volcanoes looming behind it, this is Peru's second-largest urban area and one of the country's most prosperous. In colonial days it had the largest Spanish population and the strongest European traditions; cattle and farming industries dating from that period remain principal sources of income for the region. *Arequipeños* are proud and fiercely independent people and like to think of their city as a place separate from – and superior to – the rest of the country.

In 1541 the King of Spain granted this oasis at the foot of the snow-capped volcano the title "Most Noble, Most Loyal and Faithful City of the Assumption of Our Lady of the Beautiful Valley of Arequipa." Aymara Amerindians living here beside the **Río Chili** more concisely called it Ariquepa *(sic)*, "the place behind the pointed mountain." Another legend has it that the Inca Mayta Capac was so moved by the beauty of the valley during one of his journeys that he ordered his entourage to stop. His exact words were said to be *"Ari quipay"* – "Yes, stay" in Quechua. Whatever the truth, Arequipa has grown into a magnificent city and the intellectual capital of modern Peru.

PRECEDING PAGES: gazing over the Cañón del Colca. **LEFT:** Arequipa's Plaza de Armas. **BELOW:** a woman from Chivay.

There are many ways of getting here: there are frequent flights from Lima, Cusco, Juliaca, and Tacna (on the Chilean border); and there are buses from Lima, Nacza, Cusco, and Puno. How you travel will depend on your budget, time scale, the degree of comfort you require, and how much of the country you want to see.

The heart of the city

Arequipa's **Plaza de Armas** Ⓐ is one of the most beautiful in Peru. Wander around it before you start your tour of the city, taking in the facade of the cathedral and the two-story arcades that grace the other three sides of the plaza, with its palm trees, old gas lamps, and a white stone fountain nestling in an English-style garden. *Arequipeños* congregate here for political rallies, protests, or *fiestas*. The plaza's thick stone buildings with busily carved portals, their Moorish touches evident, breathe 460 years of history. An earthquake in 2002 caused considerable damage, but most of the main historical buildings have now been restored.

Head toward **La Compañía** Ⓑ, on the southeast of the plaza. The frontispiece of this two-story Jesuit church is a compilation of columns, zigzags, spirals, laurel crowns, flowers, birds, and grapevines. into which is embroidered in rock abbreviations of the Good Friday Masses, the city's coat of arms, and the date the

massive work was completed: 1698. But a careful look shows that the European influence had its limits. The angels have Amerindian faces – one face is even crowned with feathers (open 9am–noon and 3–6pm; admission fee).

What lies inside La Compañía is equally impressive. The gilded main altar is the apogee of Peruvian baroque, and the sacristy's ceiling is covered with miniature paintings and carvings of crimson and gold. The view from the steeple is fabulous, especially at sunset when the late light casts a pink, then mauve, glow on the city's gracious white buildings. On the Calle Morán side of the church is the cloister, where stark architectural lines are broken by detailed columns, demonstrating the high level that stone carving reached during the 17th century. The Capilla de San Ignacio (St Ignatius' Chapel) is also worth a look, but check the visiting hours because they are different from those for the church.

Now retrace your steps to the massive twin-towered **Catedral ❻** (open 7am–noon and 5–8pm; free admission), rebuilt twice in the 1800s after it was destroyed by fire and earthquake – which La Compañía escaped. The cathedral's ornate exterior is misleading because the interior is unusually bare and simple, except for an elaborate chandelier. The church's organ hails from Belgium, and its elaborately carved wooden pulpit, the work of French artist Rigot in 1879, was brought to the city a century ago by a local aristocrat's daughter.

Colonial mansions

Arequipa is a delight for those interested in secular colonial architecture, for this city is full of dignified patricians' homes built in the 18th century, which have somehow withstood the tremors that regularly shake this city. The single-story structures are replete with massive carved wooden doors, French windows with

TIP

Calle Jerusalén, to the northeast of the Plaza de Armas, is a good place to change foreign currency, as it has several exchange bureaux.

BELOW: a shoeshine while digesting the news.

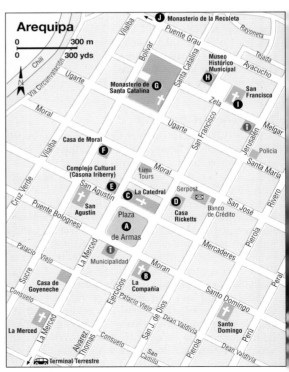

ornate grilles, and high-ceilinged rooms clustered around spacious central patios.

To see some of the best of them, cross Calle San Francisco to **Casa Ricketts Ⓓ**. Built as a seminary in 1738, this is now the Banco Continental, but there is a small museum and art gallery inside (open 9am–1pm and 4–6pm). Next, take the street round the back of the cathedral to the **Casona Iriberry**, built in the late 18th century, which houses the **Complejo Cultural Chaves la Rosa Ⓔ**. There is often something on at the complex: films, art exhibitions, and concerts. A few meters away, on the corner of Moral and Bolívar, is the **Casa Moral Ⓕ** (open 9am–4pm; entrance charge), which is also a bank, the Banco Sur, and originally named, like the street, after the venerable mulberry tree on its patio. The carvings above the door depict pumas from whose mouths snakes are slithering – the same designs found on the ceramics and fabrics of the Nazca Amerindians. Another interesting colonial house that is open to the public is the **Goyeneche Palace**.

Secret world

From Casa Moral turn right along Calle Moral, then left into Calle Santa Catalina to the 16th-century **Monasterio de Santa Catalina Ⓖ** (open 9am–4pm; entrance charge), the most astonishing site in Arequipa, which was opened to the public in 1970 after almost 400 years as a cloister. Despite the closed doors, little heed was paid to the vows of poverty and silence, at least in the early days. During its heyday this convent's sleeping cells were luxurious, with English carpets, silk curtains, cambric and lace sheets, and tapestry-covered stools. As for silence, French feminist Flora Tristan, visiting the convent in 1832, said that the nuns – daughters of aristocrats – were nearly as good at talking as they were at spending huge sums of money. Each had her own servants,

A carved detail in La Compañía.

LEFT: Virgin in Santa Catalina.
RIGHT: colonial cloisters.

Map on page 250

Santa Catalina wall painting.

BELOW: a glimpse inside Santa Catalina's cloister.

and dined off porcelain plates, with damask tablecloths and silver cutlery.

Santa Catalina takes visitors back four centuries. Entering the cloister you see the spacious patios, the kitchen and slave quarters and stone wash-tubs of this convent where entrance requirements were among the strictest in Peru. Novices had to prove Spanish origin and come up with a dowry of at least 1,000 gold pesos. The narrow streets, arches, and gardens of the convent bear their original names: Córdoba Street, its whitewashed walls stark against the pots of bright red geraniums; Zocodober Square with a granite fountain; Sevilla Street with archways and steps. There is also an impressive collection of paintings from the 17th and 18th centuries in what was formerly the community dormitory. About 30 nuns still live in the convent, which once housed up to 500.

When the convent opened its doors to the public, its anecdotes and scandals were resurrected, among them the story of Sister Dominga, the 16-year-old who entered the convent when her betrothed left her for a rich widow. The religious life did not agree with this beautiful young woman, and she staged her own death to escape. Dominga really did place the body of a deceased Amerindian woman in her bed one night and set the room on fire, but it actually happened in the **Convento de Santa Rosa**, seven blocks from Arequipa's main square, which remains cloistered. It was founded in 1747 by four nuns from Santa Catalina; nearly two dozen members of the religious order still reside there.

Close to Santa Catalina is the **Museo Histórico Municipal** ❶ (open 9am–5pm; entrance charge), which is interesting for an overview of the city's history. From here it is only a few yards to the **Iglesia de San Francisco** ❶ (open 7–11am and 5–8pm), the focus of attention every December 8 during the Feast of the Immaculate Conception. A fairy-tale coach topped with the image

of the Virgin Mary surrounded by angels and saints, usually stored in the small chapel of the Sorrowful Virgin, is paraded through the streets in a colorful procession of pilgrims carrying flowers and candles. To reach the most interesting museum in the city, the **Monasterio de la Recoleta ❶**, you must cross the Río Chili, by either the Puente Grau or the Puente Bolognesi. The monastery has a vast library of 20,000 books, many of them very old, and a collection of religious art (open 9am–noon and 3–5pm). There is also a new museum, the **Museo de Arte Contemporáneo** (Tacna y Aríca 201; open 9am–5pm; entrance charge) housed in the railway manager's house opposite the train station.

Seceding from the north

As already mentioned, *arequipeños* are a proud, even haughty lot, and their perennial attempts to secede from the rest of the country are a source of entertainment for *limeños*. They once designed their own passport and flag in a futile attempt at separatism. From Arequipa's well-educated and politically passionate ranks have come two of the country's best-known figures: the former President Fernando Belaunde Terry, and the internationally known novelist and failed presidential hopeful, Mario Vargas Llosa.

This regionalist passion peaks at the annual celebrations marking the anniversary of the city's foundation. Every August 15, *arequipeños* cut loose with parades, bullfights, and night-time revelry highlighted by fireworks. The birthday celebration is accompanied by a week-long handicrafts and folk festival. The other important festival in Arequipa is a more solemn one – the traditional religious processions of *Semana Santa*, Easter.

To unwind in Arequipa in the evening, do what the locals do: head to a *pican-*

Map on page 250

BELOW: the library of the Monasterio de la Recoleta.

tería for a cold *arequipeña* beer and some spicy food – stuffed peppers, pressed rabbit, or marinated pork. If you opt for the peppers *(rocoto relleno)*, take care – they are scorchingly hot. Tourist reactions to this spicy dish are a source of amusement for other diners and concern for restaurant owners. The beer will be accompanied by a dish of *cancha* or salty fried corn which, like potato crisps, makes you even thirstier. There is no shortage of restaurants, with something to suit all pockets, serving a wide variety of food from the local specialties already mentioned, to good *ceviche* (the typical, marinated seafood dish – Arequipa is less than two hours from the ocean), to vegetarian dishes and good pizzas.

Restored ruin

There are some interesting trips to be made outside Arequipa. One is to **Sabandía**, about 7 km (4 miles) from the city, near the pleasant suburb of Paucarpata. Here stands a flour mill, made of volcanic rock, which was built in the 17th century and restored, stone by stone, in 1973. In 1966, architect Luis Felipe Calle had restored an old mansion in Arequipa (now the main branch of the Central Bank) when he was given the task of restoring this old ruined mill outside the city. He set up a tent beside the mill and lived there for the two and a half years it took him to finish the project, which he did by referring to old documents and conducting interviews with residents who remembered when the mill had last operated nearly a half century earlier. After the restoration the bank put the *molina* up for sale – and Calle himself purchased it. "Architecture of Arequipa is a fusion. The big stone houses are humble but at the same time vigorous, a faithful reflection of the spirit of their people," said Calle, whose 17th-century property – open to visitors – is set in some of the area's most beautiful countryside.

A little farther out from the city are the thermal springs of **Yura**, 30 km (18 miles) from Arequipa in the foothills of the extinct **Volcán Chachani**. Crude cement pools fed by the sulfurous waters are open for bathing, and lunch is available at the Hotel Libertador. Two hours from the city, on the road to Lima, are the **Toro Muerto petroglyphs**, hundreds of volcanic rocks believed to have been engraved and painted more than 1,000 years ago by Wari (Huari) people living in the region. The petroglyphs show realistic depictions of llamas, condors, pumas, guanacos, dancers, and warriors.

Deeper than the Grand Canyon

Four hours away from Arequipa, and drawing almost as much tourist attention these days, is the **Cañón del Colca** , one of the world's deepest gorges cut 3,182 meters (10,607 ft) into the earth's crust. Said to be deeper than the Grand Canyon, the Colca is shadowed by snow-topped peaks – many of them volcanoes – and sliced by the silvery Río Colca. The base of this canyon is cold and windy and draws only dare-devil kayak enthusiasts and researchers. Above, at the brink of the chasm, Quechua farmers irrigate narrow terraces of rich volcanic earth in much the same way as their ancestors did centuries ago.

Though isolated, the Colca was a productive farming area even before the Incas claimed it, and when the Spanish reached the 64 km- (40 mile-) long valley where this canyon lies they found terraced fields and herds of llamas and alpacas. When the canyon became part of the route between the silver mines of Bolivia and the coast, the Colca farmers were snatched from their homes and forced to work in the mines. Later, when the railroad reached as far as Arequipa, the Colca Valley was forgotten.

When a multinational consortium began investigating the possibility of diverting the Río Colca for a desert irrigation project, eyes turned once again to this valley and its gorge. From a lost chasm trapped in a time warp, the Colca has become one of the hottest tourist attractions in southwestern Peru. There has been a modification in the valley's crops as it has more contact with the outside world. One innovation is barley, which is now grown on some terraces for use in the brewery that makes some of the rather good *Arequipeña* beer.

The canyon is an average of 900 meters (3,000 ft) deep. Perhaps the most popular section is the **Cruz del Cóndor** (Condor Crossing), where visitors scan the skies for a glimpse of the majestic birds soaring above in pairs. They use the thermal air currents produced in the early morning or the early evening, and few who visit at those times in the hope of spotting them are disappointed.

The Cruz del Cóndor is included in a variety of one- and two-day trips, which can be organized in Arequipa. En route, many of the tours take in the **Reserva Nacional Salinas y Aguada Blanca** (at 3,900 meters/12,800 ft you'll notice how thin the air seems) where groups of shy vicuñas can often be seen. Even more remote than Colca, the **Cotahuasi Canyon** has only recently been exposed to tourism. Now believed by many to exceed Colca in depth, making it the world's deepest canyon, it is a pristine area of great natural beauty ideal for adventurers and nature lovers. Accommodations can be found in the small town of Cotahuasi. ❑

Map on page 230

BELOW: memorable sight in the Cruz del Cóndor.

COLONIAL ART AND ARCHITECTURE

Once the Spaniards laid aside the sword and the musket, they began building. Wonderful examples of their architecture still grace Peru's oldest cities

After subduing the indigenous peoples, one of the conquistadors' first acts was to start building splendid churches. This symbolized their power and confidence, glorified God and provided places of worship for new converts. The earliest churches were built by the Franciscans: the first cathedral in Lima was completed in 1555, but only a decade later they considered it too small and began another. In Cusco, the church of El Triunfo was founded in 1536, the year the Spanish vanquished Manco Inca's forces at Sacsayhuamán. The first stones for Cusco's cathedral were laid in 1559. Not to be outdone, the Dominican order founded Santo Domingo on the site of the Inca Temple of the Sun, which the Spaniards had stripped of its vast wealth.

The Jesuits arrive

When the Jesuits, the most zealous of the missionaries, arrived, they started their own building program. La Compañía in Cusco, begun in 1571, rivaled the cathedral in splendor. It was virtually destroyed by an earthquake less than a century later, but rebuilt with an ornate baroque facade. La Compañía in Arequipa was initiated only in the late 17th century, by which time baroque influences were prevalent. It was predated by the cathedral and the exquisite Monastery of Santa Catalina. All were built in imitation of the great churches of Spain, with massive towers and cupolas, and arched, shady cloisters. Many had strong Mudéjar influences, blending with the innovative School of Cusco *(see side panel)*. Around the churches were the great Plazas de Armas – the one in Cusco is a magnificent example – and in the late 17th and the 18th century elegant town houses were constructed in the colonial style in all the major cities.

◁ **SCHOOL OF CUSCO**
This picaresque figure from a painting in Lima Cathedral is by an unknown 17th-century *cusqueño* artist.

△ **VILLAGE GLORY**
The gilded altar of the 17th-century Jesuit church in Andahuaylillas, a village church which resembles a cathedral in its sumptuous decoration.

◁ SANTO DOMINGO
The cloister of the Monastery of Santo Domingo, a classic example of the colonial style, which was built on the foundations of the Inca Temple of the Sun.

△ LA COMPAÑIA
The ornate frontispiece of the Jesuit church shows the blending of styles. In close-up it can be seen that the carved angels have Amerindian faces.

THE SCHOOL OF CUSCO

The School of Cusco was a 17th-century movement which blended European and indigenous motifs to create a New World art form. Archangels would be dressed in Hispanic clothes, while cherubs had Amerindian features. The master of this school was the *indígena* artist Diego Quispe Tito, examples of whose work hang in Cusco's Cathedral and Museo de Arte Religioso. The colors were rich and dark, and the themes had their dark side too, depicting martyrs' horrific deaths.

By the 18th century the style had changed, and secular subjects were introduced. The picture above *(La Niña María Milando)*, shows the evolution of the style.

▷ CUSCO'S COLONIAL ART
Colonial artists of the Cusco School depicted their subjects in deep rich colors, with a mixture of indigenous and European features and clothes.

▽ GRIM REMINDER
A detail of a magnificent mural in the church of Huaro, south of Cusco, shows a graphic portrayal of the grim reaper.

▷ SAN FRANCISCO, LIMA
This is one of the best-preserved of Lima's colonial churches. Its extensive catacombs may have given it a base solid enough to withstand the earthquakes of the 17th and 18th centuries, although it suffered badly in the 1970 quake. Now well restored, the interior has strong Mudéjar influences mingled with the baroque.

CUSCO

The ancient capital of the Inca Empire is the city most tourists want to visit, a jewel of Inca and colonial architecture standing 3,330 meters (10,900 ft) above sea level

Maps on pages 230 & 262

Amerindian vendors speak Spanish to tourists and Quechua to each other. Catholic nuns live in buildings once inhabited by Inca "chosen women." The Marcos Zapata painting of the Last Supper in the cathedral shows Christ and his apostles dining on Andean cheese, hot peppers, and roast guinea pig. **Cusco ⓯** is a city where past and present collide in an intriguing mix.

When Francisco Pizarro and his soldiers arrived nearly five centuries ago, Cusco, the capital of the Inca empire, served as home to an estimated 15,000 nobles, priests, and servants. Where now daily rail, plane, and bus services connect this city to the rest of the country, long-distance Amerindian relay runners called *chasquis* once linked the rest of Tahuantinsuyo, as the empire was called. Today, local residents have attempted to recall those glory days, relabeling streets with their original Quechua names and even calling the city Qosqo, a pronunciation closer to its original Inca name.

Center of the world

For the Incas, Qosqo meant "navel of the world," and they believed their splendid city was the source of life. Legend has it Cusco was founded by Manco Capac and his sister-consort Mama Ocllo, sent by the sun god Inti with the divine task of finding a spot where the gold staff they carried would sink easily into the ground. That place was Cusco, and there Manco Capac taught the men to farm and Mama Ocllo taught the women to weave.

The Inca empire came into being during the reign of Inca Pachacutec Yupanqui, who began a great expansion, imposing Quechua as the common language, conquering other Amerindian nations, creating a state religion and turning Cusco into a glittering capital as large as any European city. It was Pachacutec who transformed Cusco from a city of clay and straw into a thriving metropolis with grand stone buildings in the second half of the 15th century.

A modern stone statue of Pachacutec on the south side of Cusco pays tribute to the king who ruled for 40 years and was one of the empire's greatest warriors, innovators, and unifiers of Andean civilizations. His son, Inca Tupac Yupanqui, continued his work, expanding even farther the empire's boundaries.

Some of the best-loved Inca legends have been transferred to the Peruvian theater. Among them is *Ollantay* – the story of Pachacutec's most famous general. Under Ollantay's military leadership, the empire was extended into what is now Ecuador, Bolivia, Colombia, Chile, and portions of Argentina. A grateful Pachacutec promised to grant him any wish. Ollantay boldly asked for the hand of Kusi Kuyur, the monarch's daughter. But the Inca, the son of the sun,

PRECEDING PAGES: the splendid Plaza de Armas.
LEFT: narrow street in Cusco.
BELOW: home-brewed *chicha*.

could not allow a member of the monarchy to marry a commoner even though the daughter professed her love for the military leader. Ollantay rebelled against Pachacutec and was eventually ordered to be imprisoned for the remainder of his life. Kusi Kuyur refused to marry anyone else and was sent to be a chosen woman, dedicating her life to serving the sun god.

The story does not end there, however, because years later an unforeseen occurrence brought the couple together again for a happy ending. The play is staged frequently in Cusco and Lima, and is worth seeing by those who understand some Spanish.

A brief moment of glory

At its peak, Cusco, built in the shape of a puma, was a city with sophisticated water systems, paved streets, and no poverty. But it had been an imposing urban center for only about 70 years before the Spanish arrived. Of course, since the Incas left no written records, and the Spanish explanations of what they found are contradictory, theories about Cusco's design are numerous. One specialist in archeology and astronomy even speculates that one city boundary was warped to make it coincide with the mid-point in the Milky Way, reflecting the Amerindian sensitivity to astronomy and the movements of the heavenly bodies.

The Spaniards were certainly impressed by the order and magnificence of Cusco, and wrote back to Spain that it was the most marvelous city of the New World. But the Incas' cultural achievements were merely a minor distraction in comparison with the lure of their treasures: conquistadors greedily pushed their way into ancient temples and seized their gold and silver art works, which they promptly melted into bullion.

The ice festival of Qoyur Riti is held in the Cordillera Vilcanota, southeast of Cusco.

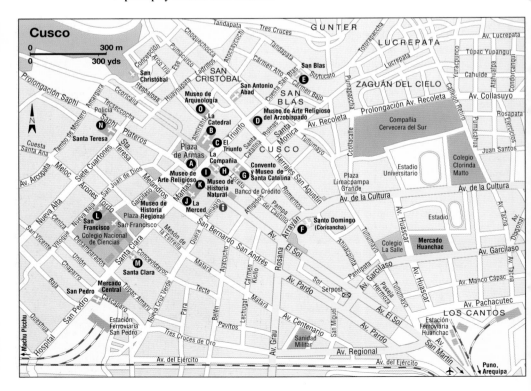

In addition to palaces and gold-filled temples, indestructible buildings, and advanced medical techniques, the Spanish soldiers found the Inca society full of skilled artisans. A storehouse of delicate, brightly colored feathers from tropical birds was used solely for the weaving of fine capes for the Inca and his priests. Rescued examples of the capes or *mantas*, which reflect the most extreme test of patience and handiwork, are found in museums in Lima. These survived because the Spanish thirst for gold was so great that they overlooked many of the empire's other treasures.

Cusco retained a level of importance for the first few decades after the Spanish Conquest. It was here that Diego de Almagro's faction of Spanish soldiers attempted to wrest control from Pizarro, and for his treachery the leader was executed on the city's main plaza. It was also here that the Spanish struggled against Manco Inca as the Amerindians made an ill-fated attempt to stop the European conquest through gallant guerrilla warfare. But by 1535 the capital of this new Spanish colony had been set up in Lima, Cusco's wealth had been stripped, and silver from Bolivia had turned attention away from this valley.

After centuries of provincial obscurity, Hiram Bingham's discovery of Machu Picchu in 1911 and the subsequent construction of a road up to that mountaintop citadel in 1948 transformed Cusco into the jumping-off point for visits to one of South America's best-known tourist attractions.

Walking into the past

The most startling and curious characteristic of Cusco at first glance is its architecture. Huge walls of intricately laid stone pay testimony to the civilization that 500 years ago controlled much of this continent. The Spaniards' attempts to

Map on pages 230–1

Service with a smile.

BELOW: Plaza de Armas, and the rooftops of Cusco.

eradicate every trace of the "pagan" Inca civilization proved too ambitious a task; the Europeans ended up putting their own buildings on the mammoth foundations of the Inca ones, often using the same stones that had been finely cut and rounded by Amerindian masons. When a massive earthquake shook the city in March 1650, the colonial walls came crashing down but the Inca foundations remained intact.

Before you start to explore this intriguing city, remember that it is more than 3,330 meters (10,900 ft) above sea level, so take it easy until you get acclimatized. Also, don't forget to buy a Cusco Visitor Ticket, which is essential for visits to historic sites in Cusco and the Sacred Valley. Bearing these two things in mind, the **Plaza de Armas** Ⓐ is a perfect place to start. In Inca times it was not only the exact center of the empire known as Tahuantinsuyo – or The Four Quarters of the Earth – but was also twice as large as it is now. Samples of soil from each of the conquered areas of the empire were joined at this spot and the plaza itself, flanked by Inca palaces, was surfaced with white sand mixed with tiny shells, bits of gold, silver, and coral.

This was the spot where important Inca religious and military ceremonies were staged. Some claim the section that remains today was a portion of Aucaypata, the Square of War, featuring a stone covered in sheets of gold where offerings were made before military actions. However, other experts disagree, and suggest it was called Huacaypata – or Weeping Square – because it was here that deceased Incas were mourned. During the early days of Spanish control, the plaza was the scene of much violence and blood-letting, such as the execution of the rebel leader Tupac Amaru II in 1781. Captured while trying to flee with his pregnant wife, Tupac Amaru was a *mestizo* whose real name was José Gabriel Condorcanqui.

BELOW: dancing in the plaza.

Map
on page
262

These days, things are quieter on the plaza, which is one of the most superb colonial squares in Latin America. Tourists study the handicrafts for sale as insistent local women sitting under blankets beneath the colonial arcades chant "*cómprame*," or "buy from me." Quality varies, but good bargains can be found. However, don't believe it when vendors claim their rugs and weavings are antique: wool does not endure indefinitely in the damp highlands. The centuries-old textiles displayed in Peru's museums were rescued from the arid coast. And if they were antique, these items should not be bought or taken out of the country.

Cusco's cathedral

The most spectacular view of the plaza comes after nightfall when dramatic lighting transforms the square. But while the night is best for outside photos, the interior of Cusco's magnificent **Catedral** ❸ can only be seen during the day (open Mon–Sat 10–11.30am and 2–5.30pm, closed Thur pm; open for worship only on Sunday, but you can go in if you are discreet). It is flanked by the church of Jesús María, to the right – also known as the Iglesia de la Santísima Trinidad – and El Triunfo (*see page 267*) to the left. Jesús María was built in the mid-18th century, which makes it one of the newer structures.

Rather confusingly, visitors are normally channeled through the main doors of El Triunfo, then turn left into the cathedral itself. Built on what once was the palace of Inca Wiracocha, and made in part from stones hauled from the fortress of Sacsayhuamán outside the city, the cathedral mixes Spanish renaissance architecture with the stoneworking skills of the Amerindians. Begun in 1559, it took a century to build and an awesome investment of money. The altar is of solid silver.

Eye-catching mailbox.

BELOW: lights at night in the Plaza de Armas.

The cathedral also contains magnificent examples of Escuela Cuzqueña (School of Cusco) paintings, including some by Diego Quispe Tito, the 17th-century Amerindian painter widely regarded as the master of the school. In the corner next to the sacristy is a painting by Marcos Zapata of the Last Supper, with Christ and his apostles dining on roast guinea pig *(cuy)*, hot peppers, and Andean cheese. A painting of Christ's crucifixion is the subject of many theories: some believe it is a 17th-century work by a member of the Cusco School; others hold that it is the work of Flemish painter Sir Anthony van Dyck; still others believe it was by a Spanish artist, Alonzo Ocano; while a final theory proposes that it is the work of various artists, because the head is out of proportion with the body. The third side-altar from the left contains a curious, but less contentious, painting of a pregnant Virgin Mary.

The city's most venerated statue is the crucified Christ known as *Nuestro Señor de los Temblores* (Our Lord of the Earthquakes), which is depicted in a painting beside the main altar. The statue was paraded around the city during the 1650 earthquake, and after the tremors eventually stopped it was credited with miraculously bringing about the end of seismic activity. Borne on a silver litter, this gift to the New World from Spain, sent by Holy Roman Emperor Charles V, is still paraded around Cusco during Easter. For the rest of the year it remains in an alcove inside the cathedral. It is blackened by the smoke of candles perpetually burning beneath it.

The cathedral's María Angola bell in the north tower can be heard up to 40 km (25 miles) away. Made of a ton of gold, silver, and bronze, the bell, which is more than 300 years old, is reportedly the continent's largest. But when it was cast it had a partner – the Magdalena, which was dropped by workers during a

BELOW: Inca masonry in Calle Loreto.

storm at the edge of Lake Titicaca, where the bells were made. Amerindians in Cusco now say that the echoes from the first peals of the María Angola each morning are actually the tolling of the Magdalena on the bottom of the lake.

Map on page 262

Cusco's first Christian church

El Triunfo ❻ (opening hours as for the cathedral) means "the triumph," and it was built in honor of the Spanish victory over the Amerindians in the great rebellion of 1536, when Cusco was under siege for many months. The uprising was led by Manco Inca, a descendant of an Inca leader, who the Spaniards assumed would be their political puppet. They were surprised, then, to find Manco surrounding the city with some 200,000 followers – against the Spaniards' 200 men and loyal Amerindians.

The turning-point of the siege was a great attack on the city, with Manco's men slinging red-hot stones to set the thatched roofs alight. The Spaniards were gathered in the old Inca armory of Suntur Huasi when it was pelted with fiery rocks. When the building did not catch fire, priests declared that the Virgin of the Assumption had appeared to put out the flames and inspire the Spaniards on to defend the city. El Triunfo – the city's first Christian church – was built on the site. The tomb containing the ashes of the indigenous historian Garcilaso de la Vega, who died in Spain in 1616 but whose remains were returned to Cusco a few years ago, can be found in this church.

A colonial courtyard.

If you turn left when you emerge from El Triunfo and walk one block up to the corner of Calle Hatunrumiyoc, literally "the Street of the Big Stones," and Calle Palacio, you will come to the **Museo de Arte Religioso del Arzobispado ❼** (open Mon–Sat 8am–11.30pm and 3–5.30pm; entrance charge). This Moorish building

BELOW: an Inca wall in the Hostal Loreto.

with complicated carvings on its doors and balconies was constructed on the site of the 15th-century palace of Inca Roca, under whose rule Cusco's schools were initiated. It used to be the Archbishop's Palace, and that is what people sometimes still call it. Just outside is the famous **Twelve Angled Stone**. A "fitting" tribute to the skill of Inca masons, this masonry masterpiece was left by Inca architects seemingly anxious to prove that no piece of granite was too irregular to be fitted without mortar. The museum houses an impressive collection of religious paintings of the Cusco School, including some by Diego Quispe Tito.

Head straight up Calle Hatunrumiyoc, and on your right you will find the **Iglesia de San Blas** ⓔ. Apart from its ornate altar San Blas is a simple church by Latin American standards, and has a beautifully carved pulpit, said to be one of the world's finest pieces of woodwork. There is some dispute about who produced it; some say it was an Amerindian leper who initiated the work after he was miraculously cured (open Mon–Sat 8–11.30am, except Thurs, daily 2–5.30pm; entrance charge). The streets around San Blas form Cusco's artists' quarter, with galleries, studios, and small shops, hostels and restaurants, and the workshops of the prolific Mendival family.

Temple of the Sun

Take any of the streets leading south from the Plaza de Armas and you will find your way to the most important place of worship in the Inca empire. Now a church, the **Iglesia Santo Domingo** ⓖ (open daily 9am–5.30pm; entrance charge), was once **El Templo del Coricancha** (or Qoricancha) – the Temple of the Sun, and the most magnificent complex in Cusco. Walls there were covered in 700 sheets of gold studded with emeralds and turquoise, and windows were constructed so the sun would enter and cast a nearly blinding reflection off the precious metals inside.

The mummified bodies of deceased Inca leaders, dressed in fine clothing and adornments, were kept on thrones of gold, tended by women selected for that honor. In the same room, a huge gold disk representing the sun covered one full wall while a sister disk of silver, to reflect the moonlight, was positioned on another wall.

Spanish chronicles recall the Europeans' astonishment when they saw Coricancha's patio filled with life-size gold and silver statues of llamas, trees, flowers, and even delicately handcrafted butterflies. Legend has it that Atahuallpa's ransom included 20 of Coricancha's life-size golden statues of beautiful women.

The Spanish historian Pedro de Cieza de León wrote a description of the patio "in which the earth was lumps of fine gold ... with stalks of corn that were of gold-stalks, leaves and ears... so well planted that no matter how hard the wind blew it could not uproot them. Aside from this there were more than 20 sheep of gold with their lambs and the shepherds who guarded them, all of this metal."

Although the temple's wealth can only be imagined, its Inca architecture can still be appreciated. Visible from inside is the perfectly fitted curved stone wall that has survived at least two major earthquakes.

Spanish chronicles also describe a fabulous Hall of

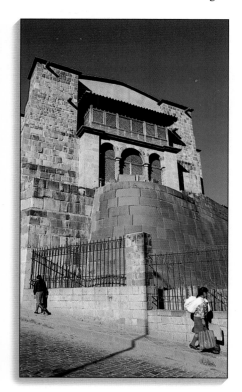

BELOW: the remains of Coricancha.

Map on page 262

the Sun in Coricancha and four chapels dedicated to lesser gods, including the moon, stars, thunder, and the rainbow. The rainbow had special significance for the Incas, which was why the Inca flag displayed all the colors of the *arco iris*, and it remains a good omen for Amerindians today. Any Peruvian child asked to draw a picture of the Sierra will invariably sketch a house with mountains in the background and a rainbow arching the sky. Current excavations at the temple of the sun promise to reveal more of its mysteries.

Chosen women

Retrace your steps toward the Plaza de Armas, and on Calle Arequipa you will find another Christian enclave that was formerly an Inca holy place. This is the **Museo de Arte y Monasterio de Santa Catalina** ❻ (open Mon–Fri 9am–5pm, Sat 9am–4pm; entrance charge), which centuries ago housed a different group of cloistered females, some 3,000 Chosen Women who dedicated their lives to the sun god. Foremost among these were the *mamaconas*, consecrated women who taught religion to selected virgins – called *acllas*. The *acllas* were taught to prepare *chicha* for use in religious ceremonies, to weave, and to pray. They made the fine robes that the Inca wore – only once – out of vicuña, alpaca, and even a silky fabric that was made from bat skins.

Attached to the convent is a museum containing works of religious art. An important contribution to the art world grew out of Cusco's mixing of the Amerindian and Spanish cultures in the often violent and bloody paintings of the School of Cusco *(see page 257)*. In many of these paintings archangels are dressed as Spaniards carrying European guns, but surrounded by cherubs with Amerindian faces, or Christ is accompanied by indigenous apostles. The Virgin Mary wears local dress, and Christ hangs on a cross decorated with Amerindian symbols.

The most beautiful church

In a city with so many churches, it is an honor to be dubbed the "most beautiful." That distinction belongs to **La Compañía de Jesús** ❼ (open daily 9–11am and 3–6pm; free admission), sitting on the southeast corner of the Plaza de Armas where once stood Inca Huayna Capac's palace. The Jesuit church, with its baroque facade, intricate interior, finely carved balconies, and altars covered in gold leaf, was started in 1571 and took nearly 100 years to complete, in part because of damage in the 1650 earthquake. During its construction, this splendid building drew so much attention that the Bishop of Cusco complained it outshone the cathedral. But by the time Pope Paul III had been called in to mediate, and had ruled in favor of the cathedral, La Compañía's construction had been completed.

To the right of La Compañía, also on the main plaza, is the university-owned **Museo de Historia Natural** ❶ (open Mon–Fri 9am–1pm and 3–6pm) with good examples of local fauna.

A few yards down the street, just past the Plaza de Armas, is the **Iglesia de la Merced** ❶ (open daily 8.30am–noon and 3.30–5.30pm except Sun; entrance charge), one of the most important churches in the city. Destroyed by the massive earthquake in 1650, this

BELOW: a typical example of *Escuela Cusqueño* art.

church was erected for a second time four years later. It contains the remains of Francisco Pizarro's brother Gonzalo, and of Pizarro's fellow conquistador Diego de Almagro, who returned to Peru after an unsuccessful search for riches in Chile, and was executed here after his failed coup attempt. There is a connected monastery and another **Museo de Arte Religioso** Ⓚ (opening hours as for the church), not to be confused with the museum of the same name in the Archbishop's Palace. This one contains several fine paintings, including a Rubens, and gold and silver altarpieces, the most ostentatious of which is a jewel-studded, solid gold monstrance.

Garden square

Continue a couple of blocks down the same street – Calle Marqués – and you will come to the **Plaza San Francisco**. This square has been planted entirely with Andean flora, including amaranth grain. Here, too, is Cusco's coat of arms, featuring a castle surrounded by eight condors. The castle represents Sacsayhuamán, and the emblem refers to the bloody battle fought there in 1536 as the Amerindians tried to defeat the Spanish conquerors. The condors flying over the castle vividly recall the scores of flesh-eating birds that, according to legend, circled over the Inca fort as the bodies of the dead piled up.

Flanking one side of the plaza is the 16th-century church and monastery, the **Iglesia de San Francisco** Ⓛ (open for Mass Mon–Sat 7am, 6.30pm and 7pm; Sun 7am, 9am, 11am and 7pm). Simple in comparison with other houses of worship in the city, it has an extensive collection of colonial art, including a painting – said to be one of the largest canvases in South America – showing the family tree of St Francis Assisi.

You may be surprised to see some signs in Cusco's tourist areas translated into Hebrew. This is because so many young Israelis travel to Peru when they come out of the army.

BELOW: street musicians, old and young.

Map
on page
262

There are two more churches that are well worth seeing, but rather difficult to get into, because both are the homes of closed orders of nuns. To see the first, turn down Calle Santa Clara, leading from the Plaza San Francisco, and you will find the 16th-century **Iglesia de Santa Clara** Ⓜ (open daily for Mass 7pm). The tiny mirrors that cover the interior are the most impressive sight in this building. In order to see the second beautiful but usually inaccessible church, the **Iglesia de Santa Teresa** Ⓝ (open daily for Mass 7am and 7pm), you must go a couple of blocks past the Plaza San Francisco, then turn right on Calle Siete Cuartones. The cloistered nuns sit at the back of the church, behind a grille, and form the church's choir. If you can't be here at these times you will have to be content with a look at the exterior of this lovely building.

Circling round behind the Plaza de Armas, on the corner of Calle Tucumán and Calle Ataúd you will find the **Museo Inka** Ⓞ (open Mon–Fri 8am–5pm Sat 9am–4pm; entrance charge), also known as the **Admiral's Palace** because it was once the home of Admiral Francisco Aldrete Maldonado. A coat of arms over its doorway belongs to a subsequent owner, the arrogant and self-important Count of Laguna, who died under mysterious circumstances. His body was found hanging in the mansion's courtyard shortly after he mistreated a priest who had complained about the count's behavior. In the same courtyard are miniature profiles of Pizarro and Spain's Queen Isabela.

There are some strange architectural features: an optical illusion is found in a corner window column, which looks like a bearded man from the inside and a nude woman from the outside, and there are mythical creatures guarding the main stairway. The building is well worth seeing for itself, as well as for the museum's newly expanded collection of pottery, textiles, and gold artifacts.

Pisac alcaldes
(mayors) blowing
conch shells to
attract villagers
to church.

BELOW: dancers at a Cusco fiesta.

Another splendid museum has opened at the Casa Cabrera in Plaza Nazarenas, the **Museo de Arte Precolumbino** (open daily 9am–11pm; entrance charge).

Before leaving Cusco and heading for landmarks outside the city, stop by the Cross Keys Pub, which is at a second-floor location at Portal Confitura 233, facing the cathedral on the Plaza de Armas. In this city of contrasts, what could be more natural than a British-owned watering-hole for offbeat travelers, cartographers, self-styled pioneers, eccentric scientists, and some of the world's most famous birdwatchers? Join them at the bar to hear an exchange of their latest adventures and consult them on out-of-the-way tourist stops. The owner, ornithologist Barry Walker, runs Manu Expeditions, which organizes nature tours in Manu National Park.

There is a wide selection of restaurants in Cusco, serving both Peruvian and international food. If you are looking for night-time entertainment as well as food, it can be found at the restaurants from which lively Andean music emanates. One of the finest floor shows takes place nightly at El Truco, where the *pisco sours* pack a hefty punch and the musicians and dancers are first-rate. Eating a plate of *anticuchos*, a delicious shish-kebab of beef heart, while watching the traditionally garbed performers singing in Quechua and playing reed flutes will make visitors temporarily forget that the Incas lost their showdown with the Spanish.

But eventually the foot-stomping dance songs will be replaced by much quieter mountain music. Locals will tell you that it was when the Spanish killed the last Inca and the sun god turned his back on his children that Andean songs became melancholy. If you are looking for something a bit more contemporary after so much history and tradition, there are several video bars in Cusco where weary tourists can select a video, order drinks, and settle down in comfort to enjoy American or other foreign movies.

Cusco's *fiestas*

Cusco holds a number of very colorful festivals; the best-known of them are in June, but there are several exceptions. One is the Christmas Eve festival called *Santorantikuy* (which means the buying of saints), when crafts and nativity sets are sold in the Plaza de Armas. Another is the celebration in Easter when Nuestro Señor de los Temblores (Our Lord of the Earthquakes), the image of Christ on the cross that is credited with saving the city from destruction during the earthquake of 1650, and which stands in the cathedral is paraded through the streets on a silver litter. Red flower petals are thrown in its wake, symbolizing the blood of Christ, and thousands of *cuzqueños* turn out along with the civic, religious, and military hierarchies of the city.

A third exception is International Workers' Day (May 1), when a parade of workers through the square continues for hours, with each group lined up behind its respective banners – from the organization of transportation workers to the union of informal street vendors *(ambulantes)*, which is made up mostly of women with their babies. This, like many ceremonies in Cusco, opens with the raising of both the red-and-

TIP

Most bars on or near the plaza offer 2 for 1 drinks during "happy hour."

BELOW: festival of *Inti Raymi.*

white Peruvian flag and the rainbow-colored standard of the Inca empire.

Corpus Christi (in honor of the Eucharist) is a movable feast, held on the Thursday after Trinity Sunday – usually in early to mid-June. Effigies of San Sebastián and San Jerónimo race into Cusco from the little towns of those names, borne on enormous litters by their devotees and led by a brass band and people carrying banners and candles. Accompanied by other statues of saints and the Virgin, brought from Cusco's *barrios* and suburbs, they are taken to the church of Santa Clara. The Plaza de Armas comes alive: large altars decorated with flowers, tin, mirrors, crosses, and images of the sun are erected and vendors set up booths with food prepared especially for Corpus Christi. These treats, well worth sampling, include *chiriuchu*, made with guinea pig, chicken, corn, cheese, eggs, and peppers; and baked *achira*, a variety of Peruvian tuber.

After High Mass, the statues are paraded around the plaza, stopping to bow at each altar – no mean feat when some of the gilded and silver-covered figures weigh up to a ton. Each parish has its own brass band, costumed dance groups and devotees, and the plaza is a mélange of color and sound. At the end of the procession comes the priest bearing the Eucharist, almost forgotten in the crush. Slip inside the cathedral if you can, because some of the old women remain there to sing Quechua hymns in the high, bird-like voices typical of traditional music. The day gets more lively as it goes on: generous quantities of alcohol are consumed, and masked devil-dancers frolic among the shrubberies.

Festival fireworks.

Bringing back the Sun

Many travelers come to Cusco for *Inti Raymi* (the Festival of the Sun) on June 24. If you are planning a visit, be sure to make hotel reservations in advance, and arrive by June 20 because the city becomes mobbed. *Inti Raymi* was the Inca winter-solstice celebration, held on June 21 or 22, which the Spanish moved to June 24, the Catholic feast of Saint John the Baptist – the Catholic Church has always been good at incorporating pagan festivities. But the fires that burn throughout the night of June 23 don't have much to do with John the Baptist. They're lit to bring back the sun during the longest nights and shortest days of the year.

In the 1940s a group of Cusco intellectuals revived *Inti Raymi*, basing their *fiesta* on colonial accounts of the Inca festival. On June 24, *campesinos*, townspeople, and travelers follow the Inca's procession from Coricancha, via the Plaza de Armas, to the fortress of Sacsayhuamán for a pageant that is no less impressive because it has an eye on tourism revenue. The regal Inca-for-a-day is borne on a litter, dressed in tinfoil and glittering gold, his guard consisting of costumed Peruvian army troops.

The fires of the empire are ceremonially relit, a llama is "sacrificed" to the sun, and music and dance groups perform, wearing hand-woven clothes that would have made Pachacutec proud. The pageant lasts for about three hours, but the city becomes a giant fair for a couple of days, full of energy and color. It's completely irresistible, but do watch out for pickpockets in the crowd. ❏

BELOW: *fiesta* face in the crowd.

THE SACRED VALLEY

*Sacsayhuamán and Ollantaytambo are awe-inspiring fortresses,
the Sacred Valley of the Incas was thought to be the biblical Eden,
and the Sunday market at Pisac is a riotous affair*

Map
on page
276

Before visiting Sacsayhuamán, the best-known of the ruins outside Cusco, and continuing to Pisac and the Sacred Valley, try going east of Cusco in the direction of Urcos – there are frequent buses which leave from near the Puno railway station. **Pikillacta ⓰**, some 30 km (18 miles) from Cusco, predates the Incas: it is a large, unrestored Wari (or Huari) ruin, probably constructed early in the 12th century, with rough stone walls more than 3 meters (10 ft) high. About 1 km (less than a mile) farther on is **Rumicolca**, the Inca gateway to the Cusco valley. In order to control access to the city, the Incas built, on Wari foundations, a wall of stone at the point where the valley narrows.

About 8 km (5 miles) farther on is **Andahuaylillas ⓱**, a charming little village with some interesting colonial houses and a 17th-century Jesuit church, extraordinarily ornate for such a small backwater, which contains some particularly fine murals. Opening hours vary but it is usually possible to find someone with a key to let you in. **Huaro**, a little farther on, is another tiny village whose church has some marvelous 17th-century murals.

Sacsayhuamán

After this detour, it's time to explore the Inca ruins closest to Cusco. You can walk or take a bus from the city to the first four sites, or you could use Pisac as a base. All Sacred Valley sites are open daily 7am–6pm. The overwhelming fortress of **Sacsayhuamán ⓲** is a bold demonstration of ancient construction skills. Made of massive stones weighing up to 17,000 kg (125 tons), this military complex overlooking Cusco has a double wall in a zigzag shape – some say to imitate the teeth of the puma figure whose head the fort may have formed. Others say it represents the god of lightning. The fort also once had at least three fabulous huge towers, and a labyrinth of rooms large enough for a garrison of 5,000 Inca soldiers. It marks the birthplace of the river that runs under Cusco, channeled through stone conduits cut to give the city an invisible water supply.

Sacsayhuamán was the focus of the Great Rebellion led by Manco Inca against the Spanish in 1536. From here, the Incas besieged Cusco for 10 months. Historians say that if Manco Inca had defeated the Spanish in Cusco, he might have saved the empire. But, no matter how valiantly his troops fought and died, the Spanish eventually wrested back control of the fort, of the old Inca capital of Cusco, and ultimately of all Peru.

Archeologists estimate that tens of thousands of workers labored on this massive structure for up to seven decades, hauling the immense stone blocks that make up its double outside walls, and erecting the nearly indestructible buildings that transformed

LEFT: Inca terracing at Pisac.
BELOW: roadside jewelry stall near Urubamba.

the complex into one of the most wondrous in all the empire. Although the outer walls remain intact, the buildings in the complex have been destroyed – in part to provide building stones for many of the structures in Cusco. Even so, visitors to the fortress can still see the so-called **Inca's Throne** from which it is said that parading troops were reviewed.

This is one of the area's most spectacular spots at which to take dawn photos, and, like much of Cusco, it provides a startling contrast of Amerindian and Christian cultures. Beside this complex, built during the reign of Inca Pachacutec, is a giant white statue of Christ donated to the city in 1944 by grateful Palestinian refugees, his arms outstretched over Cusco in the valley below. It's a good place for a picnic lunch, too: perched on almost any stone you'll have an amazing view of the red-tiled roofs of Cusco and the lush fields of the surrounding valley. The gaily decorated llamas wandering through the ruins are smelly but harmless, and the giggling children tending them will almost certainly ask you to take a photograph – be sure to give them a tip.

In response to claims by Peruvian archeologists and Inca scholars who say that Sacsayhuamán was in danger from the 100,000 tourists and Peruvians who annually attend the colorful *Inti Raymi* festival *(see page 273)* to celebrate the winter solstice, the celebrations have been moved to the esplanade facing the great walls – a move that has satisfied conservationists and those who insist that Cusco's largest celebration each year must be held in the Inca stronghold.

Some 7 km (4 miles) from Sacsayhuamán is **Qenko** ⓳, an Inca shrine with a circular amphitheater and a 5-meter (18-ft) stone block that is said to represent a puma. Its name means "zig-zag," and this ceremonial center – dedicated to the worship of mother earth (Pacha Mama) – includes water canals cut into solid

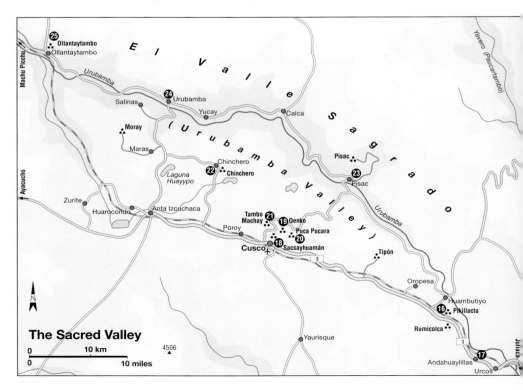

The Sacred Valley

0 — 10 km

0 — 10 miles

rock, and a subterranean room. Unlike Sacsayhuamán, which is a complex made up of huge stone blocks transported to the spot and assembled there, Quenko was carved from a huge limestone formation found at the site. Into its walls were carved typical Inca-style niches and alcoves used to display gold and holy items in pre-Hispanic times. The shrine also contains drawings etched laboriously into its stone, among them a puma, a condor, and a llama.

Farther along the road to Pisac is a smaller fortress, **Puca Pucara** ⑳, believed to have guarded the road to the Sacred Valley of the Incas. Like Machu Picchu, this pink stone complex has hillside terraces, stairways, tunnels, and towers. And to the north is **Tambo Machay** ㉑, the sacred bathing place for the Inca rulers and the royal women. A hydraulic engineering marvel, its aqueduct system still feeds crystalline water into a series of showers where once water rituals were held by worshipers of the sun. The ruins now consist of three massive walls of Inca stonework tucked into a hillside. There are Peruvian historians who say that this was used by Inca Tupac Yupanqui as a hunting lodge, in addition to being a shrine. Some claim that it was where Pachacutec received a prophetic vision of the Incas as conquerors. Others say that the water running through the aqueduct came from a holy spring, and this may have been one of the rare spots where sacrifices of children were made.

Chinchero ㉒ is an attractive village with Inca ruins, which can be visited by bus from Cusco. It has a lively market on Tuesday, Thursday, and Sunday – the latter being the best day to go. It is said that Chinchero was one of the favorite spots of Inca Tupac Yupanqui, who built a palace and had agricultural terraces cultivated here at the mouth of the Río Vilcanota. Other historians say it was an important population center in Inca times and that Tupac Inca, the

Map on page 276

BELOW: Inca festival of *Inti Raymi* at Sacsayhuamán.

Vivid cloth for sale at a village market.

BELOW: carrying a heavy load at Chinchero.

son of Pachacutec, had an estate here. If the Inca royalty were lured to Chinchero, it might have been by the commanding view of snow-capped mountains and the river below. If you are here for the Sunday market, you will notice that Amerindians use it as an opportunity to socialize as much as to buy goods. This "town of the rainbow," as it was known in pre-Hispanic days, has kept many of its ancient customs, and its inhabitants still live in centuries-old houses and wear traditional clothing.

The Sacred Valley of the Incas

Pisac ㉓ makes a good base for exploring the Sacred Valley. The valley is a delightful place: the climate is pleasant, the people are agreeable, the agricultural terracing is a marvel, and there are a number of welcoming little *hostales* in which to spend the night. Pisac is a friendly village known for its good fishing, busy Sunday market, and the ruins above the town, and it lies about 32 km (20 miles) from Cusco on a curving but decent road. There is a road up to the ruins, and you can sometimes get a ride in a taxi, but otherwise you can climb there past the mountainside terraces (Amerindian children will cheerfully serve as guides for a small fee) or hire a horse from beside the village church. At this high altitude, even the fittest travelers find themselves winded and their hearts pounding, so they are grateful when they round the bend on an isolated trail to find themselves face to face with one of the many Inca Kola vendors at the site. Steep farming terraces and dramatic architecture mark this one-time fortress city whose many features include ritual baths fed by aqueducts and one of the largest known Inca cemeteries. The stones making up Pisac's buildings are smaller than those at Sacsayhuamán, but the precision with which they are cut is amazing.

In fact, in some respects the stonemasonry is more awesome than that of the more famous ruins at Machu Picchu. There are residential buildings and towers that some scientists say may have been astronomical observation spots. Higher up, there is a second set of ruins. Owing to the style – smaller stones more haphazardly arranged – a number of theories have arisen to explain the origin of this section. Some say that it was used by servants or other community members with low social standing; another less likely theory is that it pre-dates the main part of the complex. You can use the Cusco Visitor Ticket to see the Pisac ruins.

Pisac's **Sunday market** is a riotous affair in a town where the people work hard and – apparently – play hard. The beer tent is the favorite haunt of the motley brass band that adds an increasingly out-of-tune touch to the town's festivities. Sometimes it seems that the beer tent is the favorite stop for most of the other villagers, too. For that reason, the later in the day visitors arrive, the better their chances for some congenial bargaining for the fine alpaca blankets and sweaters available (although, of course, the biggest selection is to be found earlier in the morning.) There is a less touristy market held on Tuesday and Thursday.

Urubamba

From Pisac, follow the road and the river about 40 km (25 miles) through the picturesque village of Yucay to **Urubamba ㉔**, which lies at the center of the valley. In recent years this has become a popular place to stay. The weather is milder than in Cusco, it's closer to Machu Picchu, and it makes a good center for visiting other places of interest. There are a number of hotels, cheap and not so cheap, in Urubamba itself and scattered along the valley. Urubamba is a peaceful town of flowering trees and has a strong Amerindian flavor. The coat of arms on

Map on page 276

BELOW: market day in Pisac.

Dressed for the Three Kings fiesta at Ollantaytambo.

the city hall is sufficient evidence of this; no Spanish symbols are found in the emblem, which bears pumas, snakes, and trees. It was the beauty and calm of this village that prompted the 18th-century naturalist Antonio de León Pinelo to expound on his theory that Urubamba was the biblical Eden. From here you can make trips to the salt pans at Salinas and the circular Inca agricultural terracing at Moray. You can take a bus for the first part of the way, but after that it's a hike.

Ollantaytambo

Continuing along the valley, you come to the great fortress of **Ollantaytambo** ㉕, a place of great sacred and military importance to the Incas. (The fortress can be visited using the Cusco Visitor Ticket. For details about the story of Ollantay, Pachacutec's most famous general, *see page 261*.) Here, travelers find themselves facing an elegant and intricate walled complex containing seven rose-colored granite monoliths which puzzle scientists, who say that the stone is not mined in the valley. A steep stairway enters the group of buildings, among which the best known is the so-called **Temple of the Sun** – an unfinished construction in front of a wall of enormous boulders. Portions of the original carvings on these huge worn stones can still be seen, although it is unclear if they really are pumas, as some claim. Specialists say that the unfinished condition of the temple has less to do with the Spanish destruction of Ollantaytambo than with the fact that it was simply never completed.

Ollantaytambo, strategically placed at the northern end of the Sacred Valley, also has plazas with sacred niches, shrines, an area of stone stocks where prisoners were tied by their hands, and ritual shower areas, including the **Princess's Bath**, or Baño de la Ñusta.

LEFT: Inca ruins at Pisac.
RIGHT: crafts at Pisac market.

The village's military fortification was so well planned that it took the Spanish by surprise when they arrived in search of Manco Inca during the 1536 uprising. Hernando Pizarro (a brother of Francisco) led a contingent of about 100 Spaniards and a number of Amerindians to the fort with the intention of capturing and executing the rebel leader. Chronicles say that as the Spaniards sneaked up to the fort just before dawn, they looked up to see the silhouettes of multitudes of Amerindian warriors ready to take them on. It is even said they saw Manco Inca himself, directing troops from inside the Ollantaytambo complex, mounted on a captured horse. In fact, Manco Inca's men had diverted the Patacancha river through some canals, and now they opened barriers that allowed the water to rush out and flood the plain that the Europeans were crossing. However, the Spaniards managed to escape to Cusco, where they recruited a force of 300 cavalrymen to return and confront Manco Inca. Outnumbered, he abandoned the walled city and fled to Vilcabamba, where he was eventually killed.

Ollantaytambo is perhaps the best preserved of all the Inca settlements. The old walls of the houses are still standing, and water still runs through original channels in narrow streets that are believed to date from the 15th century. In the nearby river stand the remains of an Inca bridge, and *campesinos* around the settlement live in houses that have changed very little since Pizarro's arrival. The CATCCO **Museum** has information about local history, culture, and architecture (open Tues–Sun 10am–1pm and 2–4pm; admission fee).

After exploring the Sacred Valley, the destination of most visitors is the **Inca Trail** and **Machu Picchu**. You can get a train from Ollantaytambo (either the tourist train or the local one) or take a train from Cusco and get off at Km 88 *(see page 285)*. Machu Picchu, of course, merits a chapter all to itself. ❑

Map on page 276

BELOW: view of the Urubamba Valley.

MACHU PICCHU

*Hidden from the world until 1911, this Inca refuge in the
mountains is breathtaking in every sense. Trekkers can choose the
hard way up, via the Inca Trail; others may opt for the train*

Map
on pages
230–1

O f all the popular treks in South America, the three- to five-day Inca Trail
is the one that most travelers want to do. The adventure begins with a
four-hour train ride along the Río Urubamba, a region known to the Incas
as the Sacred Valley. Legions of early-rising *campesinos*, loading and unloading their marketable goods at every station along the way, crowd together in
what begins to look more like a cattle car than a passenger train. At Qori-
huayrachina, **Kilometer 88**, the hikers' trail begins. It is no longer possible to
walk the Inca Trail independently; you must pre-arrange the trip either at home
or in Cusco. (If you want to avoid several days of arduous trekking, the train
leaving from Cusco also stops at Chalcabamba, **Kilometer 104**, 8 km/5 miles
from the Lost City, and you can get off there, but you will miss out on some
stunning scenery.)

The first 11 km (7 miles) meander through easy terrain of dusty scrub bushes,
low-lying hills, and a few rustic huts. Conserve your strength on this stretch,
because it will soon get tougher. The first barrier is the **Warmiwañusqu Pass**.
Beyond lies a wealth of Inca ruins, but struggling to the top of this 4,000-meter
(13,000-ft) pass is no small challenge. Laboring up the seemingly endless trail,
the hiker soon identifies with its name. In English it translates literally as "Dead
Woman's" pass.

From here, Inca history begins to unfold. The small
guard-post of **Runkuraqay**, overlooking the valley
and often shrouded in mist in the morning, is the first
reward offered by the Inca Trail. Farther along, the
more elaborately constructed site of **Sayajmarka**
(Dominant Town) perches atop a narrow cliff. The
fine stonework for which the Incas were justly famous
is apparent here. Snaking along the valley below is
an incredible "paved highway" made of neatly fitted
stone, masterfully constructed by a culture the Spanish conquistadors considered uncivilized.

Stunning ruins

As the trek progresses, the archeological sites become
more complex. **Puyapatamarka** (Cloud-level Town)
is fascinating for its circular walls and the finely engineered aqueduct system, which still provides spring
water to the ancient ceremonial baths. Below, the trail
offers yet another delight to the trekker.

Huge steps, a virtual stone stairway almost a half
mile in length, lead down into high jungle vegetation
where wild orchids and other exotic flowers bloom.
Curiously, this section of the trail lay undiscovered
until 1984. Until then, a modern footpath connected
this interrupted section of the Inca highway.

Tenaciously clinging to the side of a steep ravine
is the last set of ruins, and the most stunning. **Huiñay**

PRECEDING PAGES:
Machu Picchu, the
Inca citadel.
LEFT: view through
a trapezoid
window.
BELOW: walking the
Inca Trail.

Huayna presents an unbelievable picture when first seen in the distance. The ability of the Incas to construct something so complex in an area so vertical defies comprehension, yet the series of ritual baths, long stretches of terracing, and intricate stonework certainly prove what would appear to be impossible.

About two hours away lies the jewel in the crown – **Machu Picchu**. From the high pass of **Intipunku**, the Sun Gate, you get the first glimpse of the fabled city. This is the culmination of days of walking; the immersion into an ancient culture is complete. Arriving as the Incas did centuries ago, the trekker begins the final descent into Machu Picchu, sharing a path with history.

Discovering the ruins

When Hiram Bingham and his party discovered **Machu Picchu** ㉖ in July 1911, Bingham was actually searching for the ruins of Vilcabamba, the remote stronghold of the last Incas. Today we know that he had almost certainly found Vilcabamba, without realizing it, when he stumbled across the jungle-covered ruins of Espíritu Pampa, some 100 km (60 miles) west of Machu Picchu, two months before making his spectacular find on the Urubamba gorge. But Bingham saw only a small section of Espíritu Pampa, and dismissed it as insignificant. It was left to Gene Savoy, another American explorer, to investigate Espíritu Pampa when he came looking for the lost city of the Incas more than 50 years later *(see page 55)*.

Bingham was a Yale graduate, later a US Senator, who became fascinated with Inca archeology in 1909 while in Peru studying Simón de Bolívar's independence struggle. He returned with the Yale Peruvian expedition in 1911, and took the narrow mule trail down the Urubamba Gorge in July of that year.

BELOW: the ruins at Puyapatamarka, on the Inca Trail.

Melchor Arteaga, a local *campesino* (subsistence farmer) whom he met by chance while camping on the river banks, led him to the jungle-covered ruins.

Machu Picchu – Ancient Peak – was what the local people called the mountain above the saddle-ridge where the ruins were located, and its sister mountain was Huayna Picchu – Young Peak. Not only did Bingham want to call these ruins Vilcabamba, because he believed he had discovered Manco Capac's gilded city, but he also speculated that the mountain refuge was Tampu Tocco, the mythical birthplace of the Ayar brothers, the first of the Incas.

Bingham's mistake in thinking that he had found the location of Vilcabamba is understandable. Who would have imagined that there were not one, but two, lost cities in the jungle north of Cusco? But overwhelming evidence against the Machu-Picchu-as-Vilcabamba hypothesis emerged, and Bingham was presented with an enigma: if Machu Picchu was not the last refuge of the Incas, then what on earth was it?

Outpost in a lost province

Bingham carried out further explorations between 1911 and 1915, discovering a string of other ruins and a major Inca highway (now known as the Inca Trail) to the south of Machu Picchu. Later still, in 1941, the Viking Fund expedition led by Paul Fejos discovered the important ruins of Huiñay Huayna above the Urubamba Gorge, about 4.5 km (3 miles) due south of Machu Picchu. This proved that Machu Picchu was not merely a lost city, but part of an entire lost region – a fact generally ignored by popular histories. The usual account portrays Machu Picchu as a secret refuge known only to a select few, and concealed from the Spaniards. But this would have been impossible; the location

Map on pages 230–1

The train to Km 88.

BELOW: orchids brighten the mountainside.

of an entire active and populated region could not have been concealed from the Spaniards, who had many allies among the Amerindian peoples.

And yet the Spaniards did not know of Machu Picchu's existence. The only possible conclusion is that the Incas and Amerindians at the time of the Conquest did not know of it either. Somehow the city and its region were abandoned and depopulated before the conquistadors arrived, and the memory was lost even to the Incas themselves. Perhaps the area was devastated by plague, or overrun by the Antis, the hostile jungle tribesmen. But why would there be total amnesia about its location? This cannot have been accidental. The Incas had a caste of *quipucamayocs* – oral history recorders – who kept detailed accounts of the Inca past, but this was official history, and the Incas were notorious for wiping inconvenient details off the record. Perhaps this was Machu Picchu's fate: a province that rebelled and was dealt with so ruthlessly that its existence was erased from official memory.

Well, that is merely one theory that fits the known facts. Here is another: according to new evidence unearthed from Spanish colonial archives, and recently presented by the archeologist J.H. Rowe, there was a "royal estate" (a rather Western concept, but the most intelligible way to put it) of the Inca Pachacutec at a place called "Picchu," north of Cusco. This leads to an interpretation that Machu Picchu was built and populated by the *panaca* (royal house) of Pachacutec, and that the eventual disappearance of the *panaca*, a generation or so after the ninth Inca's death, led to the depopulation and abandonment of the whole region.

Signs of a pre-Inca occupation at Machu Picchu, going back 2,000 years, have recently been discovered, but there was certainly no pre-Inca city of any consequence here. If we accept that Machu Picchu was built for Pachacutec, we can speak of the construction dates of Machu Picchu with reasonable confidence. According to a widely accepted chronology, the Inca expansion began in the year 1438, after Pachacutec had defeated the Chanca invasion from the north. Various chronicles tell us that for strategic reasons (to keep the retreating Chancas out) this mountainous area was the first to be settled in the headlong rush toward empire.

The building style of Machu Picchu is "late imperial Inca," which supports this thesis, and there are no signs of post-Conquest occupation. So the whole settlement was built, occupied, and abandoned in the space of less than 100 years. The rest is speculation. And who can resist speculating when faced with something as affecting and impenetrable as the mystery of these silent stones?

Piecing together the past

What kind of settlement was Machu Picchu? John Hemming, author of *The Conquest of the Incas* – probably the best book on the subject – states that the site has only 200 habitation structures, leading him to estimate a permanent population of about 1,000 people. It is interesting that the agricultural output of the area would have greatly exceeded the needs of the population, for, beside the large extension of agricul-

The hydro-electric plant on the trail was destroyed by a massive wave of mud and water in 1998. There are plans to build a new one in Sucuni, some four hours from Cusco in the direction of Arequipa.

BELOW: the trail to Huayna Picchu.

Map on pages 230–1

tural terracing at Machu Picchu itself, there were also much larger terraced areas at Inti Pata (just behind Machu Picchu peak to the southwest), and Huiñay Huayna, along the Inca Trail. More than one archeologist has proposed that the principal material function of the Machu Picchu region was to create a reliable supply of coca leaves for the priests and royals of Cusco.

Hiram Bingham called the ruin a "citadel," existing for strategic and defensive purposes. But beside its outer walls and moat, Machu Picchu contains an unusually high proportion and quality of religious architecture. Modern opinion leans more to the view that Machu Picchu was essentially a site of spiritual and ceremonial significance, with important agricultural functions. Its strategic purposes, if any, were secondary.

Bingham's fortress idea did not prevent him from speculating that the city was a refuge of Cusco's Virgins of the Sun, an idea inspired by the revelation that more than 75 percent of the skeletal remains found there were female. This exciting piece of news has been on the lips of tour guides ever since. Yet there is one difficulty with this hypothesis: the Yale expedition found only skulls, the other bones having disintegrated in the humid climate. It is extremely hard to pronounce on the gender of a skull, particularly if, like the expedition's medical authority Dr Eaton, you are not very familiar with bones of the racial subgroup it comes from. Dr Eaton pronounced most of the skulls "gracile," and therefore, he assumed, female. But they could as easily have been young men, or men of small stature. The skulls still exist, and could be studied again by modern experts, but so far no-one has done so.

It is alleged that the terms of Bingham's permission to excavate at the site of Machu Picchu were unclear. This led to vague accusations of smuggling after he shipped all the relics back to Yale University, where most of them remain to this day. There were no precious metals, however, and it is not a visually spectacular collection, so the dispute is mainly one that concerns scholars.

Breakthroughs in archeology

Since 1985 an astonishing number of new discoveries have been made around Machu Picchu. Taken as a whole they support and expand the emerging view of Machu Picchu as the ceremonial and possibly administrative center of a huge and quite populous region. The alluring myth of Machu Picchu as some kind of Andean Shangri-la perched alone on its remote crag must now be laid to rest.

The most extensive finds have been made across the river to the northeast, on a sloping plateau known as Mandorpampa about 100 meters (330 ft) above the railroad. Its outstanding feature is an enormous wall about 3.5 meters high by 2.5 meters wide (11½ by 8¼ ft), and more than a kilometer long, which runs straight up the mountainside toward a pointed peak known as Yanantin. It was apparently built to protect the adjacent agricultural terraces from erosion, and may also have served to demarcate two areas with separate functions.

A road running along its top heads off northeast into densely forested mountains toward Amaybamba,

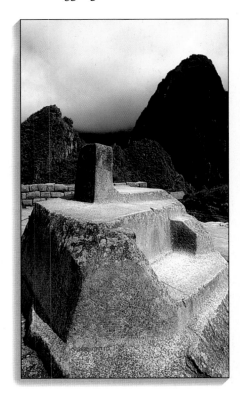

BELOW: the solar calendar at Machu Picchu.

or perhaps some other Inca settlement as yet undiscovered. Other finds on the *pampa* include quarries, circular buildings, a large number of stone mortars, and a big observation platform.

Closer to Machu Picchu itself, the sector on the north slope of Huayna Picchu, which is known as the "Temple of the Moon," has been cleared to reveal a subterranean temple, a fine wall with an imposing gateway, and an observatory directed toward the Yanantin peak.

Farther upriver, two important burial sites known as Killipata and Ch'askapata have been discovered, and the ruins of Choquesuysuy, just upstream from where the hydro-electric power station used to stand, now appear to be much larger than had been previously believed. Of all these sites only the Temple of the Moon has been opened to the public so far.

In the years following Bingham's discovery the ruins were cleared of vegetation, excavations were made, and later a railroad was blasted out of the sheer granite cliffs of the imposing canyon. Visitors began to arrive. Pablo Neruda came in 1942, and was inspired to write his most famous poem, *The Heights of Machu Picchu*. In 1948 a sinuous 12-km (7-mile) road from the river banks to the ruins was inaugurated by Hiram Bingham himself.

A walking tour of the ruins

Bingham classified the ruins into sectors, naming some of the buildings. But some of his conclusions appear wide of the mark to modern archeologists; others seem too arbitrary, resting on minimal evidence. However, for the sake of clear directions we need to name different sectors, and, since nobody has come up with a better system than Bingham's, here we go: you enter the ruins through

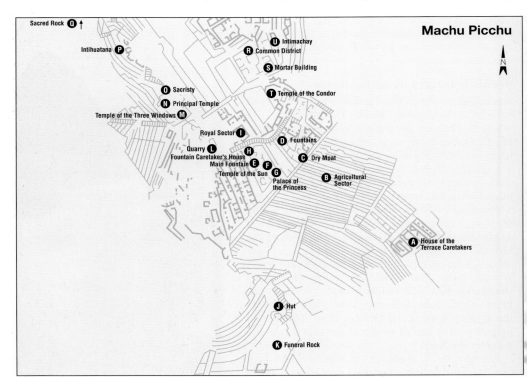

Machu Picchu

Sacred Rock **Q**
Intihuatana **P**
U Intimachay
R Common District
S Mortar Building
O Sacristy
N Principal Temple
Temple of the Three Windows **M**
T Temple of the Condor
Royal Sector **I**
Quarry **L**
Fountain Caretaker's House **H**
Main Fountain **E**
F
Temple of the Sun **G**
Palace of the Princess
D Fountains
C Dry Moat
B Agricultural Sector
A House of the Terrace Caretakers
J Hut
K Funeral Rock

the **House of the Terrace Caretakers**  **Ⓐ**, which flanks the **Agricultural Sector Ⓑ**. This great area of terracing was undoubtedly for agricultural purposes, and made the city self-sufficient in crops. The terraces end in a **Dry Moat Ⓒ**, beyond which lies the city itself.

Map on page 290

If you continue straight ahead you come to the **Fountains Ⓓ**, which are actually small waterfalls, in a chain of 16 little "baths," varying in the quality of their construction. These were probably for ritual, religious purposes relating to the worship of water. Bingham speculated that Machu Picchu might have been abandoned because this water supply dried up, or became inadequate to irrigate the terraces. The hotel consumes most of this spring water today. The **Main Fountain Ⓔ** is so called because it has the finest stonework and the most important location; it is just above you to the left as you arrive from the terraces.

Here, too, is the **Temple of the Sun Ⓕ**. This round, tapering tower features the most perfect stonework to be found in Machu Picchu. It contains sacred niches for holding idols or offerings, and the centerpiece is a great rock, part of the actual outcrop on which the temple is built. The base of this rock forms a grotto that is casually referred to as the Royal Tomb, although no bones were found there.

Recent archeo-astronomical studies have demonstrated how this temple would have served as an astronomical observatory. The rock in the center of the tower has a straight edge cut into it. This is precisely aligned through the adjacent window to the rising point of the sun on the morning of the June solstice. The pegs on the outside of the window may have been used to support a shadow-casting device, which would have made observation simpler.

The temple's entrance doorway has holes drilled about the jamb, less complex

An overloaded bus.

BELOW: explaining the finer points.

than those on a similar doorway at the Coricancha in Cusco. The adjacent building has two stories and was obviously the house of someone important. Bingham named it the **Palace of the Princess G**.

Next to the Sun Temple, just above the main fountain, is a three-walled house, which has been restored and had its roof thatched as an example of how these structures looked in Inca times. It is usually called the **Fountain Caretaker's House H** – but it's unlikely to have been a house at all, since it is open to the elements on one side. The thick stone pegs fixed high up in the wall are thought to have served as hangers for heavy objects.

Students of the more esoteric aspects of the Inca culture have suggested that this complex of adjacent structures forms a temple to the four elements: the Temple of the Sun (Fire); the "Royal Tomb" (Earth); the open-fronted Fountain Caretaker's House (Air); the Principal Fountain (Water).

The structures directly opposite the Sun Temple, across the staircase, have been classified as the **Royal Sector I** because of the roominess of the buildings, and also for the huge rock lintels (weighing up to 3050 kg or 3 tons) that in Inca architecture generally characterized the homes of the mighty.

At the top of the agricultural terraces, standing high above the city, is a lone **hut J**, which is a great place for an overall view of the ruins. It backs onto a gently sloping area known as the cemetery, because Bingham discovered numerous bones and mummies at this spot. Just a few meters from the hut lies a curiously shaped carved rock, called the **Funeral Rock K**. Bingham speculated that this had been used as a place of lying-in-state for the dead, or as a kind of mortician's slab, on which bodies were eviscerated and then left to be dried by the sun for mummification.

BELOW: limbering up on the Inca Trail.

Mysterious stone

At the top of the staircase leading up from the fountains you come to a great jumble of rocks **L** that served as a quarry for the Inca masons. There is a fascinating discovery in this sector – a partially split rock that seems to show precisely how the builders cut stone from the quarry. The rock bears a line of wedge-shaped cuts where tools were hammered in to form a crack. The problem with this rock, though, is that it was reportedly cut by a 20th-century archeologist, Dr Manuel Chávez Ballón.

Follow the ridge away from the quarry with your back to the staircase, and you come to one of the most interesting areas of the city. Here is the **Temple of the Three Windows M**. Its east wall is built on a single huge rock; the trapezoidal windows are partly cut into it. On the empty side of this three-walled building stands a stone pillar that once supported the roof. On the ground by this pillar is a rock bearing the sacred step-motif common to many other Inca and pre-Inca temples.

Next to this site stands the **Principal Temple N**, another three-walled building with immense foundation rocks and artfully cut masonry. It is named for its size and quality, and also because it is the only temple with a kind of sub-temple attached to it. This is generally called the **Sacristy O**, because it seems a suitable place for the priests to have prepared themselves before sacred rites. The stone that forms part of the left-hand door-jamb has 32 corners in its separate faces.

Ascending the mound beyond this temple leads you to what was probably the most important of all the many shrines at Machu Picchu, the **Intihuatana P**, the so-called "Hitching Post of the Sun." This term was popularized by the American traveler Squier in the 19th century, but nobody has ever unraveled the mystery of how this stone and others like it were used. Every major Inca center

Map on page 290

BELOW: Inca terraces have survived the centuries.

had one. It seems likely that the stones somehow served for making astronomical observations and calculating the passing seasons. There was at least one other "Intihuatana" in the vicinity, located near the site of the old hydro-electric power station in the valley below, to the west. The second stone was probably situated to make a specific astronomical alignment with the main one. The main Intihuatana is a sculpture of surpassing beauty. It is the only one in all Peru to have escaped the diligent attention of the Spanish "extirpators of idolatry," and luckily has survived in its original condition.

The group of buildings across the large grassy plaza below forms another, more utilitarian sector of the city. At the north end, farthest from the entrance to the ruins, you find two three-sided buildings opening onto a small plaza, which is backed by a huge rock generally called the **Sacred Rock Q** An intriguing aspect of this plaza is that the outline of the great flat rock erected at the northeast edge is shaped to form a visual tracing of the mountain skyline behind it. Then, if you step behind the *masma* (three-sided hut) on the southeast edge and look northwest, you find another rock that echoes in the same way the skyline of the small outcrop named **Uña Huayna Picchu**. In 2000, an enormous scandal broke out in Peru after a lighting crane being used during the filming of a beer commercial fell and broke part of the sacred stone. Since then, all visitors must visit the site with an official guide.

Walking back toward the main entrance along the east flank of the ridge, you pass through a large district of cruder constructions that has been labeled the **Common District R**. At the end of this sector you reach a building with two curious disk-shapes **S** cut into the stone of the floor. Each is about 30 cm (1 ft) in diameter, flat, with a low rim carved around the edge. Bingham thought these were mortars for

BELOW:
point of view.

grinding corn, but this is doubtful. True, he did find some pestle stones in the same building, but the normal mortar used by the Quechua Amerindians today is much deeper and more rounded within; also it is portable, not fixed in one spot. These "mortars" would not have served well for that function. However, nobody has suggested a more plausible explanation for these enigmatic cavities.

Just across the next staircase you come to a deep hollow, surrounded by walls and niches, which is known as the **Temple of the Condor ⓣ**. Bingham called this the Prison Group, because there are vaults below ground, and man-size niches with holes that might have been used for binding wrists. But the concept of "prison" probably did not exist in Inca society; punishments tended to involve loss of privileges, or physical suffering, or death. Some early Spaniards reported pits full of snakes or pumas into which offenders were dropped to see if they would survive, but that is hardly a prison. The complex was probably a temple. A rock at the bottom of this hollow bears a stylized carving, apparently a condor, with the shape of the head and the ruff at the neck clearly discernible.

There is a small cave known as **Intimachay ⓤ** above and to the east of the Condor Temple, which has been identified as a solar observatory for marking the December solstice. The cave is faced with coursed masonry and features a window carved out of a boulder that forms part of the front wall. This window is precisely aligned with the winter solstice sunrise, so that morning light falls on the back wall of the cave for ten days before and after that date.

Further explorations

If you arrived at Machu Picchu via Aguas Calientes rather than by the Inca Trail, there are three walks that are worth attempting. First, above the ruins to

The porters make it look easy.

BELOW: following the tracks to Machu Picchu.

Map on page 290

the southeast you can see a pass scooped out of the ridge, with a small ruin at the center. This is **Intipunku**, the Sun Gate. You can actually see the sun rise in this gateway from the western heights of the ruins at certain times of year. The trail traversing the mountainside from this point was the main Inca highway from Huiñay Huayna and other sites farther south. It is well preserved, and makes for a fairly easy climb, taking about an hour and a half there and back. The view of Machu Picchu from Intipunku is magnificent.

The second walk is to the **Inca Drawbridge**. A trail winds back from the heights of the ruins, by the cemetery, leading along the west flank of the mountain behind Machu Picchu. This trail grows narrower until it is cut into the side of a sheer precipice, and you find yourself taking each step with care. Follow it until you come to a spot so abrupt that the ancients had to build a huge stone buttress to create a ledge for the path to cross. They left a strategic gap in the middle of the buttress, bridged by logs which could be withdrawn. Beyond this point the trail quickly peters out, becoming unstable and extremely dangerous. The path has been fenced off shortly before the bridge, ever since one walker tried to hike beyond it and fell to his death. To the bridge and back is an exciting one-hour walk demanding a cool head for heights.

Hardy visitors also like to climb **Huayna Picchu**, the towering granite peak that overlooks Machu Picchu from the north. It's the original Inca path, very steep, and stepped in places. Approach it with caution – but don't be put off by the peak's fearsome appearance. You don't have to be a mountaineer. If you are reasonably active and healthy you will get to the top – and back. Everyone planning to climb Huayna Picchu must sign in at the control point along the trail leaving the principal ruins. You must set out before 2pm, as visitors are barred from starting the climb any time after that.

As you near the top of Huayna Picchu you pass through ancient terraces so inaccessible and so narrow that their value for agricultural purposes would have been negligible. It is thought that they were probably ornamental gardens, to be admired from the city below. About an hour and a half gets the average person to the peak for a stupendous view.

The **Temple of the Moon** stands inside a cavern halfway down the north face of Huayna Picchu. It was discovered in 1936 and contains some of the finest stonework of the entire Machu Picchu complex. The Inca pathway that leads to the temple forks off the main trail to the left about one third of the way up to the peak of Huayna Picchu.

Huiñay Huayna

Physically active people staying overnight at Machu Picchu can also take the **Inca Trail** to **Huiñay Huayna** *(see pages 285–6)*. The round trip takes about four hours, including some time to look at the ruins. Note that the Inca Trail fee, minus entrance fee to Machu Picchu, is charged for this hike. The journey itself is rewarding, since the trail passes through exotic tropical forest, and is well worth the effort. It is also possible to spend the night at the basic hostel at Huiñay Huayna, and return to Machu Picchu the following morning. ❑

BELOW: a view from Huayna Picchu.
RIGHT: dawn of the winter solstice at the Temple of the Sun.

LAKE TITICACA

The highest navigable lake in the world is the legendary birthplace of the first Inca and the site of some fascinating local communities such as Puno and Copacabana

Map on pages 230–1

Lima

Lake Titicaca is the world's highest navigable lake and the center of a region where thousands of subsistence farmers eke out a living fishing in its icy waters, growing potatoes in the rocky land at its edge, or herding llama and alpaca at altitudes that leave Europeans and North Americans gasping for air. It is also where traces of the rich Amerindian past still stubbornly cling, resisting in past centuries the Spanish conquistadors' aggressive campaign to erase Inca and pre-Inca cultures and, in recent times, the lure of modernization.

The turquoise blue lake was the most sacred body of water in the Inca Empire and is now the natural separation between Peru and Bolivia; it has a surface area exceeding 8,000 sq. km (3,100 sq. miles), not counting its more than 30 islands. At 3,856 meters (12,725 ft) above sea level it has two climates: chilly and rainy or chilly and dry. It gets cold in the evenings, dropping below freezing from June through August. During the day the sun is intense and sunburn is common, so take care.

Birthplace of the Incas

According to legend, this lake gave birth to the Inca civilization. Before the Incas, the lake and its islands were holy places for the Aymara Amerindians, whose civilization was centered at Tiahuanaco, now a complex of ruins on the Bolivian side of Titicaca but once a revered temple site with notably advanced irrigation techniques. Geologically, Titicaca's origins are disputed, although it was probably a glacial lake. Maverick scientists claim that it had a volcanic start; a century ago, it was popularly believed to be an immense mountain-top crater. There are a few diehards today who stick to the notion that the lake was part of a massive river system from the Pacific Ocean – but then, there are those who insist that the earth is flat.

Amerindian legend says the sun god had his children, Manco Capac and his sister-consort Mama Ocllo, spring from the freezing waters of the lake to found Cusco and the beginning of the Inca dynasty. Later, during the Spanish Conquest, the lake allegedly became a secret depository for the empire's gold. Recent aquatic expeditions have found gold figurines and other precious items, most notably around the islands of the sun and moon in Bolivia, but these were most probably thrown into the lake as ritual sacrifices.

In 1961, the oceanographer Jacques-Yves Cousteau used mini-submarines to explore the depths of the lake, but found no gold. What he did discover, to the amazement of the scientific world, was a 60-cm (24-in) tri-colored frog that apparently never surfaces. Visitors today find a region unlike anywhere else: a place of floating reed islands, ancient lifestyles, and crumbling churches, where women wear bowler hats and the men knit their own brightly colored headgear.

PRECEDING PAGES: a *totora* boat on the lake.
LEFT: selling tapestries on the Islas de los Uros.
BELOW: a lakeside llama.

Urban base

If you are approaching the area from Cusco you will probably take the train to **Juliaca ㉗**, although some tour groups travel in minibuses. Be forewarned that flights from Cusco are sometimes discontinued for no apparent reason. Juliaca is a busy town with the largest railway terminus in the country, a good airport, and plenty of places to eat, but not much else going for it except for a lively Sunday market. From here you can continue by train or go by minibus to **Puno ㉘**, a commercial center settled as a Spanish community in 1668 by the Count of Lemos. During the colonial period it was one of the continent's richest cities because of its proximity to the Laykakota silver mines discovered by brothers Gaspar and José Salcedo in 1657. The mining boom drew 10,000 people to an area not far from what is now Puno. It also brought a bloody rivalry that ended only when the iron-handed count ordered José Salcedo to be executed, and transferred Laykakota's residents to Puno.

Dance and wild costumes

At an altitude of 3,830 meters (12,630 ft), Puno is the capital of Peru's *altiplano* – the harsh highland region much better suited to roaming vicuñas and alpacas than to people. It is also Peru's folklore center, with a rich array of handicrafts, costumes, *fiestas*, legends and, most importantly, more than 300 different ethnic dances. Among the latter, the most famous is the *Diablada* (Devil Dance), performed during the feast of the Virgen de la Candelaria during the first two weeks in February. Dancers compete fiercely to outdo one another in this dance, notable for its profusion of costly and grotesque masks. The origins of the dance have become lost over the centuries, but it is believed to have started

BELOW: a bus excursion from Puno.

with pre-Inca cultures, surviving through the Inca conquest and the Spanish takeover of the country, with the costumes being modified each time.

The lavish outfits the dancers wear are as varied as the dances themselves. They range from multi-hued *polleras* (layered skirts), worn by barefoot female dancers, to the short skirts, fringed shawls and bowler hats used in the highland version of the *marinera* dance *(see page 173)*. For centuries the Amerindians in the *altiplano* were accustomed to working hard, then celebrating their special days with gusto. Many of the dances incorporate features of the most repressive times for the Amerindians, with dancers dressed as mine overseers or as cruel landowners – characters who are mocked during the festivities. It is difficult to find a month in Puno without at least one elaborate festival, which is always accompanied by music and dance.

Little of Puno's colonial heritage is visible, but there remains a handful of buildings worth seeing. The **Catedral** is a magnificent stone structure, dating back to 1757, with a weather-beaten baroque-style exterior and a surprisingly spartan interior – except for its center altar of carved marble, which is plated in silver. Over a side altar to the right side of the church is the icon of The Lord of Agony, commonly known as *El Señor de la Bala*. Beside the cathedral is the Balcony of the Count of Lemos found on an old house on the corners of Deústua and Conde de Lemos streets. It is said that Peru's Viceroy Don Pedro Antonio Fernández de Castro Andrade y Portugal stayed here when he first arrived in the city he later named "San Carlos de Puno."

On the **Plaza de Armas** are the **Biblioteca** (Library) and the municipal **Pinacoteca** (Art Gallery), and half a block off the plaza is the **Museo Carlos Dreyer**, displaying a collection of Nazca, Tiahuanaco, Paracas, Chimu, and Inca artifacts

Map on pages 230–1

Amantaní Island girls.

BELOW: the festival of the Virgen de la Candelaria, Puno.

bequeathed to the city on the death of their owner, for whom the museum is named. One of the museum's most valuable pieces is an Aymara *aribalo*, the delicate pointed-bottomed pottery whose wide belly curves up to a narrow neck. Throughout the South American continent, the *aribalo* is a symbol of Andean culture.

Views of the Sierra

Three blocks uphill from the plaza is the **Parque Huajsapata**, a hill that figures in the lyrics of local songs, and an excellent spot for a panoramic view of Puno. Huajsapata is topped by a huge white statue of Manco Capac gazing down at the lake from which he sprang. Another lookout point is found beside **Parque Pino**, at the city's north side, in the plaza four blocks up Calle Lima from the Plaza de Armas, in which stands the Arco Deústua, a monument honoring those killed in the decisive independence battles of Junín and Ayacucho.

The park is also called Parque San Juan, after the San Juan Bautista church within its limits; at its main altar is a statue of the patron saint of Puno, the Virgin of Candelaria. Also in the park is the Colegio Nacional de San Carlos, a grade school founded by a decree signed by Simón de Bolívar in 1825. It was later converted into a university, then subsequently used as a military barracks.

Two blocks down F. Arbul Street from Parque Pino is the city market, a colorful collection of people, goods, and food. Tourists should keep their eyes on their money and cameras, but it is worth a stop to see the wide selection of products – especially the amazing variety of potatoes, ranging from the hard, freeze-dried *papa seca* that looks like gravel, to the purple potatoes and yellow and orange speckled *olluco* tubers. Woolen goods, colorful blankets, and *ponchos* are on sale here, along with miniature versions of the reed boats that ply

Puno Week – the first week in November – when the town goes wild, is a celebration of Manco Capac's emergence from Lake Titicaca.

BELOW: navigating in *totora* boats.

Lake Titicaca. Among the more intriguing trinkets are the *Ekekos*, the ceramic statues of stout jolly men laden with an indefinite number of good luck charms, ranging from fake money to little bags of coca leaves. Believers say that the *Ekekos* like to smoke, and they are often found with lit cigarettes hanging from their mouths. It is also said that these images only bring luck if they are received as gifts – not purchased.

The real reason for coming to Puno is that it is the stepping-off point for exploring Lake Titicaca and its amazing array of islands, Amerindian inhabitants, and colorful traditions. Small motorboats can be hired for island visits or fishing trips – although fish stocks have declined in recent years and most lake trout is now farmed. Another fascinating relic of a different era is the *Yavari* steamship. Built by the British in 1862, it plied the lake until 1975, and is now a floating museum.

Floating islands

The best-known of the islands dotting the surface of Titicaca are the **Islas de los Uros** ㉙, artificial floating islands of reed named after the Amerindians who inhabited them, but often known simply as the Islas Flotantes. Old legends described the Uros islanders as people incapable of drowning, "like the fish and the birds of the water." The last full-blooded Uro was a woman who died in 1959. The people who live on the islands today are physically indistinguishable from mainlanders, having intermarried with Aymara- and Quechua-speaking Amerindians, and they now speak Aymara.

Poverty has prompted more and more of the people to move to Puno, and has caused those who remain to take a hard-sell approach to tourists on those

Map
on pages
230–1

BELOW: everything
is made of reeds
on the Islas de
los Uros.

islands that are most visited. But why not? They certainly need the money. Take some fresh fruit as gifts when you visit, as the islanders' diet is very basic. There is some criticism that tourism has not only opened the Uros Islands to the stares of insensitive tourists but has also destroyed much of the culture, as the Amerindians modify their handicrafts to appeal to outsiders, or abandon traditional practices to dedicate more time to the influx of outsiders, but in fact many of the floating islands are not visited, and therefore remain untouched by tourism.

Homeward-bound after a hard day.

Many traditional customs and crafts remain unchanged, and the islanders are still quite different from the rest of Peru's population. They fish, hunt birds, and live off lake plants, and the most important element in their lives is the lake reeds they use to make their houses and boats and even as the base of their islands – the largest of which are **Toranipata**, **Huaca Huacani**, and **Santa María**. The lower layers of the reed islands decay in the water and are replaced from the top with new layers, making a spongy surface that is a bit difficult to walk on. Even the walls of the schools on the bigger islands are made of *totora*. The soft roots of the reed are eaten, too, making it a pretty handy thing to have around.

Another island that lures tourists is **Isla Taquile** ㉚, the home of skilled weavers and a spot where travelers can buy well-made woolen and alpaca goods as well as colorful garments whose patterns and designs bear hidden messages about the wearer's social standing or marital status. Prices of these goods may be higher than on the mainland, but the quality is very good. The residents of this island run their own tourism operations in the hope of maintaining a degree of control over tourism and ensuring that the visits of outsiders do not destroy their delicate culture *(see page 311)*. There are no hotels on Taquile, but the

BELOW: Taquile women.

Quechua-speaking islanders open their homes to tourists interested in an overnight stay. Arrangements for such accommodations can be made with local people, who wait at the top of the steep stone staircase where the boats dock. You will find several places to eat, mostly serving simple but tasty fish and rice dishes. You can visit Taquile in one day, but it means spending much of the day on a boat, and an overnight stay is recommended.

Map on pages 230–1

Isla Amantaní

Handicrafts also play an important role in life on **Isla Amantaní**, a lovely, peaceful island even farther away from Puno than Taquile. Amantaní was once part of the Inca empire, as attested to by local ruins, and was reputedly once a prison island, before the Spanish invaded and slaughtered the islanders. The Spaniard who was granted a concession to the island used the Amerindians in forced labor, and his descendants were still in control after Peru's independence from Spain. But eventually an island *fiesta* turned violent, and the Amerindians attacked their landlord with hoes and subsequently split up the island into communally held fields.

Amantaní has opened its doors to outsiders who are willing to live for a few days as the Aymara-speaking islanders do – and that means sleeping on beds made of long hard reeds and eating potatoes for every meal. There is no running water, and night-time temperatures drop to freezing even in the summer. But those happy to rough it catch a glimpse of an Andean agricultural community that has maintained the same traditions for centuries. Some Amantaní residents live and die without ever leaving the island.

Journeys to Amantaní and Taquile commence at the Puno docks aboard sputtering wooden motorboats that are operated by the islanders. At the end of the three-hour trip, visitors are registered as guests and then assigned to a host family, which shows the way to its mud-brick or reed home set around an open courtyard decorated with white pebbles spelling out the family's name. The socializing begins when a family member who may speak a little English offers a guided walk around the island, from where the views are absolutely spectacular. Women from the island wearing traditional black-and-white lace dresses pass by with slingshots in their hands to kill scavenging birds.

Another island, **Isla Esteves**, is connected to Puno by a causeway and is best known for the luxurious but ugly Hotel Libertador Isla Esteves, which stands out like a sore thumb. It's a far cry from what used to be the main construction on the island – a prison that accommodated the patriots captured by the Spanish during Peru's War of Independence. James Orton, a naturalist and explorer who died crossing Titicaca on a steamship in 1877 is buried here; his memorial sits beside one honoring the liberation fighters who perished in the war with Spain. Orton, a professor of natural history from Vassar University, was on his third expedition to explore the Beni River in the Amazon area. The Beni's link to the Mamore River – both crucial conduits during the jungle's 19th-century rubber boom – was named the Orton in honor of the great explorer.

BELOW: a boatman wears a typical woven hat.

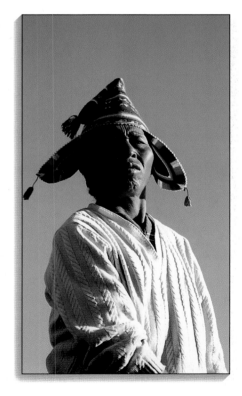

Mysterious burial chambers

Some 35 km (20 miles) from Puno is **Sillustani**, with its circular burial towers or *chullpas* overlooking **Lago Umayo**. The age of the funeral towers, which are up to 12 meters (40 ft) high, remains a puzzle. A Spanish chronicler described them as "recently finished" in 1549, although some look as if they were never completed. They were built by people of the Colla civilization, who spoke Aymara, and whose architecture was considered more sophisticated than that of the Incas, but who had been conquered by the Incas about a century before the Spanish arrived. The *chullpas* were apparently used as burial chambers for members of the nobility, who were entombed together with their entire families and possessions to take with them to the next world. This is a stunningly beautiful spot with a wealth of birdlife, and guinea pigs scuttling across the paths.

Among the wading birds to be seen around Sillustani are the Andean goose, the lapwing and, occasionally, the flamingo.

Not far away (about 20 km/12 miles from Puno) is **Chucuito**, an *altiplano* village that sits upon what was once an Inca settlement and which has an Inca sundial in the plaza. Close to the village stands the ancient fertility temple of the same name, whose most notable feature is an enclosure of giant stone phalluses. Have a look at the **Iglesia Santo Domingo** with its small museum; the church of **La Asunción** is also worth visiting.

Juli (about 80 km/50 miles from Puno), and once the capital of the lake area, has four beautiful colonial churches. Although it now appears a little strange to see so many large churches so close together, at the time when the Spanish had them built they were hoping to convert huge numbers of Amerindians to Catholicism. In addition, the Spanish were accustomed to providing one church for Europeans, one for mixed-raced Christians and yet another for Amerindians.

BELOW: celebrating a Taquile festival.

The largest – and oldest – of Juli's ornate churches is **San Juan Bautista**, with rich colonial paintings tracing the life of its patron saint, John the Baptist.

From the courtyard of the **Iglesia La Asunción** there is a captivating view of the lake. The other churches in the city are **San Pedro**, once the principal place of worship, in which a choir of 400 Amerindians used to sing each Sunday, and **Santa Cruz**, which is just beside the city's old cemetery, and is currently in the worst state of repair. Santa Cruz was originally a Jesuit church upon the front of which indigenous stonemasons carved a huge sun – the Inca god – along with more traditional Christian symbols. From Juli, the Transturin hydrofoils leave for Bolivia. The timetable is a bit erratic, and it is best to make arrangements in Puno, rather than wait until you get to Juli.

The road from Juli hugs the shore, and about 25 km (15 miles) farther on you come to the little village of **Pomata**, with its granite church of **Santiago Apóstol**.

Pilgrimage site

Copacabana, a pleasant and friendly little town on the Bolivian side of the lake, can be reached by taking a minibus ride from Puno (via Yunguyo) around the side of the lake, passing the reeds waving in the wind, shy but curious children at the bends in the road, and the ever-present brilliant blue of Titicaca. This pleasant trip sometimes involves a short ferry ride at the

Strait of Tiquina. As a pilgrimage site, Copacabana is accustomed to tourists and has a number of modest but clean restaurants and hotels, and a couple of very comfortable ones, newly built by the lakeside. It is most famous for its cathedral containing a 16th-century carved wooden figure of the Virgin of Copacabana, the Christian guardian of the lake. The statue, finished in 1853, was the work of Amerindian sculptor Francisco Tito Yupanqui, nephew of Inca Huayna Capac. Except during Mass, the statue stands with its back to the congregation – but facing the lake so that it can keep an eye out for any approaching storms and earthquakes. One of the loveliest outings in Copacabana is a dawn or dusk walk along the waterfront, watching the sky explode into color with sunrise, or slip into the blue-black of night at sunset.

Getting to Bolivia

From Copacabana, launches can be hired to visit the Bolivian islands on Lake Titicaca – the **Isla del Sol** and the **Isla de la Luna** (the Island of the Sun and the Island of the Moon). The former (also accessible via a public ferry) has a sacred Inca rock at one end and the ruins of Pilko Caima, with a portal dedicated to the sun god at the other. The Island of the Moon, which is also known as Coati, has ruins of an Inca temple and a cloister for Chosen Women.

    The bus from Puno to La Paz takes about eight hours on a newly paved road via Copacabana in Bolivia; an impressive route with great views of snowy peaks over the lake. Most buses stop for lunch in Copacabana, which has a beautiful cathedral. You can also reach Bolivia by taking a bus from Puno around the other side of the lake, via Desaguadero, a scruffy border town. This route is shorter, but is not as scenic as going via Copacabana. ❏

Map on pages 230–1

Village mayor, Isla Taquile.

BELOW: herds of llamas live around Lake Titicaca.

TAQUILE ISLAND

Lake Titicaca's Taquile Island is a harshly beautiful place whose people have retained their traditional lifestyle and values

In the 16th century Taquile was a colonial *hacienda*. After Peru's independence (in 1821) it became a prison island, but the people of Taquile gradually regained control of their lands and today they are a closely integrated community. Their language sets them aside from other Titicaca Amerindians: they speak Quechua rather than the more common Aymara.

△ **BELT CODE**
The men's embroidered belts contain coded calendars giving information about crops and marriage dates.

▽ **TILLING THE SOIL**
A couple till the soil using a foot plow little changed in style since Inca times.

FARMING, FISHING, AND KNITTING

Taquile is a very special place: the earth is a rich, reddish brown, a color that predominates in the women's clothes, and the lake a glorious vivid blue. Life seems to have changed little over the centuries: the earth is farmed with traditional implements, and crop diversification is unknown. Plenty of potatoes but few fresh vegetables or fruits are grown. Trout, the best in Peru, are fished from the lake and served in the few basic restaurants. On the hillsides stand the remains of Inca terracing.

The Taquile weaving cooperative is renowned for the quality of its garments, and the people habitually look as if they are dressed for a *fiesta*. The women wear layers of multi-colored skirts and embroidered blouses; the men sport smart waistcoats and black trousers along with the little pointed hats that they knit themselves.

The islanders enjoy fiestas, too, and whether they are celebrating Santiago (St James), which falls on July 25 or Pacha Mama (Mother Earth) in early August, high spirits, music, and plenty of *chicha* are always very much in evidence.

▷ **TAQUILE SUNDAY**
Mayors of Taquile file out of church after Sunday morning Mass. As elsewhere in Peru, Christian observances co-exist with indigenous rites.

◁ *FIESTA* **HEADGEAR**
This elaborate hat is reserved for major *fiestas*. For daily wear, most women cover their heads with simple black shawls.

▽ **COOPERATIVE VENTURES**
Taquile is famous for its weaving cooperatives, which produce a range of distinctive, high-quality garments. These are much in demand, and can be bought in the community shop on the main plaza.

CONTROLLING THE FLOW

When visitors first arrived on Taquile during the early 1970s, ferried across the lake by enterprising Puno boat-owners, the islanders decided that if change was on the way they wanted to control it. They began operating their own passenger boats, and regulating the number of people who visit the island.

The islanders will not allow the construction of hotels. Some of them open their homes to visitors, who can spend the night and share their meal for a very reasonable charge. If you want to sample their hospitality, remember that the accommodation will be pretty basic.

Realizing that their woven goods are also of interest to outsiders, the islanders now sell them on the main plaza. Prices are higher than on the mainland, but the quality is superb. It seems that the people of Taquile are making a very good job of managing tourism: enjoying the economic benefits without taking unfair advantage of their visitors.

△ **NO IDLE HANDS**
Wherever you go on Taquile you will see men knitting finely spun wool into the brightly colored stocking hats they habitually wear. Colors denote marital status and social standing.

▷ **ISLAND FASHIONS**
Taquile women dress in colorful, many-layered skirts and black shawls.

▽ **A VIEW ON THE WORLD**
Children growing up on Taquile today will inevitably find their lives affected – for good and ill – by the influx of foreign tourists. However, their parents' generation is trying hard to make tourism work while still preserving the traditional ways.

CENTRAL SIERRA

Isolated for years by geography and then terrorism, Ayacucho and the other towns of the Central Sierra are places to enjoy traditional Peru and some spectacular scenery

Maps:
Area 230
City 314

Lima

Historically, **Ayacucho** ㉛ and the central highlands have been the link between Lima, and other coastal towns, and Cusco, with the vast eastern jungle region beyond it. It is also here that much of Peru's mineral wealth is to be found, which brought both riches and hardship to the area. In the 1980s, terrorism and emergency military rule made the highland provinces unsafe and unwelcoming, but with the return of peace and the building of a breathtaking highway from Lima, the area is once again welcoming travelers who enjoy its traditional way of life, handicrafts, and often spectacular mountain scenery.

These mountains in Central Peru contain caves where, as at Pikimachay, traces have been found of the first inhabitants dating back to over 15,000 years ago. Ayacucho was also important during the Huari (or Wari) culture, which dominated the region for several hundred years before falling to the Inca in the 14th century. The Incas themselves used it as a communications center, as its river valley was on the main route up to what is now Ecuador, and south into Chile. Mining in the area continues, as it has done for centuries, with the giant Cerro de Pasco mine still being one of the world's most important producers of copper. To the north are the imposing peaks of the Cordillera Occidental, and the mysterious rock formations at Marcahuasi, which attract many visitors.

LEFT:
highland girls with
the family livestock.
BELOW: Ayacucho's
colonial entrance.

Much of this area was off-limits for travelers in the 1980s and 1990s, because Ayacucho was the center of activities for Abimael Guzmán and his Sendero Luminoso (Shining Path) guerrilla group. More than half of the 69,000 people killed by the rebel group and in the armed forces' counter-insurgency campaigns came from these provinces: the vast majority of them innocent peasants. This violence led to a massive migration to Lima and other coastal cities, and created a climate of fear and suspicion.

In recent years however, with the capture of Guzmán and the virtual disappearance of Shining Path, many people have returned and taken up their traditional pursuits. The best times to visit are during Easter Week, which is given up entirely to processions and fiestas, or the week at the end of April, when Ayacucho's patron saint is remembered with more riotous celebrations. Another festival well worth attending is the Fiesta de las Cruces in May, when the famous scissor dance is performed in which a pair of men wielding huge tailors' scissors try to cut each other's trousers.

Churches and mansions

Ayacucho was founded by Francisco Pizarro in 1540, as an important communications link between Lima and Cusco. The city was at first called Huamanga, after the local stone similar to alabaster, and is still often,

Posing on the Plaza de Armas.

BELOW: one of the city's 33 churches.

somewhat confusingly, called this by locals. The name was changed in 1824, after Republican forces finally freed Peru of Spanish troops at the nearby battle on the plain of Ayacucho. The impressive archway known as the **Arco de San Francisco de Asis**, or Arco de Triunfo, on the Jirón 28 de Julio in the city center was built in 1924 to commemorate the victory.

Ayacucho's reputation as a city with "a church on every street corner" may be exaggerated, but it does have 33 churches, most of them still in regular use. Perhaps the most impressive is the **Catedral Ⓐ** (open Mon–Tues and Fri–Sat 9am–noon and 3–5pm; Thur 4–7pm) on the Plaza Mayor de Huamanga (previously Plaza Sucre). Built in 1612, it has superb gilt altars, a silver tabernacle, and a beautifully carved pulpit. It also contains Stations of the Cross paintings brought from Rome. During the famous *Semana Santa* celebrations during Easter Week, this is one of the most visited churches in all Peru. The procession of its statues round the city by different *cofradías* or brotherhoods, rivals that of Seville in Spain. The faithful start the week on Palm Sunday with a candlelight procession when a precious statue of Christ from the cathedral is carried on the back of a white donkey. Each day after this there are more processions, with each statue from the church being revered by its own group of worshipers. At dawn on Easter Sunday, all the bells of the city celebrate Christ's resurrection, the doors of the cathedral are flung open, and 250 men carry the statue of Christ around the square.

Another outstanding church, the Jesuit **Templo de la Compañía Ⓑ** (open Mon–Sat 9am–noon) built in 1605, boasts an unusual carved facade of orange-red stone and has a lovely gilded altar. The interior also has richly carved wood and 17th-century religious paintings.

A few blocks away up Jirón 9 de Diciembre stands the **Templo de Santo**

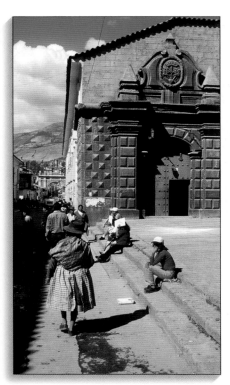

Domingo ⒞ (open Mon–Tues and Fri–Sat 9am–noon and 3–5pm; Thur 4–7pm). It has an altar richly decorated with gold leaf, but it is this church's role in history that is most significant: bells in its small towers rang out the first peals of Peru's independence following the decisive Battle of Ayacucho. Round the corner on Jirón Callao, the finest carved pulpit of all Ayacucho's churches is to be found in the **Iglesia de San Francisco de Paula ⒟** (open Mon–Sat 9am–noon and 3–7pm).

Although Spanish colonial architecture is the pride of Ayacucho, this was an important area for many civilizations prior to the arrival of the Spaniards. Five hundred years before the Incas, the Wari empire dominated these highlands, and traces of that and other influences are to be found at the **Museo Hipólito Unanue ⒠**, part of the **Instituto Nacional de Cultura** on Avenida Independencia. The museum's collection ranges from 1500 BC stone carvings to Wari ceremonial bowls, Chancay textiles, and stone and ceramic Inca pieces (open Mon–Fri 9am–1pm and 2–5pm; Sat 9am–1pm; entrance charge).

Ayacucho has several other museums that are worth visiting. **The Museo Joaquín López Antay** in the colonial **Casona Chacón** (now a bank) on the Plaza de Armas has a good collection of local art, popular objects, and photographs of the city and its surroundings (open Mon–Fri 9.30am–12.30pm and 4.30–6pm; Sat 9.30am–12.30pm). The nearby **Casona Jauregui** is another exquisitely proportioned 17th-century mansion which holds temporary exhibitions.

The **Museo Mariscal Cáceres ⒡**, housed in the elegant 17th-century **Casona Vivanco** on Jirón 28 de Julio, has a fine display of colonial paintings and furnishings. It is named after Andrés Cáceres, a young man from Ayacucho whose rapid military ascent stemmed from his successful organization of *campesinos*

Map on page 314

The inti was a currency that was introduced in 1986, but it only lasted until 1991.

BELOW: Good Friday's procession in Ayacucho.

Street art using flower petals during Ayacucho's Easter celebrations.

to resist the Chilean invaders during Peru's otherwise disastrous performance in the War of the Pacific in the 1880s. Cáceres was rewarded by being made president of Peru in 1886. The *casona* is one of the best-preserved of the colonial mansions which are the hallmark of Ayacucho (open Mon–Sat 9am–12.30pm and 2–5pm).

Another splendid mansion is the **Casona Boza y Solis** , the seat of the provincial prefecture. Built in 1740, it has a two-story interior courtyard and a wide staircase lined with beautiful imported colored tiles. It also contains the cell where the local heroine of independence, María Prado de Bellido, was held until she was executed by a Spanish firing squad in 1822 (open daily 9am–5pm).

Arts and Crafts

Ayacucho is a center for many traditional handicrafts. A good place to see artisans at work and to purchase their wares is the **Santa Ana** neighborhood behind the Alameda Bolognesi. Many of the houses here still contain family workshops, where several generations make rugs, tapestries, and carpets. Filigree and silver work as well as retablos (painted altars) of all shapes and sizes can be bought in Santa Ana and other parts of the city. Another specialty of the city are the etched *mates burilados* (gourds). These often show surprisingly complicated scenes of everyday life or from the Bible, etched onto dried gourds of every dimension. The local huamanga alabaster is also still worked with great skill into biblical scenes, cribs for Christmas and other, more modern fantasies.

Shopping is also a lively experience at the city's sprawling market a block south of Avenida San Martín. Here, stalls offer everything from handicrafts and hand-knitted sweaters, to rubber boots and hot peppers and other medicinal herbs. Delicious fresh-made bread, with cinnamon and aniseed, is sold from cloth-covered baskets, as are herbal drinks known as *emolientes*. You can safely try the bread, but it is perhaps advisable to leave the drinks to the locals: the glasses are not usually properly washed.

BELOW:
ceramic by potter Pablo Seminario.

But the local drink of *ponche* is well worth a try. This is a milk-based punch flavored with peanut, sesame, clove, cinnamon, walnuts, and sugar, and spiked with *pisco*. You could accompany this with one of the hearty local dishes such as *puca picante*, a stew made of pieces of pork, potatoes and toasted peanuts, served with rice and parsley.

Battle site

In the rolling hills 37 km (22 miles) northeast of the city is the village of **Quinua**. It was on the plain one kilometer (½ mile) outside the village that the decisive battle of Ayacucho was fought against the Spanish troops on 9 December 1824. Although outnumbered almost two to one, the Venezuelan general Antonio José de Sucre emerged victorious from the battle, which was the last fought by the Spaniards in Latin America. (Some local guides will even tell you that no battle as such was fought, since the Spanish commander Virrey de la Serna decided to avoid bloodshed and withdrew.) The place of the encounter is marked by a hideous 1970s obelisk some 44 metres (144 ft) high, built with Venezuelan oil wealth. Its one redeeming feature is the spectacular scenery to be seen from its viewing platform. The broad plain is a popular place for week-end picnics, and each December the victory is celebrated by an eight-day extravaganza. Dancing and craft exhibitions are central to the celebrations, with the scissors dance *(see page 313)* once again to the fore.

The village of Quinua itself is a center for handicrafts, and has been so successful that as many as 7,000 people now live there, most of them producing crafts of one kind or another. Almost all the red-tiled roofs are topped with good-luck symbols: small ceramic churches or pairs of bulls, made originally for festivals coinciding with the branding of cattle. These pieces are also on sale in the village's many stores, together with hand-made guitars and sculptures in huamanga stone.

Several tour companies in Ayacucho organize day trips that include Quinua and the battlefield, and also a visit to **Vilcashuamán**. This was once an important administrative center for the Inca empire, and is interesting above all for the Spanish constructions built directly on top of Inca architecture. The village is most famous for its "usnu" or ceremonial Inca pyramid, which has been preserved almost intact. Inca remains are also to be found at **Intihuatana** (a 30-minute walk from the highway). Next to a lagoon thought to have been artificially constructed by the Incas, there are the remains of a palace, a tower, a Temple of the Sun, a sacrificial stone, and a boulder carved with 17 angles.

Another stopover is at the Huari (Wari) ruins about 20 km (12 miles) outside Ayacucho on the way to Quinua. These extensive ruins, in a landscape full of tuna cactuses, are thought to be the remains of the Wari culture which flourished here between the 6th and 11th centuries. Archeologists have estimated that up to 50,000 people lived in this settlement, occupying as many as 15 different "neighborhoods". There is a small museum on site, but most of the finds have been taken to the archeological museum in Ayacucho for safekeeping.

As well as the tuna cactuses, you may also find in these high valleys the *Puya raimondi*, a strange-looking plant that lives to be a hundred years old but dramatically flowers in great profusion only after 80 years of growth. The rivers that cut the valleys around Ayacucho also offer good fishing for trout and other native species. No permit is necessary, but there are seasons for different fish – best to ask a local expert.

North from Ayacucho

Ayacucho's nearest northern neighbors – although it takes several hours to reach them – are the towns of **Huancavelica** and Huancayo. Huancavelica has a lengthy past as one of Peru's main mining towns. Silver was discovered here soon after the Spanish conquest, and through the 17th and 18th centuries it was a great creator of wealth, although many of the indigenous people who worked in the mines suffered from mercury poisoning and died very young. The mines at **Santa Barbara**, some 5 km (3 miles) outside the city, can be visited. As in Ayacucho, some of this mining wealth was spent on the city's churches. The **Catedral**

Map on page 230–1

BELOW: toffee apples for sale.

in the Plaza de Armas in the center of Huancavelica has a fine gilded altar and some baroque paintings. Nearby, **San Francisco** shows how Spanish colonial architecture became far more baroque in the 18th century, while the church and convent of **Santo Domingo** includes paintings shipped especially from Rome.

More interesting is the bustling city of **Huancayo** ㉜, situated some 400 km (250 miles) northwest of Ayacucho. The city's name means "place of stones" and from the remaining monuments it is easy to see why. Its main attractions are the **Capilla de la Merced** (open Mon–Sun 9am–noon, 3–6.30pm), the colonial church where the Peruvian constitution was signed in 1839. The people of Huancayo are also very proud that it was in their city that slavery was abolished in Peru in 1854, and the statue in the main plaza honors Mariscal Ramón Castilla, who pushed the measure through. There is also an interesting regional museum in the **Museo del Colegio Salesiano** in the El Tambo district, while the Cerrito de la Libertad is a hill overlooking the city with panoramic views. A short walk further on are the remarkable eroded stone towers known as the **Torre Torre**, which also give views over the town.

Huancayo is known throughout Peru for its boisterous festivals. The most famous – as in Ayacucho – is the Fiesta de las Cruces, which is held every May. There is also a Sunday market which brings in artisans from all the surrounding area, and is a good source of bargains. And in Huancayo, everyone has to try at least once the fabulous *pachamanca*, where a meat stew is cooked in a hole in the ground covered with hot stones.

Huancayo is also the starting point for journeys to the Mantaro Valley, which has several places well worth a visit. About 8 km (5 miles) from Huancayo is the village of **Cochas Chico**, where some of the best local handicrafts can be

Oscar Durand, the last leader of the guerrilla group Sendero Luminoso, was captured near Huancayo in 1999. This marked the end of the group's activities, which had brought death and misery to many.

BELOW:
the spectacular rail
journey from Lima
to Huancayo.

THE TRAIN TO THE SKIES

The train journey from Lima to Huancayo is one of the most spectacular in the world. The line rises 346 km (215 miles) from sea level to a height of 4,800 meters (16,000 ft) at the Ticlio pass, and is said to be the highest in the world. There are 26 stations, 61 bridges and 67 tunnels through the Andes. Construction of the railway started in the late 1800s by the US engineer Henry Meiggs, and took over 40 years to complete. It is an engineering wonder – but to pay for it, the Peruvian government of the day almost went bankrupt. Principally it was for transporting copper and zinc from mines in the Andes and farm produce from the valleys.

The passenger service was stopped in 1992 due to terrorist activity, but a limited passenger service has now resumed. The train only makes special journeys once a month between April and October (during the dry season), so it is vital to book in advance. The journey takes 12 hours.

bargained for. There is also the Convento de Santo Ocopa, founded some 250 years ago as a training place for missionaries who were setting off to evangelize in the vast Amazon regions of Peru. In the convent there is a precious library, with some texts dating back to the 15th century. Further north, the **Santuario Warivilca** is a fortified ruin from the days of the Wari empire.

The mountains here form the beautiful Cordillera Huaytapallana, which is 17 km (11 miles) long and has five peaks over 5,000 meters (16,400 ft) high, with many important glaciers. The highest of the peaks is the Nevado Lasuntaysuyo, which is always covered in snow.

Some 40 km (25 miles) from Huancayo is the small town of **Jauja**. This is famous above all for being the capital of Spanish Peru before Lima was founded, and for the expression *país de Jauja*, referring to a never-never land of milk and honey. Its narrow streets and blue-painted houses seem to reflect hundreds of years of unhurried existence. Boats can be rented by the hour to take you to the nearby Laguna de Paca.

Some 170 km (105 miles) north of Huancayo is a favorite destination for keen bird-watchers: the **Reserva Nacional de Junín**. The lakes here abound with aquatic birds and the large Andean species.

The northernmost town of any importance in the central highlands is **Huanuco**. Previously part of the Wari and then the Inca culture, the modern city was founded by Gomez de Alvarado in 1539. It has always been the market center for a mainly agricultural and wooded region, and maintains much of its slow charm today. The central square or Plaza de Armas has a 19th-century sculpture by an Italian designer but, unlike many other Peruvian cities, its cathedral is modern, dating from 1966. Two older churches though are the **Iglesia San Cristobal**, the first built by the Spaniards, which is adorned with fine wood carvings, and the **Iglesia de San Francisco**, first constructed in 1560 but remodeled in the 18th century in neoclassical style (open daily 6–10am and 5–8pm). This sleepy town comes to life during carnival week, celebrated here in August. And in January, it is host to the *danza de los negritos*, when dancers wear black masks to represent the black slaves imported to work in the silver mines, most of whom died out.

Five kilometers (3 miles) outside Huanuco stands **Kotosh** and its famous **Templo de las Manos Cruzadas**. As the name suggests, this temple, believed to be several thousand years old, has carvings of crossed hands on the walls. According to some archeologists, this is a sign that the ancient people who lived here had a dual vision of the universe.

Also close to Huanuco are the amazing, colossal rock formations of **Marcahuasi**. These are a magnet for rock climbers, but have also bred several strange theories that they represent huge human profiles sculpted by a people who inhabited the earth before mankind. The copper rich stones are reported to have protective properties, and are said to shield visitors from negative energy. A large flat plain in the middle of the formations is the scene each year (July 28–30) of a local festival bringing together music and dance groups from all the surrounding villages. ❑

Map on page 230–1

BELOW: vicuñas run in the Andean highlands of the Central Sierra. **OVERLEAF:** the Madre de Dios region from the air.

INSIGHT GUIDES

TRAVEL TIPS

CONTENTS

Getting Acquainted

The Place

Area 1,285 sq. km/496,100 sq. miles
Capital Lima
Highest Mountain Nevado Huascáran (6,768 meters/ 22,205 ft)
Principal waterways River Amazon, Lake Titicaca
Population 27.5 million
Language Spanish, Quechua
Religion Roman Catholic
Time Zone GMT –5hrs
Currency Nuevo Sol (S/)
Weights & Measures Metric
Electricity 220/240v
International Dialing Code +51

Politics and Economy

In June 2001, Alejandro Toledo was elected president of Peru. His election finally ended more than a decade of rule by Alberto Fujimori (1989–2000), who fled to Japan in disgrace when allegations of widespread corruption and abuses during his period in office came to light *(see page 67)*. Perhaps the one lasting achievement of the Fujimori regime was its success in combating the extremist groups. The leader of the Shining Path guerrilla movement, Abimael Guzmán, was captured in 1992, which led to the collapse of the group. Then in 1996–97, the leaders of the Tupac Amaru rebel group were wiped out to end the siege of the Japanese ambassador's residence. After these two successes, political violence in Peru virtually ceased, although human-rights groups criticized many of the government's tactics, including

the imprisonment of thousands of people merely on suspicion of links with terrorist groups, the suspension of civil liberties, and the armed forces' involvement in massacres, especially in remote rural areas.

The Toledo government set up a Truth and Reconciliation Commission to investigate these charges. Its final report, published in 2003, estimated that some 69,000 people had died in the political violence of the years 1980–2000. At the same time, investigations continue into the extent of the corruption that occurred during the governments headed by Fujimori and the head of his intelligence services, Vladimiro Montesinos. The charges against the two men run from organizing death squads to arms smuggling, profiting from the illegal drugs trade, to embezzlement, corruption of officials, and gross misuse of public funds.

Since coming to power Alejandro Toledo, who is the first elected president of Andean indigenous extraction, has been attempting to restore confidence in Peru's politicians by bringing in reforms. In late 2002, the first regional elections were held, in an attempt to change the massive centralization of funds and political power in the capital. He has also tried to use Peru's strong growth to help alleviate poverty, with programs to distribute food and build new housing in rural areas. After so many years of violence and corruption, most Peruvians are now happy to enjoy their newly rediscovered democracy, even though the economic benefits have yet to be felt.

Population

Of a population of 27.5 million, as many as 8 million live in the Greater Lima area. The highest density is in the coastal areas (55 percent of the total); 34 percent, mostly direct descendants of the

Inca culture, live in the Highlands; and 11 percent live in the eastern jungle area.

About 45 percent of the population are Amerindians, 32 percent *mestizos*, 12 percent whites *(criollos)* and 2 percent blacks and Asians.

The national languages are Spanish and Quechua, and Aymara is also spoken by Amerindians living around Lake Titicaca.

Despite the economic upswing achieved through Fujimori's neoliberal politics, the dreadful living conditions of most Peruvians haven't changed.

Ten million suffer from the consequences of malnutrition while about the same number have no clean drinking water. The infant mortality rate in Peru is one of the highest in South America.

Climate

Peru has wet and dry seasons, although on the coastal desert strip it is always dry. However, Lima suffers a bizarre weather condition prevailing from April to November called the *garúa*, a damp cold mist which obliterates the sun and sours everyone's mood. August is the worst month for this, with temperatures around 13°C–17°C (55°F–62°F). The rest of the year, Lima enjoys sunshine and moderate temperatures from 20°C–26°C (69°F–79°F).

Towns like Nazca on the western slopes of the Andes are dry and hot all year round, but the central Andes experiences distinct wet and dry seasons. The best time to visit the highlands – and for most people, that means the best time to visit Peru generally – is between May and September when views of the mountains are crystal clear. Although the days

Time Zones

Lima is five hours behind Greenwich Mean Time and therefore coincides with Eastern Standard Time in the USA.

are bright and clear, nights can be bitterly cold and temperatures can fall to 0°C (32°F). During the rest of the year, the weather is warmer but wetter, and the Andes are often obscured.

In the Amazon Basin, the wet season lasts from January–April, when landslides and flooding are a constant problem. During the dry season, May–October, it might not rain for weeks at a time (although there might be short showers every day). Daytime temperatures average 23°C–32°C (81°F–90°F), with night-time lows averaging 20°C–26°C (69°F–79°F).

However, unexpected cold fronts called *friajes,* which come up from the south, are unique to the southern rainforests and can bring a few days of wind and rain with spring-like daytime temperatures of 13°C–18°C (55°F–65°F) and night-time lows of 10°C (50°F). Although this weather condition is unusual, it is said to have a beneficial effect on the wildlife of the region.

Planning the Trip

What To Bring

Peru being a country of such diversity, what you bring depends on your itinerary. For example, those planning adventure travel will need specific items such as tents that other travelers can do without. Bring warm clothes for the Sierra, light clothes for the jungle and a combination for the coastal deserts, which are warm by day and cool at night. *See "Climate", above, for more details.*

Items that are difficult to obtain in Peru include: your personal medical supplies; a strong money belt; sunscreen; good books in English; and any electronic equipment you use. Bring your camera and some film, although most types of film are widely available.

What To Wear

Good traveling clothes should be comfortable and durable and preferably made of natural fiber, although one or two synthetics in the form of evening wear that won't wrinkle in your suitcase come in handy for those formal nightspots. Take some good walking shoes that won't look too out of place in a casual restaurant.

One rarely regrets traveling light, especially in a land where clothes shopping is a dream. Remember all those alpaca sweaters and leather goods – you can buy as many warm clothes as you like when you arrive. However, it is almost impossible to get shoes in large sizes.

The most appropriate clothing for a jungle trip is long-sleeved shirts and trousers of close-woven material. These protect the wearer

from most biting insects. A hat gives valuable protection while traveling on the river or birdwatching on the lakes. Mountaineers and hikers should not forget to bring good walking shoes, warm clothes, and equipment because there is a shortage of trekking supplies in Peru. Avoid olive-green trousers and military-style jackets; Peruvians could get the wrong idea.

Visas and Passports

Visas are not required by citizens of South American countries, European countries, the United States of America, Canada, Japan, Australia, or New Zealand.

All visitors, however, must have a passport and are issued with an entry stamp and tourist card on arrival in Peru. These are valid for 90 days and the card must be surrendered to immigration on departure. These tourist cards can be extended for 30 days, for a fee of US$20 and presentation of a return ticket, in Migraciones at the Dirección Nacional de Migraciones in the Oficina de Migración, Av. España 7, Breña, Lima tel:01 330 4111/01 330 4114.

Health

The most serious illnesses to guard against are yellow fever and malaria, which both occur in jungle areas of the north and south Amazon, and malaria on parts of the coast. There have been outbreaks of yellow fever in Puerto Maldonado, so visitors should ensure they are vaccinated. Visitors are advised to consult their physician about anti-malarial drugs before leaving home. Malarial mosquitoes only bite at night so always use a mosquito net when sleeping in jungle towns and keep covered up as much as possible between dusk and dawn. Cholera is not a great threat: tourists risk infection only if they have direct body contact with acutely or chronically infected people. Vaccination against cholera is possible but can't replace elementary hygiene precautions *(see tips below concerning eating and drinking, control of flies, avoiding dirty accommodation and public swimming pools).*

Hepatitis A is caught by ingesting contaminated food or water. Be cautious about seafood; stick to bottled drinks, peeled fruit and good-quality restaurants, thereby ensuring your standard of hygiene. Two shots taken six months apart should protect against Hepatitis A for ten years (one shot works for six months).

A less serious and much more common condition for travelers in Peru (or any third-world country, for that matter) is upset stomach and diarrhea – often caused by a change in culture and diet, unclean water or utensils, or simply the change of place. Traveling itself places extra pressure on the immune system, so take it easy until you feel stronger. In most cases, the symptoms will improve after a day or so of fasting and drinking plenty of fluids (hot tea without milk is ideal). If the more serious condition of dysentery develops (i.e. any blood or pus in the stool), you should see a doctor.

Don't be surprised if your exaltation at flying into Andean mountain cities is followed by a less pleasant sensation called *soroche* or altitude sickness. In most cases the symptoms are very mild – fatigue, shortness of breath, slight nausea, and headache. The best prevention and cure is to lie down for a few hours upon arrival at your hotel and then slowly introduce yourself to physical activity. Coca tea, available in all highland hotels and restaurants, also helps. If the symptoms are severe – i.e. vomiting, rapid irregular pulse, insomnia – take it seriously and descend immediately to a lower altitude (although this usually happens only to mountain climbers).

Medical Services

Good hotels will have reliable doctors on call. The following clinics in Lima have 24-hour emergency service and an English-speaking staff member on duty:
Clínica Anglo Americana,
Alfredo Salazar s/n, San Isidro,
tel: 221 3656/221 2240.

Heat of the Sun

The tropical sun might feel very gentle but it can burn you to a crisp. Ultra-violet rays are particularly powerful at high altitudes; wearing a brimmed hat as well as sunglasses, and using a high-factor sun screen will all help protect you from the glare. High humidity dehydrates the body; drink plenty of liquid and add salt to your food.

Clínica Internacional,
Jr. Washington 1475, Lima,
tel: 433 4306.
Clínica Javier Prado,
Av. Javier Prado Este 499, San Isidro,
tel: 440 2000.
Emergency Hospital Casimiro Ulloa,
Av. República de Panamá 6355,
San Antonio, Miraflores,
tel: 241 2789/242 7133.
Clínica San Felipe
Av. Gregorio Escobedo 650,
Jesús María,
tel: 463 0909
Clínica Tezza
Av. El Polo 570, Monterrico, Surco,
tel: 435 6990; 24 hours,
tel: 437 1310
Maison de Santé
Av. Chorrillos 171–173, Chorrillos,
tel: 467 1310/467 0753
Travel insurance which covers the cost of an air ambulance should be taken out before you start your trip.

Money

Since 1986 Peru has twice introduced a new currency to stop depreciation. In 1991 the nuevo sol (s/) replaced the shrinking inti at a ratio of 1 to 1 million. The annual inflation rate steadied during the 1990s after the hyper-inflation of the 1980s. The exchange rate in 2004: US$1 = s/3.45.

There is no shortage of money-changing facilities in Lima, formal and otherwise – if you don't mind haggling on street corners. On the Plaza San Martín, in downtown Lima, hundreds of outdoor bankers run alongside the traffic – the rate is usually a little better than in the

banks. It is legal to change with these *cambistas*, who generally wear a blue jacket and carry a calculator, and usually quite safe – although if you don't feel comfortable with it, there are plenty of alternatives. Banks will change your currency at the slightly inflated "official" rate and good hotels have exchange services or will send a hotel courier to one of the *casas de cambio* for a better rate (remember to give him a tip). Travel agents accept payment in some foreign currencies and exchange small amounts.

The Banco de Crédito and the Banco de la Nación are recommended for any international banking business such as receiving US dollars from overseas. Ask for a *liquidación por canje de moneda extranjera* (cash in exchange for foreign currency).

It is convenient to carry some US cash as well as your travelers' checks, credit cards, or cash advance card (although Lima, Cusco, Arequipa, and Iquitos have every money-changing facility). It is not always possible to change checks, and cash dollars get a better rate, although you run the risk of theft. American Express will replace lost travelers' checks only in Lima.

Make sure that you don't carry more cash than your insurance policy covers you for, or you will be penalized for being under-insured in the event of a claim.

Local currency can be obtained via credit/debit cards using the ATM machines of the following banks:
Banco de Crédito ATM
For Visa and Plus cards
Banco Latino ATM
For MasterCard and Cirrus cards
Banco de la Nación ATM
For Visa cards.
Interbank ATM
For Visa and Plus cards.

CREDIT CARDS

Credit cards such as Diners Club, Visa, American Express, and MasterCard are accepted by good hotels and restaurants. There are branches of Diners, MasterCard and Visa in Lima.

To report credit-card loss in Lima, call:

Visa: 108 Operator Collect Call: (001) 410 581 0120
Diners Club: 221 2050
MasterCard: (1-800) 307 7309
American Express: 441 4744

Offices in Cusco:
MasterCard: Banco Latino, Calle Almagro 125
Visa: Banco de Crédito, Av. Sol 189

Getting There

By Air

Jorge Chávez airport lies around 16 km (10 miles) from the center of Lima. Minibuses (Airport Express) leave regularly for Miraflores. Guests of bigger hotels can use the hotel shuttle service. There is an international departure tax of US$28.

Peru is well connected by international flights. From Europe, direct flights to Lima are available with Iberia and KLM.

American Airlines make daily flights from Canada and the US via Miami. These same airlines, plus Continental Airlines, also fly direct from major cities including New Jersey, Dallas, Houston, and Los Angeles.

There is no shortage of flights to other South American countries. Lloyd Aero Boliviano flies between Cusco and La Paz, Bolivia, twice a week. To travel to and from Mexico use either Aero México, Mejicana, LACSA, or Copa.

The best route from Australia or New Zealand is probably with the Aerolineas Argentinas direct flight to LA, connecting with Lima. There are also weekly flights from Sydney and Auckland to Santiago in Chile (via Tahiti with Qantas or UTA, connecting with Lan-Chile to Santiago, stopping over at Easter Island). In Santiago, change for Lima.

By Sea

Few people arrive at Lima's port of Callao by ocean liner or freight ship. The limited services available are expensive and inconvenient in comparison to flying.

By Land

Peru has borders with Chile, Bolivia, Colombia, Brazil, and Ecuador. The border crossing with Chile is at Tacna on the Peruvian side, Arica on the Chilean; taxis regularly make the crossing and some long-distance buses operate between Lima, Quito, Santiago de Chile, and Buenos Aires. Tickets for such marathon journeys sometimes include food and overnight accommodation.

From Bolivia, efficient minibus services will take you from La Paz to Puno. The journey from Ecuador is also straightforward: take a bus to the border at Huaquillas and walk through to Tumbes. Other buses operate from there, but note that the "international service" advertized in Quito still requires a change of bus at the border, unless you are traveling with the Ormeño bus company, so it is actually more expensive and occasionally much less convenient than doing the trip in stages.

All rail links abroad have been closed due to a lack of profitability.

Airline Offices

Overseas

Air passes for cheap domestic travel within Peru are sometimes available from travel agents specializing in South America

Exito
1212 Broadway Ave, Suite #910
Oakland, CA 94612.
tel: 800-655 4053
fax: 510-655 4566
www.exitotravel.com
Journey Latin America
12 & 13 Heathfield Terrace,
Chiswick, London W4 4JE.
tel: 020-8747 8315

fax: 020-8742 1312
e-mail: sales@journeylatinamerica.co.uk
South American Experience
47 Causton Street, Pimlico,
London SW1P 4AT.
tel: 020-7976 5511
fax: 020-7976 6908
e-mail: info@southamericanexperience.co.uk
Peru's largest airline, **Aero Continente**, has been suspended until a replacement insurer can be found.

In Peru

ACES
Jorge Chávez 400, Miraflores
tel: 447 1311; fax: 447 3021.
Aero Condor
Juan de Arona 781, San Isidro
tel: 441 1354/222 4130.
Aeroflot
Martir Olaya 201, Of. 350, Miraflores
e-mail: aeroflot_ventas@terra.com.pe
Aeroméxico
Vía Principal 155, Piso 7, Centro Empresarial Torre Real 3, San Isidro
tel: 421 3500;
e-mail: aeromexicoventas2@terra.com.pe
Air Canada
Av. Reducto 945, Miraflores
tel: 241 2342/241 2074.
Air France
Av. José Pardo 601, Of. 601, Miraflores
tel: 444 9285; fax: 444 9313.
Alitalia
Mártir Olaya 129, Of. 1702, Miraflores
tel: 447 3899.
American Airlines
Av. Canaval y Moreyra 390, 1st floor, San Isidro
tel: 211 7000/575 1547
www.aa.com

A Reminder

Don't forget to hang on to the tourist card that you fill out when you arrive in Peru. You'll need to hand it in to immigration when you leave. And don't spend the last of your money on souvenirs before making for the plane: remember that airport tax of US$25 is payable on international flights, and a small fee is necessary on domestic flights.

Flight Information

Lima Airport (Aeropuerto Internacional Jorge Chávez):
517 3100
National and international flights: 595 0666

Avensa Servivensa
Av. Bolognesi 291, Miraflores
tel: 241 8280; fax: 241 8278.
Avianca
Centro Comercial Boulevard Los
Olivos, Av. Paz Soldán 225, Of. C-5
Mezzanine, San Isidro
tel: 221 7530/221 7822.
Aviandina
Aeropuerto Internacional Jorge
Chávez, Edificio Central
tel: 447 8080; fax: 484 0244;
e-mail: aviandina@pol.com.pe
British Midland
Arístides Aljovín 472, Miraflores
tel: 444 4441; fax: 445 5479.
Continental Airlines
Victor Andrés Belaunde 147,
Of. 110, San Isidro
Av. Larco 1315, Miraflores
tel: 221 4340/222 7080.

Reading Addresses

The following may help you find
your way around the addresses
listed in this book:

Av. *(Avenida)* = avenue
Calle = street
Edificio = building
Hostal = cheap hotel (not a hostel)
Jr. *(Jirón)* = way/street
Of. *(Oficina)* = office
Pasaje = passage/alley
Piso = floor/story
s/n *(sin numéro)* = no number
Urb. *(Urbanización)* = area or
neighborhood

Copa Airlines
Av. Dos de Mayo 741, Miraflores
tel: 610 0808; fax: 610 0810.
Cubana de Aviación
Jr. Tarata 250, Miraflores
tel: 241 0555; fax: 241 0554.
Delta Air Lines
Swissotel Lima, Via Principal 180,
Centro Empresarial Real, San Isidro
tel: 211 9211.
Iberia
Av. Camino Real 390, Of. 902,
Torre Central del Centro Camino
Real, San Isidro
tel: 411 7800/411 7801.
Japan Airlines
Av. Central 717, Piso 11a, San Isidro
tel: 221 7501.

KLM
José Pardo 805, 6th floor,
Miraflores
tel: 242 1240/421 9500.
Lan
José Pardo 513, Miraflores
tel: 213 8200.
Lan Peru
José Pardo 513, Miraflores
tel: 213 8200; fax: 446 3157.
Lloyd Aereo Boliviano
Av. Pardo 231, Miraflores
tel: 241 5210/444 0510.
Lufthansa
Av. Jorge Basadre 1330, San Isidro
tel: 442 4455/442 4466;
e-mail: lhlim@terra.com.pe
TACA Perú
Comandante Espinar 331, Miraflores
tel: 213 7000/446 0033
TANS Perú
Av. Arequipa 5200, Miraflores
tel: 241 8519; fax: 445 7107.
Servivensa
Av. Bolognesi 291, Miraflores
tel: 241 8280.
Varig Brazil
Camino Real 456, Of. 803,
Torre Real, San Isidro
tel: 442 4361; fax: 442 1191;
e-mail: varig@terra.com.pe

Practical Tips

Security & Crime

As Peru's urban centers have
swollen, so has petty crime.
Pickpockets and thieves have
become more and more common in
Lima and Cusco. It is recommended
that tourists do not wear costly
jewelry and that watches be
covered with a sleeve. Thieves have
become amazingly adept at slitting
open shoulder bags, camera cases,
and knapsacks; keep an eye on
your belongings.

All kind of confidence tricksters
pull ever more imaginative ruses;
some pose as policemen, others
work together with bus and taxi
drivers or use diversionary tactics
to get hold of your valuables.
Special care is needed at railway
stations and airports. Go out at
night in small groups if possible.
Visits to the shanty towns *(pueblos
jóvenes)* on the outskirts of the
cities are very dangerous.

Officials also warn against
dealing with anyone calling your
hotel room or approaching you in
the lobby or on the street, claiming
to represent a travel agency or
specialty shop. Avoid contact with
over-friendly strangers who may
want to get you involved in criminal
deals. Be aware that drug dealing
is a crime that results in a long
prison sentence.

Driving alone and after dusk is
not advisable. Don't hitch-hike. For
journeys overland choose only
well-known and established bus
companies and take care that
you are always able to identify
yourself: carry your passport
at all times.

There is little or no activity by
rebel groups these days, and
incidents of violence involving

foreign tourists are few and far between. There is army activity in the coca-growing regions of the Andes, but these are extremely remote.

The border dispute with Ecuador in Peru's northern Amazon region has been settled peacefully. It is still advisable for tourists to cross the frontier in this area at official checkpoints.

Expeditions and trekking tours should ideally be undertaken in larger groups and accompanied by a local and experienced mountain guide. It is a good idea to notify a reliable third party of your destination and home address before leaving for a long trekking tour. For more specific inquiries, contact your embassy or the **South American Explorers' Club**, Av. República de Portugal, 146 Breña, Lima, tel: 425 0142.

Emergency Numbers

In case of an accident, attack, emergency, etc., call:
● **General emergency** 105; 103 general information; 116 fire emergencies *(see also page 324 for medical services)*
● **Radio Patrulla** (police radio control and emergency service). In Lima: tel: 475 2995/225 0202.
● **Dirección Nacional Contra El Terrorismo** (DINCOTE) terrorism and hijacking. In Lima: tel: 433 3684/ 433 0403/433 9861.

Police

A special security service for tourists recognizable by white braid worn across the shoulders of the uniform was created by the Guardia Civil, now called Policía Nacional del Perú (PNP). The tourist police are very helpful, and have special English speakers on duty. You can find them in Lima, especially in the downtown area.

Security Tip

Leave your valuable jewelry at home and don't carry cameras or Walkmans in public areas.

The office of the tourist police in Lima is in the Museo de la Nación, Av. Javier Prado Este 2465, Floor 5, San Borja, tel: 476 7708.
In Cusco: Calle Saphi in the Delegación de Policía, 2 blocks from the Plaza, tel: 249 652.
In Arequipa: Calle Jerusalén 315–A, tel: 251 277.
In Iquitos: Iquitos Airport, tel: 235 371.

Weights & Measures

Peru uses the metric system. Here's a table to help you convert to the imperial system.

To Convert:	Multiply By:
centimeters to inches	0.4
meters to feet	3.3
kilometers to miles	0.6
kilograms to pounds	2.2

Electricity

Peru uses 220 volts, 60 cycles AC, except Arequipa which is on 50 cycles. The major hotels provide 110-volt outlets in bathrooms for the use of shavers only.

Business Hours

Most stores open Mon–Fri 10am–8pm with a long lunch break between 1pm and 4pm.

Banks are open only in the morning 9am–12.30 or 1pm during summer (Jan–Mar). For the rest of the year there is also afternoon trading between 3pm and 6pm, although the hours often change. *Casas de cambio* (exchange houses) open 9am–6pm, while money changers are on the footpaths nearly 24 hours a day.

Newspapers

The major daily newspapers in Lima are: *El Comercio*, *La República* and *Expreso*. *Caretas*, a weekly magazine, is also a good source of information.

Newspapers Online
El Comercio:
www.elcomercioperu.com.pe
Expreso:
www.expreso.com.pe

Telephone Codes

The code for Peru is 00 51. Below are the codes for the most important Peruvian cities (without the "0" from within Peru).
Arequipa: 054
Ayacucho: 064
Cajamarca: 044
Chachapoyas: 044
Chiclayo: 074
Cusco (and Machu Picchu): 084
Huancavelica: 064
Huancayo: 064
Huaraz: 044
Ica: 034
Iquitos: 094
Lima: 01
Pisco: 034
Puno: 054
Tacna: 054
Trujillo: 044

La República:
www.larepublica.com.pe
Caretas:
www.caretas.com.pe

Telephone

The main offices of Telefónica del Perú are in Av. Arequipa 1155, Santa Beatriz, tel: 210 1412. Offices are open Mon–Fri 8am–3pm. Carabaya 937, Plaza San Martín, Central Lima; Infocentro: Av. Jorge Basadre 592, Piso 2, San Isidro. Open daily 6am–11pm. Bell South and TIM also provide services.

Peru has direct dialing for international calls from all public telephones, which makes calls much cheaper than from your hotel. Telephone cards can be bought at newsstands, from street vendors near the public telephone boxes, or in shops. International access codes: MCI (0-800) 50010, AT&T (0-800) 50000, Sprint (0-800) 50020.

For local calls you can use either coins or telephone cards. *(See box on this page for codes.)*

Postal Services

The central post office in Lima, called Serpost, at Conde de Superunda 190, tel: 427

8531/427 8876, opens Mon–Sat 8.15am–1pm and 2–7.30pm, Sun 8am–1pm.

You can have mail sent here c/o Lista de Correos. Take your passport for identification when you go to collect it. There is a parcel collection office at Tomás Valle Cuadra 6, Los Olivos (near the airport), tel: 533 1340. There are branch post offices in other districts of Lima:

Airport office: Jorge Chávez, International Airport; open 24 hours.

Miraflores office: Petit Thouars 5201, tel: 445 0697; Mon–Sat 8am–8.45pm, Sun 9am–2pm.

San Isidro office: Libertadores 325, tel: 440 0797; Mon–Fri 8am–7pm, Sat 9am–2pm, Sun closed.

Courier Services

DHL International, Los Castaños 225, San Isidro, tel: 221 1133/221 2474; Av. José Pardo 620, Of. 1, Miraflores, tel: 517 2500, fax: 614 2500.

Federal Express, Pasaje Mártir José Olaya 260, Miraflores, tel: 242 2280.

OLVA Courier, Av. Argentina 2566, tel: 336 5400.

SkyNet, Natalio Sánchez 125, 2nd floor, Lima, tel: 433 1717.

TNT International Express Av. Libertadores 199, San Isidro, tel: 222 0555.

Websites

www.hotelstravel.com/peru Hotel listings and tourist information in English.

www.magicperu.com Comprehensive site, with information on politics, tourism, and ecology, through to investment opportunities in Peru.

www.peru.com News, general information, and a travel agency, in English and Spanish.

www.perutravelnet.com Online hotel bookings, and an excellent range of articles on places of interest. In English and Spanish.

UPS, Pasaje Tello 241, Miraflores, tel: 264 0105.

World Courier, Schell 343, Of. 206, Miraflores, tel: 446 4646.

American Express

American Express clients can have mail sent to: Amex, c/o Lima Tours, Av. Pardo y Aliaga 698, San Isidro, tel: 222 2522. Take your passport as identification for this, as well as for the *lista de correos* (poste restante) at the post office. Members of the South American Explorers' Club can also have mail held for them at Casilla 3714, Lima 100, Peru.

Internet Centers

Lima
Dragon Fans: Pasaje Tarata 230, Miraflores and Av. Grau 8th block, Barranco. Open daily 8am–10pm.

Gambaru S.A.C. Angamos Este 158, Miraflores tel: 446 2644

Interaxis Pasaje Tarata 277, Miraflores. Open daily 8am–10pm.

Microstudio Diagonal 218, Miraflores tel: 241 2701

Plazanet Café Internet Av. 28 de Julio 451, Miraflores tel: 447 3995/446 0540

Serinec General Suarez 287, Miraflores tel: 444 5297

Telematic Net Jr. Junin 355, Miraflores

Cusco
Telser: Telefónica del Peru, Calle del Medio 117

Red Cientifica Peru: Portal Comercio (near Trotamundos)

Daveli Net Portal de Panes 127

Ukukus Calle Plateros 316

Latin net Santa Catalina Ancha first block.

Huaraz
Portal Net Av. Luzuriaga 999

Arequipa
CHIPS Internet: San Francisco 202a
Net Central: Alvarez Thomas 219

Trujillo
Several Internet cafés on Calle Pizarro, one block from the plaza.

Useful Addresses

TOURIST OFFICES

Lima
Calle 1 Oeste s/n Edificio Mitinci, 13th floor, Corpac, San Isidro, tel: 224 9355; e-mail: postmaster@prom.peru.gob.pe

There is also a 24-hour complaints line for tourists. From Lima: 224 7888; outside Lima: freephone 0800-42 579.

Lima Tourist Information Center: Jr. Conde de Superunda 169, 5th floor, open Mon–Fri 9am–4pm; Paseo de los Escribanos 145, Palacio Municipal; open daily 10am–6pm; tel: 427 4848/ 427 6080.

Miraflores Tourist Information Center: Av. Larco 770 (Ricardo Palma Cultural Center), Miraflores; open Mon–Fri 8am–4.30pm; tel: 446 3959.

Tourist Information Booth, Parque Kennedy, Miraflores; open daily 9.30am–6.30pm.

Also worth visiting is the **South American Explorers' Club** for up-to-date information: Av. República de Portugál 146, tel: 425 0142. Mon–Fri 9.30am–5pm or write to Casilla 3714, Lima 100, Peru.

Outside Lima
Arequipa: Plaza de Armas, tel: 211 021, ext 113. Open 8am–5pm.

Cajamarca: Dirección de Turismo, Conjunto Belén 650, tel: 822 997.

Casa de Guías (Guides' House): Parque Ginebra 28G, Apartado 123, Huaraz–Ancash, tel: 721 333.

Chiclayo: San José 733 y Plaza de Armas, tel: 233 132.

Cusco: Mantas 118, tel: 263 176, Open Mon–Fri 8am–7pm, Sat 8am–1pm. There is an information office at Cusco airport, and a complaints office in the city:

Indecopi, Portal de Carrizos 250, tel: 252 974. Open daily 8am–7pm.

Huaraz: Av. Luzuriaga 459, tel: 721 521. Mon–Fri 8.30am–12.30pm and 2.30–3.30pm.

Nazca: The Hotel Nazca on Av. Lima 438, is the main source of local information, tel: 422 085.

Puno: Calle Lima y Deústua (corner of Plaza de Armas), tel: 353 804. Mon–Fri 8am–12.30pm and 2.15–5.30pm.

Trujillo: Libertravel, Calle Independencia 548, tel: 205 632.

Outside Peru

For tourist information before you go, contact the **Peruvian Embassy** in your home country:

Australia: 9th floor, 197 London Circuit, Canberra ACT 2601, tel: 062-257 2953, fax: 062-257 5198

Canada: 130 Albert St, Suite 1901, Ottawa, Ontario, tel: 613-238 1777; fax: 613-32 3062

UK: 52 Sloane St, London SW1X 9SP, tel: 020-7235 1917; fax: 020-7235 4463

USA: 1700 Massachusetts Av. NW, Washington DC 20036, tel: 202-833 9860; fax: 202-659 8124.

Embassies and Consulates

Argentina
Av. 28 de Julio 828, Lima, tel: 433 3381.
Visas Mon–Fri 9am–noon.

Australia
Victor A. Belaunde 147, Via Principal 155, building 3, Of. 1301, San Isidro, tel: 222 8281.

Bolivia
Los Castaños 235, San Isidro, tel: 442 3836.
Visas Mon–Fri 9am–1pm.

Brazil
Av. José Pardo 850, Miraflores, tel: 421 5660.
Visas Mon–Fri 9am–12.30pm.

Canada
Libertad 130, Miraflores, tel: 444 4015.
Visas Mon–Fri 8.30am–11.30am/Tues and Thur 2pm–4pm

Chile
Av. Javier Prado Oeste 790, San Isidro, tel: 221 2080.
Visas Mon–Fri 9am–1pm.

Colombia
Av. Jorge Basadre 1580, San Isidro, tel: 441 0954.
Visas Mon–Fri 9am–1pm.

Ecuador
Las Palmeras 356, San Isidro, tel: 440 9941.
Visas Mon–Fri 9am–1pm and 3pm–6pm.

Ireland
Angamos Oeste 340, Miraflores, tel: 446 3878/242 1942
Visas Mon–Fri 10am–2pm

Japan
Av. San Felipe 356, Jesús María, tel: 218 1130.

Netherlands
Av. Principal 190, 4th floor, Santa Catalina, La Victoria, tel: 476 1069.

South Africa
Via Principal 155, Of. 801, San Isidro, tel: 440 9996

UK
Natalio Sánchez 125, 12th floor, tel: 433 4738.
Visas 8.30am–noon.

United States
Av. La Encalada s/n, cuadra 17, Monterrico, Surco, tel: 434 3000.
Visas 9am–11am.

Getting Around

Orientation

Lima, the "City of Kings," is Peru's gateway to the rest of the country (although Cusco and Iquitos have now begun promoting their own international airports).

If time is limited, Lima has the facilities to organize your itinerary so you can fly directly to any major destination with your reservations or tour confirmed beforehand. Machu Picchu and the Sacred Valley might be the one essential destination for some, while others travel for months to experience the wide diversity of cultures between the coastal regions, the Andes, and the Amazon.

Lima itself is divided into districts, each with its own distinctive character. Downtown Lima has grandiose plazas, mansions, and restored historical Plaza Mayor, although there is a certain amount of street crime.

In the more glitzy suburbs of Miraflores and San Isidro, there is better security. New shopping complexes and landscaped gardens make this a complete contrast.

Barranco is an upmarket beach suburb where some artists have their workshops, giving it a bohemian reputation. Open-air cafés and restaurants have live jazz and creole music, while the crumbling old mansions give the tree-lined streets a relaxed ambience.

Maps & Street Plans

The **Touring Club de Perú**, César Vallejo 699, Lince, tel: 221 2432, is the best source for maps and information. General maps are available from **The South American Explorers' Club** at Av. República de Portugal 146, Breña, tel: 425 0142.

Maps and street plans can also be bought at the kiosk, bookshops and at the **Instituto Geográfico Nacionál**, Aramburú 1190, Surquillo, tel: 475 3030, ext. 122; open Mon–Fri 8am–4.30pm.

The Yellow Pages of Telefónica del Perú has street maps of Lima Metropolitana, and Callao.

From the Airport

Getting to and from Lima airport is easiest in the care of your tour organizer, or using the hotel shuttle: **Transhotel**, Logroño 132, Miraflores, tel: 448 2179, airport tel: 518 011. **CM Tours**, tel: 275 0612. **VIP International Service S.A.**, tel: 446 4821.

There is an official taxi desk outside the Arrivals area (before going through the barrier). Taxis to central Lima cost US$10–15 and to Miraflores US$15. Otherwise once past the Arrivals barrier, there are plenty of taxi drivers waiting, but be prepared to bargain.

In Cusco and other cities, taxis into town are very cheap but make sure you agree on a price before starting your journey.

Public Transportation

Lima's public buses can only really be recommended for a one-time cultural experience. Flagging one down is a feat in itself – then you must survive the jostling crowds and pickpockets.

There are thousands of privately run minibuses stopping and starting every few seconds, but why bother with this slow form of transport when private taxis are cheap? Make sure you agree on the fare before entering the taxi.

Car Rental

Certain regions are better appreciated with your own mode of transport, such as the Callejón de Huaylas, a 200-km (125-mile) long valley nicknamed the "Peruvian Switzerland" for its glaciers, lakes, and snowy peaks. The town of

Huaraz is a 6-hour drive from Lima on well-surfaced roads.

You don't need an international driving license to rent a car: just a valid driving license from your own country, a passport, and credit card.

Car Rental Agencies
Avis Rent A Car
Av. Javier Prado Este 5235, Camacho, La Molina.
tel: 434 1111.
Bolognesi 599, Miraflores
tel: 242 6631.
Lima airport: 575 1637.
Calle Palacio Viejo 214, Arequipa
tel: 212 123.
Av. del Sol 808, Cusco
tel: 248 800.
Budget
Av. La Paz 522, Miraflores or Av. Canaval y Moyeyra 569, San Isidro
tel: 441 9458.
Lima airport, tel: 442 8703/575 1674 (24 hours), fax: 441 4174.
Dollar Rent a Car
La Paz 438, Miraflores
tel: 444 4920.
Lima airport: 575 1719.
Hertz Rent A Car
Arístides Aljovín 472, Miraflores.
tel: 444 4441.
Inka's Rent A Car
Cantuarias 160, Miraflores.
tel: 447 2583.
Lima airport: 575 1390
National Car Rental
Av. España 449.
tel: 433 3750.
Lima airport: 575 1111
Touring and Automobile Club of Peru, César Vallejo 699, Lince, tel: 221 2432, fax: 441 0531.

Domestic Travel

Most travelers prefer to fly between major destinations, but overland travel in Peru is not always as problematic as imagined. For example, the coastal Pan-American Highway is fully paved and worked by regular, comfortable buses. However, roads in the Andes are generally unpaved and buses range from reasonable to back-breaking. The journeys are cheap and colorful with some amazing scenery, if you have the time and inclination.

By Air
There are several domestic airlines providing daily services to most cities, with little qualitative or price difference. Sometimes air passes are available for cheap flights within Peru. *(See listings for **Lan Peru**, TANS, and TACA **Peru** on page 325.)*

Domestic airlines are sadly unreliable in meeting their flight schedules. Times are often changed and, in the case of remote destinations, occasionally cancelled due to lack of interest; you often will not find out until you are at the airport. Other small, new airlines that operate for a while and then close down, fly to smaller places and remote jungle airstrips.

It's best to book in person at the reservations office, or through a good travel agent who will confirm your tickets. Tales of travelers being bumped off flights are legion: it is best to re-confirm your ticket 72 hours in advance, otherwise you might simply disappear from the airline computer.

For domestic flights there is an airport tax of US$3.50 at all airports.

For travelers who don't want to do the three- or four-day trek or take the train to Machu Picchu, a helicopter transfer service operates from Cusco to Aguas Calientes. Conservationists oppose this service, however, as the noise disturbs the wildlife (as well as the tranquility of the site).
Helicuzco
Jr. Arias Araguez 369, Miraflores, tel: 445 6126; fax: 444 8708; Calle Triunfo 379, Piso 2, Cusco, tel: 227 283; fax: 227 283.

By Rail
Train journeys are very popular with all types of travelers. Relatively comfortable and well-serviced "first-class" carriages are available (book through Lima Tours or other agencies); very cheap seats can also be booked but they can be quite unreliable and slow. The trips provide valuable glimpses of rural life and views of magnificent landscapes. In recent years, the

journey from Puno–Cusco has become particularly popular.

The Lima–Huancayo passenger service, the world's highest train journey, is unfortunately no longer operating.

To reach the ruins at Machu Picchu, there are several options: the modern *Autovagón* departs from Cusco early for Machu Picchu (get off at Aguas Calientes) and returns in the afternoon. Travel agents in Cusco sell all-inclusive day tickets for the trip. The "Hiram Bingham" is the most expensive, but you are paying for a package which includes your guide and food. Visitors who want to walk the Inca Trail to the ruins must take a bus with a tour agency.

Peru Rail in Cusco: tel: 232 672; reservations tel: 221 992.

By Bus

Numerous buses operate morning and evening departures to most cities. Reliable companies include:
Ormeño,
Av. Javier Prado Este 1059, Lima 13 (domestic and international routes), tel: 472 1710; fax: 470 6474.
Carlos Zavala 177, Lima (domestic), tel: 427 5679.
Cruz del Sur,
Jr. Quilca 531, Central Lima, tel: 424 1005;
Paseo de la República 801, La Victoria (by National Stadium), tel: 433 6765;
Av. Javier Prado 1109, San Isidro, tel: 225 6163/225 6200 (terminal for their luxury buses);
Jr. Lucar y Torre 573, Huaraz, tel: 723 532.
Tepsa
Av. Javier Prado Este 1091, Lima tel: 470 4664.
Jr. Lampa 1237 1241, Lima, tel: 427 5642.
Civa
Av. 28 de Julio corner of Paseo de la República,
tel: 332 5236/332 5264.

By Boat

Boats can be taken from the bay of Paracas to the Ballestas Islands, home of sea lions, Humboldt penguins, and various sea birds.

From Puno, there are tranquil excursions by boat across Lake Titicaca to the islands of Taquile and Amantaní, and the floating islands of Uros, made entirely of reeds.

In the Amazon, a motorized canoe along the winding, muddy waterways is the only way to travel.

By Taxi

Taxis in Peru have no meters – you simply bargain on a rate, preferably before even getting in. In smaller cities you may prefer to walk, but in Lima taxis are often essential and very cheap. Try:
Lima Driver: tel: 266 0459
Tata Taxis SRL: tel: 274 5151
Taxi Fono: tel: 422 6565
Taxi Real: tel: 470 6263
Taxi Seguro: tel: 275 2020
Note that your hotel will arrange taxis for you if you ask. This is more expensive, but very secure. If you don't speak much Spanish and don't fancy bargaining on the street, this can be the best option.

On Foot

Downtown Lima is definitely best explored on foot. Now that the city has a new look and street vendors have nearly been eradicated it's a pleasure to stroll from the Government Palace to the museums and colonial mansions, all contained within several blocks. Sit for a while in the Plaza Mayor or Plaza San Martín and gain true insights into the Limeño character. Always watch out for your belongings.

Trekking is one of Peru's great attractions. Most famous is the four-day Inca Trail to Machu Picchu; an organized group will include hired carriers who set up camp and cook ahead of your arrival. *(See the feature on "Adventure in the Andes" page 123 for more information.)* Not all excursions require a high level of expertise. Tour operators can also arrange shorter and less tiring walking tours in the Sacred Valley, or in the area around Cusco.

Where to Stay

Hotels

LIMA

Downtown Area
Sheraton Lima Hotel & Towers
Paseo de la República 170,
tel: 315 5022; fax: 315 5024
A comfortable, modern hotel, with the usual Sheraton good service. At the edge of downtown Lima – not a safe area to walk at night. **$$$**
Hotel Riviera
Av. Garcilaso de la Vega 981
tel: 424 9438; fax: 424 7102
www.cybernt.com.pe
A good traditional hotel, but the area is not very pleasant. **$$$**
Gran Hotel Bolívar
Jr. de la Unión 958,
Plaza San Martín
tel: 428 7672; fax: 428 7674
e-mail: bolivar@terra.com.pe
Opulent, old-style comfort. Within easy walking distance of historic sites but not a safe area at night. **$$**
Hotel Kamana
Camana 547
tel: 426 7204; fax: 426 0790
e-mail: kamana@amauta.rcp.net.pe
Comfortable and modern, rooms with private bathroom in heart of downtown Lima. **$$**
Hotel Residencial Europa
Jr. Ancash 376, Plaza San Francisco
tel: 427 3351
Budget hotel in the heart of downtown Lima; clean, with shared bathrooms, lively atmosphere, and popular with backpackers. **$$**

Price Guide

Prices are all for double rooms:
$$$ US$100 plus
$$ less than US$100
$ US$50 or under

Hostal España
Jr. Azángaro 105
tel: 428 5546/427 9196;
e-mail: fertur@terra.com.pe
Clean, with shared bathrooms.
A fun atmosphere for
backpackers. **$**

La Posada del Parque
Parque Hernán Velarde 60
tel: 433 2412; fax: 332 6927
e-mail: monden@telematic.com.pe
Old mansion in quiet cul-de-sac,
with antiques and artworks; big
rooms with private bathroom. **$**

Hostal Las Artes
Chota 1460
tel: 433 0331
e-mail: artes@telematic.com.pe
Good budget hotel in downtown
Lima in an old restored mansion.
Rooms with or without bathroom. **$**

Miraflores

Miraflores suburb is the commercial
center of Lima and home to affluent
Peruvians. Shops, nightclubs,
restaurants, and businesses
abound.

Miraflores César
La Paz 463, Miraflores
tel: 444 1212; fax: 444 4440
e-mail: cesarreservas@terra.com.pe
Luxury hotel. Pool, gym, sauna. **$$$**

Miraflores Park Plaza
Av. Malecón de la Reserva 1035
tel: 242 3000; fax: 242 3393;
e-mail: res-parkplaza@peruorientexpress.
com.pe
The most luxurious hotel in
Miraflores, with ocean view. **$$$**

Las Américas
Av. Benavides 415
tel: 241 2820; fax: 444 1137
e-mail: amerihtl@chavin.rcp.net.pe
A hotel for executives. Well placed
in the heart of Miraflores. **$$$**

Hotel Antigua
Av. Grau 350
tel: 241 6116; fax: 241 6115
e-mail: hantigua@amauta.rcp.net.pe
Attractive colonial house, with
restaurant, bar, gym, sauna, jacuzzi,
and conference rooms. **$$**

Hostal El Patio
Diez Canseco 341
tel: 444 2107; fax: 444 1663
www.hostalelpatio.com
Very nice colonial-style hotel in the
heart of Miraflores. **$$**

Miramar Ischia
Malecón Cisneros 1244, Miraflores
tel: 444 6969/446 8174
fax: 445 0851;
e-mail: ischia@bellnet.com.pe
Attractive, friendly hotel, with sea
view. Not far from downtown
Miraflores. **$$**

Hostal Señorial
Jose Gonzalez 567
tel/fax: 444 5755
e-mail: senorial@viabcp.com
Colonial-style house in quiet street,
with garden and patio. Comfortable
rooms and friendly atmosphere. **$$**

Hotel La Castellana
Grimaldo del Solar 222
tel: 444 3530; fax: 446 8030
www.toursperu.com/lacastellana
Conveniently located colonial
house, with restaurant and
courtyard; comfortable rooms. **$$**

Hostal José Luis
Francisco de Paula de Ugariza 727
tel: 444 1015; fax: 446 7177
www.telematic.edu.pe/users/hsjluis
Private house in safe neighborhood.
Most rooms with private bathroom
and refrigerator. Excellent value.
Must reserve in advance. **$**

Casa de los Sánchez
Av. Diagonal 354, Parque Kennedy
tel: 444 1177
www.casadelossanchez.com
Upper end of budget accommodation
in heart of Miraflores. Rooms with
private bathroom. **$**

The Witches Guest House
Bolognesi 364
tel: 241 8835
Cheap backpackers' hostel, with
shared rooms, in a good location. **$**

**Flying Dog Backpackers Bed &
Breakfast**
Jr. Diez Canseco 117
tel: 445 2376;
e-mail: flyingdog@mixmail.com
Close to Parque Kennedy. **$**

San Isidro

The residential "garden" of Lima,
also the home of its prestigious golf
and country clubs.

Hotel los Delfines
Calle los Eucaliptus 555
tel: 215 7000; fax: 215 7070
www.losdelfineshotel.com
Luxury hotel with casino and
nightclub. **$$$**

Swissôtel
Via Central 150, Centro Empresarial
Camino Real
tel: 421 4400; fax: 421 4422
e-mail: reservations.lima@swissotel.com
Very elegant, with a Swiss-style
restaurant. **$$$**

Sonesta Posada El Olivar
Pancho Fierro 194
tel: 221 1210; fax: 221 2141
www.sonesta.com
Quiet location in one of Lima's last
wooded areas; with a pool, coffee
shop, and restaurant. **$$$**

Hotel San Isidro
Av. Pezet 1765
tel: 264 2019; fax: 264 3434
e-mail: hsisidro@terra.com.pe
A quiet, traditional hotel in the
garden neighborhood. **$$**

Sonesta Posada del Inca
Av. Libertadores 490
tel: 222 4373; fax: 222 4370
www.sonesta.com
Comfortable and elegant. **$$**

Youth Hostel Malka
Los Lirios 165
tel: 442 0162
Open 24 hours. Shared rooms. **$**
e-mail: hostelmalka@terra.com.pe

Barranco

Attractive residential suburb beyond
Miraflores, with many colonial
buildings around its social hub, the
leafy Plaza Barranco.

Mochilero's Backpackers Hostel
Pedro de Osma 135
tel: 477 4506;
e-mail: backpacker@amauta.rcp.net.pe
Dormitories in beautiful colonial
building, just off Plaza Barranco and
near to all the great Barranco bars.
Great value. **$**

La Quinta de Alison
28 de Julio 281
tel: 247 6430; fax: 247 1515
Private bathrooms, cable TV, close
to Plaza de Barranco. **$**

THE NORTH

Huaraz

Hotel Andino
Pedro Cochachín 357
tel: 72 1662; fax: 72 2830
reservations in Lima:
tel: 445 9230; fax: 241 5927

Comfortable hotel with excellent service and stunning views. **$$**

Baños Termales Monterrey
Av. Monterrey, parte alta
(Km 7 from Huaraz)
tel: 721 717;
reservations in Lima: tel: 425 1670
With thermal springs; set in pleasant green surroundings. **$$**

El Patio
Av. Monterrey
Carretera Huaraz Caraz Km 6
tel: 724 965.
reservations in Lima: tel: 449 6295; fax: 448 0254
Peaceful country setting – just down the road from baths. **$$**

El Tumi
Jr. San Martin 1121
tel: 721 913/721 784
A comfortable place for budget travelers. **$**

Hotel Colomba
Jr. Francisco de Zela 278
tel: 721 501
Friendly, family-run bungalows within pleasant garden. A little run-down. **$**

Albergue Alpes Andes
Casa de Guías, Parque Ginebra 28G
tel: 721 811; fax: 722 306
Comfortable but simple hotel. An excellent place for information about mountain treks. **$**

Casablanca
Tarapaca 138
tel: 72 2602; fax: 72 4801;
reservations in Lima:
tel: 421 9131; fax: 421 8504;
e-mail: cashotel@telematic.edu.pe
Modern and clean; good service. **$**

Edward's Inn
Bolognesi 121
tel/fax: 722 692
Friendly family-run place. Edward is a good source of information on climbing and trekking. **$**

Hostal Quintana
Mariscal Caceres 411
tel: 726 060.
Rooms with or without bathroom. Hot water. Good-value hotel. **$**

Trujillo
Libertador Trujillo
Jr. Independencia 485, Plaza de Armas
tel: 232 741; fax: 235 641;

reservations in Lima:
tel: 442 1996; fax: 442 2988;
e-mail: reservas@libertador.com.pe
Good-value accommodation in a beautiful building in central location, with an excellent Sunday buffet. **$$**

Los Jardines Bungalows Hotel
América Norte 1245
tel: 222 258;
reservations in Lima: tel: 463 2056
Large hotel with bungalow accommodation and swimming pool, on the outskirts of town. Good for families with young children. **$$**

Los Conquistadores
Diego de Almagro 586
tel: 203 350; fax: 235 917
Comfortable, with bar and restaurant. **$$**

Price Guide

Prices are all for double rooms:
$$$ US$100 plus
$$ less than US$100
$ US$50 or under

Hostal Trujillo
Grau 581
tel: 243 921
Budget hotel, clean, rooms with private bathroom. **$**

Huanchaco, Trujillo
Hotel Bracamonte
Los Olivos 503
tel/fax: 461 266
Bungalows, converted caravans, or camping. Pool and restaurant. **$**

Cajamarca
Hostal Laguna Seca–Baños Termales
Av. Manco Capac, Baños del Inca
tel: 823 149; fax: 823 915;
e-mail: hotel@lagunaseca.com.pe
Renovated *hacienda* 6 km (4 miles) from Cajamarca with thermal baths in the privacy of your room. **$$**

Sierra Galana
Jr. Comercio 773
tel/fax: 82 2470;
reservations in Lima:
tel: 446 3652; fax: 445 1139
Well located in the center of town and very comfortable. **$$**

El Ingenio
Av. Via de Evitamiento 1611–1709
tel: 827 121; fax: 828 733
Just outside town; relaxed. **$$**

Hostal Cajamarca
Dos de Mayo 311
tel: 821 432
Old colonial house with patio. Private bathrooms and hot water. **$**

Chiclayo
Garza Hotel
Av. Bolognesi 756
tel: 228 172; fax: 228 171;
e-mail: garzahot@inkanet.com.pe
Modern and efficient, with a swimming pool. **$$**

Gran Hotel Chiclayo
Av. Federico Villareal 115
tel: 234 911; fax: 223 961;
e-mail: ventasghch@kipu.rednorte.com.pe
Business hotel close to town center. Air conditioning, hot tub, cable TV, business center, casino. **$$**

Tumi de Oro
L Prado 1145
tel: 227 108
Clean budget hotel; rooms with or without bathroom; hot water. **$**

Piura
Los Portales Hotel
Libertad 875
tel: 323 072
Right on the main square. **$$**

Punta Sal
Punta Sal Club Hotel
Panamericana Norte Km 1192, Tumbes
tel/fax: 540 088
Resort hotel with smart beach bungalows. **$$**

Iquitos (Northern Amazon)
Acosta I
Corner of Huallga and Calvo de Araujo
tel/fax: 231 761;
reservations in Lima:
tel: 421 9195; fax: 442 4515
Has a swimming pool and a good restaurant. **$$**

Hotel El Dorado
Jr. Napo 362
tel: 232 574; fax: 23 2203
Modern hotel with swimming pool half a block from Plaza de Armas. **$$**

Hotel Eunice
Arica 780
tel: 233 405
Has large rooms and friendly
service. **$$**
Real Hotel Iquitos
Malecón Tarapaca s/n
tel: 231 011; fax: 236 222
Amazing views of the river. **$$**
Hobo Hideout
Putumayo 437
tel: 234 099
The place for backpackers. **$**

THE SOUTH

Pisco
Hotel Paracas
Av. Paracas 173, Paracas
tel: 227 022; fax: 242 8541
reservations in Lima:
Libertad 120, 2nd floor, Miraflores
tel: 446 5079; fax: 447 6548;
e-mail: hparacas@terra.com.pe
Beachside bungalows, tennis
courts, and pool; arranges
excursions to the peninsula. **$$$**
Hostal Posada Hispana
Av. Bolognesi 236
tel/fax: 536 363
e-mail: andesad@ciber.com.pe
Clean and friendly, good-value
budget hotel. Rooms with private
bathroom and hot water. Also has
a travel agency. **$**

Price Guide

Prices are all for double rooms:
$$$ US$100 plus
$$ less than US$100
$ US$50 or under

Ica
Las Dunas
Av. La Angostura 400
tel: 231 031/256 231;
reservations in Lima: Invertur,
tel: 221 7020; fax: 442 4180
e-mail: reservas@invertur.com.pe
A holiday resort, complete with
horseback riding and private
airstrip for Nazca Lines flights.
$$$
Hotel Mossone
Huacachina, 5 km (3 miles) from Ica
tel: 213 630; fax: 236 137;

reservations in Lima: Invertur
tel: 221 7020; fax: 442 4180
e-mail: invertur@invertur.com.pe
Attractive colonial-style hotel overlooking the lagoon. Good service
and excellent food. **$$**
Hotel Ocujaje
Carretera Panamaricana Sur,
Km 336
tel: 22 0215
reservations in Lima:
tel: 444 4191; fax: 444 4059
Pleasant restored winery/farm in
the middle of the desert,
operating wine and *pisco* distillery.
$$

Nazca
Hostal de la Borda
Km 447, Panamericana Sur
tel/fax: 522 750;
reservations must be made in Lima:
tel: 440 8430; fax: 440 8430
Near the airfield, *hacienda* with
garden, swimming pools, hot
showers, and friendly service. **$$**
Nazca Lines Hotel
Jr. Bolognesi s/n
tel: 522 293; fax: 522 112;
reservations in Lima: Invertur
tel: 221 7020; fax: 442 4180
e-mail: invertur@invertur.com.pe
Comfortable and clean, with a
swimming pool. **$$**
Hostal Las Líneas
Jr. Arica 299
tel: 522 488
Just off Plaza de Armas. Small
rooms, hot showers; restaurant has
a surprisingly varied menu. **$$**
Hostal Alegría
Jr. Lima 164
tel: 522 702; fax: 523 431
e-mail: alegria@nazcaperu.com
www.nazcaperu.com
Simple but good bungalows with
private bathroom; quiet garden;
popular with backpackers. **$**

Arequipa
Posada del Puente
Av. Bolognesi 101
tel: 253 132; fax: 253 576
e-mail: hotel@posadadelpuente.com
Friendly and small, with river
views and good restaurant. **$$$**
Hotel Libertador
Plaza Bolívar, Selva Alegre
tel: 215 110; fax: 241 933

reservations in Lima:
tel: 442 0166/442 1995
e-mail: arequipa@libertador.com.pe
The most traditional hotel in
Arequipa, just out of town, by
Parque Selva Alegre. Great
breakfast on the terrace; pool,
soccer, Jacuzzi, sauna, gym. **$$$**
Holiday Inn
Camino al Molino s/n Sabandia
tel: 448 383; fax: 448 344
e-mail: holiaqp@LaRed.net.pe
Resort just outside Arequipa in the
country, with view of El Misti
volcano. Pool, horseback riding,
hiking, conference rooms. **$$**
La Posada del Monasterio
Santa Catalina 300
tel/fax: 21 5705
Colonial building with modern
extension, opposite Santa Catalina
Convent. Great view of city.
Pleasant living room with open
fire. Garden and patio. **$$**
El Portal Hotel
Portal de Flores 116
tel: 812 782
reservations in Lima:
tel: 40 6447/40 6155
e-mail: reserva@portalhotel.com.pe
On the Plaza de Armas, with
excellent views and roof-top
swimming pool. **$$**
Casa Grande
Luna Pizarro 202, Vallecito
tel: 214 000
Old house with a good family
atmosphere. In a quiet area. **$$**
Hostal La Casa de Mi Abuela
Jerusalem 606
tel: 241 206; fax: 242 761
e-mail: giardinotours@chasqui.LaRed.net.pe
Constantly receives rave reviews.
Large complex of bungalow-style
rooms in garden setting. **$**
Hotel El Balcón
García Calderon 202, Vallecito
tel: 286 999
Pleasant and good value, colonial-
style hotel, just outside the center
of town. Comfortable. **$**
Hotel Conquistador
Mercaderes 409
tel: 212 916; fax: 218 987
Pleasant colonial building and
friendly service. **$**
Hostal Belén
Av. Bolognesi 132
tel: 253 625; fax: 201 419

Simple but fun hotel; rooms give onto central patio. **$**

Colca Canyon
Lodge Yanque
Reservations in Arequipa: Zela 212
tel: 245 199
e-mail: colcalodge@grupoinca.com
Near Yanque, in peaceful setting with swimming pool. Great for horseback riding, hiking, cycling, or just relaxing. **$$**
Casa Andina B&B Colca
Huayna Cápac s/n, Chivay
Colca
tel: 531 020. **$$**
Part of a new chain of bed and breakfast hotels in the Colca Valley. **$$**
Hostal Rumillacta
Chivay
tel: 521 098
Attractive cabins three blocks before the plaza, if entering the village from Arequipa. Rooms with private bathroom; restaurant. **$**

Puno (Lake Titicaca)
Hotel Libertador Isla Esteves
Isla Esteves
tel: 353 870; fax: 367 879
reservations in Lima:
tel: 442 1066/442 1995
fax: 442 2988
www.libertador.com.pe
Large modern building with an excellent view of Lake Titicaca. **$$$**
Sonesta Posada del Inca
Sesqui Centenario 610, Sector Huaje-Puno
tel: 364 111/364 112
fax: 363 672
reservations in Lima: tel: 222 4777; fax: 422 4345
www.sonesta.com
Same chain as Sonesta Posada del Inca in Lima, Cusco, and Yungay. **$$$**
Casa Andina B&B Lago Titicaca
Jr. Grau 270
tel: 367 520
A newly-built hotel with 35 rooms offering bed and breakfast facilities close to the lake. **$$**
Colón Inn
Jr. Tacna 290
tel/fax: 351 432
e-mail: colon@mail.cosapidata.com.pe
Warm and comfortable with a pleasant restaurant. **$$**

Hostal Hacienda
Jr. Deústua 297
tel/fax: 356 109
Attractive old colonial house. Comfortable. **$$**
Hotel Sillustani
Jr. Lambayeque 195
tel: 351 881; fax: 351 431
e-mail: sillustani@inkanet.com.pe
Clean and friendly. Ask for a heater for your room. **$$**
Hostal Europa
Alfonso Ugarte 112
tel: 353 023
Popular with backpackers. Problematic showers. **$**
Hostal Q'oñiwasi
Av. La Torre 119
tel: 353 912
Opposite train station. Basic but clean and warm. Usually hot water. **$**
Hostal Pukara
Jr. Libertad 328
tel/fax: 368 448
e-mail: pukara@computextos.net
Friendly, comfortable, family-owned small hotel in the center of Puno. **$**
Isla Suasi
Calle Arequipa 387
tel: 622 772/351 417
www.suasi.com
A privately owned island on the north-east shore of Lake Titicaca in the district of Conima. **$$$**

Cusco
Don't be daunted by the number of hotels in Cusco. The competition is high and so is the quality.
Monasterio de Cusco
Calle Palacio 136, Plaza Nazarenas
tel: 241 777;
reservations: tel: 237 111
reservations in Lima:
tel: 221 0826; fax: 421 8283
www.monasterio.orient-express.com
Elegant colonial building; immaculate service. **$$$**
Hotel Libertador Cusco
Plazoleta Santo Domingo 259
tel: 23 1961; fax: 23 3152
e-mail: cuzco@libertador.com.pe
www.libertador.com.pe
reservations in Lima:
tel: 442 0166/442 1995.
Top-class hotel in 380-year-old building; well-furnished and efficient. **$$$**

Sonesta Posada del Inca
Portal Espinar 142
tel: 227 061; fax: 248 484
reservations in Lima: tel: 222 4777
fax: 422 4345
www.sonesta.com
Comfortable, with excellent service. **$$**
Hotel El Dorado Inn
Av. El Sol 395
tel: 231 232
reservations in Lima:
tel: 472 1415
Pleasant if a bit noisy. Good service and restaurant. **$$**
Hotel Royal Inka I
Plaza Regocijo 299
tel: 223 876/231 067; fax: 234 221
www.royalinkahotel.com
Close to the main plaza, and housed in a National Historical Monument. **$$**
Hotel Royal Inka II
Calle Santa Teresa 335
tel: 222 284/223 876; fax: 234 221
reservations in Cusco, tel: 234 221
www.royalinkahotel.com
Attractively situated on the upper plaza, with good service. More expensive, but more comfortable than Royal Inka I. **$$**
Hotel Los Andes de América
Calle Garcilaso 234–236
tel: 222 253; fax: 240 275
www.cuzcoandes.com
Centrally heated, comfortable rooms arranged around an interior courtyard. Helpful staff; excellent buffet breakfast included. **$$**
Hotel Ruinas
Calle Ruinas 472
tel: 260 644; fax: 236 391
www.hotelruinas.com
Comfortable hotel, some rooms with great view of Nevado Ausangate. **$$**
Hostal Corihuasi
Suecia 561
tel/fax: 232 233
e-mail: corihuasi@amauta.rcp.net.pe
Attractive colonial-style house two blocks away from the Plaza de Armas, with warm and quiet rooms. Friendly service; good view from breakfast room. Hot water. **$**
Hotel Los Niños
Meloq 442
tel: 231 424
e-mail: ninos@correo.dnet.com.pe

Attractive renovated colonial building with courtyard. Friendly, clean, and comfortable. Profits from hotel go toward projects to help street children. **$**

Hostal El Balcón
Tambo de Montero 222
tel: 236 738; fax: 225 352
e-mail: balcon@peru.itete.com.pe
Great views of Cusco, with a bar and sauna. Take a taxi back at night (situated in an isolated area). **$**

Hostal Amaru
Cuesta San Blas 541
tel/fax: 225 933
Clean and friendly hotel. Rooms with or without private bathroom. **$**

Hostal Rikch'arty
Tambo de Montero 219
tel: 236 606
Budget hotel with shared rooms and bathroom. Great value, with garden and views. **$**

Machu Picchu
Machu Picchu Sanctuary Lodge
By Machu Picchu ruins
tel: 211 038/211 039; fax: 211 053
reservations in Lima:
tel: 221 0826; fax: 421 8283
e-mail: res-mapi@peruorientexpress.com
Streamlined modern hotel next to the entrance to the ruins. Used by many large tour groups. **$$$**

Aguas Calientes
Machu Picchu Pueblo Hotel
Km 110, 5 minutes from town; reservations in Cusco:
tel: 245 314; fax: 244 669
reservations in Lima, Andalucía 174, Miraflores, tel: 422 6574
fax: 422 4701
e-mail: reservas@inkaterra.com.pe
Very comfortable bungalow accommodation surrounded by cloud forest. Gardens and pool. Good restaurant. **$$$**

Hotel Machu Picchu Inn
Av. Pachacutec
tel: 211 057; fax: 211 011
reservations in Lima, tel: 421 9018
fax: 421 8283
e-mail: monasterio@protelsa.com.pe
Comfortable hotel. **$$**

Hostal Machu Picchu
Av. Emperio de los Inkas 127
tel: 211 034; fax: 211 065

Good, basic, and clean. Private bathrooms with hot water. Next to the railway line. **$**

Gringo Bill's
(Hostal Q'oñi Unu)
Just off Plaza de Armas
tel: 211 046
Friendly, relaxed hotel. Rooms with or without private bathroom. **$**

Urubamba Valley
Incaland
Av. Ferrocarril s/n, Urubamba
reservations in Cusco:
tel: 201 126/201 127
fax: 201 117
reservations in Lima: tel: 421 1175
www.enperu.com
Comfortable rooms, reliable hot water supply, swimming pool. **$$**

La Posada del Libertador
Plaza Manco II 104, Yucay
tel: 201 115; fax: 201 116
Charming colonial building with extra rooms and a good restaurant built around gardens. Ask here about balloon flights over Sacred Valley (US$300, 45 minutes). **$$**

Sonesta Posada del Inca
Plaza Manco II 123, Yucay
tel: 201 346/201 107
fax: 201 345
reservations in Lima: tel: 222 4777; fax: 422 4345
www.sonesta.com
Luxuriously converted monastery; museum and gardens on-site. **$$**

Monasterio de la Recoleta
Jr. la Recoleta
tel/fax: 201 004
reservations in Lima: 424 9438
www.hotelessanagustin.com.pe
17th-century monastery just outside Urubamba. **$$**

Ollantaytambo
El Albergue
Next to rail station
tel/fax: 204 014
Simple, relaxing hostel. Shared bathroom with hot water. **$**

CENTRAL SIERRA

Ayacucho
Ayacucho Hotel Plaza
Jr. 9 de Diciembre 184
tel: 812 202

Built round a courtyard on the Plaza de Armas, perhaps the best hotel Ayacucho has to offer. **$$**

Hotel Crillonesa
Calle Zazareo 56
tel: 812 350
Comfortable and clean, with good views of the city from rooftop. **$$**

Hostal Santa Rosa
Jr. Lima 166
tel: 812 083
Centrally situated, with good service. **$**

Lodges

A wide range of jungle trips are available, from one-day excursions to much longer expeditions. You can start either from Iquitos in the northern jungle or from Puerto Maldonado in the south. Prices start from around US$40 per person per day for all-inclusive packages. It's a good idea to check what's on offer before you jump on board – there are good and bad operators (see page 223).

NORTHERN JUNGLE

ACEER (Amazon Center for Environmental Education and Research), on the Sucusari River in the Amazon Biosphere Reserve near Iquitos, has comfortable accommodations in 20 double-occupancy rooms, with research and study facilities. A 500-meter (1,600-ft) canopy walkway is suspended among the treetops for viewing the wildlife. Enquiries: Explorama Tours (see below).

Amazon Camp and Cruises,
Requena 336, Iquitos
tel: 233 931; fax: 231 265
reservations in Lima:
tel: 265 9524/471 5287
One-night/two-day lodge stays, or more adventurous expeditions and

river cruises available, including trips on M/V *Arca* from Iquitos to Leticia in Colombia.

Anaconda Lara Lodge,
Fénix Viajes, Pevas 215, Iquitos
tel: 239 147/233 430; fax: 232 978
Some 40 km (25 miles) upstream from Iquitos on the Río Momón.

Explorama Lodge & Explornapo Camp
Av. La Marina 340, Iquitos
tel: 252 526/252 530
fax: 252 533;
reservations in Lima: tel: 244 764
fax: 234 968;
e-mail: amazon@explorama.com
Offers two-day packages with optional extra days. Managed by the well-organized Explorama Tours, the Explornapo Camp is well situated for sighting fauna. It offers a good balance of comfort and penetration of the jungle for those who wish to experience the Amazon with a fairly structured itinerary.

Yacumama Lodge
Sargento Lores 149, Iquitos
tel: 235 510;
www.yacumama.com
Comfortable lodge on Río Yarapa, 177 km (110 miles) upriver from Iquitos; 3-night/4-day itineraries.

Paseos Amazónicos (Amazonas Sinchicuy)
Pevas 246, Iquitos
tel: 233 110; fax: 231 618
reservations in Lima:
tel: 241 7576; fax: 446 7946
Sinchicuy Lodge is on Río Sinchicuy, 1½ hours from Iquitos. Nature hikes and evening excursions on the river are offered.

SOUTHERN JUNGLE

Manu
Manu Lodge
Manu Nature Tours, Pardo 1046, Cusco
tel/fax: 252 526
e-mail: mnt@amauta.rcp.net.pe
The only lodge inside the Parque Nacional El Manu. More expensive than some of the lodges, but it's comfortable, and an excellent spot for birdwatching.

Manu Expeditions
Av. Pardo 895, Miraflores

tel: 226 671; fax: 236 706
e-mail: manuexpe@amauta.rcp.net.pe
Run by ornithologist Barry Walker. Camping trips into the reserve, led by knowledgeable guides. Offer customized trips into other areas/lodges in the southern jungle.

Tambopata-Candamo Area
Cusco Amazónico Lodge
Julio C. Tello C13
Urb. Santa Monica
tel: 235 314; fax: 244 669
e-mail: amazonico@inkaterra.com.pe
On the Río Madre de Dios, 15 km (9 miles) from Puerto Maldonado. Package includes trekking in the lodge's private reserve.

Eco Amazonia Lodge
Portal de Panes 109, Of. 6
tel: 236 159
e-mail: unsaac.edu.pe
Two hours downriver from Puerto Maldonado, with oxbow lakes and tree canopy access.

Explorers' Inn
Plateros 365, Cusco
tel: 235 342
reservations in Lima: tel: 447 8888
www.peruviansafaris.com
Good chance of observing wildlife from this location, about 60 km (38 miles) from Puerto Maldonado on the Tambopata River.

Tambopata Jungle Lodge
Av. Pardo 705
tel: 225 701; fax: 238 911
e-mail: postmaster@patcuzco.com.pe
Offers a good chance of observing wildlife; situated 4 hours upriver from Puerto Maldonado on Tambopata River.

Tambopata Research Center
Rainforest Expeditions
Av. Aramburu 166, 4B, Miraflores, Lima
tel: 421 8347; fax: 421 8183
e-mail: postmast@rainforest.com.pe
6–7 hours hours upriver from Puerto Maldonado on Tambopata River. Spartan but comfortable accommodation, low-impact native architecture; 15-minutes' walk from the world's largest macaw clay lick.

Where to Eat

What To Eat

Peru's *criolla* cuisine evolved through the blending of native and European cultures. *A la criolla* is the term used to describe slightly spiced dishes such as *sopa a la criolla*, a wholesome soup containing beef, noodles, milk, and vegetables.

Throughout the extensive coastal region, seafood plays a dominant role in the creole diet. The most famous Peruvian dish, *ceviche*, is raw fish or shrimp marinated in lemon juice and traditionally accompanied by corn and sweet potato. Other South American countries have their own version of *ceviche* but many foreigners consider Peru's to be the best. *Corvina* is sea bass, most simply cooked *a la plancha* (griddled), while scallops *(conchitas)*, and mussels *(choros)*, might be served *a lo macho*, in a shellfish sauce. *Chupe de camarones* is a thick and tasty soup of salt- or freshwater shrimp.

A popular appetizer is *palta a la jardinera*, avocado stuffed with a cold vegetable salad or *palta a la reina*, stuffed with chicken salad. *Choclo* is corn on the cob, often sold by street vendors at lunchtime. Other Peruvian "fast food" includes *anticuchos*, shish-kebabs of marinated beef heart; and *picarones*, sweet lumps of deep-

Price Guide

Prices are all for two people excluding wine:
$$$ More than US$40
$$ US$25–US$40
$ less than US$25

fried batter served with molasses. For *almuerzo*, or lunch, the main meal of the day, one of four courses might be *lomo saltado*, a stir-fried beef dish, or *aji de gallina*, chicken in a creamy spiced sauce.

Peruvian sweets include *suspiro de limeña* or *manjar blanco*, both made from sweetened condensed milk, or the ever-popular ice cream and cakes. There are many wonderful fruits available in Peru, notably *chirimoya* (custard apple), *lúcuma*, a nut-like fruit, delicious with ice cream, and *tuna*, which is the flesh from a type of cactus.

What To Drink

Peru's national drink is *pisco sour*, which consists of grape brandy, lemon, egg white, and a dash of cinnamon. Try the famous, potent *catedral* at the Gran Hotel Bolívar in Lima. In many Peruvian towns the soft drink *chicha morada*, made with purple maize, is popular. It's different from the *chicha de jora*, the traditional home-made alcoholic brew known throughout the Andes. The lime green *Inka Kola* is more popular than its northern namesake, but Coke, Pepsi, Orange Crush, Sprite, and Seven-up can all be found.

The *jugos* (juices) are a delightful alternative to sodas and there are many choices available. Instant Nescafé is often served up even in good restaurants, although real coffee can be found. Tea drinkers would be advised to order their beverage without milk, to avoid receiving some odd concoctions.

The inexpensive beers are of high quality. Try Cusqueña, Cristal, or Arequipeña. Peruvian wines can't compete with Chilean quality, but for a price, Tabernero, Tacama, Ocucaje, and Vista Alegre are the reliable names.

Where To Eat

LIMA

Lima offers a huge choice of restaurants, but the following are among the most reliable, providing high-quality food and service:

Traditional Fare

The most traditional of Andean foods is *cuy*, guinea pig, which is roasted and sometimes served with a peanut sauce. Another specialty of the Sierra is *pachamanca*, an assortment of meats and vegetables cooked over heated stones in pits in the ground. Succulent freshwater trout is plentiful in the mountain lakes and rivers.

International
Carlin
La Paz 646, Miraflores
tel: 444 4134
Mon–Sat noon–4pm and 7pm–midnight.
Cozy restaurant, equally popular with residents and tourists. **$$$**
Le Bistrot de mes Fils
Av. Conquistadores 510, San Isidro
tel: 422 6308
Mon–Fri 1–3.30pm and 7pm–midnight; Sat 7pm–midnight.
A real French bistro with great food. **$$$**
Ambrosia
Hotel Miraflores Park Plaza, Malecón de la Reserva 1035, Miraflores
tel: 242 3000
Mon–Fri noon–4pm, Sat 7pm–1am.
Tempting gourmet cuisine. **$$$**
La Gloria
Calle Atahualpa 201, Miraflores
tel: 445 5705
Mon–Sat 1–4pm and 8pm–1am, Sun closed.
Delicious Mediterranean food. Quality commensurate with price. **$$$**

Seafood
La Costa Verde
Barranquito Beach
tel: 477 2413/477 2424
One of the best, for food and atmosphere. **$$$**
La Rosa Naútica
Espigón 4, Costa Verde, Miraflores
tel: 447 0057
Daily 12.30pm–2am.
Lima's most famous seafood restaurant. Located at the end of an ocean boardwalk with Pacific views. **$$**

Criolla
Las Brujas de Cachiche
Bolognesi 460, Miraflores
tel: 444 5310/447 1883
Mon–Sat noon–midnight, Sun noon–4pm.
Good creole food. **$$**
El Señorio de Sulco
Malecón Cisneros 1470, Miraflores
tel: 441 0183;
www.ssulco@mail.cosapidata.com.pe
Daily noon–midnight.
Exquisite Peruvian cuisine on the quayside. **$$$**
Restaurante Huaca Pucllana
Gral. Borgoño Cdra. 8
tel: 445 4042
High-class Peruvian cuisine in pre-Inca pyramid site. **$$**

Chinese
Chifa Capon
Ucayali 774
Traditional restaurant in downtown Chinatown. **$**
Chifa Kun Fa
San Martín 459, Miraflores
tel: 447 8634. **$**
Typical Peruvian-style Chinese food.
Chifa Lung Fung
Av. República de Panama 3165
tel: 441 8817
One of the city's best Chinese restaurants, with interior garden. **$**

French
L'Eau Vive
Ucayali 370
tel: 275 612
Mon–Sat noon–3pm and 7.30–10.15pm.
Fine provincial dishes prepared and served by nuns. The sky-lit inner courtyard is one of Lima's most pleasant settings for lunch (the nuns – and customers – sing Ave Maria, nightly at 10pm). **$$**

Italian
La Trattoria
Manuel Bonilla 106, Miraflores
tel: 446 7002
Mon–Fri 1–3.30pm and 8–11.30pm.
Delicious Italian pasta. **$$**
Valentino
Manuel Bañon 215, San Isidro
tel: 442 2517/441 6174
Mon–Fri and Sun noon–3pm and

7.30–11pm, Sat 7.30–11pm.
Excellent Italian cusine. **$$**

Japanese
Matsuei Sushi Bar
Manuel Bañon 260, San Isidro
tel: 422 4323/442 8561
Mon–Sat noon–3pm and 7–11pm.
Excellent Japanese food. **$$$**

Steak
La Carreta
Rivera Navarrete 740, San Isidro
tel: 442 2690
Daily noon–midnight.
Excellent Argentine beef. **$$**
La Tranquera
Av. Pardo 285, Miraflores
tel: 447 5111
Daily noon–midnight.
Good steaks in kitsch ranch-style
dining room. **$$**
Martin Fierro
Malecón Cisneros 1420,
Miraflores
tel: 441 0199.
Argentine beef. Big buffet on Sun.
$$

Pizza
"Pizza Street," just off Diagonal, is
lined with good-value pizzerias.

Cafés
La Tiendecita Blanca – Café Suisse
Av. Larco 111, Miraflores
tel: 445 9797/445 1412
Daily 7am–midnight.
The best tea shop in town. **$$**
Cafe Olé
Pancho Fierro 115, San Isidro
tel: 440 7751/440 1186
Mon–Sun 7.30am–2am.
Smart café, good coffee, and
snacks. **$$**
Bohemia
Santa Cruz 805, Ovalo Gutierrez,
Miraflores
tel: 445 0889/446 5240
Excellent salads, sandwiches and
main dishes. **$$**
Café Café
Martín Olaya 250, Miraflores
tel: 445 1165
Open daily until late.
Trendy cafe with lattes,
cappuccinos, and many other
types of coffee. Good sandwiches.
$$

Café Haiti
Diagonal 160, Miraflores
Favorite hangout for Lima's writers
and artists.

Vegetarian
Bircher-Benner
Diez Canseco 487, Miraflores
tel: 444 4250
Open Tues–Sat 8.30am–10.30pm.
Inexpensive and good. **$**
Natur
Moquegua 132, just off Jirón de la
Union, Central Lima
tel: 28 5540
Open Mon–Sat 9am–9pm.
Good, meat-free Peruvian food. **$**

Ice Cream
Heladería 4D
Angamos Oeste 408, Miraflores.
Mouthwatering Italian ice cream.
$
Ben and Jerry's
Larco Mar Comercial Center,
Malecón Cisneros at end of Av.
Larco, Miraflores.
The genuine US-branded ice-cream,
for homesick North Americans. **$**

AREQUIPA

This attractive city has maintained
a reputation for style and
affluence. There are a number
of good restaurants around the
Plaza de Armas and cafés can
be found in the first block of
San Francisco.
El Fogón
Santa Marta 112
tel: 214 594
Specializes in barbecued chicken.
$
Sol de Mayo
Jerusalén 207 (Yanahuara district)
tel: 254 148
Good lunchtime menu of Peruvian
specialties such as *rocoto relleno*
(stuffed hot peppers), and *ocopa*

(potatoes in a spicy sauce with
melted cheese). **$$**
Tradición Arequipeña
Av. Dolores 111, José Luis
Bustamante y Rivero
tel: 242 385
Good Arequipeña food. **$$**
La Cantarilla
Tahuaycani 106 (Sachaca district)
tel: 251 515
Traditional Arequipeña and
international food. Sit outside for
lunch of freshwater shrimps. **$$**
Pizzeria Los Leños
Jerusalén 407
Oven-baked pizzas. Popular.
Evenings only. **$**
Cafe Forum
San Francisco 156
Popular meeting place. **$**
Govinda (Madre Natura)
Jerusalén 505
Cheap, good vegetarian set lunch. **$**

AYACUCHO

Alamo
Jr. Cusco 215
Local chicken and meat dishes a
specialty.
Restaurant Tradicional
Calle San Martin 406
International and Peruvian food in a
friendly atmosphere. **$$**
Restaurant La Casona
Jr. Bellido
Pork dishes and highland food. **$**
Restaurant Turistico
Jr. 9 de Diciembre 396
Good value for lunch. **$**

CUSCO

Sample the succulent pink trout,
prepared in many of the Peruvian and
international restaurants. There is
always a new establishment to be
found within the main plaza's portals.
Good restaurants also provide
exciting Andean music and dance.
Cafés around the plaza serve *mate
de coca*, chocolate cake, and hot
milk with rum on chilly nights.
El Ayllu
Portal de Carnes 203 (beside the
cathedral)
tel: 232 357

Virtually a Cusco institution, a popular place with older *cusqueños*, with tasteful decor and background classical and jazz music. Excellent breakfasts of ham and egg, toast, and fruit juice, or yoghurt, cakes, teas, and good coffee. **$**

El Truco
Plaza Regocijo 247
tel: 232 441
Mon–Sat noon–11pm
Catering to most of the large tour groups, this nightly dinner and show is the most elaborate in Cusco and very good value. **$$**

Inka Grill
Portal de Panes 115, Plaza de Armas
tel: 262 992
daily 8am–12pm
Upmarket international restaurant. Excellent food and service. **$$**

Kusikuy
Plateros 348
tel: 262 870
Typical local food including roast guinea pig. **$**

La Yunta
Portal de Carnes 214
tel: 235 103
Great juices, salads and pizzas. **$**

Al Grano
Santa Catalina Ancha 398
tel: 228 032
Good Asian food including vegetarian curry. Also great cookies. **$**

Kin Taro
Heladeros 149
tel: 226 181
Cheap, excellent Japanese food. Sit upstairs on floor with cable TV. **$**

Greens
Tandapata 700, above Plaza San Blas
tel: 243 379
The best curry in Peru. Also delicious British-style Sunday Roast (on Sunday afternoons – make reservation). **$**

El Mochica
Bolívar 462
tel: 465 022
Fine *criolla* cooking. **$**

Pacha-Papa
120 Plaza San Blas
tel: 241 318/233 190
Highly recommended restaurant serving traditional Peruvian food. **$**

Trotamundos
Portal de Comercio 177 (upstairs)
tel: 232 387
Good coffee, snacks and meals. **$**

Cross Keys Pub
Plaza de Armas
tel: 233 865
Typical British Pub with pub grub. Great meeting place. **$**

HUARAZ

Monte Rosa
Av. Luzuriaga 496
Pizza and international food. **$**

Restaurante Plaza
Jr. Lima 125
Traditional cuisine, mostly for locals. **$**

Pizzeria Bruno
Luzuriaga 834
Authentic Italian pizza. French owner Bruno. **$**

Price Guide

Prices are all for two people excluding wine:
$$$ More than US$40
$$ US$25–US$40
$ less than US$25

Alpes Andes
Casa de Guias, Plaza Ginebra
tel: 721 811
daily 7am–11pm
Good for breakfast. Cozy in the evening. **$**

Siam de los Andes
Gamarra esq Juan de Morales
tel: 728 006
daily 5–10pm
Thai cuisine, stir-fries and curries. **$**

Café Andino
Juan de Morales 753.
A relaxing place for coffee and cake, US-run, with a book exchange. **$**

TRUJILLO

There is a concentration of cheap, clean restaurants near the market, including several good *chifas* – Chinese restaurants – and several vegetarian places on Bolívar.

Big Ben
España
tel: 221 342
Delicious seafood and meat dishes. Also **Big Ben** in Huanchaco, Av. Larco 836. Urb. El Boquerón, tel: 461 869. **$$**

De Marco
Francisco Pizarro 725
tel: 234 251
Peruvian and international cuisine. Popular for ice creams and desserts. **$**

Parrillada Tori Gallo
Av. Bolognesi s/n
tel: 257 284
Good grilled meat. Sometimes has live music on Saturday night.

ICA

La Cueva
Domingo Elias 286, Urb. Luren
tel: 224 975
Good mixed cuisine. **$$**

NAZCA

La Taberna
Jr. Lima 321
tel: 522 322
Popular with *gringos*. Good food and lots of graffiti on the walls.

CAJAMARCA

El Cajamarques
Amazonas 770
tel: 822 128
Good food in colonial setting. **$$**

Los Faroles
In Hostal Cajamarca,
Jr. Dos de Mayo 311
Live music in the evenings, local food. **$$**

El Batán
Del Batan 369
tel: 926 025
Good local and international food. Live music at weekend. ~There's an art gallery on the first floor. **$$**

Salas
Jr. Amalia Puga 637
tel: 822 876
Popular with locals; inexpensive regional dishes. **$**

CHICLAYO

Fiesta
Av. Salaverry 180 (in 3 de Octubre district)
Excellent local dishes. **$$**
Las Tinajas
Av. Elías Aguirre 957
Delicious seafood. **$**
Romana
Balta 512
tel: 223 598
Popular place, good local food. **$**

CHACHAPOYAS

Restaurant Matalacha
Jr. Ayacucho 616
Inexpensive meals, big portions. **$**
El Tejado
Plaza de Armas, Grau 534
Large set meals. **$**
Yana Yaku
Ortiz Arrieta 532, Plaza de Armas.
Pleasant café overlooking plaza. **$**

PUNO

Don Piero
Lima 364
Popular restaurant with locals and *gringos*. **$**
Pizzeria del Buho
Jr. Libertad 386
(and also Lima 347)
tel: 356 223
Cozy small restaurant specializing in wood oven-baked pizzas. **$**
Internacional
Libertad 161
Popular with tour groups.
International and Peruvian dishes available. **$**

Attractions

Round Trips & Tours

Lima Tours is the main tour organizer in Peru, with branches in every tourist region. They offer tours to all parts of the country mentioned in this book – for example to Cusco and Machu Picchu, Arequipa, the Amazon, the North, and Lake Titicaca.

Lima Tours also keeps up to date on new events, and offers theme trips: for example, tours to the Sipán archeological dig; and have exclusive rights on visits to some colonial houses in Lima (including evening dinners in 17th-century mansions, etc). It's worth dropping by their modern offices in Calle Belén and asking for one of their brochures:

Lima Tours, Belén 1040, Lima
tel: 424 5110; fax: 330 4488;
e-mail: info@limatours.com.pe
Mon–Fri 8.30am–5.15pm and Sat–Sun 8.30am–3pm.
Also at Av. José Pardo 392, Miraflores, tel: 241 7551;
fax: 241 2611;
e-mail: vacacionperu@limatours.com.pe
Class Adventure Travel for well-organized tours and private groups throughout Peru.
Grimaldo del Solar 463, Miraflores
tel: 444 2220
fax: 241 8908
e-mail: info@cat-travel.com
www.cat-travel.com
Aracari Travel Consulting SRL
Av. José Pardo 610 # 802, Miraflores, tel: 242 6673;
fax: 242 4856;
e-mail: info@aracari.com
www.aracari.com
Specialize in arranging escorted group tours and accommodations in Chachapoyas and the northwest of the country.

Trekking

Preparation The country looks most beautiful in the dry season from May to September when the weather is good. Assembling a group in Cusco is possible – try using the notice board hanging in the tourist office in Portál Mantas 188. Members of South American Explorers' club can find other trekking companions through the notice boards at the Lima and Cusco club houses.
Equipment Essential for trekking tours are: backpack, strong walking shoes, sleeping bag, thermal mat, tent, and cooker. Some adventure travel agencies rent all the equipment; such places are quite easy to find. The gear is inexpensive but the quality is often bad. You should check your equipment carefully before starting.

The nights tend to be very cold but it is easy to get sunburnt during the day in the Andes. Don't forget a hat and a high-factor sunscreen, although you can now buy this in Peru. If you wish you can hire a porter to carry your luggage up the Inca trail. Mule guides *(arrieros)* can be found

Adventure Travel

Apart from Lima Tours, recommended specialist adventure travel companies for river running, trekking, and jungle expeditions include:

● **Explorandes**
Calle San Fernando 320, Miraflores
tel: 445 0532; fax: 445 4686;
e-mail: postmaster@exploran.com.pe
● **Amazonas Explorer**
PO Box 722,
Cusco
tel: 22 5284; fax: 23 6826;
e-mail: www.amazonas-explorer.com
● **Inti Travel (in USA)**
1212 Broadway Av.,
Suite # 910,
Oakland, CA 94612
tel: 1-800 655 4053;
www.wonderlink.com/inti

everywhere in the Cordillera Blanca, and their service is not expensive.

Food Buy your food in the larger towns because there is not a great choice in small villages. A chain of *supermercados*, *bodegas*, and street markets sell food such as dried fruit, cheese, fruit, instant soup, and tinned fish. Drinking water should be treated with iodine, although even quite remote places sell bottled water.

Altitude sickness The onset of altitude sickness can be diminished by sticking to a few rules. Avoid alcohol, excessive eating, and getting physically tired out in the first few days. Drinking lots of liquid helps the body adjust. Sugar, for example from sweets and glucose mixtures, stimulates the metabolism and aspirin helps headaches. *Mate de coca*, a coca-leaf tea, is supposed to be the best universal remedy, and is widely available in cafés and restaurants.

Nazca

For flights over the Nazca Lines in light aircraft, reservations can be made with **Aero Cóndor** at the airport or their office in town.
In Lima flights can be booked at:
Jr. Juan de Arona 781, San Isidro
tel: 441 1354/440 1754;
fax: 442 9772;
e-mail: acondor@ibm.net
Information after office hours,
tel: 941 8675.
Aero Ica
In Nazca airport or at Hotel La Maison Suisse
tel: 522 434.
Aero Ica (In Lima)
Diez Canseco 480B, Miraflores
tel: 446 3026; fax: 242 2140.
Aero Paracas
In Nazca airport
tel: 522 688.

Arequipa

Most attractions in Arequipa are accessible on foot and easily appreciated as an independent traveler, although if you don't have

much time, city tours are available, which include the Santa Catalina Monastery and other points of interest. Day tours into the mountainous terrain include the Colca Canyon, climbing the El Misti volcano, viewing the petroglyphs at El Toro, bathing in local thermal springs, and visiting Cotahuasi.

The following companies offer traditional and adventure tours around Arequipa and to the Colca Canyon:
Lima Tours
Santa Catalina 120
tel: 242 293; fax: 228 481;
e-mail: limatours-aqp@LaRed.net.pe
Ideal Travels
Ugarte 208
tel: 245 199; fax: 242 088 ;
e-mail: idealperu@terra.com.pe
Giardino Tours
Jerusalen 604A
tel: 221 345/241 206;
fax: 242 761;
e-mail: giardinotours@terra.com.pe
Holley's Unusual Excursions
tel/fax: 258 459;
e-mail: angoho@LaRed.net.pe
An interesting option: English owner Anthony Holley knows the area inside out and runs 4-wheel drive excursions for up to six people.
Amazonas Explorer
PO Box 333, Arequipa
tel: 212 813; fax: 220 147;
e-mail: info@amazonas-explorer.com
For first-class rafting and mountain-biking trips try Amazonas Explorer. The English/Swiss owners are experts in alternative adventure.
Hilton Travel
Santa Catalina 102
tel: 227 297; fax: 242 761;
e-mail: hiltontravel@wayna.rcp.net.pe
Condor Travel
Puente Bolognesi 120
tel/fax: 218 362;
e-mail: condormisti@condortravel.com.pe
Sky Viajes y Turismo
San Francisco 319
tel: 205 124/281 731;
e-mail: skyaqp@terra.com.pe

Puno (Lake Titicaca)

Tours can be taken around the lake, to the ruins at Sillustani, Chucuito, and the town of Juli. Contact:

Turpuno
Jr. Lambayeque 175
tel: 352 001; fax: 351 431;
e-mail: turpuno@viaexpresa.com
Offer free transport to Juliaca if you buy air travel from them.
Edgar Adventures
Jr. Lima 328
tel: 353 444; fax: 354 811;
e-mail: edgaradventures@hotmail.com
Kafer Viajes y Turismo
Jr. Arequipa 179
tel/fax: 352 701;
e-mail: kafer@punonet.com
Solmar Tours
Jr. Arequipa 140
tel: 352 586; fax: 351 654
Many travelers take the short boat ride across Lake Titicaca to the Floating Islands. Simply go to the dock where boats leave regularly. It is a 3-hour boat ride to the tranquil islands of Taquile or Amantaní. Boats leave between 8 and 9am.

Cusco

The first thing to do is to purchase a Visitor Ticket, a combination entry pass to all the historic buildings of note. It includes fourteen different sites, but each site can only be visited once. The ticket can be bought from the tourist office on the corner of Calle Garcilaso and Plaza Regocijo.

Tour operators in Cusco fall into two categories: those offering standard tours of Cusco and the surrounding ruins and market villages; and those operating adventure tours such as trekking, climbing, river running, and jungle expeditions.

CULTURAL TOURS

Lima Tours
Jr. Machu Picchu D24,
Urb. Manuel Prado
tel: 228 431; fax: 221 266;
e-mail: litocus+@amauta.rcp.net.pe
Condor Travel (Cusco)
Calle Saphi 848 A
tel: 226 605; fax: 231 161;
e-mail: condorcuzco@condortravel.com.pe

ADVENTURE TOURS

Trek Peru
Jr. Ricardo Palma N-9 Santa Monica
tel: 252 899; fax: 238 591;
e-mail: trekperu@terra.com.pe
Peruvian Andean Treks
Av. Pardo 705
tel: 225 701; fax: 238 911;
e-mail: postmaster@patcuzco.com.pe
Explorandes
Av. Garcilaso 316 A, Wanchac
tel: 238 380; fax: 233 784;
e-mail: postmaster@exploran.com.pe
Inti Travel (in USA)
1212 Broadway Ave, Suite 910,
Oakland, CA 94612
tel: 1-800 655 4053;
e-mail: info@intitravel.com
www.wonderlink.com/inti

The following organize trips into
Manu from Cusco:
Manu Expeditions
Av. Pardo 895
tel: 226 671; fax: 236 706;
e-mail: manuexpe@amauta.rcp.net.pe
Manu Nature Tours
Av. Pardo 1046
tel: 252 721; fax: 234 793.
Branch office at: Portal Comercio
195, Plaza de Armas
tel/fax: 252 526;
e-mail: mnt@amauta.rcp.net.pe
Pantiacolla Tours (**Manu Biosphere
Reserve**)
Calle Plateros 360, Cusco
tel: 238 823; fax: 252 696;
e-mail: pantiac@terra.com.pe

The following organize trips into
Tambopata Reserve from Puerto
Maldonado:
Peruvian Safaris
Explorers Inn, Calle Plateros 365
tel/fax: 235 342;
e-mail: safaris@amauata.rcp.net.pe
Rainforest Expeditions (Lima)
Av. Aramburú 166 Dep. 4B,
Miraflores, Lima
tel: 221 4182; fax: 421 8183;
e-mail: rainfore@amauta.rcp.net.pe

Huaraz

For tours to Chavín, Pastoruri, other
day trips and longer treks:
Huaraz Chavín Tours
Av. Luzuriaga 502
tel: 721 578/722 602;
e-mail: chavin-t@telematic.edu.pe
Explorandes
Av. Centenario 489
tel/fax: 721 960;
e-mail: postmaster@exploran.com.pe
Montrek
Av. Luzuriaga 646, 2nd floor,
tel/fax: 721 124
Montañero Aventura y Turismo
Parque Ginebra 30-B
tel: 726 386; cellphone: 613 751;
fax: 722 306;
e-mail: aventuraperu@hotmail.com
Andean Sport Tours
Av. Luzuriaga 571
tel: 721 612

For mountain biking:
Mountain Bike Adventures
Lucar y Torre 520/538 or
Julio Arguedas 1246
tel: 724 259;
fax: 724 888 attn: Julio Olaza;
e-mail: olaza@mail.cosapidata.com.pe

Trujillo

For tours to the five major
archeological sites:
Condor Travel
Jr. Independencia 533
tel: 244 658; fax: 255 975;
e-mail: condortru@condortravel.com.pe
Guía Tours
Independencia 580
tel: 245 170; fax: 246 353.
Trujillo Tours
Jr. Diego de Almagro 301
tel/fax: 257 518.

Chachapoyas

Vilaya Tours
Jr. Grau 624 (or ask at the Gran
Hotel Vilaya)
tel: 777 506; fax: 778 154;
e-mail: info@vilayatours.com
www.vilayatours.com

Chiclayo

Important new archeological sites
such as Sipán can be reached with
Lima Tours or:
Indiana Tours
Colón 556
tel: 222 991; fax: 225 751;
e-mail: indianatours@terra.com.pe

Cajamarca

Tours of the city include
numerous colonial churches,
thermal baths at Baños del Inca,
and the Ventanillas de Otuzco.
Contact:
Cumbe Mayo Tours
Jr. Amalia Puga 635
tel/fax: 922 938.
Clarín Tours,
Jr. Del Batán 161
tel/fax: 826 829;
e-mail: clarintours@yahool.com
Atahualpa Inca Tours
Jr. Amazonas 760, Of. 01
tel: 824 4147; tel/fax: 827 014
Cajamarca Travel
Jr. Amazonas 570, Of. 7
tel: 830 074; fax: 828 642;
e-mail: cajamarcatravel@si.computextos.net

Iquitos

There are many interesting sights
in and around the city as well as
jungle expeditions.
Explorama Lodges
Av. La Marina 340
tel: 252 526/252 530;
fax: 252 533;
e-mail: amazon@explorama.com
Amazon Tour and Cruises
Requena 336
tel: 233 931; fax: 231 265.
Reservations in Lima:
Francisco de Zela 1580, Of. 1
tel: 265 9524; fax: 471 5287.
Yacumama Lodge
Sargento Lores 149, Iquitos
tel: 235 510;
www.yacumama.com
Paseos Amazónicos
Calle Pevas 246, Iquitos
tel: 241 7576/446 7946 (Lima)

Ayacucho

Morochucos Travel
Av. 28 de Julio 147, Portal
Union 32
tel: 815 382; fax: 811 441;
e-mail: morochucos@terra.com.pe

Culture

For details of museums, *see* chapters, pages 149–317.

Galleries

Lima
The best art and antique establishments are in the areas of San Isidro, Miraflores, and Barranco.

Banco Continental, Tarata 201, Miraflores, tel: 444 0011. Mon–Sat 11am–9pm.

Camino Brent, Burgos 170, San Isidro, tel: 422 2205. Mon–Sat 4–8pm.

Centro Cultural de la Pontificia Universidad Católica (PUCP) Camino Real 1075, San Isidro, tel: 222 6899.

Forum, Larco 1150, Miraflores, tel: 446 1313. Mon–Fri 10am–1.30pm and 5–9pm, Sat 5–9pm.

Galería de la Municipalidad de Miraflores, Av. Larco 3rd block, tel: 444 0540.

Galeria Municipal Pancho Fierro Pasaje Santa Rosa 126, Lima, tel: 427 0835.

Instituto Culturál Peruano Norteamericano (ICPNA) Av. Angamos Oeste 160, Miraflores, tel: 446 1841/242 7358.

Museo de Arte, Paseo Colón 125, tel: 423 4732. Tues–Sun 9am–5pm.

Porta 725, Porta 725, Miraflores, tel: 447 6158. Mon–Fri 10.30am–1.30pm and 3.30–7.30pm. Sat by appointment.

Praxis Arte Internacional, San Martín 689, Barranco, tel: 477 2822. Mon–Sat 5–9pm.

Trapecio, Larco 143, Mezzanine 2, Miraflores, tel: 444 0842. Mon–Fri 10.30am–12.30pm and 5–9pm, Sat 5–9pm.

Theaters & Music

ICPNA Instituto Culturál Peruano Norteamericano, Av. Arequipa 4798 corner of Av. Angamos, Miraflores, tel: 241 1940.

Centro Cultural de la Pontificia Universidad Católica (PUCP), Av. Camino Real 1075, San Isidro, tel: 222 6899.

Teatro Larco, Av. Larco 1036, Miraflores, tel: 447 1341.

Teatro Británico, Bellavista 529, Miraflores, tel: 447 1135.

Teatro Municipal, Ica 300, Lima. Burnt down in 2000, but performances are still staged here.

Check the Cultural section of *El Comercio* newspaper for details.

Architecture

Many of Lima's architectural jewels from the colonial era are slowly being repaired. The city council has initiated a program to restore old buildings by looking for money from private investors. During 1998 they made a start with the ornate balconies, as part of a program called "Adopt a Balcony," and some of the results can already be seen in the streets around the Plaza Mayor.

The following colonial-style buildings can be visited:

Casa Alíaga, Jr. de la Unión 224, Lima, tel: 427 6624. The 16th-century house of Jerónimo de Aliaga, one of Pizarro's original 168 conquistadors. Still occupied by the Aliaga family, but tours can be arranged through Lima Tours.

Casa de los Marqueses de la Riva, Ica 426, Lima, tel: 428 2642. Visits by appointment only. Owned and run by the Entre Nous Society.

Casa de la Riva Agüero, Camaná 459, Lima, tel: 427 9275. Mon–Fri 1–8pm, Sat 9am–1pm. Free entry. The first floor contains the archives and library of the Catholic University; the second floor is a small but fine folk-art museum.

Casa Courret. The 1865 art-nouveau house of the French photographer Eugène Courret, hidden away above the modern storefronts on the busy Jirón de la Unión.

Public Holidays & Festivals

January
January 1 – New Year's Day (national holiday).

January 15–20 – Lima Foundation Week. Official celebrations of the founding of Lima by the Spanish conquistador Francisco Pizarro on January 18, 1535.

January 24–31 – *Festival de la Marinera*, Trujillo. Annual traditional dance competitions.

February
February 1–15 – *Cruz de Chalpon*, Chiclayo. Handicraft and commercial fair in the nearby prilgrimage center of Motupe.

February 8–14 – *Virgen de la Candelaria*, Puno. "La Mamita Candicha," the patron of Puno, is honored with folklore demonstrations. Thousands participate in the parades, dances, fireworks, and music of this important religious event.

February (every Sunday) – Carnival, Iquitos. Colorful masquerades and typical *La Pandilla* dancing take place throughout the city.

Mid-February – Carnival, Puno and Cajamarca. Pre-Lent carnival is celebrated throughout Peru, but especially in these cities, with *La Pandilla* dancing and traditional festivities.

March/April
March 1–5 – *Fiesta de la Vendimia*, Ica. The grape harvest of the Ica Valley is celebrated with parades, dances, and revelry.

March/April – *Semana Santa* (Easter/Holy Week). Among the nationwide commemorations is the spectacular procession in Cusco in honor of *El Señor de los Temblores*, held on Holy Monday and Thursday. The people of Tarma make carpets of flowers to cover the streets for their evening processions. (Half day holiday on Maundy Thursday, full day holiday on Good Friday.)

April
Third week – National Contest of *Caballos de Paso*, Lima. This

exhibition and contest in Mamacona, 30 km (18 miles) south of Lima, involves horse breeders from the most important regions of Peru.

May

May 1 – Labor Day and *San José* (St Joseph's Day) (national holiday).
May 2 – *Cruz Velacuy*, Cusco. The crosses in all the churches of Cusco are veiled and festivities take place.
May 2–4 – *Las Alasitas*, Puno. Important exhibition and sale of miniature handicrafts.

June

First week – Mountaineering Week in the Andes, Huaraz. The Callejón de Huaylas and the Cordillera Blanca provide the majestic settings for the National and International Ski Championships, as well as many other adventurous activities.
Mid-June – Corpus Christi, Cusco. One of the most beautiful displays of religious folklore, the Procession of the Consecrated Host is accompanied by statues of saints from churches all over Cusco.
June 24 – *Inti Raymi* (Festival of the Sun), Cusco. This ancient festival is staged at the Sacsayhuamán Fortress, and involves Inca rituals, parades, folk dances, and contests. *San Juan* (St John's Day) is celebrated throughout the Andes.
June 29 – *San Pedro y San Pablo* (St Peter's and St Paul's Day; national holiday).

Concerts

In Lima, the Philharmonic Society presents celebrated international orchestras and soloists from April to October. For further information check the cultural section of *El Comercio*, or contact: Porta 170, Of. 301, Miraflores, tel: 457-395/242-6396, Mon–Fri 9am–1pm and 4pm–6pm (9am–1pm only March–April). Sponsors well-known North American and European orchestras.

July

July 15–17 – *La Virgen del Carmen*, Cusco. Festivities are held throughout the highlands, especially colorful in Paucartambo, 255 km (160 miles) from Cusco.
July 28 & 29 – Peru's Independence celebrations (public holiday).

August

August 13–19 – Arequipa Week. This is the city's most important annual event. Festivities include folkloric dances and handicraft markets, and climax with a fireworks display in the Plaza de Armas on the 15th.
August 30 – *Santa Rosa de Lima* (public holiday).

September

September 18 – Unu Urgo Festival, Urcos and Calca (near Cusco). Ceremonies, Andean music, dancing, and parades.

October/November

October 7–20 – *El Señor de Luren*, Ica. Thousands of pilgrims pay homage to the town patron, with the main procession on the 17th.
October 8 – Commemoration of the Battle of Angamos (national holiday).
October 18, 19, & 28 – *El Señor de los Milagros*, Lima. A massive procession in honor of Lima's patron saint, on the 18th.
October/November – Bullfighting Season. An international competition is held at the Plaza de Acho, in the oldest bullring in the Americas.

November

November 1 – *Día de Todos los Santos* (All Saints' Day; national holiday).
November 1–7 – Puno Jubilee Week. Puno celebrates its founding by the Spanish, followed by a re-enactment of the emergence of the legendary founders of the Inca Empire, Manco Capac and Mama Ocllo, from the waters of Lake Titicaca. This week sees the best of Puno's folkloric festivities.
November 29 – Zaña Week, Chiclayo. Week of celebrations for the foundation of Zaña include

folklore shows, sporting events, and exhibitions of *Caballos de Paso*.

December

December 8 – *La Concepción Inmaculada* (Immaculate Conception; national holiday).
December 24 – Festival of *Santu Rantikuy*, Cusco. Andean toy and handicrafts fair in the main plaza.
December 24 & 25 – Christmas (half-day national holiday on 24th, full day on 25th).

Cinema

Peru's film industry is very small, but going to the cinema is popular and there are movie houses in all the larger towns, often showing US films in English, with Spanish subtitles. Sometimes the Spanish language wins out, though, and it's the *gringos* who have to be content with the subtitles.

Lima

Multicines StarVision El Pacífico, Av. Diagonal (corner of Av. José Pardo), Miraflores, tel: 444 9964.
Cinemar, Centro Cultural Jockey Plaza, Av. Javier Prado Este block 42, Monterrico, Surco, tel: 434 0034.
Multicines Larco, Centro Cultural LarcoMar, Parque Salazar, Miraflores, tel: 446 7336.
Romeo y Julieta, Pasaje Porta 132, Miraflores, tel: 444 0135.
Filmoteca de Lima, Museo de Arte, Lima, tel: 4423 4732.
El Cine, Centro Cultural PUCP, Camino Real 1075, San Isidro, tel: 222 6899.

Nightlife

Live Music

Lima

Lima offers some of the best music from all over Peru. Not only are there good groups performing Andean folk music, but there are Afro-Peruvian bands, salsa, the more recent *techno-cumbia* dance music, and some jazz bands. The *peñas* which put on Andean folk music get very crowded at the weekends, as do the *salsadromos* where young Peruvians love to dance the night away.

Peña Hatuchay, Trujillo 228, Rimac (across the bridge from the center of town). The best night out for budget-conscious travelers and anyone else who is willing to get into the informal spirit. Colorful decor and a great variety show. Shows on Fri and Sat 9pm.

Barranco is Lima's Bohemian suburb of cafés, bars, and live music, including:

El Ekeko, Av. Grau 266, Barranco, in front of the Municipal Park, tel: 247 3148.

La Estación de Barranco, Pedro de Osma 112, Barranco, tel: 247 0344. Tues–Sat, shows at 11pm.

Video Bars

Video bars have become very popular in Cusco, catering to hordes of backpackers, tired out from the Inca Trail. Snacks and drinks are served while you watch videos, usually in English with Spanish subtitles. Bars come and go, so there would be little point in recommending particular spots, but people will accost you in the Plaza de Armas with flyers for the latest places.

Manos Morenas, Pedro de Osma 409, Barranco, tel: 467 0421/ 467 4902. A restaurant with good Peruvian food. Wed and Thurs nights they have an Afro–Peruvian dance group, "Negro," and Fri–Sat general Peruvian music.

Brisas del Titicaca, Walkuski 168, tel: 423 7405. Folk dancing from all over Peru. Popular with the locals. Very authentic and cheap.

Sachún, Av. del Ejército 657, Miraflores, tel: 441 0123/441 4465. Tues–Sat traditional Andean and Afro-Peruvian dances.

For jazz, latin jazz, and rock, try:

El Dragón, Av. Nicolás de Piérola block 1, Barranco.

La Casona de Barranco, Av. Grau 329, Barranco.

Jazz Zone, Av. La Paz 656, Pasaje El Suche, Miraflores, tel: 242 7090

Cusco

Cusco has some of the best *peñas* in South America, with a range of Andean styles (some of the bands are internationally known). They're mostly around the Plaza de Armas and easy to find because of the blaring music. Two *peñas* sharing the same staircase on the south-western side of the plaza are probably the best place to start.

Several restaurants around the plaza (such as the Roma and El Truco) also have live music – just stroll around and listen. Many of the larger hotels also stage folkloric shows. Folkloric venues include:

Ukukus, Calle Plateros 316, tel: 242 951.

El Truco, Plaza Regocijo 261, tel: 235 295.

Amadeus Taberna, Parque Ginebra.

Huaraz

Tambo Taverna, José de la Mar 776.

Montrek Disco – Sucre (just off Plaza de Armas) in converted cinema.

Nightclubs/Discos

Lima

Discoteca Gótica, Larco Mar, Miraflores. One of Lima's best clubs.

El Grill del Costa Verde, Restaurant Costa Verde, Playa Barranquito s/n,

Barranco, tel: 441 3485. Fancy disco attached to restaurant.

La noche, Av. Bolognesi 307, Barranco. Popular with smart young *limeños*.

Teatrix, Larco Mar, Miraflores. Trance and other dance music.

Cusco

Ukukus, Plateros 316. Late afternoon movies, live local bands, followed by disco.

Mama Africa, Portal Belén 115. Movies, internet café, hip music.

Kamikaze, Plaza Regocijo 274. Live band around 10pm followed by Western disco-rock/pop music. Happy hour before live band.

Bars

Lima

La Noche, Av. Bolognesi 307, Barranco, tel: 477 4154. Attractive, lively bar; great meeting place.

O'Murphy's Irish Pub, Schell 627, tel: 242 4540. Pub grub and good atmosphere.

Amnesia, Pasaje Sanchez Carrión 153, tel: 477 9577. Another lively bar full of *limeños*.

Cusco

Los Perros, Tecsecocha 436. Trendy bar for cocktails and beers, with couches. Great mix of music.

Rosie O'Grady's, Santa Catalina Ancha 360, tel: 247 935. Attractive smart Irish Bar with good food and Guinness.

Cross Keys Pub, Plaza de Armas. Typical British Pub, with darts.

Shopping

In Lima, as well as in the many regional marketplaces, the best quality and value lies in handcrafted products. *(See the feature on "How Crafts Have Adapted" for more information.)* This particularly applies to gold, silver, and copper work, as well as Peru's rich textile goods – such as alpaca garments and woven tapestries. Many tourists also take home reproductions of pre-Columbian ceramics, with gourds being a great favorite.

Visitors to the jungle may have the opportunity to purchase traditional handicrafts, including adornments (necklaces worn for tribal dances), utensils (baskets, food bowls, hunting bags), and weapons (bows, arrows, spears). However, never be tempted to buy skins, live animals, or arrows decorated with parrot feathers. This trade is often illegal and has direct consequences in destroying wildlife populations.

Apart from *artesanías*, quality shopping goods can only be found in the commercial streets of Miraflores and San Isidro, where suppliers for international brands keep a limited stock at very high prices. For bargains in electronics, you would do better to cross the southern border into northern Chile and its *Zona Franca* (Duty Free) complexes.

It is quite easy to get camera supplies in Lima. You may also be surprised to find alkaline batteries and film for your camera in the Lake Titicaca area, or in a market in the Andes. But, just to be sure, always bring extra supplies. There are very good color labs for developing film in the big cities. For black and white film it's better to take it back home to be developed.

Each region has its own distinctive crafts, but if your time is limited, you'll find that many cultures are well represented in Lima. There are a number of shops within an attractive courtyard at "1900," Belén 1030, just down from Plaza San Martín. Two other recognized centers of quality merchandise are at El Alamo, 5th block of La Paz, Miraflores, and El Suche, the 6th block of La Paz in Miraflores.

Markets

Outdoor markets offer the best bargains although quality varies and one needs to be wary of pickpockets. The best ones are **Mercado Indio** in Av. La Marina, from blocks 6 to 10 on your way to the airport, or at Petit Thouars 5242, Miraflores, both in Lima.

Also in Lima, a relaxed artists' market with canvasses of varying quality is on Parque Kennedy in the heart of Miraflores.

PERUVIAN CRAFT

Lima

Artesanías del Perú, Jorge Basadre 610, San Isidro, tel: 440 1925. Mon–Sat 11am–7.30pm.
Antisuyo, Jr. Tacna 460, Miraflores, tel: 447 2557.
Kunturwasi, Ocharán 182, Miraflores, tel: 242 9469/444 0557. Mon–Sat 11am–7.30pm.

Alpaca products are well worth buying, as long as you are prepared to hand-wash them with great care. Vendors will often tell you their goods are made from alpaca "bebé." This does not mean baby alpacas, but refers to the wool taken from the throat of the animal, where it is at its finest and softest.

Most woolen jumpers sold as alpaca are usually a more hard-wearing mix of llama wool and synthetic fibers.

Adexport S.R. Ltda, Calle Q 256, Los Jazmines, Miraflores, tel: 448 2366.
Artesanías Pachacútec, Cantuarias 240, Miraflores, tel: 241 0086.
Cerámica y Artesanía, Conde de Superunda 239, tel: 427 1760.
Mercado Artesanal, Av. Petit Thouars Block 52, Miraflores.

CLOTHING WITH PERUVIAN DESIGNS

Lima

Club Peru, Conquistadores 946, San Isidro.
Silvania Prints, Conquistadores 915, San Isidro, tel: 422 6440. Mon–Fri 9.30am–6pm; Sat 9.30am–2pm. Also at Diez Canseco 376, Miraflores. Mon–Sat 10.30am–1pm and 4.30–7.30pm.

ALPACA, LEATHER AND FUR

Lima

Alpaca 111 S.A. (English spoken), Av. Larco 671, Miraflores, tel: 447 1623, and at: Camino Real Shopping Center, Level A, Shop 32–33, San Isidro.
Royal Alpaca, La Paz 646, store 14–15, El Suche Commercial Center, Miraflores. Mon–Sat 9.30am–9.30pm, Sun 11am–7pm.

Arequipa

Alpaca 111, Jerusalem 115, tel: 212 347.
El Zaguán, Santa Catalina 120A, tel: 223 950.

Cusco

Alpaca's Best, Plaza Nazarenas 197, tel: 245 331. Mon–Fri 9.30am–9.30pm.
La Casa de la Llama, Calle Palacio 121, tel: 240 813. Daily 9am–10pm.

GOLD AND JEWELRY

Lima

Casa Welsch, Monterosa 229, Chacarilla, Surco, tel: 372 6688;

fax: 438 6848. Mon–Fri 10am–1pm and 4–7.30pm.

Cabuchón, Libertadores 532, San Isidro, tel: 442 6219. Mon–Fri 10am–1pm and 4–8pm.

Camusso, Libertadores 715, San Isidro, tel: 422 0340/221 1594. Mon–Fri 9am–1pm and 3.30–7.30pm. Sat 9am–1pm.

The major hotels often house exclusive jewelry and *artesanía* stores, such as H. Stern Jewelers, with outlets at the Hotel Gran Bolívar, the Lima Sheraton, Miraflores Cesar's Hotel, the Gold Museum, and the International Airport.

BOOKS

There is not much in the way of good English-language bookshops in Peru. The following will have titles in English and are the best bets *(see also English Books under Further Reading, page 350)*:

Lima

Zeta Bookstore SRL, Comandante Espinar 219, Miraflores.
Special Book Services, Av. Angamos Oeste 301, Miraflores, Lima 18.

Arequipa
Special Book Services, Calle Rivero 115 A, Cercado.

Cusco
Special Book Services, Av. El Sol 781 A.

Edible Gifts

The harvesting of wild Brazil nuts is a major economy of the jungle and does not destroy its ecosystem. Fresh Brazil nuts are richer in flavor than processed nuts as they still contain many of their natural oils. Large bags of ready-shelled nuts can be bought very cheaply, either plain or with a less-healthy sugar coating.

Sport

Participant

Lima Tours can arrange visits to **El Pueblo Inn**, a country club 11 km (7 miles) east of Lima, specifically for sporting activities such as tennis, golf, horseback riding, and swimming. Another agency to try is: **Sudex Tours S.A.**, Av. 28 de Julio 1120, Miraflores, tel: 242 7272, fax: 241 5988.

Ask about other 18-hole golf courses at Country Club de Villa, Granja Azul and La Planicie. For ten-pin bowling and pool playing, go to the Brunswick Bowl, Balta 135, Miraflores.

A great variety of sports is available to tourists outside Lima. Horseback riding is popular in the Sierra, where horses can easily be hired. Fly fishing in Andean lakes and streams is a rewarding pastime and there is excellent deep-sea fishing off Ancón, north of Lima.

Spectator

The main spectator sports in South-American countries are soccer (football), horse racing and, to a lesser extent, bullfighting.

Association football matches take place at the National Stadium (Estadio Nacional), Paseo de la República in downtown Lima, which seats 45,000.

Horse racing takes place most weekends and some summer evenings at the Monterrico Racetrack at the junction of the Panamerican Highway South with Avenida Javier Prado in Lima. Take your passport to get access to the members' stand.

Language

Useful Words and Phrases

There are a few interesting local variations of the Spanish *(castillano)* familiar to many. An expression you will hear everywhere, and which is difficult to translate, is *no más. Siga no más* for example, means "Go ahead." *Come no más* means "Just eat it (It'll get cold/it's nicer than it looks, etc.)." You will soon get the hang of it.

Vowels
a as in apple
e as in bed
i as in police
o as in got
u as in rude

Consonants
Consonants are approximately like those in English, the main exceptions being:
c is hard before **a**, **o**, or **u** (as in English), and is soft before **e** or **i**, when it sounds like **s** (as opposed to the pronunciation of **th** as in think used in Spain). Thus, *censo* (census) sounds like senso.
g is hard before **a**, **o**, or **u** (as in English), but where English **g** sounds like **j** – before **e** or **i** – Spanish **g** sounds like a guttural **h**.
g before **ua** is often soft or silent, so that *agua* sounds more like awa, and Guadalajara like Wadalajara.
h is silent.
j sounds like a gutteral h.
ll sounds like y.
ñ sounds like ni, as in onion.
q is followed by u as in English, but the combination sounds like k instead of like kw. **¿Qué quiere Usted?** is pronounced: Keh kee-ehr-eh oostehd?

r is often rolled.

x between vowels sounds like a guttural h, e.g. in México or Oaxaca.

y alone, as the word meaning "and", is pronounced ee.

Note that ch and ll are each a separate letter of the Spanish alphabet; if looking in a phone book or dictionary for a word beginning with ch, you will find it after the final c entry. A name or word beginning with ll will be listed after the final l entry.

If you speak no Spanish, here are some basic words to help you get around:

My name is Mary *Me llamo María*
What is your name? *¿Como se llama?*
Hello, how are you? *¿Hola, qué tal?*
I'm very well, and you? *Muy bien. ¿Y usted?*
Very well, thank you *Muy bien, gracias*
Good morning *Buenos días*
Good afternoon *Buenas tardes*
Goodnight *Buenas noches*
Welcome *Bienvenido*
Hello *¡Hola!*
Bye *Adios*
See you later *Hasta luego*

How are you? *¿Qué tal?*
Very well *Muy bien*
Thank you *Gracias*
Don't mention it *De nada*
Please *Por favor*
Excuse me *Perdón*
Yes *Sí*
No *No*
What is this? *¿Que es esto?*
How much is this? *Cuánto es?*
Expensive *Caro*
Cheap *Barato*
Where is the tourist office? *¿Dónde está la oficina de turismo?*
Straight on *Todo recto*
To the left *a la izquierda*
To the right *a la derecha*
Town Hall *Ayuntamiento*
Bank *Banco*
Library *Biblioteca*
Bookshop *Librería*
Art Gallery *Sala de Exposiciones*
Pharmacy *Farmacia*
Bus stop *Parada de Autobús*
Train station *Estación de tren*
Post office *Correos*
Hospital *Hospital*
Church *Iglesia*
Hotel *Hotel*
Youth hostel *Albergue*
Camping *Camping*
Parking *Aparcamiento*
Sports ground *Polideportivo*

Square *Plaza*
Discotheque *Discoteca*
Beach *Playa*
At what time...? *¿A qué hora?*
Late *Tarde*
Early *Temprano*
I am hot *Tengo calor*
I am cold *Tengo frio*

Days of the Week

Note that the Spanish form takes a lower-case initial letter.

Monday *lunes*
Tuesday *martes*
Wednesday *miércoles*
Thursday *jueves*
Friday *viernes*
Saturday *sábado*
Sunday *domingo*

Months of the Year

Note that the Spanish form takes a lower-case initial letter.

January *enero*
February *febrero*
March *marzo*
April *abril*
May *mayo*
June *junio*
July *julio*
August *agosto*
September *septiembre*
October *octubre*
November *noviembre*
December *diciembre*

Questions/Complaints

There is no hot water *No hay agua caliente*
I would like a quieter room *Quiero una habitación mas tranquila*
Are there any vegetarian dishes? *¿Hay comidas vegetarianas?*
I feel ill *Me siento mal*
I need a doctor *Necesito un médico*
May I use the phone? *¿Puedo telefonear?*

Numbers

1	*uno*	30	*treinta*
2	*dos*	40	*cuarenta*
3	*tres*	50	*cincuenta*
4	*cuatro*	60	*sesenta*
5	*cinco*	70	*setenta*
6	*seis*	80	*ochenta*
7	*siete*	90	*noventa*
8	*ocho*	100	*cien*
9	*nueve*	101	*ciento uno*
10	*diez*	200	*doscientos*
11	*once*	300	*trescientos*
12	*doce*	400	*cuatrocientos*
13	*trece*	500	*quinientos*
14	*catorce*	600	*seiscientos*
15	*quince*	700	*setecientos*
16	*dieciséis*	800	*ochocientos*
17	*diecisiete*	900	*novecientos*
18	*dieciocho*	1,000	*mil*
19	*diecinueve*	2,000	*dos mil*
20	*veinte*	10,000	*diez mil*
21	*veintiuno*	100,000	*cien mil*
25	*veinticinco*	1,000,000	*un millón*

Further Reading

General

The novels of Peru's high-profile writer and former presidential candidate, Mario Vargas Llosa, provide an interesting insight into the country's psyche. *Aunt Julia and the Scriptwriter*, which has also been made into a film, and *The Time of the Hero* are probably the most readable. *The Green House* is set in Peru's Amazon and *Death in the Andes* (Faber, 1996), explores the effects of terrorism on various rural communities.
Cut Stones and Crossroads, by Ronald Wright. Viking Press, 1984 (also in Penguin). Considered the best travel book on the country in recent years.
Exploring Cusco, by Peter Frost. Nuevas Imágenes S.A., 1999 (fifth edition). Comprehensive coverage of the Cusco region by a 30-year resident.
Martín Chambi: Photographs of Peru 1920–1950, by Martín

English Books

The South American Explorers' Club has a good library for all things South American. Members of the club can utilize the free book exchange of paperbacks. The ABC bookstore in Centro Comercial San Isidro, in Paseo de la República, provides newspapers, magazines, guide books, and coffee-table books in English, French, and German. Keep in mind these items will be more expensive than at home.
 El Virrey, Miguel Dasso 141, San Isidro, is an excellent book shop where politicians and intellectuals go shopping. It has a great stock of publications on Peru plus a new section of books in English. *(See also page 348)*

Chambi. Banco de la República. A collection of shots by Peru's most famous photographer.
The Dancer Upstairs, by Nicholas Shakespeare. Picador, 1997. A fascinating account of Shining Path leader Abimael Guzmán's final attempt to avoid capture.
The White Rock, An Exploration of the Inca Heartland, by Hugh Thomson. Weidenfeld and Nicolson 2001. How the lost cities of the Incas have been re-discovered.
Faces of Latin America, by Duncan Green. Monthly Review Press, 1997. Bestselling introduction to the history and culture of Latin America.
Peru: Paths to Poverty, by Michael Reid. Latin American Bureau, 1985. A cogent, readable interpretation of modern Peruvian history.
The Peru Reader: History, Culture, Politics, by Orin Starn, Carlos Degregori, Robin Kirk (eds). Latin America Bureau, 2000. A collection of essays and extracts that gives a portrait of Peru's social history through the 20th century.

Archeology & Pre-Inca Cultures

The Adobe Sculptures of Huaca de los Reyes, by Michael E. Moseley and Luis Watanabe. Archaeology 27: 154–61 (1974).
Chan Chan: Peru's Ancient City of Kings, by Michael E. Moseley and Carol J. Mackey. National Geographic 143/3: 318–44 (1973).
Chavin: and the Origins of Andean Civilization, by Richard Burger (ed.). Thames and Hudson. A thorough study by British archeologists of one of Peru's most fascinating pre-Inca cultures.
Early Ceremonial Architecture in the Andes, Christopher B. Donnan (ed.). Dumbarton Oaks Research Library and Collection, 1985.
An Early Stone Carving from Pampa de las Llamas-Moxeke, Casma Valley, Peru, by Thomas Pozorski and Shelia Pozorski. Journal of Field Archaeology 15/3: 114–19 (1988).
Lines to the Mountain Gods: Nazca and the Mysteries of Peru, by Evan Hadingham. Random House, 1987.

Nazca: Eighth Wonder of the World? by Anthony Aveni. British Museum Press.
The Nazca Lines: A New Perspective on their Origins and Meaning, by Johan Reinhard. Editorial Los Pinos, 1988 (fourth edition). An exploration of the different theories about the famous desert lines.
Peruvian Prehistory, by Richard W. Keatings (ed.). Cambridge University Press, 1988.

Inca Society

Comentarios Reales de los Incas, by Inca Garcilaso de la Vega. Buenos Aires, 1943. Classic 16th-century accounts by *mestizo* chronicler (in Spanish).
The Conquest of the Incas, by John Hemming. Penguin, 1983. The best modern account of the fall of the Inca Empire. Extremely readable style, brings the history of Peru to life. Hemming has also written a coffee-table book called *Monuments of the Incas* with black and white photography by Edward Ranney. Both are classic introductions to understanding Peru.
The Incas and their Ancestors, by Michael E. Moseley. Thames and Hudson, 1991. Fascinating research into how the Inca empire flourished.
Historia del Tahuantinsuyu, by María Rostworowski de Diez Canseco. Lima, 1988. Modern, non-imperialist view of the Incas (in Spanish).
Inca Architecture, by Garziano Gaspairini and Louise Margolies. Bloomington, 1980. The most complete book on the subject.
The Inka Road System, by John Hyslop. New York, 1984. First-hand account of the author's investigations.
Lords of Cusco, by Burr Cartwright Brundage. Norman, Oklahoma, 1967 and *Empire of the Incas*, by Burr Cartwright Brundage. Norman, Oklahoma, 1963. Two highly tendentious but well-written and researched accounts.
Realm of the Incas, by Victor W. Von Hagen. New York, 1957. Still one of the better accounts of Inca daily life.

Colonial History

Daily Life in Colonial Peru, by Jean Descola. Trans. by Michael Hern. George Allen & Unwin, 1968.
Harochiri: An Andean Society under Inca and Spanish Rule, by Karen Spalding. Stanford University Press, 1984.
Peru: A Cultural History, by Henry E. Dobyns and Paul L. Doughty. Oxford University Press, 1976.
The Quechua in the Colonial World, by George Kubler. Handbook of South American Indians by Julian H. Steward (ed.) Vol 2: 331–410. Smithsonian Institution, 1946.
Vision of the Vanquished: The Spanish Conquest through Indian Eyes, by Nathan Wachtel. Harvester Press, 1977.

Machu Picchu

Antisuyo, by Gene Savoy. New York, 1970. Fascinating book, long out of print, by a man with an incredible nose for lost cities.
Arqueología de la America Andina, by Luis G. Lumbreras. Lima, 1981. A search for connections in Andean culture (in Spanish).
Lost City of the Incas, by Hiram Bingham. New York, 1972. Classic account of Bingham's explorations. Outdated theories, but a great read.
Machu Picchu, an Inca Citadel, by Hiram Bingham. New York, 1979. More details of Bingham's discoveries.

Other "Lost Cities"

El Paititi, El Dorado, y las Amazonas, by Roberto Levillier. Buenos Aires, 1976.
The Golden Man: The Quest for El Dorado, by Victor W. von Hagen. Glasgow, 1974.
The Search for El Dorado, by John Hemming. London, 1978.

Amazon Jungle

The Cloud Forest, by Peter Matthiesson. Penguin, 1987. Account of travel on the Amazon and through the cloud forest of Peru.

In the Rainforest, by Catherine Caufield. University of Chicago Press, 1989. Depressing but readable investigation into the depletion of the rainforest.
Tropical Nature, by Adrian Forsyth and Ken Myiata. Scribner & Sous, 1984. An excellent introduction to life and death in a New World rainforest.
An Annotated Checklist of Peruvian Birds, by T. Parker. Buteo Books, 1982.
A Guide to the Birds of Colombia, by Steve Hilty. Princeton Press, 1986. The most useful identification guidebook for birds in this area.
Rainforests: A Guide to Tourist and Research Facilities at Selected Tropical Forest Sites, by James L. Castner. Feline Press. The title is self-explanatory.
At Play in the Fields of the Lord, by Peter Matthiesson. Matthiesson's novel of uncontacted tribes and missionaries set in the department of Madre de Díos.
People of the Sacred Waterfall, by Michael Harner. Harner's celebrated ethnography of the head-shrinking Jivaro Amerindians in northeast Peru.
The Wizard of the Upper Amazon, by Ralph Lamb. His true account of a boy captured by Amerindians in northern Peru and his apprenticeship as a shaman.

Other Insight Guides

The whole subcontinent, from Colombia to Tierra del Fuego, is captured between the covers of **Insight Guide: South America**, with up-to-date information on all the major countries. Other Insight Guides on South America include **Venezuela**, **Ecuador** (and the Galápagos), **Brazil**, **Rio de Janeiro**, **Argentina**, **Buenos Aires** and **Chile**, each with Insight Guides' incisive journalism and stunning photography.

    Insight Guide: Amazon Wildlife, one of the series' nature guides, brings to life the fantastic flora and fauna of this great natural area.

    Insight Pocket Guides, each with a full-size fold-out map, offer special itineraries to help visitors get the most from a limited stay,

while Compact Guides pack surprisingly comprehensive detail into a handy pocket-sized format. Titles on South America include **Pocket Guide Peru**, **Compact Guide Chile** and **Compact Guide Rio de Janeiro**.

    Insight also produce numerous guides to Central America and the Caribbean.

Feedback

We do our best to ensure the information in our books is as accurate and up-to-date as possible. The books are updated on a regular basis, using local contacts, who painstakingly add, amend and correct as required. However, some mistakes and omissions are inevitable and we are ultimately reliant on our readers to put us in the picture.

    We would welcome your feedback on any details related to your experiences using the book "on the road". Maybe we recommended a hotel that you liked (or another that you didn't), as well as interesting new attractions, or facts and figures you have found out about the country itself. The more details you can give us (particularly with regard to addresses, e-mails and telephone numbers), the better.

    We will acknowledge all contributions, and we'll offer an Insight Guide to the best letters received.

Please write to us at:
    Insight Guides
    PO Box 7910
    London SE1 1WE
    United Kingdom
Or send e-mail to:
insight@apaguide.co.uk

ART & PHOTO CREDITS

Photography by Eduardo Gil except:

Martin Adler/Panos Pictures 313
AKG London 24
Aurora/Katzpictures 74/75
Alejandro Balaguer/Biosfera 130,
188, 232, 244
Jim Bartle 20/21, 125, 192, 198
André and Cornelia Bärtschi 96,
204/205, 206, 209, 211, 215,
218, 219, 220, 320
Mariana Bazo/Reuters 73
Suzy Bennett/Alamy Images
318
Yann Arthus-Bertrand/Corbis 263
Tibor Bognar/Alamy Images 156
Courtesy of Brüning Museum 33
Huw Clough 255
Sue Cunningham 14, 124, 151R,
187, 222, 233, 312
Dunstone Slide Library 223
Greg Epperson/Photolibrary.com
123
Michael Fogden 132
Michael & Patricia Fogden 221T
Peter Frost/Apa 77, 90, 120, 122,
254, 272, 297, 307, 316
Gebhard/Laif/Katzpictures 127
Getty Images 70
Eduardo Gil/Courtesy of Brüning
Museum back cover bottom
Eduardo Gil/Courtesy of Gold
Museum, Lima 30, 31
Eduardo Gil/Courtesy of Larco
Herrera Museum, Lima 28, 29
Eduardo Gil/Courtesy of Museo
Nacional de Antropologia y
Arqueologia, Lima back cover
centre, 100/101
Gonzalez/Laif/Katzpictures
136/137, 152
Andreas Gross back flap bottom,
18, 19, 68, 158, 171, 196, 237,
243, 245T, 252T, 278T, 295T, 302
Michael Guntern 88, 260, 284,
304, 305
Adriana von Hagen 86, 210, 216
Blaine Harrington III 152T, 153
Martin Henzl 287
Andrew Holt Photography 267T,
280T
Dave G. Houser 186T

Jeremy Horner/Corbis 266
Huber/Laif/Katz 155, 163
Mark A. Johnson/Corbis 265
Martin Kelsey 134
Eric Lawrie 1, 8/9, 10/11, 12/13,
89, 109, 110, 117, 138/139,
170T, 194T, 262T, 271T, 273T,
273, 303T, 309T, 314T, 315, 316T,
317
John Warburton-Lee 314
Charles & Josette Lenars/Corbis
107
Lima Times 62, 63, 64
John Maier Jr. 6/7, 16/17, 71,
180, 270R, 291, 296
Luiz Claudio Marigo 95
Mediolmages/Powerstock 157
Lynn A. Meisch 285
Tony Morrison/South American
Pictures 242
Pilar Olivares/Reuters/Corbis 85,
295
Susanna Pastor 185
Tony Perrottet 104, 149, 263, 267,
279, 289, 303, 317T
Photofrenetic/Alamy 84, 154
Heinz Plenge 32, 97, 106, 131,
133, 135L, 166, 167, 176, 177,
186, 207, 208, 213, 217,
228/229, 252, 275
Heinz Plenge/Courtesy of Brüning
Museum 26, 27
Sepp Puchinger/Alamy 126
Raach/Laif/Katz 81, 184, 194,
277
Reuters/Corbis 66, 319
Rex Features 25, 68, 294
Galem Rowell/Corbis 195
Anibal Solimano/Getty Images 72
SuperStock/Powerstock 144/145
Tafos/Susanna Pastor 121, 210T
Topham Picturepoint 46, 69, 277
Tophoven/Laif/Katz 264, 292
Renzo Uccelli 112
Mireille Vautier 47, 172T, 181,
197, 201, 238T, 245, 251T, 291T
Francesco Venturi/Kea front flap
top, 287T
Betsy Wagenhauser 52, 128,
190/191, 193, 199, 200, 202,
203, 235, 286

Map Production Berndtson &
Berndtson Productions
© 2005 Apa Publications GmbH & Co.
Verlag KG (Singapore branch)

Cartographic Editor **Zoë Goodwin**
Design Consultants **Klaus Geisler**
Picture Research **Hilary Genin,
Monica Allende**

Index

*Numbers in italics refer
to photographs*

A
B
C
D
F
G
H
I
J
a
b
c
e
f
g
h
i
j
k
l

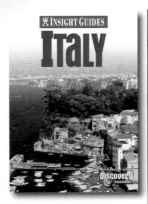

INSIGHT GUIDES

The classic series that puts you in the picture

Alaska
Amazon Wildlife
American Southwest
Amsterdam
Argentina
Arizona & Grand Canyon
Asia's Best Hotels & Resorts
Asia, East
Asia, Southeast
Australia
Austria
Bahamas
Bali
Baltic States
Bangkok
Barbados
Barcelona
Beijing
Belgium
Belize
Berlin
Bermuda
Boston
Brazil
Brittany
Brussels
Buenos Aires
Burgundy
Burma (Myanmar)
Cairo
California
California, Southern
Canada
Caribbean
Caribbean Cruises
Channel Islands
Chicago
Chile
China
Colorado
Continental Europe
Corsica
Costa Rica
Crete
Croatia
Cuba
Cyprus
Czech & Slovak Republic
Delhi, Jaipur & Agra
Denmark

Dominican Rep. & Haiti
Dublin
East African Wildlife
Eastern Europe
Ecuador
Edinburgh
Egypt
England
Finland
Florence
Florida
France
France, Southwest
French Riviera
Gambia & Senegal
Germany
Glasgow
Gran Canaria
Great Britain
Great Gardens of Britain
   & Ireland
Great Railway Journeys
   of Europe
Greece
Greek Islands
Guatemala, Belize
   & Yucatán
Hawaii
Hong Kong
Hungary
Iceland
India
India, South
Indonesia
Ireland
Israel
Istanbul
Italy
Italy, Northern
Italy, Southern
Jamaica
Japan
Jerusalem
Jordan
Kenya
Korea
Laos & Cambodia
Las Vegas
Lisbon
London

Los Angeles
Madeira
Madrid
Malaysia
Mallorca & Ibiza
Malta
Mauritius Réunion
   & Seychelles
Mediterranean Cruises
Melbourne
Mexico
Miami
Montreal
Morocco
Moscow
Namibia
Nepal
Netherlands
New England
New Mexico
New Orleans
New York City
New York State
New Zealand
Nile
Normandy
North American &
   Alaskan Cruises
Norway
Oman & The UAE
Oxford
Pacific Northwest
Pakistan
Paris
Peru
Philadelphia
Philippines
Poland
Portugal
Prague
Provence
Puerto Rico
Rajasthan

Rio de Janeiro
Rome
Russia
St Petersburg
San Francisco
Sardinia
Scandinavia
Scotland
Seattle
Shanghai
Sicily
Singapore
South Africa
South America
Spain
Spain, Northern
Spain, Southern
Sri Lanka
Sweden
Switzerland
Sydney
Syria & Lebanon
Taiwan
Tanzania & Zanzibar
Tenerife
Texas
Thailand
Tokyo
Trinidad & Tobago
Tunisia
Turkey
Tuscany
Umbria
USA: The New South
USA: On The Road
USA: Western States
US National Parks: West
Venezuela
Venice
Vienna
Vietnam
Wales
Walt Disney World/Orlando

℞ INSIGHT GUIDES

The world's largest collection of visual travel guides & maps